SLAVISTIC PRINTINGS
AND REPRINTINGS

260/3

THE ECUMENICAL WORLD OF ORTHODOX CIVILIZATION

RUSSIA AND ORTHODOXY: VOLUME III

Essays in honor of Georges Florovsky

ANDREW BLANE

Editor

Thomas E. Bird

Associate Editor

1974

MOUTON

THE HAGUE · PARIS

PREFACE

Though intended as a work in its own right, this book is also meant to serve as one of three volumes which form a *Festschrift* in honor of Georges Florovsky. The first is devoted to Florovsky's life and thought; the second and third, respectively, to the fields in which he has made his fullest and finest contributions to scholarship — Russian religious culture and Orthodox ecumenical thought.

The articles were solicited for the individual volumes with these themes in mind. It was thereby hoped that each study would be much more than a collection of disparate writings bound only by honorific occasion. As for the language of the various essays, commonality has been of little concern. Here diversity rules, with the language of original composition retained in the final publication. The purpose is less to underline the international character of the contributing community than to preserve a multi-tongued and cosmopolitan flavor in keeping with the life and scholarship of Georges Florovsky.

Of necessity, an enterprise of this magnitude has been long in the making. Hardships and compromises have been inevitable; but it is gratifying to record that the final reality surpasses the original dream. To the contributors, to the general editor, and to the publisher, whose longsuffering patience has been nothing short of stoic, the editor offers his profound gratitude. Others to whom heartfelt thanks belong are Sharon Arndt, Martha Mock, Sylvaine Casalis, Marina Keijzer, Rima Shore, and Ursula Hoffman for technical assistance; to Nina Birnbaum, Madelaine Morris, and Natasha Belinkova for editorial advice; and, most especially, to Masha Vorobiov for wise counsel and suve support whatever the moment or place. Without all these, this volume — and its companions — would never have come forth to do honor to a good and worthy man and, hopefully, to further the life of the mind.

Andrew Blane

TABLE OF CONTENTS

BAPTISMAL THEOLOGY AND PRACTICE IN ROME
AS REFLECTED IN JUSTIN MARTYR

GEORGE H. WILLIAMS

Much has been written on baptism in Justin Martyr because his account of it in *I Apology* 61 is a notably early record of the practice.[1] Yet because of the relative simplicity of this rite as he describes it here *for pagans* as compared with the greater theological and liturgical complexity of the same rite in Rome as somewhat later set forth *for the faithful* by Hippolytus in the *Apostolic Tradition* and in Carthage by Tertullian in *De baptismo*,[2] some scholars have tended to picture baptism in Justin's day and milieu as a rather plain and straightforward exercise, even when they have also secondarily taken into account all dispersed references and possible allusions to baptism in Justin's *Dialogue with Trypho the Jew*. If, however, the *Dialogue* were to be given preeminence over the *I Apology*, as being written *for Jews* of various degrees of observance, who themselves, in any case, all practised proselyte baptism, then, in giving due weight to Justin's use of scripture adduced during the dialogue within the schism, as it were, or among the factions of the biblical λαός[3] in

---

[1] The fullest recent account of baptism in Justin is that of André Benoît, "Justin et les Apologètes", *Le Baptême chrétien au second siècle: La Théologie des Pères* (*Études d'Histoire et de Philosophie Religieuses*) (Paris/Strasbourg, 1953), ch. vii.

[2] Tertullian, author of the oldest monograph on baptism (*De baptismo*, c. 200), lists most conveniently in *De carnis resurrectione*, 8.3, all the components or moments of the paschal baptismal action: lustration, sealing, imposition of hands, illumination by the Spirit, and the eucharist. This was not necessarily the sequence, however, even in Carthage.

[3] Hans von Campenhausen, *Die Entstehung der christlichen Bibel* (Tübingen, 1968); Helmut Köster, "Septuaginta und Synoptischer Erzählungstoff im Schriftbeweis Justins", dissertation (Heidelberg, 1956); Pierre Prigent, *Justin et l'Ancien Testament* (*Études Bibliques*) (Paris, 1964); G. T. Armstrong, *Die Genesis in der Alten Kirche* (Tübingen, 1962); J. Smit Sibinga, *The Old Testament Text of Justin Martyr, I. The Pentateuch* (Leiden, 1963); Willis A. Shotwell, *The Biblical Exegesis of Justin Martyr* (London, 1965); Arthur J. Bellinzoni, Jr., *The Sayings of Jesus in the Writings of Justin Martyr* (Leiden, 1967).

their pagan setting, we would find in Justin quite a liturgically and theo-logically complex baptismal rite.

The circles to whom Justin directed the *Dialogue* were, indeed, ac-quainted with several "liturgical" and other actions for proselytes besides ablutionary baptism. The Jewish initiatory rite for proselytes[4] included instruction, the seal of circumcision for males, baptism of both males and females, and — in the earlier period — the sacrifice of a dove. At the same time, for progeny within the covenant of Abraham there was still the circumcision of infant males on the eighth day, for which within the new covenant in Jesus Christ baptism had become the replacement.[5] Because this, as it were, merely confirmatory baptism of the progeny of a household of Christian faith to some early Christians, presumably per-haps especially to those of Jewish origin, seemed to be different in purport and perhaps even form from the elaborated baptismal rite for adults converted from the nations (which included catechetical instruction, exorcism,[6] unction, illumination, and the seal of the Spirit), there is still some difficulty for scholars, especially given the variant ecclesiastical traditions out of which most come to assess the still inconclusive ancient evidence, to sort out the data variously suggesting or even fully document-ing believers' baptism, pedobaptism, and the baptism of a whole house-hold.[7] Some scholars discover in the rite a distinguishable moment that could be identified as a sealing or a confirmation (eventually separable as a separate sacrament).[8]

[4]   David Daube, "A Baptismal Catechism", *The New Testament and Rabbinic Judaism* (London, 1956), 106-140.
[5]   Hans-Joachim Schoeps, *Theologie und Geschichte des Judenchristentums* (Töin/ Tübingen, 1948); Einar Molland, "La circoncision, le baptême et l'autorité du décret apostolique", *Studia Theologica* IX (1955), 1-39.
[6]   Franz Joseph Dölger, *Der Exorzismus im altchristlichen Taufritual* (Paderborn, 1909).
[7]   Joachim Jeremias, *Infant Baptism in the First Four Centuries* (London, 1960) (original German, 1960); Kurt Aland in reply, *Did the Early Church Baptize Infants?* (London, 1962) (original German, 1961); Jeremias in refutation and restatement, *The Origins of Infant Baptism* (= *Studies in Historical Theology* I) (London/Naperville, Ill., 1963) (original German, 1962).
[8]   Gregory Dix, *The Theology of Confirmation in Relation to Baptism* (Westminster, 1946); L. S. Thornton, *Confirmation: Its Place in the Baptismal Mystery* (London, 1954); Leonel L. Mitchell, *Baptismal Anointing* (London, 1966); G. W. H. Lampe, *The Seal of the Spirit: A Study in the Doctrine of Baptism and Confirmation in the New Testament and the Fathers*, 2nd ed. (London, 1967); Cyril Pocknee, *Water and Spirit: A Study in the Relation of Baptism and Confirmation* (London, 1967); and the discussion as to whether there was a separate moment of sealing at baptism in the second century among J. E. I. Oulton (no), Gregory Dix (yes), and E. C. Ratcliff (yes) in *Theology* L (1947), 86-91; LI (1948), 7-12; and *ibid.*, 133-139, entitled by Ratcliff, "Justin Martyr and Confirmation".

Thus, despite the comprehensiveness and the detail of recent and earlier inquiries bearing on the theory and practice of baptism in the writings of Justin, something more can still be said by taking into account somewhat more fully than hitherto (1) the still quite Jewish and Jewish-Christian milieu of the community of faith out of which Justin writes; (2) the possibility that within it or within Justin's memory or acquaintance a distinction could still be felt among three degrees or formulas of baptism: for Jewish converts to Christ, for the progeny of (Gentile and Jewish) Christian households, and for Gentile converts to Christian Israel; (3) the moral rigorism and radical (though not ultimate) dualism of Justin, which would have made of the extended penitential-initiatory-salvific baptism for pagans a decisive moment in the exercise of the recovered use of free will in working out in fear and trembling one's salvation from death, and the eschatological flame; which event (4) would have strongly affected his conception of redemption, communal discipline, and eschatology; hence (5) the likelihood that many of his scriptural argumentations presumably with the several sectors of Hellenistic Judaism as represented by Trypho and his companions rely on passages long prominent in catechetical instruction and baptismal exhortation, and therefore that many of them can be pressed for clues as to the conception and practice of baptism according to Justin and in his community of faith; (6) that, with respect to the prominence in Justin's allusion to baptism of both light and fire, our recognition of a cultual sense of illumination, in addition to the cognitive, moral, and eschatological meanings, does not require that one yield to a *religionsgeschichtlich* interpretation here, as though Justin and his church borrowed the terminology and cultual accoutrements of φωτισμός[9] from the mystery cults, since the term surely had strong scriptural antecedents and sanctions and possibly even contemporary Jewish analogues; and finally (7) that, in the awesome rite, if we are correct about its true character within his milieu, Justin, teacher of catechumens (upon whom he was perhaps wont to lay his own hand in blessing) and spirited adversary

---

[9] Carl-Martin Edsman, *Le Baptême de feu* (= *Acta Seminarii Neotestamentici Upsaliensis* IX) (Leipzig/Uppsala, 1940); Per Lundberg, *La Typologie baptismale dans l'ancienne Église*, ibid. X (Leipzig/Uppsala, 1942); Augusto Segovia, S.J., *La Iluminacion bautismal en el antiguo cristianismo* (Granada, 1958); and J. Ysebaert, *Greek Baptismal Terminology: Its Origins and Early Development* (Nijmegen, 1962).

It has been reflection on my experiences and observations of Passion Week, including its paschal luminosity, in Athens, the Phanar, Thessalonica, and Mount Athos in 1961, in a degree of personal participation made possible directly and indirectly by Father Florovsky, that has induced me to study the luminosity in Justin's record of annual paschal baptismal eucharist. See also nn. 44, 60.

of both Gnostic Christian and philosophical rivals in and about his school near the Timothean bathhouse, was perhaps indirectly (sofar as the extant works go) countering the claims of Valentinus, for example, about the necessity of a sacramental act of ἀπολύτρωσις to carry the ordinary psychic Christian to the pneumatic level through the bestowal of the Spirit.[10]

1. THE COSMIC AND SCRIPTURAL SETTING OF JUSTIN'S UNDERSTANDING OF THE TRIPARTITE PENITENTIAL-INITIATORY BAPTISM FOR CONVERTS FROM PAGANISM

Justin Martyr understands convert baptism, which he commonly calls illumination, as a personal moment of inner kindling of the mind and heart situated in personal history in a sequence beginning with the cosmic fire-light at creation and recurring in the salvific fire-light at Jesus' own baptism. The latter is the paradigm and sanction for the rite of baptismal

---

[10]   Valentinus taught in Rome c. 136-165 A.D. In Valentinian Gnostic Christianity "redemption" has the specialized meaning of a laying on of hands in the bestowal of the Spirit. This conception of a superior stage of baptism or a confirmation that leads to something higher for the merely psychic Christian is especially well documented in the Valentinian Coptic Gospel of Philip. See the discussion in Jacques E. Menard's text, translation, and commentary, L'Evangile selon Philippe (Strasbourg/Paris, 1967), 25-29. Origen had to deal with Valentinian ἀπολύτρωσις in the hermeutics and sacramental theology of Heracleon, discussed by Elaine Hiesey Pagels, "The Herme-neutical Debate between Origen and Heracleon in Origen's Commentary on the Gospel of John", Ph.D. thesis (Cambridge, 1970). Since Justin only used ἀπολύτρωσις once in his surviving works, we cannot pursue the problem here further but only suggest the Gnostic ceremony as a possible context besides that of the Jewish baptism in which to understand the extraordinary amount of scriptural texts adduced in the Dialogue particularly that could have been connected with baptism. In the single usage of the key term (Dialogue 81.1) Justin refers to the tree of life in paradise and the cross and continues: "Moses was sent with a rod ἐπὶ τῆν ... ἀπολύτρωσιν of the people, and holding this in his hands at the head of the people divided the sea [Ex. 14:6], and by means of this he saw water springing from the rocks."

   On the laying on of hands by teachers like Justin (cf. the Valentinian Gnostic Ptolemy in his Letter to Flora, apud Epiphanius, Panarion, 37.7), see Arnold Ehrhardt, The Apostolic Succession (London, 1953), and "Jewish and Christian Ordination", Journal of Ecclesiastical History V (1954), 125-138, esp. in reference to Dialogue 49.6-7. Here it is a matter of the succession of the Spirit from Moses through Joshua to John the Baptist, over against the absence of the Spirit in the rabbis, since according to the Jewish view prophecy has ceased. Although in this chapter Justin does not use either the technical term Χειροτονία nor the Valentinian word for the ritual laying on of hands in bestowing the gift of the Spirit to a psychic for the completion of his redemption, that is, effectually redemption (ἀπολύτρωσις), in any case it is a discussion in the context of the prophetic and spiritual status of John the Baptist and hence also of catholic as distinguished from Gnostic Christian baptism in the line of the Baptist, Christ, and the Apostles.

lustration, rebirth, and illumination by which one might be saved from the destructive fire of the Latter Day to enjoy the blessed light of eternal salvation.

Justin opens the *Dialogue* (1.5)[11] by identifying within range of his discourse a group on either side of what he regards as the true Christian position. On the one side are those like the Stoics who acknowledge an eschatological fire but hold, after the conflagration, "that you and I shall live again [exactly] as we are living now, without having become either better or worse" (cf. *II Apology* 7.3). On the other side are Middle Platonists or even Christian Gnostics, he does not specify, who "premising that the soul is immortal and incorporeal, think that even if they have committed any wrong they will suffer no punishment (for the incorporeal is incapable of suffering), and again, as the soul itself is (by nature) immortal, they have no further need for God" (*Dialogue* 1.5; cf. 80.4 where the direct immortalists opposed are probably Marcionites; and 35.1-6, where various Gnostics are pilloried).

Justin believes in both an aboriginal and an eschatological punitive-purificatory fire-light, associated with the Spirit of both the pre-existent, the incarnate, and the judgmental Word-Son-Christ; and he understands the whole sacramental transaction of "baptism", from catechetical instruction to the Paschal communion, as the way in which Jesus Christ, the light to the Gentiles, made it possible for one to participate in that Light and to be saved from that Light in its eschatological aspect as a punitive Fire (cf. *I Apology* 45.1, 6; *II Apology* 1.2; 7.2, 5; 8.4; *Dialogue* 49.3).

[11] The critical texts used for the *Dialogue* and the *Apologies* are: Johannes C. T. Otto, ed., *Iustini philosophi et martyris Opera quae feruntur omnia*, 3rd ed. (Jena, 1877), 2 vols., the first in two parts, with extensive notes, constituting volumes in the *Corpus Apologetarum Christianorum saeculi secundi*; and Edgar Goodspeed, ed., *Die ältesten Apologeten: Texte mit kurzen Einleitungen* (Göttingen, 1914), to be supplemented by his *Index Apologeticus sive clavis Iustini Martyris operum aliorumque Apologetarum pristinorum* (Leipzig, 1912). Many other editions and translations have been consulted, but for the translations of the *Apologies* into English the standard version in the American edition of *The Ante-Nicene Fathers* I (Buffalo, 1885) has been adduced (into which the chapter subdivisions of Goodspeed and occasional modifications of the translation have been introduced without notice) and for the translations of the *Dialogue* that of A. Lukyn Williams has been adduced, *Justin Martyr: The Dialogue with Trypho: Translation, Introduction, and Notes* (London, 1930).

In the completion of this study I was greatly stimulated by the bibliographical assiduity and scholarly insights of all the members of my Justin Martyr Seminar at Harvard Divinity School in 1967: Leonard Buck, Donald Espinosa, Nicholas Finke, S.J., Manfred Waldemar Kohl, Alan Kolp, Alastair Logan, Michael McCann, Mrs. Wendy Ross, and especially Father John W. Howard, S.J., who also generously helped me with the final draft of this paper.

That Justin pictures this Light-Fire as at creation is evidenced in the two chapters in the *I Apology* (59 and 60) which lead to his explicit description of baptism (61). Arguing that Plato in the *Timaeus* drew upon Moses' account of creation, after quoting "Let there be light" (Genesis 1:3), Justin goes on to imply that Plato and the Greeks in general also followed Moses with respect to the realm of Erebus, through which souls had to pass to Hades: "For a fire is kindled by my anger, and it burns to the depths of Sheol, devours the earth and its increase, and sets on fire the foundations of the mountains" (Deuteronomy 32:22). That Justin holds that God prepared the eschatological fire at creation is reinforced by his repetition of the same Deuteronomic passage in the next chapter, where he says that the passage was inspired by the spirit of prophecy with respect to the selectively punitive (rather than the totally destructive Stoic) conflagration: "He [Moses] spoke thus: 'Everlasting fire shall descend, and shall devour to the pit beneath'" (60.1). Now this "everlasting fire" seems, in Justin's mind, to be the punitive aspect of the same Spirit of God, "a third power", which at creation "moved over the waters" (Genesis 1:2) and which Pseudo-Plato in *II Letter* called "the third around the third".[12] To be sure, Justin does not here expressly call either "the second power" (λόγος/υἱὸς τοῦ θεοῦ, ἡ μετὰ τὸν πρῶτον Θεὸν δύναμις) light or "the third power" (the Spirit) fire. But such a differentiation between the invisible and ineffable God the Creator and the two angelic powers above the primordial chaos (the cruciform Logos and the hovering Spirit) is implied in the assimilation of the cosmogony of the *Timaeus* to that of Genesis. Such an interrelationship between Logos/light and Spirit/fire is noted by Justin at other moments in the history of salvation.

A second citation of Deuteronomy 32:22 within a few lines (60.9), as the primordial provision of the eschatological fire, occurs in the context of Justin's trying to show that in the *Timaeus* Plato was but garbling Moses when he said that God placed "the Son" "crosswise in the universe" (60.1, 5, 7)[13] during the cosmogony, and that the passage in Moses on which Plato was allegedly drawing was Numbers 21:4-9 (60.2-4), wherein it is recounted that in the wilderness near the Red Sea Moses warded off serpents and other creeping assailants by means of a fiery Serpent placed on a pole (Justin says out of brass he made a type of the cross and placed it *over* the holy tabernacle). How could Justin have thought Plato to have been influenced by such a passage so far removed from the account of chaos and creation in Genesis? One explanation

---

[12]   *II Epistle* 312E.
[13]   *Timaeus*, 36BC.

would be that Justin himself and his community of faith had come to apply this passage to the baptismal water which they thought of as representing not only the Jordan but also the primordial flood. They would, accordingly, have identified the wilderness of Sinai with the cosmic abyss at creation (the *tohu* and *bohu* of Genesis 1:2; cf. wilderness as *tohu* in Job 12:24 and Psalm 107:40).[14] The realms of the wilderness of the desert and the wilderness of many waters, which lie curbed under the earth in Hebraic cosmology, were the haunts of serpents, monsters of the deep, dragons, and all manner of crawling things, and notably the chief of all demons, *Sata-nas*, which Justin understands (*Dialogue* 103.5) etymologically to mean the Apostate Serpent (*sata* = in Hebrew 'to be faithless'; in Aramaic also 'to be rebellious'; in Syriac also 'to decline from religion' + Samaritan *nash*; Hebrew *nāchāsh* = 'serpent').[15]

Justin, who mentions the Logos in the shape of a × (cross) over the cosmic deep three times (61.1, 5, 7), may allude also to some cruciform gesture of consecration of the baptismal waters. In any case, Justin was the only Apologist to use σταυρός, emphasizing the historic crucifixion under Pontius Pilate.[16] But he also frequently used the more mythical term ξύλον and may have been the first Christian to have linked the σταυρός of Calvary and the ξύλον of Paradise (*Dialogue* 85.1).[17] In the following chapter (86) Justin collects Old Testament instances of dividing, crossing, purifying, or sweetening bodies of water (the Red Sea, the Jordan, springs) and may therein allude to a practice later known to have been observed in the consecration of the baptismal font.

The Cross, Water, and Fire before the Landing of Noah

Justin (*Dialogue* 138.1-3) was the first to see in the Ark of Noah made of quadrangular wood (Genesis 6:15 LXX) a type of the cross (rather

[14] To be sure, Prudentius Maran, instead of taking the desert as the symbol of the primordial abyss, takes "the holy tabernacle" as the symbol of the universe, rightly noting that in fact Justin imports into his reading of Numbers 21:4-9 both the specificity of the pole equalling a cross and the placement thereof over (ἐπί) the holy tabernacle. Migne, *Patrologia Graeca* VI, col. 418, n. 66. Justin's reading at this point could reflect a special, possibly cultual extension of the text at baptism or another textual tradition of LXX. The holy tabernacle in any case does not appear in other references to the cross raised in the desert, namely in *Dialogue* 91.4 (where the language approaches John 3:14); 94.1; 104.1-3; 112.1.

[15] The same in Irenaeus, *Adversus haereses*, v. 21.2; *Praedicatio apostolica*, 16.

[16] G. Q. Reijners, O.S.C., *The Terminology of the Holy Cross in Early Christian Literature as Based upon Old Testament Typology* (= *Graecitas Christianorum Primaeva* II) (Nijmegen, 1965), 35.

[17] Reijners, p. 41; passage quoted above in n. 10.

than the Church),[18] which he, of course, as with so many other σταυρός/ ξύλον texts, connects with baptism.[19] Justin also finds in righteous Noah a figure of Christ for baptizands. "For Christ, being the Firstborn of every creature, has also become again the head of another race, which was begotten anew of Him by water and faith and wood" (*Dialogue* 138.2; cf. 19.4). There is no fire here or light; but he might elsewhere (in lost works) have seen in the olive branch in the bill of the dove (Genesis 8:11) a symbol of the benign oil and potential light of the Holy Spirit or in the burnt offerings at the altar erected by Noah[20] after leaving the Ark (8:20) a type of the eucharist following baptism. Justin uses details in the story of the Deluge in the context of the rite of baptism to convince Trypho that the eight persons saved within the Ark typify the very day, the eighth,[21] on which Christ as the true Noah annually becomes the head of the neophytes on Easter morn (*Dialogue* 138.1 f.).

Joshua the High Priest

Justin finds types of Jesus in two Joshuas: in the son of Nun and successor of Moses fighting the Amalekites while Moses' hands were held up in prayer to form a cross (Exodus 12:12f.; *Dialogue* 90.5), and in Joshua the high priest with dirty garments (Zechariah 3:1-5; *Dialogue* 115-116).

We shall concentrate on the second as most clearly connected with baptism. Although Justin quotes Zechariah 2:10-3:2, he stresses only the last part of the text and its sequel, not directly quoted, through 3:10. It is quite possible that we can overhear at this point an adapted baptismal homily on the taking off of the filthy garments of pagan wickedness and the literal donning of fresh raiment after the baptized has escaped the consequences of sin "like a brand plucked out from the fire" (Zechariah 3:2). That this discussion in *Dialogue* 115-116 is baptismal in its fundamental allusion is borne out by the fact that it is immediately followed by a discussion of the eucharist of the bread and the cup (117.1), which does not obviously come out of the text being expounded, but which would have in any homily based thereon following baptism.

Since the whole treatment of the Zecharian passage may throw light on the baptismal practice of which Justin is expounding a scriptural

---

[18] Reijners, p. 45.
[19] Reijners, pp. 33-47, noted several times.
[20] Cyril F. Pocknee, *Cross and Crucifix* (= *Alcuin Club Tracts* No. 32), Plate 17.33 shows a dove holding an object resembling a paint-brush in its claw and making the monogram Chi-Rho, Calixtus, 3rd century epitaph, described also in Mitchell, 94.
[21] Jean Daniélou, *La semaine hebdomadaire*.

sanction, we shall look at it more closely. The high priest Jesus (Joshua) of the prophecy faced Satan (Zechariah 3:1) and had his filthy garments removed to be replaced by rich apparel (v. 4). Jesus Christ, the true high priest, himself with *holy* garments, "puts off all the filthy garments wherewith we were clothed" (116.1). Justin continues:

Yet the devil stands over against us, ever opposing us, and wishing to draw all unto himself. And the angel [possibly the Holy Spirit] of God, that is to say the power of God which was sent us by Jesus Christ, rebukes him, and he departs from us. [2] And we have been plucked out as from *fire* (Zechariah 3:2), when we were purged from our former sins, and also from the affliction and the *burning* (πύρωσις; cf. I Peter 4:12),[22] wherein both the devil and all his servants *burn* us. For from them again does Jesus the Son of God pluck us. Also he has engaged to clothe us with the clothing prepared for us, if we practice His commandments; and He has promised to provide an everlasting kingdom. [3] For ... we, who by the name of Jesus have as one man believed on God the Maker of the universe, and have by the name of His first-born Son stripped off our filthy garments, that is to say, our sins [being like Joshua, a brand plucked from the fire], for we were set on *fire* (πυρωθέντες) by the Word of his calling (cf. Jeremiah 23:29), are now the true high priestly race of God (*Dialogue* 116.1-3).[23]

Justin completes the section with more about this high priestly race, which leads into a specific discussion of the Christian eucharist,[24] and then anticipates the resurrection and Last Judgment "when He raises all up, and sets some as incorruptible and immortal and free from all sorrow in an everlasting kingdom that will never cease, and sends others away into everlasting punishment by fire" (*Dialogue* 117.3). All of this makes it certain that we have before us considerable detail about the meaning and practice of baptism in the name of (1) God the Maker, (2) Jesus the Word (linked with fire in the allusion to Jeremiah 23:29 "Is not my Word like fire ...?"), and presumably (3) the Holy Spirit, the angel and power sent by Jesus Christ to rebuke Satan. A double function of fire is recurrent in Justin, now to enkindle faithfulness, now to purge sin. In the context of the stripping off of old garments and of being clothed in new garments on emergence from the baptismal font, Justin somehow sees the New Joshua's garments, the robe of Christ, as covering the baptizand plucked symbolically from some searing flame of the Spirit to escape thereby the eschatological fire of the same Spirit.

[22]   See Emily Sanders, "Πύρωσις in I Peter 4:12", Harvard Th.D. thesis (Cambridge, 1966).
[23]   Discussed by Benoît, 150, 183.
[24]   *Dialogue* 117.1 and 3: "At the thanksgiving of the bread and the cup ... at the remembrance of their food, both dry and liquid, in which also the suffering which the Son of God has suffered for their sake is brought to mind".

Elijah as Both a Baptismal and an Eschatological Figure

In adducing Elijah, the fire motif at baptism becomes for Justin quite explicit. Elijah, as priest and prophet, the anointer of Elisha, the fore-runner of the Messiah and destined in Jewish expectation (by the time of Justin) to be the anointer of the Messiah[25] (*Dialogue* 8.4), in having once called down first water and then fire upon the wood on Mount Carmel (I Kings 18:38), was a baptismal figure[26] identifiable at once with the worsting of the demons of paganism and their priests and with John the Baptizer and anointer of Jesus as the suffering and hidden Messiah.[27] For example, after quoting Elijah, "I have yet seven thousand men, who never bowed knee to Baal",[28] Justin says (in *Dialogue* 39.1) that in submitting to penitential baptism on the model provided by John-Elijah, "leaving the way of error ..., being *enlightened* (φωτιζόμενοι) by the name of Christ", neophytes in the process "also receive gifts" of the Spirit, detailed in a way to suggest those in Isaiah 11:2 (*Dialogue* 39.2).[29]

Satan, Water, Fire, and the Spirit at the Paradigmatic Baptism and Disguised Anointment of Jesus as the Messiah

Justin's account of the baptism of Jesus is the oldest allusion to John the Baptist outside the canonical New Testament. John the Baptist himself could draw upon two scriptural traditions with respect to judgmental fire: the fiery breath or sword in the mouth (cf. Revelation 11:5; 19:15) and the fiery lake, river, or torrent (Daniel 7:10; IV Ezra 13:10f.).[30]

[25] Joseph Klausner accepted Justin's testimony at this point as conclusive evidence of this Jewish tradition dating back at least into the second century, *Die Messianischen Vorstellungen* (Berlin, 1903), 62.

[26] Lundberg, 2: "Le paradigme d'Elie en tant que paradigme du baptême".

[27] E. Sjöberg, "Justin als Zeuge vom Glauben an den verborgenen und leidenden Messias im Judentum", *Interpretationes ad Vetus Testamentum pertinentus*, Festschrift für S. Mowinckel, ed. N. Dahl and A. Kapelrud (Oslo, 1955).

[28] Section 1; also *Dialogue* 46-6. The whole passage is nearer to Romans 11:3f. than to I Kings 19:10, 14, 18.

[29] Here Justin conflates certain of the gifts of I Cor. 8f. with those of Isa. 11:2, while retaining the number seven. Elsewhere Justin thinks of a single gift of the Spirit for all the baptized. In the other reference to Elijah, where the polemic is directly anti-Jewish (46.6f.), Justin still associates the (baptismal) renunciation of "sacrifice" to those to whom we used to sacrifice, "namely to Satan and all his demons", with belief "that God will raise us up by His Christ, and will make us incorruptible and free from suffering, and immortal".

[30] Carl H. Kraeling, *John the Baptist* (New York/London, 1951); Joachim Jeremias, "Der Ursprung der Johannestaufe", *Zeitschrift für neutestamentliche Wissenschaft* XXIII (1929), 312-320; J. Bornemann, *Die Taufe Christi durch Johannes: Feuer- oder*

Similarly there were two scriptural traditions about the role of the Spirit of God: to empower men to witness to the truth and to rout the forces of evil (cf. Mark 3:23-30; II Thessalonians 2:8).[31] Also there was a rabbinical interpretation of proselyte baptism as a possible substitute for circumcision and understood as a symbolic reenactment for the would-be Israelite of Israel's collective passage through the Red Sea and across the Jordan (cf. I Corinthians 10:1f.).[32] Finally, there was a tradition that understood baptism as death and suffering (cf. Mark 10:30; Luke 12:20; Romans 6:3).

We may understand John's original conception of baptism in the Jordan as representing both the Red Sea and the Jordan crossing (under Joshua), whereby Jews might willingly submit to the torrent symbolic also of the acceptance of the imminent judgment which he proclaimed for the unrighteous in Israel. The sense of John's original baptismal exhortation can be recovered thus: "I baptize you with water for repentance, and if you repent not in my baptism, He, the Messiah, will destroy you with his fiery breath or spirit."[33]

Justin, close to some Baptist traditions (cf. *Dialogue* 80.4) and several Jewish Christian traditions (*Dialogue* 47.1, 3, 4; 48.4; cf. 88.3), introduces a reading[34] from the Gospel of the Nazarenes or of the Ebionites, with whom he is not in accord, christologically, possibly because in it alone he finds a reference to baptismal fire. Justin writes:

[W]hen Jesus came to the river Jordan, where John was baptizing, when Jesus went down to the water, fire was even kindled (πῦρ ἀνήφθη) in the Jordan, and when He was rising up from the water the Holy Spirit fluttered down upon Him as a dove (*Dialogue* 88.3).

Lichterscheinung; Joseph Thomas, *Le mouvement Baptiste en Palestine et Syrie* (Gembloux, 1935); and in preparation, David Flusser, *Johannes der Täufer*, Arbeiten zur Geschichte des späteren Judentums und des Urchristentums, III.

[31]   Kraeling, 58-64.

[32]   Kraeling, 105 with rabbinical references, n. 13. See Jean Jacques von Allmen, *Vocabulary of the Bible* (London, 1958) (proselytes had to pass through the Red Sea and the Jordan; cf. *Manual of Discipline*) and Oscar Cullmann, *Baptism in the New Testament* (Chicago, 1950).

[33]   Kraeling's conjecture, p. 63. II (IV Ezra) 14:39 speaks of a cup of inspiration "with water, but the colour of it was like fire". See David Syme Russell, *The Method and Message of Jewish Apocalyptic, 200 BC-AD 100* (London, 1964), 172. Cf. above at n. 29.

[34]   The fullest form of the account of *super aquam ignis* derived from *Pauli Praedicatio* survives in a quotation in Pseudo-Cyprian, *De rebaptismate*. Edsman, 142-147. See Edgar Hennecke/Wilhelm Scheemelcher, *The New Testament Apocrypha*, tr. by R. McL. Wilson, 2 vols. (Philadelphia, 1964), I, 146f., 157; II, 92f.

This reference to fire on the Jordan, in the two Jewish Christian Gospels, reappears in the form of "a great light" shining from the water in two Old Latin MSS of Matthew and in Tatian's *Diatessaron*.[35] Possibly from the Jewish-Christian tradition Justin also preserves the original wording of Psalm 2:7 as uttered from heaven at the baptism: "Thou art my Son; this day I have begotten thee" (*Dialogue* 88.8; 103.6).[36]

In his accounts (*Dialogue* 49f.; 88) of John at the baptism of Jesus, Justin works with elements in the tradition not preserved in the canonical gospels. Notable is Justin's representation of John at the Jordan seated (καθεζόμενος; *Dialogue* 49.3; 51.2; 88.7) as teacher, rather than standing in the act of baptizing "or anointing" Jesus. It is just possible that Justin found this position of John seated as teacher conformable to what obtained in the extended ritual of which Justin gives an account; for he indicates that administrators or helpers of various kinds carry out the immersions of children, men, and women, and thereupon conduct them to the προεστὼς τῶν ἀδελφῶν, in whom we might be seeing the bishop seated in the center of his co-presbyters, prepared to seal or confirm the baptism with his hand on the head of each baptizand and to offer prayer and deliver a baptismal homily, prior to presiding over the eucharistic action of the assembly of neophytes and the faithful. If the *seated* president of the brethren confined his baptismal role to the sealing of those immersed by others elsewhere, before proceeding with the eucharist, one can find it plausible that just as in his eucharistic role the bishop represented Jesus Christ at the table, so here the seated προεστώς represented John the Baptist καθεζόμενος,[37] teaching in his homily about the fierce wrath to come from which the neophytes have just been saved by immersion in a symbolic (primordial Abyss, Red Sea, and) Jordan.

Justin understands that Elijah had reappeared in John *seated* by the River Jordan, as a teacher of Judah, calling for the baptism of repentance, a forerunner of the Messiah to be crucified, who "also would come". As Judge, "Christ is about to come in glory out of heaven" (*Dialogue* 49.3) to baptize "with the Holy Ghost and with fire". Justin holds that

---

[35] Cited by Ephraem Syrus (d. 306) and Ishodad of Merv (c. 850). Lukyn Williams, 187, n. 4.

[36] In the latter place, Justin says the words are "recorded in the Memoirs of the Apostles". Luke 3:23 has this reading in Codex Bezae, also the Old Latin, and others.

[37] Bishop Ignatius of Antioch sometimes thought of himself as representing God the Father (e.g. *Trallians* 3.1), sometimes as Jesus Christ the Son (e.g. *Trallians* 2.1). If the bishop as teacher preached from his chair on penitential baptism and fire to come like John seated at the Jordan, we can do no better than to think of his homily as something like *II Clement*, which greatly stresses the eschatological fire.

the first advent of the Spirit at the baptism at Jordan was "without glory", like the first advent of the Messiah as suffering servant, but that the second advent of the Spirit, like that of the judicial Christ, will be attended by "fire unquenchable" (*Dialogue* 49.7; 54.1).

Jesus did not submit to baptism, according to Justin, because he was in need of being cleansed of sin or because he needed the coming down of the Holy Spirit, but rather to set an example of going down and rising from water, whereby persons following him might appropriate the achievement of the cross (*Dialogue* 88.4). Justin does not have a doctrine of an infectious original sin. Adam fell "under death and deceit of the serpent" (cf. *Dialogue* 79.4; 112.3; 124.3), "each man [thereafter] acting ill by his own fault" (88.4).[38]

2. THE TRIPARTITE BAPTISM OF GENTILES: ILLUMINATION AS EXPERIENCED AND EXPLAINED BY JUSTIN

For Justin the baptismal action at the font involves, in a sequence not yet fully clarified, the renunciation of *Sata-nas* and the demons[39] (fallen angels, their demi-human offspring, and all creeping things which are manifestations of the same fallen nature), exorcism, cleansing, symbolic death and resurrection, the bestowal of the Spirit or the gift/gifts of the Spirit.

Justin's tripling (*Dialogue* 13.2) in his quotation of the Isaiah injunction (52:1): "Depart, depart, depart from unclean things", might well reflect liturgical usage at the triune baptism (the Hebrew and LXX use "depart" only twice). Justin holds that Isaiah 1:16-20, "Wash yourselves ... though your sins be as scarlet", in *I Apology* 44.4; 61.7f. and the *Dialogue* 44.4, is a prophecy of Christian baptism. His special phrasing in *I Apology* 61.4: "Except ye be born again (ἀναγεννῆθετε), ye shall not enter the kingdom of heaven", echoing Matthew 11:3 but with the influence of John 3:5, may reflect a baptismal formulary in use at Rome at the time.[40]

We shall continue, in any case, with the fire-light motif. The fire-light

---

[38] On individual accountability for sins, see further *Dialogue* 124.4; 140.4.
[39] I. F. Andres, *Die Engellehre der griechischen Apologeten des zweiten Jahrhunderts und ihr Verhältnis zur griechisch-römischen Dämonologie* (= *Forschungen zur christlichen Literatur- und Dogmengeschichte* XII) (Paderborn, 1914), 1-35; H. Wey, *Die Funktionen der bösen Geister bei den griechischen Apologeten des zweiten Jahrhunderts* (Winterthur, 1957); and Russel, "Angels and Demons", *op. cit.*, ch. ix.
[40] Cf. Jeremias, *Infant Baptism*, 51 ff.

motif in the annual paschal repetition of the baptism at Jordan is prominent in Justin's distinctive designation of baptism as φωτισμός, which
must be understood as at once illumination by the Logos or Spirit and
the salvific experience of fire as purgation to forfend against the punitive
fire of the Last Days. One can accept in Justin a scriptural revelatory
(noetic), a moral, and also a cultual aspect of illumination without
yielding to the theory that he was drawing upon a technical term of the
mystery religions and that there was some glaring light contrived to
impress Christian initiates.[41]

Justin may well allude to his own baptismal conversion when he tells
Trypho that, after conversing with the Old Man near Ephesus, "straight-
way a fire was kindled (πῦρ ανήφθη; the exact expression used about
fire on the Jordan as quoted above from *Dialogue* 88.3) in my soul, and
a passionate desire possessed me for the prophets, and for those great
men who are the friends of Christ" (*Dialogue* 8.1). Elsewhere he becomes
more specific and says that in baptism the neophytes are "enlightened
by the name of this Christ" and dowered with gifts of the Spirit (*Dialogue*
39.2). In *Dialogue* 122.1, 4, 5 Justin refers to the Isaian prophecy (49: 6)
of the Light to the Gentiles and of their salvation and argues against
the Jews: "You think that these words refer to the stranger and proselyte
[to Judaism] but in fact they refer to us who have been *illumined* by
Jesus..., us Gentiles, whom he has *illumined*." Thereupon he quotes
Psalm 2: 7 f. with a possible *arrière pensée* that at each paschal baptism,
imitating that at Jordan, the baptizand is regenerated as a son of God
(cf. *I Apology* 61.4). In *I Apology* 61.10-13, where he is expressly describing the whole baptismal transaction from catechetical instruction
to the first communion, Justin describes baptism as illumination in the
context of his commenting on the tripartite baptismal formula (most
commonly) used:

[10] [T]here is named, at the water, over him who has chosen to be born again
and has repented of his sinful acts, the name of God the Father and Master
(δεσπότης) of all. Those who lead to the washing the one who is to be washed
call on God by this term only ... [12] This washing is called *illumination*
(φωτισμός) since those who learn these things are illumined within. [13] The
illuminated one (φωτιξόμενος) is also washed in the name of Jesus Christ, who

---

[41]   The most recent studies reject as unsubstantiated a dependency upon the vocabulary
or practice of the mysteries. Segovia, *op. cit.*; Ysebaert, *op. cit.* It is not certain
whether Justin read Philo who, in any case, also spoke of the divine gleam by which
"the eye of understanding is dazzled" (*De opificio mundi*, 71); of the thankful confessor of
God's praise "pervaded by fire (πεπύρωται)" (*Legum allegoriae*, i.84); of the body of
the ecstatic "enkindled (πεπυρωμένον)" (*De ebrietate*, 147).

was crucified under Pontius Pilate, and in the name of the Holy Spirit, who through the prophets foretold everything about Jesus (*I Apology* 61.10-13).

At this point in the writings of Justin we have the plenary or triune baptismal formula for Gentile converts, who, in contrast to Jews, first of all have to have been illumined by scriptural revelation concerning the ineffable Creator. It is just possible that it was baptism in the name of God that constituted the moment of illumination in the strict sense, for after baptism in the name of the nameless δεσπότης the baptizand is already called φωτιζόμενος. After the tripartite baptismal action, the neophytes were presumably covered with baptismal garments before being conducted into the presence of "the president of the brethren" presumably for the episcopal sealing and for the eucharist.

In his account in *I Apology* 59.61-66 of the baptismal transaction ending in the eucharistic fellowship Justin does not expressly mention any forms of lighting in connection with the actual practice of baptism. Yet we assume with good reason that baptism took place during the Easter vigil, namely, at night, and that elementary illumination would have in any case been necessary both where the water was and where presumably the main body of the brethren, assembled with the president, awaited the neophytes. Twice in the account a distance is fixed between these two locales: "Then they are led ... where there is water" (*I Apology* 61.1) and "[W]e, after we have thus washed him ..., lead him to those who are called brethren where they are assembled" (65.1). But besides minimal illumination by torches, or lamps, or candles at the water and at the larger assembly, there might well have been symbolic light or flame. Justin perhaps cannot go so far as to tell the pagan world exactly what the initiation rite is, but he unwittingly provides clues; for he interrupts his sober account of baptism to cope with demonic imitation of the Christian lustration and illumination (62-64)[42] before resuming his account of the baptism (65.1 f.) and of the eucharist (65.3-66.3), which is in turn followed by a (however, very much briefer) allusion to pagan (Mithraic) imitation of this aspect of the paschal sacramental action (65.4).

Before drawing attention to what Justin's anti-pagan apologetic may disclose indirectly about otherwise unmentioned aspects of the baptismal transaction of his community, we should remark that a *lucernarium*, the ancestor of the paschal candle (which is lowered into blessed water),

---

[42] Cf. Cullen I. K. Story, "Justin's Apology I: 62-64: Its Importance for the Author's Treatment of Christian Baptism", *Vigiliae Christianae* XVI (1962), 172-178, who stresses the triune God and the noetic element in baptism in this section continuous with what Justin has already said about Christian baptism.

is known to have been borne by Romans in funeral procession and placed
by Christians at the tombs of martyrs, and that, in somewhat later usage,
after being lit with new fire, the paschal candle was acclaimed on Holy
Sabbath as the Light of Christ.[43]

In the excursus *I Apology* 62-64 on how the demons have imitated the
Christian baptismal transaction, Justin is clearly preoccupied with fire.
He adduces the appearance of Christ to Moses in the burning bush in
the wilderness (Exodus 3:1-12). He may well be doing this because he
is trying to explain perhaps as much to Christians as to the pagan world
the prominence of some kind of flame at some point in the baptismal
transaction. Since symbolic flame beyond the mere need of nocturnal
illumination is clearly connected in Justin's references with the place
where there is water, we do well to begin our extrapolation from the anti-
pagan excursuses with what Justin says about water (*I Apology* 64).

In dealing with what is presumably a counterfeit or analogy to some
aspect of the Christian sacramental action, Justin says that the demons
instigated the practice of setting up the images of Kore as daughter of
Zeus at spring-heads, notably at Eleusis, in imitation of Moses' account
(Genesis 1:2) of the Spirit hovering upon the face of the waters, and he
refers back to his own treatment of this in *I Apology* 59.3; 60.6. The
parallel between Spirit and Kore, goddess of springs, would have been
all the more natural to a person or a community aware that the Semitic
word behind πνεῦμα is feminine in gender. Expressly conscious of gender,
Justin then goes on to say that the demons have also "craftily feigned
that Athena was the daughter of Zeus, not by sexual union ... the first
ἔννοια" (64.5) and thereupon he ridicules this absurd feminizing conceptual counterfeit of the Logos-Son.

One can plausibly conjecture, especially in view of Justin's reference
back to his earlier discussion of the primordial waters at creation, that
at the place "where there is water", in scriptural words, by sacred gestures
and with lights, not expressly mentioned, the celebrants set forth symbolically their understanding of that water as at once the face of the
deep at creation and the laver and womb of regeneration. What is more
plausible than that under the starry sky, expressly chosen by astronomical

---

[43] F. Dölger, "Lumen Christi", *Antike und Christentum* V (1936), 1-43; B. Capelle,
"La procession, du Lumen Christi au Samedi-Saint", *Revue Bénédictine* XLIV (1932),
104-119; A. Olivari, "Vom Ursprung der römischen Taufweihe", *Archiv für Liturgie-
wissenschaft* VI (1959), 62-78; and Aileen Guilding, *The Fourth Gospel and Jewish
Worship: A Study of the Relation of St. John's Gospel and the Ancient Jewish Lectionary
System* (Oxford, 1960), esp. 104-110 on the water and light passages for the Feast of
Tabernacles related expressly to Christian baptism.

calculations as the night of the full moon after the vernal equinox, the baptizands and the faithful would be solemnly mindful of what had been revealed to them about God invisible and ineffable (ἄρρητος, *I Apology* 61.1; cf. *Dialogue* 127.2), ποιητὴς τῶν ὅλων (*Dialogue* 56.4), δεμιουργός (*I Apology* 63.7), πατὴρ ὁ οὐράνιος/πάντων/τῶν ὅλων (*I Apology* 15.8; 63.11), and δεσπότης (*I Apology* 12.9; 65.3), and his two Angels and agents, "the second" and "the third δύναμις": the Logos-Son-Wisdom-Christ and the Holy Spirit.

It is significant that in the surviving decorations of the two oldest baptistries, one connected with the house church of Dura Europas (c. 232) and another at San Giovanni in Fonte in Naples (c. 400), the starry sky of the original locale of outdoor paschal baptism is reproduced in the cupolas, and a Roman tombstone (c. 400) for a small boy preserves the same archaic baptismal scene of a starry sky out of which the colomboid Holy Spirit descends with water spilling from its beak.[44] Even though illumination might well have had primarily a cognitive and moral sense, i.e., initiation into the revelation of the Creator of the universe and his universal moral law, it is not necessary (in order to accept Justin's basic account and purpose) to exclude from the baptismal action and from the procession to the water and back such nocturnal illumination as could also have served a symbolic role in keeping with the mystery of regeneration and the acceptance of God as the Creator and sustainer not only of the Creation in general with its sun, moon, and stars but also of each soul.[45] Thus it is quite possible that behind Justin's evocation of both Genesis and the *Timaeus* near the beginning (*I Apology* 49, 50) of his

[44] The latter in the museum in Aquileia is pictured in F. van der Meer and Christine Mohrmann, *Atlas of the Early Christian World* (London/New York, 1955), plate 397. For the iconography of baptistries, see Lucien De Bruyne, "La décoration des baptistères paléochristiens", *Miscellanea Liturgica in honorem L. Cuniberti Mohlberg*, 2 vols. (= *Bibliotheca "Ephemerides Liturgicae"* XXII) (Rome, 1948), esp. p. 193.

[45] The fact that the baptizands "are led (ἄγονται) by us" (*I Apology* 61.3) and that after each one has been joined to us. "we lead (ἄγομεν) to the brethren" (65.1) surely suggests a nocturnal procession. Cf. the quotation in *Dialogue* 122.1 from Isaiah 42:16 ("And I will lead [ἄξω] the blind in a way they know not ... and turn the darkness before them into light") in a chapter that has altogether five uses of "enlighten". The man blind from birth at Bethsaida (Mark 8:22-26; cf. John 9:5), blind Bartimaeus (Mark 10:46-52 and parallels), and the possibly blind paralytic at the pool of Bethsaida (John 5:3-9) are represented in the baptistry of Dura Europas, the catacomb of Calixtus (chapel A 3), and a fourth-century sarcophagus in the Museo delle Terme in Rome, Van der Meer and Mohrmann, plates 50, 52, and 398. The baptizands were clearly conducted in a nocturnal procession with some kind of illumination to and from the baptismal waters. In Orthodoxy this paschal-baptismal procession survives today (even though baptistries are no longer constructed separate from the churches and even though baptisms are no longer performed) on Easter Eve, when the congrega-

account of baptism (*I Apology* 61) and his excursus on demonic counter-
feits of baptism (*I Apology* 62-64) are some real light and fire (differen-
tiated perhaps as a lantern and a torch) used in the consecration of the
baptismal water (the former plausibly in a crosswise motion to make
a ×), and hence as symbols respectively of the Logos, illuminating the
world through the *traditio legis*,[46] and of the Spirit destined with Christ
after their second advent to punish the wicked after the Last Judgment.

That the Logos-Son-Angel-Christ was represented by some kind of
fire at the watery site is most clear in the otherwise inexplicably extended
and misplaced discussion of Christ as the fire in the burning bush (Exodus
3:1-12). In his discussion (*I Apology* 62.3) of this passage in the context
of describing purportedly *to pagans* the initiatory practice of Christians,
Justin is unaccountably preoccupied with arguing *against the Jews* that
the fiery theophany is that of Christ as Angel or Apostle (*I Apology* 63.5;
cf. *Dialogue* 128.1),[47] rather than the invisible and ineffable God, the
Father. Justin's persistent concern to defend the invisibility and ineffability of the transcendant God comes out remarkably at this point in
his (possibly) purposeful inversion of the Matthaean word (11:27) thus:
"No one knoweth the invisible Father but the Son; nor the Son, but the
Father, and they to whom the Son revealeth Him" (*I Apology* 63.3, 13;
Dialogue 100.1).[48]

It can be conjectured, since he seems to be defending a baptismal

---

tion hurries from the basilica with tapers, spreading illumination from "the sleepless
light" on the altar and pressing instinctively around the no longer baptismally func-
tional βρύση (βρύσις) or δεξαμενή before returning to the basilica for the midnight
Easter liturgy. Cf. n. 60.

[46] The figure of Christ as teacher seated in heaven, revealing the law (*traditio legis*),
is pictured in the ancient baptistry in Naples. De Bruyne, *op. cit.*, 192. Johannes
Kollwitz, "Christus als Lehrer und die Gesetzesübergabe an Petrus in der konstantin-
ischen Kunst Roms", *Römische Quartalschrift* XLIV (1936), 45-66 and E. Weigand,
"Die Spätantike Sarkophagskulptur im Licht neuerer Forschungen", *Byzantinische
Zeitschrift* XLI (1941), 104-164, who in passing argues against Josef Wilpert that the
figure of Jesus Christ in the *traditio legis* is seated not on the mount but in heaven.
It is possible that a connection between the *traditio legis* scene and baptism may be
found, for example, in Justin's understanding of Jesus Christ as a God and Lord and
Angel (other than and less than ποιητής τῶν ὅλων, *Dialogue* 56.4), announcing or
giving the Law to the illuminands in *Dialogue* 122.4 (those illumined by the Law) and
122.5 (Christ illuminating the Gentiles with the Law). See above at n. 44.

[47] Cf. Philo, who understood the Logos or even *logoi* to be present in the bush,
De somnis i.69; *De vita Moses* i.66, etc.

[48] The reversal of Father and Son in the Matthaean text is found also in Marcion (?),
Irenaeus, and later Fathers. But neither Leon E. Wright, *Alterations in the Words of
Jesus as Quoted in ... the Second Century* (Cambridge, 1952), nor Arthur Bellinzoni,
The Sayings of Jesus in the Writings of Justin Martyr (Leiden, 1967), sees any theological
motivation in Justin's inversion.

practice against the pagan practice of taking off shoes at a shrine for libations and lustrations, that the catechumens before immersion did remove their shoes and kneel before the presence of symbolic flame, just as Moses knelt unshod before the burning bush. Moreover, since Justin quotes (*I Apology* 63.8) the voice from the fiery theophany, identified by Justin with that of the Logos-Son-Christ, as bidding Moses go down into Egypt and bring forth His people (Exodus 3:6), one may conjecture that it was at this moment that garments were removed from the baptizands and that they were immersed in the waters which could be interpreted as at once the primordial Abyss, the Red Sea, and the Jordan.

That, before the exorcism and consecration, the waters were felt also to be symbolically the abode of Satan and slithering demons from which the baptizands were to be snatched with the abyss behind them sealed off is suggested by the recurrent reference to the serpentine character of *Sata-nas*.[49] In a cluster of three Dominical *logia* (*Dialogue* 76.4-6) adduced in connection with exorcism, an integral part of the whole baptismal transaction,[50] Justin prefers the serpentine *Sata-nas* to the Matthaean reading *devil* in the eschatological command (25:41): "Depart into the outer darkness, which the Father prepared for *Sata-nas* and his angels" (*Dialogue* 76.5). Justin also vividly amplifies (*Dialogue* 76.6) the Dominical asseveration in Luke 10:1-9 and puts it appropriately in the present rather than perfect tense: "I *give* you authority to tread upon serpents and scorpions *and centipedes*, and *on every form* of the Enemy's power." And Justin goes on to affirm that in fact as the result of the crucifixion under Pontius Pilate "we who believe on Jesus our Lord ... exorcise all the demons and evil spirits, and thus hold them subject to us" (*Dialogue* 76.6).[51] During exorcism "the demons today tremble" (*Dialogue* 30.3; 85.2), because Christ overcame the demons "in the time of Pontius Pilate" (*Dialogue* 30.3; 85.2).

But Justin knew that even Jesus himself, as he ascended from the waters of the Jordan, was immediately tempted by *Sata-nas* (*Dialogue* 103.6).

3. A POSSIBLY SIMPLER (UNIPARTITE) BAPTISM FOR CONVERTS FROM JEWRY

It is plausible in a mixed Jewish-Gentile Christian milieu with recent

---

[49] For Justin's etymology, see above at n. 14. For the sealing up of the demonic waters (in reference to the Odes of Solomon), see Lampe, 113.
[50] Dölger, *Der Exorzismus*.
[51] In *Dialogue* 30.3 and 85.2 the efficacy of Christian exorcism is also connected with the crucifixion, symbolically reenacted at the Paschal baptism.

memories of eucharistic and social relations troubled by dietary scruples
on the part of many (of Jewish antecedents) that "Samaritan"-born Justin
could write of his own community of faith, presumably in Rome:

> ... we who ... would not eat with those of other race ..., now since the mani-
> festation of Christ have a common life (*I Apology* 14.4).

Justin was well acquainted with the position and the writings of the
Ebionites "of *our* race", with whose Christology expressly he did not
agree (*Dialogue* 48.4), as well as with those of other Jewish-Christian
and Jewish sects.

The proximity of Christians and Jews in Justin's community of discourse is further suggested by the fact that, though in general Justin
disallows a second penance after penitential baptism, he makes an exception for relapsed Christians of *Jewish* origin. Though tempted after
baptism like Jesus himself by Satan, Christians are under continuous
mutual oversight in the observance of the commandments of the high
priestly race[52] and should be ejected from the community for sinful be-
havior. Justin is more of a rigorist than his older contemporary in Rome,
Hermas, and the possibly Roman homilist of repentance of *II Clement*,
and turns on those Christians "who say that even though they be sinners
..., God the Lord will not impute sin to them" (*Dialogue* 141.2).[53] But
one very serious point, which for former pagans would come under the
grave heading apostasy, for converts from Judaism is mitigated thus:

> But they [Jews] that once professed and recognized that this is the Christ, and
> *do not repent before death*, cannot, I declare, in any wise be saved (*Dialogue* 46.4).

This extraordinary asseveration, albeit in a negative form, about Christians who relapse — not to paganism but to their (ancestral) Judaism —
is given in the general context (*Dialogue* 47) of Justin's making a number
of distinctions with respect to concentric circles or degrees of Judaism[54]

---

[52] Cyril Richardson, "The Meaning of πολιτευταί [distinguished from πολῖται] in
Justin; *I Apology* 65.1", *Harvard Theological Review* XXIX (1936), 89-91; Clarence
Lee, "The Sacerdotal Ethics in Early Christianity", Harvard Th.D. Thesis (Cambridge,
1966).
[53] Justin even exhorted the pagan emperors to punish Christian heretics. *I Apology*
16.14. On Justin's rigorism in comparison with Hermas, see Benoît, 158.
[54] On the various circles of Jews and proselytes, cf. Theodor Zahn, "Studien zu
Justinus Martyr", in *Zeitschrift für Kirchengeschichte* VIII (1886), 59f. On Justin's
effort, against intra-Christian groups such as Marcionites and Gnostics, to preserve the
universal moral element in the Old Testament, which in fact had always appealed to
both prospective Jewish and Christian proselytes from among the Gentiles, see von
Campenhausen, 74, 106, 195f.

impinging on or related to the Christian community: (1) Jews who in their synagogues anathematize Christians; (2) Jews who, having once accepted Jesus as Christ, return to Moses; (3) Christian Jews (by birth) who accept Jesus as the Messiah but who compel Gentile converts to live in accordance with the law or refuse to have communion with them; (4) Jews who accept Jesus as Christ, maintain the ceremonial laws of Moses as well as "those ordinances [in the Old Testament] of the practice of righteousness and of piety which are everlasting and in accordance with nature" (and therefore to be observed also by Gentile Christians), but who do not impose the ceremonial law on fellow Christians of Gentile origin and willingly join them in conversation and at meals; (5) Christian Gentiles who comply with the Jewish legalistic demands of group three (above); (6) Christians of Jewish antecedents who refuse to follow anything but the moral law of the Old Testament and do not perpetuate the rite of circumcision for their Christian progeny; and (7) Jewish proselytes of pagan background, initially attracted to, and versed in, the moral law of the Old Testament and practising at least some of the ethical code of Hellenistic Jewry, but now hovering between a definitive submission to Judaism through the painful rite of circumcision and a no less decisive incorporation into that plenary and painless Christian "Judaism" through baptismal "circumcision" in Jesus as the Messiah and Lord of the Law.

We began our account of the theology and practice of the baptismal transaction in Justin by noting the very close connection between Jews in various stages of attitude toward Jesus and Gentile Christians, of which this classification of seven circles is ample demonstration. It is in a milieu of this "ethnic" and "interfaith" complexity that we must situate Justin's theology and practice of baptism. In this very section (*Dialogue* 47.1) Justin expressly speaks of Christian Gentiles as having "been circumcised by Christ", that is, as having been baptized in a rite which is in part the New Covenantal equivalent of circumcision. Elsewhere (*Dialogue* 43.2) he says more directly that "we [Gentiles] received it [circumcision] by our baptism", quite appropriately on (the eve of the) eighth day (Easter Sunday). It is a "second circumcision" (*Dialogue* 12.3). It is a πνευματική circumcision (*Dialogue* 43.2) of the kind undergone by Adam, Abel, Enoch, Noah, Lot, and Melchizedek (*Dialogue* 19.2-4). It is understood as accompanied by the action of the Holy Spirit (*Dialogue* 29.1) which makes the Jewish form of proselyte baptism (mere ablution in cisterns with all kinds of legalistic specifications) "useless" (*Dialogue* 19.2-5; 46.2). (Justin may also have in mind that the Gnostic ἀπολύτρωσις, with the alleged supplementary bestowal of the Spirit, is supererogatory.)[55]

All this information about concentric and partly intersecting circles of Jewry and the Christian community, and the evident preoccupation with circumcision and its Christian equivalent, baptism, allow us to conjecture that we are, in the extant writings of Justin, at a significant point in the evolution of baptismal theology and practice in the differentiation of the Church from Jewry. Here, indeed, it is possible for Justin, despite his moderate anti-Jewish polemic, to feel that he as a Gentile Christian, faithful now to the divine-natural law of God the Creator revealed by the Logos-Son-Christ-Angel in the Old Testament, and admitted to the high priestly or royal-priestly people — not by circumcision but by baptism in fire and the Spirit — is still not so uniquely privileged in his possession of the Old Testament. For Justin evidently conceded that an hereditary devotee of the invisible ποιητής, δεμιουργός, πατήρ, δεσπότης, even after committing apostasy with respect to Jesus as the Christ (the unique Son and Messenger of that God), might yet, by repentance "before death", hope for salvation (cf. *Dialogue* 46.4 as quoted above). And yet, Justin himself, as a Gentile Christian similarly apostasizing, would be lost forever, because he would have departed presumably not only from Jesus as the Christ, but also from God the Creator (whom that same Christ revealed to former Gentiles like himself).

If we are right in our surmise that Justin felt that there was a distinction between Gentile and Jewish Christian apostasy, he may well have known also of some other prevailing distinction (now lost to our view) between the baptism of recruits from paganism with a tripartite formula and of Jews with merely an unipartite formula in the name of Christ by or in the Holy Spirit (as in Acts 2:38; 8:16 f.; 10:47 f.; 19.5 f.).[56] And if this proselyte baptismal procedure, primarily an ablution, persisted as a substitute also for circumcision with respect to the progeny of both Jewish and Gentile members of the church, then we can conjecture three degrees and possibly formulations of baptism in use at the time of Justin, each influencing the other, until at length the elaborate usage with respect to converts from among the Gentiles with its tripartite formula at immersion would have altered the formula also for the baptism of Christian offspring, and by that time the special baptismal formula hypothesized for Jews who had only to accept Jesus as the Christ in the Spirit would have passed into desuetude. It may have been in the midst of a comparable develop-

---

[55]   See n. 10 above.
[56]   Harry A. Wolfson, *The Philosophy of the Church Fathers*, 2nd ed. (Cambridge, 1964), 143-147.

ment, in anticipation of uniform usage, that the author of Ephesians 4:5 enjoined "one baptism" along with "one Lord, one faith, and one God and Father".[57]

Admittedly what we have clearly outlined in Justin's surviving writings is only the most distinctive and dramatic form of the baptismal transaction with its tripartite formula, the kind that was by his time the most common, and the one through which Justin himself as a Gentile passed. But we do have a reference (*Dialogue* 39.2) to the fact "that every day some [?Jews] are becoming disciples unto (μαθητευόμενοι εἰς) the name of Christ and are being enlightened by (φωτιζόμενοι διά) the name of Christ". That Gentile converts were generally baptized on paschal eve might suggest that Jewish converts to Christ could have been solemnized at any time, which is indeed the clear impression of the early baptismal activity recorded in Acts.

We have been assuming all along that the baptismal theory and practice in Rome as reflected in Justin might well be seen in the framework of the baptismal rite as set forth somewhat later in the *Apostolic Tradition* of Hippolytus (although the author thereof might prove to have been but an Alexandrian sojourner in Rome)[58] and, accordingly, that children were first immersed and then the men, followed by the women. It has been commonly assumed, moreover, that these children could just as well be the progeny of converts as of the faithful (I Cor. 7:14 on presumably baptismal consecration of an unbeliever's progeny). But the fact that they come first in the Hippolytean order could be a way of segregating the progeny of the faithful from the more elaborate baptismal ritual for converts. However this may have been, Justin himself only once intimates baptism of children when in *I Apology* 15.6 he writes of "many men and women of the age of sixty and seventy years who have been disciples (ἐμαθητεύθησαν) of Christ from childhood (ἐκ παίδων)". As the word presumably for being baptized is the same as that for Jewish converts to Christ in *Dialogue* 39.2,[59] it is not implausible to see in the sole reference to infant baptism in Justin but the counterpart of several baptisms of Jews in Acts and elsewhere *in the name of Christ* (alone), a rite much more readily extended to the progeny of Jews becoming followers of Christ than

---

[57] Edgar Goodspeed, *The Meaning of Ephesians* (Chicago, 1933); R. Batey, "The MIA ΣΑΡΧ Union of Christ and the Church", *New Testament Studies* XIII (1966/67), 270-280.

[58] Jean M. Hanssens, *La Liturgie d'Hippolyte* (=*Orientalia Christiana Analecta* CLV) (Rome, 1959).

[59] Cf. Jeremias, *Infant Baptism*, 72.

to pagans becoming illuminated by the scriptural revelation of the Creator God.

There is also indirect evidence of baptism in the name of Jesus Christ alone in the response of a Justin pupil in the trial before the prefect of the city Rusticus, Hierax "from Iconium in Phrygia". To the question about his parentage he replied: "The true father of us in the Christ and [our] mother is faith in him".[60] Hierax, as quite possibly of Jewish origin, stressed as a Christian preeminently the κύριος = πατήρ and πίστις = ματήρ (cf. Ephesians 4:5f.). The closest parallel, however, to his extraordinary affirmation of the paternity of Christ (sanctioned uniquely by Isaiah 9:6, the messianic "Everlasting Father") is the possibly Roman homily, *II Clement*. In the context of a good deal of reference to baptism and to the seal thereof (7.5; 8.6), repentance, and the eschatological fire, the homilist refers to Jesus Christ as one who "had given us light", "Father ... [who] has called us sons" (1.4). The ecclesiological context of the Clementine homily suggests a congregation of mixed Gentile and Jewish background. The other parallel to Hierax' reference to Christ as Father is in the Jewish-Christian Pseudo-Clementine *Homily* 3.14, where Jesus Christ is referred to as "father for his children", "our Father and Prophet". Hierax, who said that he revered and worshipped "the same God" where the antecedent is Christ, and said that this Christ was his Father (through baptism), implied in answer to the prefect that he had been a Christian before coming to Justin ("I was a Christian, and will be a Christian") and said further that after the death of his earthly parents, he "was driven from Iconium in Phrygia". It is pertinent to recall that this Iconium was a Jewish center with a synagogue, where Paul and Barnabas had preached and which was twice revisited (Acts 13:51-14:6, 20f.; 16:2-18:23). It is in this section of Acts (18:24-19:10) where we learn of the Jewish Christian evangelist Apollos of Alexandria, Ephesus, and Corinth, who "knew only the baptism of John" (Acts 18:25) but who "powerfully confuted the Jews in public, showing by the scriptures that the Christ was Jesus" and where we also learn of disciples like him in Ephesus, whom Paul, on discovering them baptized "in the name of the Lord Jesus", laid hands on for the reception of the Holy Spirit and the gift of tongues (19:5).

[60] *Acta martyrii Justini et sociorum*, ed. Otto, III, 274; Rudolf Freudenberger, "Die Acta Justini als historisches Dokument", *Humanitas-Christianitas*, Festschrift für Walter von Löwenich (Witten, 1968), 24-31. Interestingly, in Pseudo-Justin, *De resurrectione* 5 (Otto, III, 591 B) "unbelief" is called "their [i.e., the opponents'] mother".

Although there is surely nothing in the name of Hierax or his fellow students to suggest a Jewish background, he came from a city where both Jews and Jewish Christians were numerous, from a region once familiar with Jewish disciples of John the Baptist who had been baptized in the baptism of repentance in the expectation of the Messiah and who had at the hands of Paul submitted to baptism "in the name of the Lord Jesus", that is, by a formula appropriate for Jews, who already believed in God as Creator of the universe and who had already submitted to the ablutionary-penitential baptism of John. We can only conjecture that the teacher of Hierax, the first outside the canonical New Testament to mention John the Baptist, knew about an earlier and perhaps still current form of baptism for Jews as distinguished from the tripartite formula for former Gentiles like himself.[61]

From what Christian baptism saved adult Gentiles, adult Jews, and Christian progeny was the eschatological fire of the "great and terrible day of the Lord" (*Dialogue* 49.1,2; *II Apology* 7.2,5; and others). How they were saved through Christ's action and through believer's baptism in appropriating the benefits of that action, that is, Justin's theory of atonement or redemption or salvation, is not so clear. Justin understood Jesus to have been not only the Paschal Lamb but also both of the two Passover goats (one respectively for each of his two advents) suffering at once as the goat for the sacrifice and the scapegoat (*Dialogue* 40.4). More directly Justin says that the Father of the universe purposed that His own Christ should receive in Himself the curses of all, on behalf of men of every race, knowing that He would raise Him up after being crucified and dying (*Dialogue* 95.2).

Thus, because of his manifest proximity to Jewry and to scriptural and rabbinical tradition, Justin is best understood in his abundant reference to baptism as giving direct or indirect testimony to three degrees of baptism: for Jews, for Christian progeny, and for Gentile converts. His theology of baptism, especially for this last group, was sustained by a profound conviction as to the cosmological and eschatological setting of sacramental salvation through the Logos-Messenger of the Creator God by whom his heart had been strangely kindled in faith and his spirit has been

---

[61]   One of the other pupil companions of Justin, Euelpistos, came from Cappadocia. It is of interest that the only companion with a Latin name, Liberianus, may have been putting a slightly different accent on his faith as a Christian, when he stressed that he worshipped τὸν μόνον ἀληθινὸν θεόν, which might set him apart from the more Christocentric responses of the other companions.

delivered from ἀνάγκη (*Dialogue* 45.1; *I Apology* 44.1; 61.10). Justin understood baptism as illumination by the Light that saves man from the eschatological Fire.

In this regard, as Father Florovsky reminds us, John 1:1-17 is in the Eastern rite the lesson for (the originally baptismal) Easter liturgy and not for Christmas, as in the Latin rite. Pointing out that Justin stressed the contingency of the soul as creature (against Middle Platonism) and its continuous dependence upon grace for its divinely willed immortality, Professor Florovsky has (drawing more particularly upon Maximus the Confessor) restated what seems to have been in effect the *regent* principle of Justin: "The Light is the Word that illuminates the natural minds of the faithful; but as a burning fire of the judgment ... He punishes those who, through love of the flesh, cling to the nocturnal darkness of this life".[62]

---

[62] "Resurrection of Life", being the Ingersoll Lecture on the Immortality of Man at Harvard Divinity School (10 April, 1951), *Bulletin* of the Harvard University Divinity School XLIX, No. 8 (Cambridge, Massachusetts, 1952), 20; for Justin therein, 7-11 *passim*.

THE IDENTIFICATION OF *EX NIHILO* WITH EMANATION
IN GREGORY OF NYSSA*

HARRY A. WOLFSON

From the fourth century on, whenever Church Fathers stressingly point
to the distinction between the Word and the world as a distinction between that which was generated from God and that which was created
from nothing, they aim, we may assume, not only at the Arian conten-
tion that the Word was created from nothing but also at the Plotinian
view that the world was generated, that is, emanated, from God. It is
this double target that is aimed at by Athanasius in a passage where he
contrasts the Word with the world. The Word, he says, is a "generated
being" (γέννημα) or a "son" and, as such, he is "the proper offspring
(γέννημα) of the essence", "not subject to will", and hence is one who
"must always be". In contradistinction to this, the world is a "created
thing" (ποίημα), and "created things (τὰ γενητά) cannot be eternal, for
they are from nothing", made by God "when He willed (ὅτε ἠθέλητε).[1]
It is also this double target that is aimed at by John of Damascus in a
passage where, speaking of the generation of the Word and alluding to
its distinction from the creation of the world, he says: "Generation is
beginningless and eternal, being the work of nature [that is, not of will]
and coming forth of the Father's own essence, ... while creation, in the
case of God, being the work of will, is not co-eternal with God, for it is
not natural that that which is brought into existence from nothing should
be co-eternal with that which is beginningless and everlasting."[2]

A direct rejection of the theory of emanation as conceived of by the
Neoplatonists is to be found in Basil's comment on the verse "In the
beginning God made (ἐποίησεν) the heaven and the earth" (Gen. 1:1).

* By request of the author, this article, originally composed for this Festschrift, has
also appeared in *Harvard Theological Review* 63 (1970), 53-60. Copyright 1970 by the
President and Fellows of Harvard College.
[1] *Orationes adversus Arianos* I, 29 (PG 26, 72 A-C).
[2] *De Fide Orthodoxa* I, 8 (PG 94, 813 A).

Playing upon the use of the word "made", which he contrasts with the words "worked" (ἐνήργησεν) and "formed" (ὑπέστησεν) that could have been used, he rejects the view of "many" who, while imagining that "the world co-existed with God from eternity", still "admit that God is the cause of it, but an involuntary cause, as a body is the cause of the shadow and the flame is the cause of the brightness".[3] The term "many" quite evidently refers to Neoplatonists, whose view, exactly as reported here by Basil, may be constructed out of the following statements in Plotinus:

(1) "If something exists after the First, it must come from Him either directly or mediately",[4] by which he means that of all the things that exist after God, Intelligence emanates from God directly, Soul emanates from Him indirectly through Intelligence, and the world emanates from Him also indirectly through Intelligence and Soul.

(2) "Since we hold that the world is eternal and has never been without existence", the "Intelligence" — and by the same token also God and the Soul — is "prior" to the world "not as in time" but "in nature", that is to say, it is prior to the world in the sense that it is "the cause of it".[5]

(3) "They are wrong ... who believe that the world was generated by the deliberate will of him who created it",[6] the implication being that the world came into existence by a process of generation which was without will.

(4) Generation is "a radiation of light ... like the bright light of the sun ... which is being generated from it", and like the "heat" which radiates from "fire", and other similar examples.[7]

Basil, in contradistinction to Plotinus, describes the creation of his own belief as God's bringing things "from nothing into existence".[8]

From all this we gather that, as conceived of by the Fathers, the differences between Neoplatonic emanation and their own traditional belief in creation are three: (1) emanation is from God; creation is from nothing; (2) emanation is an eternal process; creation is an act in time; (3) emanation is by nature; creation is by will. I shall now try to show

---

[3] *Hexaemeron* I, 7 (PG 29, 17 BC).
[4] *Enneads* V, 8, 12.
[5] *Enneads* III, 2, 1. On "prior in nature" in the sense of "cause", cf. Aristotle, *Categores*, 12, 14b, 11-13.
[6] *Enneads* V, 8, 12.
[7] *Enneads* V, 1, 6. Among the examples used here by Plotinus as illustrations of necessary causality there is no mention of the example of a body and its shadow, which is used by Basil in the passage quoted above at n. 3. But it must have been a common example. It is thus used in the Arabic version of the *Enneads*, the so-called *Theology of Aristotle* (ed. Dieterici, p. 112, l. 10).
[8] *Epistolae* VIII, 11 (PG 32, 264 B).

how Gregory of Nyssa, by making emanation an act in time and of will, has identified it with creation *ex nihilo*, thus probably being the first to make that identification.[9]

Gregory of Nyssa's own conception of creation is fully unfolded in the following statement: "We believe that the power of the divine will is sufficient to bring things from nothing (ἐκ τοῦ μὴ ὄντος) into existence."[10] This statement he subsequently repeats by saying that, according to the commonly accepted doctrine of faith, "the universe came into existence from nothing (ἐκ τοῦ μὴ ὄντος)".[11] It is to be remarked that in both these statements, as well as in the statements quoted above from Athanasius and John of Damascus and Basil, the Greek phrase which I have translated "from nothing" literally means "from non-existence" or "from the non-existent" but, in Patristic literature, that phrase is used in the technical sense of *ex nihilo*, of which the Greek literal equivalent, ἐξ οὐδενός, is used by Hippolytus.[12] Gregory of Nyssa thus explicitly expresses himself as believing in creation *ex nihilo*. Still in the very same context he also says that, according to Holy Scripture, "the genesis of all things is from God (ἐκ τοῦ θεοῦ)".[13]

Now, by itself, Gregory's statement that "the genesis of all things is from God" could be taken to mean that the creation of the world had been in the thought of God from eternity but that when He actually came to create the world He created it out of nothing. However, from the objection quoted by Gregory himself as having been raised against this statement of his, as well as from the way in which he answers that objection, it is quite clear that he means by this statement literally that, according to Scripture, God created the world out of Himself by an emanation like that conceived of by Plotinus, except that in Gregory's use of it the emanation had a beginning in time and it was an act of the divine will.

The objection against his statement that "the genesis of all things is from God" is ascribed by Gregory of Nyssa to certain "contentious argufiers" (ἐριστικοί), whose own view was that "matter is co-eternal

<hr/>

[9] For later attempts at identifying creation *ex nihilo* with emanation, see my paper "The Meaning of *Ex Nihilo* in the Church Fathers, Arabic and Hebrew Philosophy, and St. Thomas" in *Mediaeval Studies in Honor of Jeremiah Denis Matthias Ford* (1948), 355-370; Gershom Scholem, "Schöpfung aus Nichts und Selbstverschränkung Gottes" in *Eranos* 35 (1957), 87-119; and my paper "The Meaning of *Ex Nihilo* in Isaac Israeli" in *Jewish Quarterly Review* 50 N.S. (1959), 1-12.

[10] *De Hominis Opificio* 23 (PG 44, 212 C).

[11] *De Hominis Opificio* 24 (213 C).

[12] *Refutatio Omnium Haeresium* X, 33, 8, p. 290, l. 8 (ed. P. Wendland).

[13] *De Hominis Opificio* 23 (209 C).

with God".[14] The reference is quite evidently to those well-known followers of Plato who, unlike Plotinus, interpreted the pre-existent matter
of their master's teachings to be not an eternal emanation from God
but rather something independent of God and co-eternal with Him.
Their argument against his statement is quoted by Gregory as follows:
"If God is in His nature simple and immaterial, without quality, without
magnitude, and without composition ... in what way can matter be born
from the immaterial, or a nature which is dimensional from that which
is non-dimensional?"[15] His critics then go on to argue that, "*if*", in
order to explain the origination of matter from God, Gregory assumes
that "something material was in God", then the question is, "How can
He be immaterial while including matter in Himself?".[16] Gregory's critics
thus assume that by his statement that "the genesis of all things is from
God" he means emanation from God's essence after the analogy of
Plotinus' theory of emanation. In fact, the very objection raised against
Gregory's statement reflects a tentative objection raised by Plotinus
himself against his own theory of emanation. As phrased by Plotinus,
it reads: "How from the One, as we conceive it to be, can any multi-
plicity or duality or number come into existence",[17] or "How can the
variety of things come from the One which is simple and which shows,
in its identity, no diversity and no duality?"[18]

That his critics understood correctly the true meaning of his statement
may be gathered from Gregory's answer to their objection. His answer
falls into two parts, corresponding to the two parts of the objection.

In the first part of his answer, while admitting that he meant by his
statement a theory of emanation like that of Plotinus and while admitting
also that this statement would imply that matter emanated from God
who is immaterial, he sidesteps the objection simply by pleading ignorance
of the way in which God moves His wondrous act of creation to perform.
To quote: "In obedience to the teaching of Scripture, we believe that all
things come from God (ἐκ τοῦ θεοῦ); but, as to the question how they
were in God, a question beyond our reason, we do not seek to pry into
it, believing as we do that all things are within the capacity of God's
power, even to bring nothing (τὸ μὴ ὄν) into existence"[19] or, as he ex-

---

[14]   *De Hominis Opificio* 23 (209 C).
[15]   *De Hominis Opificio* (209 D-212 A).
[16]   *De Hominis Opificio* (212 A).
[17]   *Enneads* V, 1, 6.
[18]   *Enneads* V, 2, 1.
[19]   *De Hominis Opificio* 23 (212 B).

presses himself elsewhere, to bring things "from nothing (ἐκ τοῦ μὴ ὄντος) into existence".[20]

The second part of his answer is introduced by him as follows: "It might perhaps be possible, by some skill in the use of words, to convince those who mock at our statement on the score of matter not to think that there is no answer to their attack on it."[21] The "skill in the use of words", by which he is trying to answer this objection, refers to the argument by which he is trying to show (1) that anything of material existence is a combination of various properties, each of which is an intelligible object (νοητόν); (2) wherever these intelligible properties come to be combined with one another, they produce bodily existence; (3) that it is these intelligible properties that emanate from God, who is an intelligible being (νοητός); (4) that God gives existence to the intelligible properties, so as to enable them to emanate from Him and produce bodily existence; (5) that the combination of these emanated intelligible properties with one another produces the material nature underlying bodily existence.[22] The implication of all this is that, just as the combination of the intelligible properties with one another after their emanation from God produces the crass matter of the various bodies, so also their totality during their existence in God forms an "intelligible matter". Accordingly, what Gregory does in this second part of his answer is to admit, for the sake of argument, that in God there is what Plotinus calls "intelligible matter" (ὕλη νοητή), constituted of intelligible properties, but to maintain, in opposition to Plotinus, that the emanation of these intelligible properties from God, as well as their combination and transformation into the crass matter of the corporeal world, was by an act of divine will and in time.

Thus the Christian traditional belief in a volitional and temporal act of creation *ex nihilo* is interpreted by Gregory of Nyssa to mean a volitional and temporal act of emanation from God. Now from a comparison of his statement that God brings all things "from nothing (ἐκ τοῦ ὄντος) into existence"[23] and his statement that "all things come from God (ἐκ τοῦ Θεοῦ)",[24] it is quite evident that the phrase "from nothing" in the former statement is used by him in the sense of the phrase "from God" in the latter statement. But what does he mean by his use of the term "nothing", of which the underlying Greek μὴ ὄν literally means

---

[20] Cf. above at n. 10.
[21] *De Hominis Opificio* 23 (212 C).
[22] *De Hominis Opificio* 24 (212 D-213 B).
[23] Cf. above at n. 10 (plus at n. 11).
[24] Cf. above at n. 19.

"non-existence", as a description of God? Certainly he could not mean by it literally that God is nothing in the sense of His being non-existent. What then does he mean by it?

An answer to this query, I believe, is to be found, again, in the second part of his answer to his critics, the part in which his answer may be described as being only *ad hominem*. According to that part of his answer, the term "nothing" in the phrase "from nothing" quite evidently refers to the "intelligible matter" in God prior to its emanation from Him. But here, evidently aware that in Plotinus the "intelligible matter" is described as "existent" (ὄν)[25] and as "substance" (οὐσία),[26] which certainly does not mean that it is "nothing", Gregory makes two statements from which one may infer an explanation for his description of intelligible matter as nothing. In the first of these statements, using the term "qualities" for "properties", that is, "intelligible properties", he says that, if matter is divested of these qualities, then, "by itself, it can in no way at all be grasped by reason".[27] The second statement reads: "If each of these intelligible properties should be taken away from the substratum, then the whole concept of the body would be dissolved",[28] that is to say, would be reduced to nothing. Though the matter which is explicitly mentioned in the first statement and is implied in the second statement refers to the matter underlying bodies in the world, it may be reasonably assumed that, throughout his discussion of the subject, whatever he says about the matter underlying bodies is true also of the intelligible matter in God prior to its emanation. Thus matter, including the intelligible matter in God prior to its emanation, is described as "nothing" in the sense of its being "by itself" incapable of being "grasped by reason" or incapable of existing in our mind as a "concept"; in short, in the sense of its being incomprehensible.

Thus, according to the second part of his answer, where for the sake of argument Gregory admits that there is in God an intelligible matter, the phrase "from God" in his statement that "the genesis of all things is from God" and the phrase "from nothing" in his statement that "the universe came into existence from nothing" both mean from the intelligible matter, which "intelligible matter" is called by him "nothing" because of its being "incomprehensible". I shall now try to show how also according to the first part of his answer, where the phrase "from God"

---

[25] *Enneads* II, 4, 16.
[26] *Enneads* II, 4, 5.
[27] *De Hominis Opificio* 24 (212 D).
[28] *De Hominis Opificio* (213 A).

and "from nothing" in the same two statements of his mean from the essence of God, that "essence of God" is similarly called by him "nothing" because of its being "incomprehensible".

It happens that the incomprehensibility as well as the ineffability of God as to His essence is the common belief of the Fathers, and Gregory of Nyssa himself gives expression to it in his statement that God "cannot be grasped by any term or by any thought, or by any other mode of comprehension".[29] In the light of this, is it not reasonable to assume that the term "nothing" which is applied by Gregory to God in the first part of his answer is used by him in the sense that there is "nothing" whereby God's essence can be comprehended and described? In fact, about four centuries later, John Scotus Erigena, whose open advocacy of the identification of *ex nihilo* with emanation is exactly like the view which I have tried to elicit from the implications of certain statements in Gregory of Nyssa, explains the term "nothing" in its application to God as being used by him in the sense of the incomprehensibility and the ineffability of God. And here is how Erigena arrives at this explanation.

He begins by stating that "nothing" (*nihil*) means "non-existence" (*non esse*).[30] This, as we have noted above, is the common meaning of "non-existence" (μὴ ὄν) as used by the Greek Fathers. But the fact that Erigena found it necessary to make that statement is significant. It alludes to the two meanings which Aristotle assigns to "non-existence". One is that which he describes as being "non-existence accidentally" (τὸ οὐκ ὄν κατὰ συμβεβηκός), and this he applies to matter. The other is that which he describes as being "non-existence essentially" (καθ᾽ αὑτήν), and this he applies to "privation" (στέρησις), which, in this connection, he uses in the sense of the absence of form,[31] in contrast to "privation" in the sense of the "forcible removal of anything";[32] and it is with reference to what he considers here as essential non-existence that he says elsewhere that "non-existence" (τὸ μὴ ὄν) is "nothing" (μηδέν).[33] It is, therefore, "non-existence" in its essential sense and as applied by Aristotle to "privation" in the sense of the absence of form that Erigena has reference to in his statement that "nothing" means "non-existence".

He then goes on to show that the term "nothing", which, in his identi-

[29] *Contra Eunomium* (PG 45, 461 B).
[30] *De Divisione Naturae* III, 5 (PL 122, 634 B).
[31] *Physics* I, 9, 192a, 3-5.
[32] *Metaphysics* V, 27, 1022b, 31.
[33] *De Generatione et Corruptione* I, 3, 318, 15; cf. *Physics* I, 9, 192a, 5-6.

fication of the phrase "from nothing" with the phrase "from God", is applied to God, has the meaning of "privation" in the sense of the absence of form to which Aristotle applies essential non-existence or nothing. But, having in mind Aristotle's statement that "by form I mean the essence of each thing",[34] he concludes his attempt to explain his use of the term "nothing" as a description of God by saying that that term, in its application to God, "means the privation of the total essence",[35] that the expression "the privation of the total essence" means "the universal negation of relation, and essence or substance, or accident, and, in general, the negation of all that can be spoken of or thought of",[36] and that such a "universal negation" is to be applied to God, for God "cannot be spoken of or thought of".[37]

It is by this use of the term "nothing" in the sense of "the negation of all that can be spoken of or thought of" that Gregory of Nyssa, I imagine, would explain his interpretation of the traditional description of creation as being "from nothing" to mean that it is "from God", for God, as it is commonly believed by the Fathers, is in His essence ineffable and incomprehensible.

[34] *Metaphysics* VII, 7, 1032b, 1-2.
[35] *De Divisione Naturae* I, 3 (443 A).
[36] *De Divisione Naturae* III, 22 (686 CD).
[37] *De Divisione Naturae* I, 15 (463 B).

THE RELATION OF THE INCARNATION TO SPACE
IN NICENE THEOLOGY

T. F. TORRANCE

> ... And in one Lord Jesus Christ, the only-begotten Son
> of God, begotten of the Father before all worlds, God of
> God, Light of Light, being of one substance with the
> Father, by whom all things were made; who for us men
> and for our salvation came down from heaven, and was
> incarnate by the Holy Ghost of the Virgin Mary, and was
> made man, and was crucified also for us under Pontius
> Pilate; He suffered and was buried, and the third day He
> rose again, according to the Scriptures, and ascended
> into heaven, and sitteth on the right hand of the Father.
> And He shall come again with glory to judge both the
> quick and the dead; whose Kingdom shall have no end ...

When the Nicene-Constantinopolitan Creed speaks about Jesus Christ
who was born of the Virgin Mary and crucified under Pontius Pilate
as "of one substance with the Father" (ὁμοούσιον τῷ πατρί), it is clearly
affirming that God Himself in His own being is actively present with us
as personal Agent within the space and time of our world. Thus "came
down from heaven" (κατελθόντα ἐκ τῶν οὐρανῶν) is predicated of God
Himself in the being of the Son. How are we to understand this *spatial*
language in its application to the redemptive movement of God in the
Incarnation (not to speak of its use in relation to the ascension and the
heavenly session of Christ, or indeed of His coming again)?

So far as the statements of the Creed itself are concerned three things
may be said right away. (1) In spite of the insistence of the Creed that
He who was born of the Virgin Mary is one and the same as He who
was born before all worlds, it is not saying that the humanity of Christ
was preexistent or that it came down. Likewise, when the Creed speaks
of the historical events in the experience of the incarnate Son, in suffering
and death and resurrection, and identifies Him with the One through
whom all things were made, it is not projecting historical happening into

the eternal Being of God. (2) The "came down from (ἐκ) heaven" must be interpreted in accordance with "God from (ἐκ) God, Light from (ἐκ) Light".[1] That is to say the *relation* between the actuality of the incarnate Son in space and time and the God from whom He came cannot be spatialised. God dwelling in heaven is essentially a theological concept like "God of God", and is no more a spatial concept than God dwelling in Light. (Even if we could conceive of a heaven of heavens we could not think of it as containing God.) It is the Biblical way of thinking that is employed here. God is the Maker of heaven and earth and of all things visible and invisible, and thus of the whole realm of space, but the relation between God and space is not itself a spatial relation. Hence the "came down" of the Creed is not in any sense to be construed as a journey through space. It is true that the mythological synthesis of God and the cosmos,[2] with its confusion between the presence of God and upper space, is to be found in the anonymous *De mundo* (falsely attributed to Aristotle) that gained currency in the second and third centuries and corrupted proper understanding of Ptolemaic cosmology. But this conception of intervening space between God and man is as far removed from Nicene theology as anything could be.[3] God is transcendent to the world He has made and remains transcendent even in the incarnation of the Son. (3) While the *homoousion* of the Son with the Father expressed the conviction that what He was toward us in His incarnate activity He was inherently, and therefore antecedently and eternally, in Himself, the conjunction of "came down" with "for us men and our salvation" makes it clear that the involvement of the Son in our lowly condition is to be understood as an act of pure condescension on His part and not as an indication of imperfection in Him. He was not creaturely or space-conditioned in His own eternal Being, but He humbled Himself to be one with us and to take our finite nature upon Himself, *all for our sakes.*[4] This is what patristic theology called His "economic condescension", i.e., the way in which God chose out of transcendent freedom and grace to effect the salvation of mankind.

These credal affirmations are clearly meant to be positive statements intelligibly correlated with the self-revelation of God in Jesus Christ, enshrining concepts that have objective truth corresponding to them be-

---

[1]   Hilary, *De Trinitate* VI, 12 (J. P. Migne, *Patrologia Latina* X, 165 ff. — hereafter *PL*).
[2]   Cf. H. Vogel, *Das Nicaenische Glaubensbekenntnis* (1963), 74 f.
[3]   See *De mundo* (ed. W. L. Lorimer), 391 a f., 399 a, 400 a, and the like.
[4]   Cf. T. H. Bindley, *The Oecumenical Documents of the Faith*, ed. F. W. Green (1950), 37, and John Burnaby, *The Belief of Christendom* (1959), 79.

cause they are grounded finally in the nature and activity of God Himself. Thus in spite of the hymnic character of the Creed, its language cannot be treated as if it were merely symbolic (or indeed essentially symbolic), employing simply aesthetic, non-conceptual forms of thought that are related to God in a detached, oblique way, but that derive their meaning and justification mainly through coordination with the religious imagination and self-understanding of the Church. Rather is the language to be regarded as essentially signitive, employing conceptual forms that are intended to refer us to God in a direct and cognitive way and that have their meaning and justification precisely in that act of objective intention.[5] There should be little doubt that the Nicene Fathers were convinced that the disciplined statements they made in formulating the Creed were rightly and properly related to what they signified, namely a basic conceptuality that did not vary with the many forms of man's own devising but one that was controlled by the reality intended.

This makes it all the more important for us to understand carefully the way in which spatial language is used in such statements. If they are merely symbolic, then the spatial element in them can be interpreted quite easily, in a merely metaphorical or tropical sense, yet at the expense of any conceptual correlation. But if they are essentially signitive, then the conceptual content of the statements must have some real correlation with God's own inherent intelligibility through which they fulfil their intention not only of indicating His reality but of affording us, in some measure at least, definite cognitive apprehension of God in His own nature and activity. Of course the words and concepts that we use are human and creaturely, with a human and creaturely content, for they belong to our existence in this world and partake of the limits of nature. If they are to be used to speak of God, they must be stretched and extended beyond the range of the creaturely and phenomenal world for which they were formed in the first place; otherwise they can only serve to exclude everything except purely natural knowledge.[6] We are aware of something similar to this in the advance of natural science where we must be prepared to do violence to our ordinary forms of speech and thought if we are to apprehend and absorb what is genuinely new.

---

[5] Contrast the approach of Paul Tillich, who constantly opposed "symbols" to "signs", and argued that the knowledge of faith was basically "non-conceptual". Cf. the admirable discussion of David H. Kelsey, *The Fabric of Paul Tillich's Theology*, 41 ff.
[6] This point was constantly made by Hilary in his exposition of Nicene theology. See *De Trinitate* I, 10-19 (*PL*, X, 31-39); II, 5-7 (*PL*, X, 53-57); III, 8 and 24-26 (*PL*, X, 80 and 92-94); IV, 2 and 14 (*PL*, X, 97 and 107); V, 1 (J. P. Migne, *Patrologia Graeca* X, 130 — hereafter *PG*); and so forth.

We have to devise new languages and step up to higher levels of thought in order to push knowledge beyond the limits of ordinary experience, yet all this remains within the limits of nature, for we ourselves belong to nature and are unable to rise above it. We cannot of ourselves transcend the necessities of finite apprehension. Scientific violence is an even more stringent requirement in theology, for a considerable shift in the meaning and reference of our ordinary terms and conceptions is necessary if they are really to indicate God Himself. But if that is to happen, the violence to which our ordinary forms of speech and thought are subjected must come from beyond us. They must be opened up from above, as it were, for anything that we do to push our words and concepts beyond the boundary of creaturely being can only take a mythological form, that is, by way of projecting the creaturely content of our concepts as such onto God. To be more precise, if human forms of thought and speech are to have a transcendental reference to what is really beyond them, this reference must be given to these forms by God Himself. That is why authentic theological statements have an orientation beyond themselves in the coming of the Word of God and through assimilation to that Word are taken up to a higher level of understanding where they partake of "a new dimension which they do not possess of their own accord".[7]

On the other hand these theological statements must retain some genuine connection with our plain, straightforward language, for if the concepts they embody are completely detached from those that are found in our ordinary knowledge and language, then the statements can no longer mean anything to us, much less convey anything to others. This is of course also characteristic of natural science, for the highly abstract denotations which we have to develop therein to lift the range and level of our knowledge cannot be cut adrift from physical language based on our old concepts of space and time, because it is through this physical language alone that the applicability of scientific concepts and terms to existence, and thus their truth, can be shown.[8] Thus while scientific concepts need to be extended in order to lay hold of what is really new they cannot be allowed to take off into an arbitrary world of their own, but they must be held in a structure of levels in which lower levels are opened to higher levels and the higher are controlled through coordination with the lower. The connection between the levels, by the very nature

---

[7]   Edward Schillebeeckx, *Revelation and Theology*, 135; also 132-138.
[8]   Cf. the discussion of W. Heisenberg, *Physics and Philosophy* (1958), 167 ff.

of the case, can be made only after new knowledge has been gained and new concepts have been formed.[9]

Now it cannot be otherwise in a disciplined theology. The scientific function of theological statements is to offer a rational account of knowledge beyond the limits of merely this-worldly experience through the use of acknowledged concepts taken from this world, and in this way to help our minds get some hold upon such knowledge, even though it is more than we can grasp in terms of this-worldly concepts. Theological statements properly made are operational statements directing us toward what is new and beyond us but which cannot be wholly indicated or explained in terms of the old. Hence as long as theological concepts must retain their creaturely content we cannot claim to lay hold of the divine reality by means of them; nevertheless they must be employed in the service of our knowledge of God in an act of direct intention in which their creaturely content is not ascribed to God, but becomes the medium of transcendental reference to Him. This takes place as under His self-revelation, i.e., God's own inherent intelligibility forces itself upon our apprehension, stretching and enlarging it so that we are directed through and beyond the creaturely content of our concepts to God Himself in His divine mode of being and activity. Theological statements operate, then, with essentially *open concepts* — concepts which, though relatively closed on our side of their reference through their connection with the space-time structures of our world, on God's side are wide open to the infinite objectivity and inexhaustible intelligibility of His divine being. Or to put it another way, the kind of conceptuality characteristic of theology is one in which our acts of cognition are formed under the pressure of the transcendent reality they intend to know so that the intelligible content of what is disclosed constantly bursts through the forms we bring to it in order to grasp it.

1

It is not possible within the dimensions of this essay to examine in detail the notions of space that the Christian Church found in contemporary culture and adapted for itself as it developed its own understanding and articulation of the relation between God and the world that is proclaimed in the Gospel. But without at least some summary statement of the notion of space prevalent in Greek thought, and in particular as developed

[9]   Cf. E. H. Hutten, *The Ideas of Physics* (1957), 64.

in the writings of Plato, Aristotle, and the Stoics, our exploration of the relation of the doctrine of Incarnation to the idea of space in Nicene theology would obviously lack a critical point of reference.

The popular and most persistent notion of space found in Greek thought from the earliest times was that derived by analogy from the vessel that may hold wine, water, air, or some other "body". A receptacle or container of this sort might be called a *place*, for place is that into which and out of which things pass, or are made to pass, or which encompasses them when they are in it. This notion of space was applied to the known universe, and what was beyond it was held to be the void. It was within this rather simple but universally held notion of space that the philosophers and scientists put forward their more reasoned views. Plato treated the receptacle concept of space rather metaphorically and developed something like a relational account of space, pointing out the difficulty of projecting the idea of space conceived within the sensible world beyond its boundary with the intelligible world. Aristotle, on the other hand, who misunderstood Plato, returned to the notion of the receptacle but thought of it and the matter it contained as interdependent, and so defined place as the innermost unmoved limit of the container. Place is what contains and limits that of which it is the place. Thus Aristotle offers a predominantly volumetric concept of space. The Stoics preferred to think of space in terms of that which occupies place, and sought to think through the whole container-contained idea by means of an active principle in which they conceived of body as making room for itself through an innate source of motion to make up the whole of the ordered universe, which they saw as set in the infinite void. But this had the effect of identifying God with the rationality that animated the cosmos and even of delimiting Him as coincident with the cosmic body as a whole, while, when linked with the Aristotelian separation (χωρισμός) between terrestrial and celestial mechanics, it had the effect of retarding the science of the heavens until comparatively modern times. Other conceptions of space did gain currency in the ancient world, such as those of the atomists and Epicureans, but, as we see in the *De rerum natura* of Lucretius, they were largely variations upon the old theme of the vessel, with space becoming the infinite container of bodies. But nevertheless the conceptions of the Platonists, the Aristotelians and the Stoics tended to prevail (sometimes assimilated closely to one another) and to provide the general basis for future theories.

What did early Christian theology make of all this? How far was it indebted to Greek notions of space? Or did it merely quarry from them in its search for scientific tools with which to develop its own concepts at those points where the Christian message forced the Church to think out the relation of the saving presence and activity of God to our human existence in the space and time of this world?

2

We shall examine the teaching of Origen by way of answering these questions, not only because he was immensely influential among Nicenes and Arians alike, but because it was in Alexandria, with which he was mostly associated, that the teaching of the different schools in philosophy and science had been merged (e.g. by Poseidonius) as perhaps nowhere else, and because Origen himself was so deeply steeped in this cultural tradition. It is not surprising, therefore, to find the familiar Greek notions of container (περίεχον) and place (τόπος) coming naturally to him when he wrote of anthropology, cosmology, or theology. Porphyry spoke of him as essentially Greek in his theology and cosmology, although Christian in his way of life,[10] but in doing so failed to take into account a supreme factor that led Origen to rethink and adapt the ideas he had learned in the schools — his doctrine of God. Unlike the "God" of the Greeks, the God who is revealed and known only through Jesus Christ and the Holy Spirit, the God who is a triad in His own unity and eternity, is completely transcendent in substance, existence, and perfection. Yet this transcendent God, and only He, can at once also be fully and freely immanent throughout the created universe without being limited or restricted by it.[11] In His own Being, as Father, as Son, or as Holy Spirit, He is αὐτοθεός, and so αὐτοαλήθεια, αὐτοσοφία, αὐτοδικαιοσύνη, αὐτολόγος, αὐτουργός, and the like.[12] This means that we must think of God strictly and consistently in accordance with His self-existent nature and majesty as God, and we must have as our "rule of piety" *to think nothing unworthy of Him.*[13]

---

[10] See A. A. T. Ehrhardt, "Origen, Theologian in the Cataclysm of the Ancient World", *Oikoumene: Studi Palaeocristiani Publicati in Onore del Concilio Ecumenico Vaticano II* (Catania, 1964), 283.

[11] See especially *De principiis* I, Preface and ch. I; and IV, IV.1f. GCS ed. P. Koetschau, *Origines*, vol. V. (Hereafter citations are made with reference to the volumes of GCS edition.)

[12] *Commentary on John* 2.2; *Contra Celsum*, numerous references listed by Koetschau in *Sachregister* II, 463.

[13] *De principiis* V, 32.18; 73.14f.; 132.8; 144.12ff.; 208.11f.; 31f.; 227.13f.; 228.13f.; 241.28; 273.1; 310.18; 322.11,29; 328.29f.; 345.6. Cf. *Contra Celsum* II (VII, 42), 193.13f.

God created all things out of nothing and gave them their order — all things that are, are made by God, so that there is nothing that is not created except the nature of the Father, Son, and Holy Spirit.[14] He created things invisible as well as visible, non-somatic as well as somatic; He created intelligible as well as sensible realities.[15] As the transcendent source of all that is not God or of all that is outside of Him it may even be said that God Himself does not participate in being, since all else participates in Him (ἀλλ᾽ οὐδὲ οὐσίας μετέχει ὁ θεός/ μετέχεται γὰρ μᾶλλον ἢ μετέχει, καὶ μετέχεται ὑπὸ τῶν ἐχόντων 'πνεῦμα θεοῦ').[16] There is therefore nothing created or material in God. He is not to be regarded in any sense as "body", so that we cannot worthily think of Him through the kind of forms and shapes we derive from the contemplation of created and physical existents. We may know Him only by thinking away the created and physical, and — in a simple, intuitive act of the intelligence — by penetrating through all worldly forms and terms, even those supplied to us in the Holy Scriptures.[17] God is therefore, so far as our creaturely forms and concepts are concerned, ineffable, indescribable, and incomprehensible, for He transcends even "eternal intelligence" and is comprehended only by, and through, the Son and the Holy Spirit.[18]

Grounded in this doctrine of God, Origen entered into critical dialogue with Greek thought. It is true that there can be no infinite void, for "God is everywhere and in all things". Yet this requires some qualification. If we are to think in accordance with God's nature, we cannot speak of Him being "in" things in the same way as we do of created realities.[19] Thus while we must say that "there is no place empty of God" (οὐδεὶς τόπος κενὸς τοῦ θεοῦ),[20] we must also say that "God is not in a place" (οὐκ ἐν τόπῳ ὁ θεός).[21] The same applies, as we shall see, to God the Son in the sense that He cannot be confined to a physical place.[22] God is not contained by anything, for on the contrary He contains all (θεὸν τὸν περιέχοντα τὰ ὅλα).[23] There is a sense in which one might

14   De principiis V, 9.13f.; 50.14f.; 271.12ff.; 273.1ff.; 359.9f.
15   De principiis V, 21.13f.; 86.5ff.; 159.4ff.; 289.11ff.; 347.15f.
16   Contra Celsum II, 134-135.
17   De principiis V, 20.1ff.; 21.10ff.; 112.15ff.; 131.14ff.; 282.12ff.; 347.5ff.; 350.7ff.
18   De principiis V, 20.5ff.; 21.10ff.; 54.4ff.; 55.1ff.; 272.7ff.; 345.23f.; 346.11ff.
19   De principiis, 283.5f. This applies particularly to a rejection of the idea that God is "in" any evil.
20   Contra Celsum I, 277.29ff.
21   Contra Celsum II, 284.14f.; 186.8.
22   De principiis V, 191.1ff.; 351.1f.; 18f.
23   Contra Celsum I, 365.19; II, 184.17.

speak of the universe as "an immense, monstrous animal held together by the power and reason of God as by one soul" because God fills heaven and earth and by His will "contains" it from being mastered by corruption.[24] "God is the Parent of all things, filling and containing the entire universe with the fullness of His power."[25] But this is to be conceived not (as did the Stoics) in the manner of a bodily container (οὐχ ὡς σῶμα δὲ περιέκον περιέχει), for it is the "body" that is contained by the divine power that embraces and encompasses everything.[26]

On the other hand, Origen does clearly accept the Stoic principle that comprehension and limitation go together, because what is not determinate or limited (πεπερασμένον) is incomprehensible. That is why God is incomprehensible, for He is immeasureable and far transcends all our thoughts about Him.[27] He is Platonist enough to insist that the mind does not need a sensible magnitude in order to think,[28] but he is aware of a logical problem in the notion of the infinite — if we are to think mathematically *ad infinitum*, we cannot at the same time put a limit to infinite progression; on the other hand, the finite mind cannot think of what is without beginning and without end. What Origen does is to turn the Stoic principle around by insisting that it is the fact that *God comprehends all things* that limits them, giving them beginning and end, and thus making them comprehensible.[29] "Every creature, therefore, is distinguished before God by being confined within a certain number or measure, i.e., within number in the case of rational beings or measure in the case of corporeal matter."[30] Moreover, Origen claims, very daringly, if the power of God were infinite (ἄπειρος) in the sense thus indicated, He could not even know Himself, since the infinite is by its nature incomprehensible (τῇ γὰρ φύσει τὸ ἄπειρον ἀπερίληπτον). In this sense, then, God's power is limited (πεπερασμένην), but self-limited, in the limitation of the creation through its subjection to His comprehension, oversight, and providence.[31] Hence Origen pleads: "Let no one stumble at the statement, if we put measures (μέτρα) even to God's power, for to encompass infinite things happens to be an inherent impossibility (ἄπειρα γὰρ περιλαβεῖν τῇ φύσει ἀδύνατον τυγχάνει). But once those

[24]   *De principiis* V, 108.11ff.; 124.1ff.
[25]   *De principiis*, 108.30.
[26]   *Contra Celsum* II, 141.11f.
[27]   *De principiis*, 20.7f.
[28]   *De principiis*, 21.14f.
[29]   *De principiis*, 272.16f.
[30]   *De principiis*, 360.10f.
[31]   *De principiis*, 164.3f.

things which God himself has inclosed in His grasp have been limited, factual necessity serves to determine the extent of their limitation. For by His power He contains or comprehends all things (ἐμπεριέχει τὰ πάντα), but He Himself is contained or comprehended by the mind of no creature."[32]

Origen seems to have overlooked that the eternity of God is different from any mathematical infinity, for since God is not in a genus with anything He cannot be thought of within the same calculus as an infinite series. But Origen was trying "by a logical answer to preserve the rule of piety".[33] This, however, created a real dilemma for him. By pushing back questions endlessly one after the other we reach the conclusion that God was always almighty and always exercising His power, that there was no beginning to His power or its exercise. But we cannot even speak of God as almighty without assuming the existence of the universe.[34] Either we think of God as progressing to almightiness or we assume that the creation was always there for the exercise of His power and care.[35] On the other hand, it would be an impiety to think of matter (or that which under-lies bodies) as uncreated and co-eternal with the uncreated God. Origen admits to a conflict in our human thoughts and reasoning, but he seeks an exit from the difficulty by speaking of creation as always present and existent in and through its *prefiguration* in the divine Wisdom.[36]

Origen further distinguishes in Platonic fashion between the two realms of the intelligible and the sensible, the invisible and the visible.[37] In Biblical language this is the distinction between heaven and earth, or the other-world and this world. He will not have it, however, that the other-world is simply a realm of thought. For we must take seriously the Biblical teaching that the Saviour came from the other-world and that the saints go to it.[38] "But whether that world which the Saviour wishes us to know is one separated and widely divided from this in respect of space, quality, or glory, or whether, as it seems to me more likely, it excells in glory and quality but is nevertheless *contained within the compass of this world*, is not certain, and is, I think, still rather strange for human thoughts and minds."[39] Origen goes on to speak of the other-world as comprising

[32]   *De principiis*, 359.16f.; 360.1f.
[33]   *De principiis*, 273.1f.
[34]   *De principiis*, 40.14f.; 41.1f.; 65.9f.; 66.1ff.
[35]   *De principiis*, 42.1ff.; 110.7ff.
[36]   *De principiis*, 67.3f., 12f.
[37]   *De principiis*, 91.11f.; 92.1ff.; 289ff.; *Contra Celsum* II, 90.19ff.; 198.6ff.
[38]   *De principiis*, 121.20ff.
[39]   *De principiis*, 122.7ff.; 190.1f.

seven "worlds" or "heavens", one sphere beyond the other.

Just as with us the heaven contains all things that are under it, so that one, they say, with its vast magnitude and indescribable compass holds together the spaces of the other spheres by a more magnificent ambit, so that all things are within it as this world of ours is under the sun ... It is within that heaven that the "earth" which our Saviour promised to the meek and gentle in the Gospel is contained and enclosed.[40]

Origen's difficulty here is reminiscent of that which faced Plato, for like him he will not think of the χωρισμός as local separation or physical distance, yet he is concerned not to discard entirely spatial concepts when speaking of the other-world. Hence he speaks not only of a "heavenly place" (τόπος οὐράνιος),[41] but of a "superheavenly place" (τόπος ὑπερουράνιος),[42] as well as of an "earthly place" (τόπος περίγειος).[43] Earlier in the De principiis he had insisted that mind does not need physical space. It acts in accordance with its rational nature, and is not hindered by diversity of places (ex locorum diversitate) from fulfilling its own activities. It is not physical but intelligible magnitude that the mind needs (indiget sane mens magnitudine intelligibili) for its development and advance.[44] That is, the concept of place or space must be formed in accordance with the nature of the occupying agent. This, argues Origen, is the principle we must follow in thinking out the nature of spatial concepts in theological statements about God if we are to think worthily of Him.

This problem becomes particularly acute when we speak of the Incarnation as the coming of the Son of God from the other-world of God to us in this world, and then of His returning to God. But before we examine Origen's treatment of this there is something else that we must take into account, namely, that in creating rational beings in this world God has involved them in physical existence. Thus bodily nature is needed to support the lives and uphold the movements of spiritual and rational minds. Life without a body is found only in the divine Trinity.[45] Moreover, bodies are needed for diversity and individuation in this world.[46] Rational

---

[40] De principiis, 123.2ff.
[41] Contra Celsum I, 270.22; II, 89.32; 130.6; 196.3.
[42] Contra Celsum II, 362.25.
[43] Contra Celsum I, 41.25; 111.6; II, 129.24,28; 201.14. Cf. also σωματικὸς τόπος II, 182.32; 183.30f.; 351.4ff.
[44] De principiis, 21.13ff.; 22.4ff.; 23.1ff.
[45] De principiis, 112.2f.; 22.21f.; 86.5f.
[46] De principiis, 109.9f. See also 166.6f., where Origen indicates that God makes use of man's fall in His purpose of diversification. Souls were created alike and equal, of the same nature (169.25; 239.3f.).

natures of this kind are necessarily subject to change and alteration, for they are endowed with the power of free and voluntary movement.[47] When somehow rational souls took the way of evil, they embarked on a course of withdrawal from God and of privation. As a punishment, they were incarcerated in their bodies and subjected to futility by being bound to what is not their proper nature.[48] It is in this context that Origen reverts most to the Greek habit of speaking of the material body as confining what it contains within fixed limits.[49] Now rational souls can move only in two directions, downward or upward; in going downward they become more and more confined within the limits and darkness of material existence, but in going upward they move into openness and light. It is a movement from restrictive space into wide intelligible magnitudes, from earthly space to heavenly space. One is the way of privation, the other the way of fullness in God. Yet this does not involve local transition from one place to another so much as the spiritualisation and illumination of human existence until it is rendered transparent and open to God's fullness.[50] What rational beings required in their fallen and confined condition was the help of God Himself, but if salvation was to come it could not take place by the pressure of some necessity or by force, but by word, by reason, and by teaching.[51] Thus the incarnation of the Son of God is regarded by Origen as the injection of the Word and Wisdom of God into the constrained and captive condition of humanity in order to break man out of his confinement and restore him to the fullness of God. And it is from this ground that he thinks through the problem of spatial and temporal concepts in Christian theology.

Certainly this was the line that Origen later took in debate with Celsus in his attack upon the Christian belief that God Himself comes down to men.[52] So far as God Himself is concerned, Origen insists that in coming down to us God who fills heaven and earth does not leave His own seat (τὴν ἑαυτοῦ ἕδραν, reverting thereby to the Platonic term), and His coming down or His condescending to us must be understood tropolog-

---

[47]   *De principiis*, 165.17 ff.
[48]   *De principiis*, 63.10 ff.; 81.1 ff.; 91.5 f.; 96.1 f.; 97.1 f.; 104.8 f.; 160.19 f.; 165.22 f.; 275.1 ff.; 238.19 f.; 239.1 ff.; *Contra Celsum* II, 201 f.
[49]   *De principiis* V, 64.12 f.; 96.11; 97.3 f.; 171.3; 260.21; 282.13 f.
[50]   *De principiis*, 23.1 f.; 84.22 ff.; 85.1 ff.; 89.12 f.; 90.1 f.; 91.1 f.; 101.28 f.; 102.1 f.; 169.18 ff.; 174.11 f.; 181.1 ff.; 182.1 f.; 190.1 ff.; 191.5 ff.; 240.20 ff.; 241.1 ff.; 242.12 ff.; 260.15 ff.; 261.1 ff.; 262.17 f. Cf. Athanasius, *Contra gentes*, 23 (*PG*, 25.48 b).
[51]   *De principiis*, 278.24 f.
[52]   *Contra Celsum* I (IV, 2-5), 275.9 ff.; 277.14 ff.

ically or in a figurative sense.[53] But in regard to the Incarnation, he has this to say:

Even, then, if the God of the universe descends with Jesus into human life by His power, and even if the Word who "was in the beginning with God", and who was Himself God, comes to us, He does not go away from where He was, nor does He leave His throne, as though one place were deprived of Him, and another which previously did not possess Him were filled (οὐκ ἔξεδρος γίνεται οὐδὲ καταλείπει τὴν ἑαυτοῦ ἔδραν, ὡς τινὰ μὲν τόπον κενὸν αὐτοῦ εἶναι ἕτερον δὲ πλήρη, οὐ πρότερον αὐτὸν ἔχοντα). The power and divinity of God comes to dwell among men through the man whom God wills to choose and in whom He finds room (ἐν ᾧ εὑρίσκει χώραν) without changing from one place (τόπον) to another or leaving His former place (χώραν) empty and filling another. Even supposing that we do say that He leaves one place and fills another, we would not mean this in any spatial sense (οὐ περὶ τόπου τὸ τοιοῦτον ἀποφανούμεθα).[54]

Certainly Christ, the incarnate Son of God, is with us "locally here below on earth" (μεθ᾽ ἡμῶν τῶν τοπικῶς κάτω ἐπὶ τῆς γῆς), but "He is also with those who cleave to Him everywhere, and is indeed also everywhere with those who do not know Him."[55]

In similar manner in the *De principiis* Origen places both these statements side by side because the nature of the case demands it. In the Incarnation the only-begotten Son of God who was God, who was hypostatically the Wisdom and Word of God, came to earth and was made man, although *He still remained what He was*, namely God. Begotten of the Father, He was yet without "beginning", not only of the sort that can be distinguished by periods of time, but of the other sort conceivable by the mind alone. God of God, Light from Light, He really became man, was born and suffered in truth, and not in appearance only, and truly rose again from the dead.[56] Origen's characteristic way of expressing this is bipolar: He became man, without ceasing to be God. He emptied Himself, but thereby displayed to us the fulness of the Godhead.[57] "Although brought within the narrow compass of a human body (*brevissimae insertus humani corporis formae*) the Son of God showed from the likeness of His works and His power to those of God the Father the immense and invisible greatness that was in Him."[58] He was made in the form of a servant in order to subject us in Himself to the Father.[59] As such He is

---

[53] *Contra Celsum* I, 275.14f.; 282.18f.
[54] *Contra Celsum* I, 277.26f. (tr. Henry Chadwick, *Origen: Contra Celsum* [1953], 187).
[55] *Contra Celsum* II, 13.9f.
[56] *De principiis* V, 10.5f.; 28.13ff.; 29.11f.; 38.1ff.
[57] *De principiis*, 38.17f.
[58] *De principiis*, 39.6; 43.5ff.
[59] *De principiis*, 79.1ff.; 276.12ff.; 277.1ff.

the Mediator, the only-begotten Son of God, yet the first-born of all creation.

Of all the marvellous and splendid things about Him there is one that utterly transcends the limits of human wonder and is beyond the capacity of our weak mortal intelligence to think of or understand, namely, how this mighty power of the divine majesty, the very Word of the Father, and the very Wisdom of God, in which were created "all things visible and invisible", can be believed to have existed within the compass of that man (*intra circumscriptionem eius hominis*) who appeared in Judaea; yes, how the Wisdom of God can have entered into a woman's womb and been born as a little child and uttered noises like those of crying children; and further, how it was that He was troubled, as we are told, in the hour of death, as He Himself confesses when He says, "My soul is sorrowful even unto death", and how at the last He was led to that death which is considered by men to be the most shameful of all — even though on the third day He rose again.[60]

When, therefore, we see in Him some things so human that they appear in no way to differ from the common frailty of mortals, and some things so divine that they are appropriate to nothing else but the primal and ineffable nature of Deity, the human understanding with its narrow limits is baffled, and struck with amazement at so mighty a wonder that it knows not which way to turn, what to hold to, or whither to betake itself. If it thinks of God, it sees a man; if it thinks of a man, it beholds one returning from the dead with spoils after vanquishing the kingdom of death. For this reason we pursue our contemplation with all fear and reverence, as we seek to prove how the reality of each nature exists in one and the same person, in such a way that nothing unworthy or unfitting may be thought to reside in that divine and ineffable existence, nor on the other hand may the events of His life be supposed to be the illusions caused by deceptive fantasies. But to utter these things in human ears and to explain them by words far exceeds the powers we possess either in our moral worth or in mind and speech. I think indeed that it transcends the capacity even of the holy Apostles.[61]

The fact that theology must speak in a way appropriate to and worthy of the divine and the human natures of Christ means that theology is forced to speak in a rather paradoxical manner about *space*. Earlier in the *De principiis* Origen had come up against a similar problem in relation to *time*. Here, after having said that "the Holy Spirit would never have been included in the unity of the Trinity, that is, along with God the unchangeable Father, and with His Son, unless He had always been the Holy Spirit", he added: "Of course these terms which we use such as 'always' or 'has been', or any similar terms bearing a temporal significance, must be interpreted with reservations and not pressed; for they relate to

---

[60] *De principiis*, 139.15.

[61] *De principiis*, 140.25f.; 141.1ff. (tr. G. W. Butterworth, *Origen on First Principles* [1936], 109f.).

time; but the matters of which we are now speaking, though described in temporal language for the purposes of discussion, in their essential nature transcend all idea of time".[62] The same question is raised in the fourth book with regard to the Son as well.

This phrase that we use, that there never was a time when He did not exist, must be accepted with a reservation. For the very words "when" or "never" have a temporal significance, whereas the statements we make about the Father and the Son and the Holy Spirit must be considered as transcending all time and all ages and all eternity. For it is this Trinity alone which exceeds all comprehension, not only of temporal but even of eternal intelligence. The rest of things, however, which are external to the Trinity, must be measured by ages and periods of time. The fact, therefore, that the Word is God, and was in the beginning with God, must not lead anyone to suppose that this Son of God is contained in any place (*in loco aliquo contineri*); nor must the fact that He is Wisdom, or Truth, or Righteousness, or Sanctification, or Redemption; for all these need no place in which to act or work, but each of them must be understood as referring to those who have a share of the Word's power and effectiveness.[63]

Origen explains that when we are brought through redemption and sanctification to be "with Christ", this does not mean that we take leave of physical space, but rather that we will "remain in some place situated on earth" (*in aliquo loco in terra posito*), for it is we who will be changed, passing through a series of "abiding places" into the nearer presence and fullness of God in Christ.[64] "Christ Himself, however, is everywhere and is active throughout the universe. We are not to understand Him any longer as being in that narrow limit to which He was confined for us and for our sakes, i.e., not in that circumscribed state which He had among men when He was located in our body on earth in such a way that He could be thought of as enclosed in some one place (*in uno aliquo circumsaeptus loco*)."[65] For saints to reach that place where He now is means that without leaving earth they will have a purified vision enabling them to penetrate even to celestial regions in their understanding of the truth.[66]

Origen acknowledged that this position involves serious problems in regard to Biblical interpretation, and so he set himself to deal with that before further consideration of the problem of space and time.[67] The main

[62] *De principiis*, 54.9f. (tr. G. W. Butterworth, 33).
[63] *De principiis*, 350.18ff.; 351.1ff. (tr. G. W. Butterworth, 316).
[64] *De principiis*, 190.1f.
[65] *De principiis*, 191.1-4.
[66] *De principiis*, 191.5f.
[67] *De principiis* V (IV, 1-IV), 292ff.

point he makes in his hermeneutical discussion is that the Scriptures
themselves partake of this two-fold character, for they are both "somatic"
and "pneumatic" since they refer us beyond sensible and bodily matters
to God Himself. Hence we have to interpret their statements worthily in
accordance with the nature of the God whom they reveal. Biblical statements have thus a two-fold reference: to what is temporal and spatial,
and to what is beyond time and space. We cannot break through the
physical sense of the Scriptures without the direct help of God and the
enlightenment of His Spirit, but when our ears and eyes are trained and
adapted to the divine truth we will be able to interpret the Scriptures in
accordance with their deeper message, without necessarily disparaging
their more obvious sense. If, however, we try to interpret all Biblical
statements on the same level, we will come up against absurdities and
contradictions so impossible as to be quite unworthy of God. On the
other hand, we have to remember that we are up against certain necessities of our finite minds, and we have to beware of trying to think beyond
rational limits.[68] No doubt in dealing with the Scriptures, as Philo earlier
had done with the Old Testament, Origen went much too far in allegorical
interpretations, while at the same time under the influence of Platonic
philosophy he tended to disparage the physical and temporal aspects of
the Gospel as "shadow" compared to the timeless "realities" in God.
But his intention was sane and sound, i.e., to think consistently as far as
he could of God in accordance with the nature of God, since to do anything else would be an act of impiety. Thus at the end of his "digression"
on hermeneutics, Origen says,

It was intended to show that there are certain things, the significance of which
just cannot be explained properly in human language but which are made clear
more through simple understanding than through any properties of words. It
is to this rule that understanding even of the divine writings must be kept, in
order that the things said there may be judged not according to the meanness
of the speech but according to the divinity of the Holy Spirit who inspired this
composition.[69]

What then do we mean when we speak of the Son of God being "in" a
place, or of Christ being "in" St. Paul, or "in" Peter or John, whether they
are on earth or "in heaven" as "in" Michael or Gabriel? From the fact
that He is "in" people in heaven and in earth it is evident that "the
divinity of the Son of God is not shut up in any place, otherwise in so far
as it was in one place it would not be in another (*divinitas filii dei non in*

---

[68] *De principiis*, 345-346, 350.10f.
[69] *De principiis*, 347.23f.

loco aliquo concludebatur, alioquin in ipso tantum fuisset et in altero non fuisset); but if in accordance with the majesty of its incorporeal nature it is shut up in no place, then in no place is it understood to be wanting".[70] There is a difference, on the other hand, that must be taken into account: He is not present in all beings in the same way, for He is more openly present in some than in others, but this is a presence that is to be understood from the side of their sharing in God's Word and Wisdom, and therefore is one that depends on their merits.[71] We are to be sure talking here of the Son of God through whom all things, visible and invisible, have been made, so that we have to understand His presence primarily in accordance with His own creative agency.[72]

What then of the *bodily* advent and the *incarnation* of the only-begotten Son of God?

It is not to be thought that all the majesty of His Deity was shut within the limits of a very small body (*intra brevissimi corporis claustra conclusa est*) so that all God's Word, His Wisdom, substantial Truth and Life were divided from the Father or forced and confined within the smallness of His body (*vel a Patris divulsa sit vel intra corporis illius coercita et circumscripta brevitatem*), nor is that majesty to be thought of as operating nowhere else. The cautious confession of piety ought to be between these two, in the belief that nothing of Deity was wanting in Christ, and in the conviction that there was no separation at all from the substance of the Father, which is present everywhere.[73]

Origen sees a clear instance of this in the Gospel when John the Baptist says of Christ in His bodily absence, "There stands one among you whom you know not, who comes after me, the latchet of whose shoes I am not worthy to unloose."[74] "Certainly it could not be said of one who was absent, so far as His bodily presence was concerned, that He stood in the midst of those to whom He was not present in a bodily way. From this it is shown that the Son of God was both *wholly* present in His body and *wholly* present everywhere (*Unde ostenditur quia et in corpore totus et ubique totus aderat filius dei*)."[75]

This does not mean that only part of the Deity of the Son of God was in Christ while the other part was elsewhere or everywhere. That would be to misunderstand the nature of incorporeal and invisible substance, Origen argues, to which partition and division do not apply. "For He is

---

[70] *De principiis*, 351.18f.
[71] *De principiis*, 351.7f.; 23f.; 352.1f.
[72] *De principiis*, 352.4ff.
[73] *De principiis*, 352.15f.
[74] John 1:26-27.
[75] *De principiis* V, 352.25f. Cf. *Contra Celsum* II (V, 12), 13.1ff.

in all things, and through all things, and above all things, in the mode of which we have already spoken, i.e., in accordance without understanding of Him as Wisdom or Word or Life or Truth, by which all local confinement is undoubtedly excluded (*omnis sine dubio conclusio localis excluditur*)."[76] Origen thus rejects the application to the Incarnation of any container view of space defined in terms of its immovable limits, and any receptacle view of the self-emptying or *kenosis* of the Son that involves an emptying however partial of material content out of Him. The incarnation involves the *whole* Son of God, so that, difficult though it may be, we must think of Him as *wholly* present in the body He assumed, and yet as *wholly* everywhere in accordance with His divine nature. This is explained from the side of the agency of the Son who for the sake of our salvation came among men, assuming not only a physical body but a human soul, in order to fulfil the divine *economy*.[77] Here in this unique mode of presence and activity in the Incarnation we have manifested the way in which the saving purpose of God is taken within human and worldly existence.[78]

Origen now sets himself to offer some kind of explanation of this. He reverts to an argument he had developed earlier to show that, far from being eternal and unchangeable, essential matter (the substance underlying every body throughout the universe) is capable of change and can pass from one given quality into another.[79] He adds to this the idea, already noted, that it is through God's own comprehending of what He had made that He imparts to this creation its rational and determinate qualities.[80] Now in Jesus Christ it is the Word and Wisdom of God that have become incarnate, that Word and Wisdom through which all things visible and invisible, corporeal and rational, were created and given their order and form. Hence we have to think of the redemptive activity of God in Christ as part of His whole economy, because redemption and creation come together in the incarnate Son. The work of the Son and of the Father are one and the same, so that in His Incarnation the Son continues the work of the Father.[81] In view of this, it is clear that we are to think of the relation of the Incarnation to space in accordance with the creative and determining agency of the Incarnate

---

[76] *De principiis*, 353.5f.

[77] *De principiis*, 353.8f.

[78] See *De principiis* V, 28.1ff. and *Contra Celsum* II, 150.2.

[79] *De principiis*, 109.9ff.; 110.1ff.; 111.1ff.; 356.21f. and 357.1ff. Here Origen claims a certain agreement with the atomists (18f.). See also 358.26f. and 359.1ff.

[80] *De principiis*, 45.10ff.; 46.1f.; 139.1ff.

[81] *De principiis*, 359.16f.; 360.1ff.

One. Even when He unites Himself to us in the body and is encompassed in a bounded human life, by His very nature and activity He springs it open; and He can accomplish this for He is Himself the Source and Creator of all material body throughout the universe and contains all time and space in the power of His Word.

How does this affect us? In reply Origen concludes the *De principiis* by claiming that we may partake in this liberating and emancipating activity of Christ through rational community or kinship with Christ. "As the Son and the Father are one, so also the soul which the Son assumed and the Son Himself are one (ὥσπερ ὁ υἱὸς καὶ πατὴρ ἕν εἰσιν, οὕτω καὶ ἥν εἴληφεν ὁ υἱός ψυχὴν καὶ αὐτὸς ἕν εἰσιν)."[82] The human soul, then, is not only the medium, as it were, of His union with a creaturely body, but the medium of our union with Him.[83] We rational beings have thus a kind of "blood-relationship" with God through Christ, and through that relationship we have a share in divine Truth. The Father, the Son, and the Holy Spirit are not related to the universe like Aristotle's "Unmoved Mover", for they stand in a relation of knowledge to themselves as well as to all created things. By sharing in the incarnate Word and Wisdom of God we are given to share in that divine knowledge. By its nature the rational mind has been placed in a body and must advance from sensible things, which are bodily, to things beyond sense, which are incorporeal and intelligible, but this advance is actually made possible through the bodily Incarnation of the Son of God, and through the rational teaching He imparts to us. And this is the way, as Origen has already explained, in which we may ascend to heavenly places and thus, without leaving our physical location on earth, be emancipated from the narrow confinement of dark material existence in which we have been involved through evil. To be saved means to have our place on earth opened out to the kind of place where Christ is; to be saved means to be brought to share in the fulness of God and thus to reach true magnitude and space of mind in communion with Him.

3

There can be no doubt that Origen did a great deal to help the Christian Church toward an articulate understanding of the Gospel with a philosophical grasp of some of the most difficult problems. But Origen's thought

[82] *De principiis*, 354.15-16.
[83] *De principiis*, 361-364.

represents the penultimate stage before Nicaea. There was not a little in his teaching that was unacceptable, particularly in the areas of anthropology, angelology, and cosmology, with his grand theory of the creation, fall, and restoration of rational souls, while his allegorical exegesis opened the door to many fancies. But as his teaching was purified of its speculative ideas, it became clear that he had prepared the ground for a scientific theology which could meet the Church's need. Such a theology emerged at Nicaea and was defended and advanced most formidably by Athanasius in the East and Hilary in the West. It will be sufficient for our purpose, in rounding out this essay, to note the principal points regarding our theme that are to be found in the writings of Athanasius.

First (1), it is once again the transcendence of God that is quite fundamental to Athanasius who maintained it with great force in his youthful *Contra gentes* over against all heathen notions of deity. Yet he insisted no less on the immanence of his transcendent God, while rejecting the philosophical notion of the divine Logos as a cosmological principle. The Word of God is the personal, living, and active Self-Word (αὐτο-λόγος) through whom all things visible and invisible were created out of nothing, and who orders and holds the universe together by binding it into such a relation to God that it is preserved from breaking up into nothingness or dropping out of existence, while at the same time imparting to it light and rationality. He leaves nothing void of His power (μηδὲν ἔρημον τῆς ἑαυτοῦ δυνάμεως).[84] Since this God is both One and Lord of heaven and earth there can be no other "god" beside Him such as the demiurge of Gnostic dualism. "Where would such a god be, if the one true God fills all things in His embrace of heaven and earth?"[85] In the nature of the case it is nonsensical to ask such questions about God, whether He is without place (χωρὶς τόπου) or whether He is in place (ἐν τόπῳ). To put these questions is to presuppose that God can be thought of in a way parallel with ourselves.[86]

In the second place (2), for Athanasius it is with the Incarnation that the problem of spatial concepts in theology arises. "The 'asomatic' and incorruptible and immaterial Word of God comes into our spatial realm although He was not far off before (παραγίνεται εἰς τὴν ἡμετέραν χώραν, ὅτι γε μακρὰν ὢν πρότερον). For no part of the creation was void of Him (αὐτοῦ κενὸν), but He fills all things everywhere, while

---

[84] *Contra gentes*, 40-42 (*PG*, 25.81 c, 84 b).
[85] *Contra gentes*, 6 (*PG*, 25.43 b).
[86] *Contra Arianos*, 1.23 (*PG*, 26.60 b-c).

remaining present with the Father. But He does come in loving and revealing condescension to be with us men."[87] Here again we have the paradox that the Son or Word of God is fully present with us in our space and time and yet remains present with the Father. He is actively engaged, deploying Himself throughout the universe in all its dimensions, "above in the act of creation, below in the act of incarnation".[88]

For He was not shut up in the body (οὐ γὰρ δὴ περικεκλεις μένος ἦν ἐν τῷ σώματι). And He was not in the body in such a way as not to be elsewhere, nor did He move the body in such a way that the universe was left void of His activity and providence. But the most unexpected thing (τὸ παραδοξότατον) is that Word though He is, He was not contained by anything but He Himself rather contains all things (οὐ συνείχετο μὲν ὑπό τινος, συνεῖχε δὲ τὰ πάντα μᾶλλον αὐτός). And just as while He is present *in* the whole of creation, He is "outside" everything in respect of His essential being but is "in" all things in respect of His own powers (ἐκτὸς μὲν ἐστι τοῦ παντὸς κατ'οὐσίαν, ἐν πᾶσι δέ ἐστι ταῖς ἑαυτοῦ δυνάμεσι),[89] giving order to the universe, extending His providence to all and in all things without being contained (περιέχων τὰ ὅλα καὶ μὴ περιεχόμενος) but being wholly and in every respect in His Father alone (ἀλλ' ἐν μόνῳ τῷ ἑαυτοῦ πατρὶ ὅλος ὢ κατὰ πάντα) — so also while being present in a human body and giving life to it Himself, He was quite consistently giving life to the universe as well: He was "in" every event and yet "outside" the universe (ἐν τοῖς πᾶσι ἐγίνετο, καὶ ἔξω τῶν ὅλωνἦ). Moreover while He made Himself known from the body through His works He was not unmanifest through His activity in the universe.[90]

Athanasius considers here the analogy of the human soul and body, and

---

[87] *De incarnatione*, 8 (*PG*, 25.109 a); 14 (*PG*, 25.120 c); *Sermo major de fide*, 7 (*PG*, 26.1268 b). See further *Contra Arianos*, 1.43. Our being made "one body with Christ" has the effect of introducing us into the realms (εἰς χώρας) of the heavenly powers and beings (*PG*, 26.99 b).

[88] *De incarnatione*, 16 (*PG*, 25.124 c).

[89] Cf. Clement, *Stromata*, II.2: "He who is Himself far off has come very near — oh unspeakable wonder. 'I am a God that draws near', says the Lord. He is far off in respect of His essence (πόρρω μὲν κατ'οὐσίαν) — for how can what is begotten ever approach the Unbegotten? — but He is very near in power, that by which all things are embraced ... For the power of God is always present, actually impinging upon us, in oversight, beneficence and instruction ... For God is not in darkness or in place but is above both space and time, and the property of events (οὐ γὰρ ἐν γνόφῳ ἦ τόπῳ ὁ θεός, ἀλλ'ὑπεράνω καὶ τόπου καὶ χρόνου καὶ τῆς τῶν γεγονότων ἰδιότητος). Therefore neither does He ever dwell in a part, either as containing or as contained (οὔτε περιέχων οὔτε περιεχόμενος), either by limitation or by division. 'For what house will ye build me? saith the Lord'. On the contrary, He has not even built one for Himself, since He cannot be confined (ἀχώρητος). Even if the heaven is said to be His throne, not even thus is He contained (οὐδ' οὕτω περιέχεται), but He rests delighted in the creation." (Ed. Otto Stählin, GCS, II, pp. 115-116). Cf. Athanasius, *Sermo major de fide*, 29 (*PG*, 26.1284 b-c).

[90] *De incarnatione*, 17 (*PG*, 25.125 a-b).

of its relation in function to what is outside the body.[91] But this analogy does not hold, for man is unable through his thought, for example, to influence the revolution of the heavenly bodies.

Surely the Word of God was not in this man in that way, for he was not bound to His body, but rather was Himself master of it in such a way that He was in this particular body and yet was participant in all events, and while He was outside the universe, He abode in His Father alone. And this was the wonderful thing that while He went about freely as a man, as Word He was the life-giving Source of all things, and as Son He was together with the Father. Hence not even when the virgin gave Him birth was He passive, nor was He defiled by being in the body but rather sanctified it. For not even by being in all things does He partake of their nature but on the contrary is Himself the source from which they are quickened and sustained.[92]

A fundamental point here is that when the Word or Son of God became man, assumed from us a human body, and therefore shared our physical space, *He remained* what He ever was,[93] so that the spatial ingredient in the concept of the Incarnation must be interpreted from the side of His *active and controlling occupation* of bodily existence and place. Space is a predicate of the Occupant; it is determined by His agency, and is to be understood in accordance with His nature. He cannot therefore have the same space-relation (χώρα) with the Father as we creatures have; otherwise He would be quite incapable (χωρεῖν) of God.[94]

Third (3), according to Athanasius the Son of God through His relation with us fulfils the part of a Mediator (μεσίτης) even in regard to space-relations between men and God, for mere creatures are unable to make "room" (χωρεῖν) for God in their natures, and far less are they able to endure the Creator in their created beings. But this bridge is supplied in the Incarnation of the Son.[95] While He took from the virgin Mary a human body, He purified it and made it "capable of giving room for the whole fulness of the Godhead bodily" (τὸ χωρῆσει δυνάμενον ἄχραντον σῶμα πᾶν τὸ πλήρωμα τῆς θεότητος σωματικῶς), as well as of bearing human suffering when He gave Himself willingly for the whole world.[96] The relation between the Son and the Father cannot be

---

[91]   Cf. *De incarnatione*, 42-43 (*PG*, 25.172 a; 173 a) and Plato, *Politicus*, 273 d.

[92]   *De incarnatione*, 17 (*PG*, 25.125 b-c).

[93]   This was the point made so strongly by Origen, and was later taken up by the whole Church. Cf. also *Contra Apollinarium* II, 3,7, or 16: μένων ὅ ἤ, which is certainly Athanasian, if not from Athanasius himself (*PG*, 26.1136 b; 1144 a; 1160 a).

[94]   *Contra Arianos* III, 18 (*PG*, 26.360 b); also *Ad Serapionem* II, 4 (*PG*, 26.629 b-d, 632 a); and *De synodis*, 26 (*PG*, 26.733 b).

[95]   *Contra Arianos* II, 26 (*PG*, 26.201 b); *De decretis*, 8 (*PG*, 25.457 b).

[96]   *Sermo major de fide*, 13 (*PG*, 26.1269 c).

thought out in terms of a receptacle (ἀγγεῖον) notion of room or space. That would mean that we think out the problem simply in terms of bodies and containers, which was precisely what the Arians were guilty of, a material approach, in which they thought of the Father and the Son as each filling the emptiness of the other (... ὥσπερ ἐν ἀγγείοις κενοῖς ἐξ ἀλλήλων πληρούμενοι. ὥστε τὸν μὲν υἱὸν πληροῦν τὸ κενὸν τοῦ πατρός, τὸν δὲ πατέρα πληροῦν τὸ κενὸν τοῦ υἱοῦ).[97] That is to say, a receptacle notion of space can only lead to a false kenoticism which does not do justice to the "fullness" and "perfection" of either the Father or the Son, for it fails to think of them in accordance with their natures. The relation of the Father with the Son and the Son with the Father must be thought out in terms of "abiding" and "dwelling", in which each wholly rests in the other: "I in the Father and the Father in Me", as the Lord expressed it.[98] This is the doctrine of the περιχώρη-σις, in which we are to think of the whole being of the Son as proper to the Father's essence, as God from God, Light from Light.[99] Creaturely realities are such that they can be divided up in separated places (ἐν μεμερισμένοις τόποις), but this is impossible with the Uncreated Source of all being, with Father, Son, or Holy Spirit, who wholly dwell in one another and who each have room fully for the others in the one God.[100] Since then "the Son was ever with the Father, for He is in the bosom of the Father, and the bosom of the Father was never void of the Deity of the Son",[101] it follows that Christ the Incarnate Son is the "place" where the Father is to be known and to be believed, for He is the "place" (or the "locus") where God is to be found. But "place" here, of course, must be interpreted in accordance with the nature of God and of His activity in revelation and redemption through the Incarnation.

We thus come to the fourth (4) of Athanasius' principles, namely, that "terms must be taken in one way through their reference to God and understood in another way in their reference to men (ἄλλως ἐπὶ θεοῦ τὰς λέξεις λαμβάνομεν, καὶ ἑτέρως ἐπὶ τῶν ἀνθρώπων ταύτας δια-νοούμεθα)".[102] God is not as man and man is not as God. Thus even

---

[97] Contra Arianos III, 1 (PG, 26.324 b).
[98] Contra Arianos III, 1 (PG, 26.321 b-c, 324 a). Cf. De decretis, 26 (PG, 25.464 a).
[99] Contra Arianos III, 3 (PG, 26.328 a ff.). See A. Robertson's notes, Nicene and Post-Nicene Fathers IV, Athanasius, pp. 393 and 395.
[100] See Ad Serapionem III, 4 (PG, 26.629 b-d, and 632 a). Cf. also Cyril of Alexandria, Thesaurus, 51, and Jerome, Commentaria in Ezekiel III, 12: "Filius locus est Patris, sicut et Pater locus est Filii". (Cited by Robertson, loc. cit.).
[101] Expositio fidei, 2 (PG, 25.204 a-c); Contra Arianos III, 4 (PG, 26.377-80).
[102] De decretis, 11 (PG, 25.411 c).

if the same terms in the Holy Scriptures are used of God and of man, nevertheless we must learn to interpret them *differently* in accordance with the nature of each of the subjects indicated (κατὰ τὴν ἑκάστου τῶν σημαινομένων φύσιν).[103] Or as Athanasius puts it elsewhere: "For terms do not take away from His nature, but rather that Nature changes the terms while attracting them to itself (οὐ γὰρ αἱ λέξεις τὴν φύσιν παραιροῦνται, ἀλλὰ μᾶλλον ἡ φύσις τὰς λέξεις εἰς ἑαυτὴν ἕλκουσα μεταβάλλει). For terms are not prior to essences, but essences are first and terms second."[104]

In accordance with this principle, we have to take into account the difference between the activity of that which is by nature self-existent and that which by nature is contingent and derivative. If, then, men do not create as God creates, we have to think differently of divine and human occupants of space. "Men who are not capable of self-existence are enclosed in place as contingent things (ἐν τόπῳ τυγχάνοντές εἰσι περιεχόμενοι) and consist in the Word of God. But God is Self-existent, enclosing all things and enclosed by none (ὁ δὲ θεὸς ὤν ἐστι καθ' ἑαυτόν, περιέχων τὰ πάντα, καὶ ὑπ' οὐδενὸς περιεχόμενος), and He is 'in' all things according to His goodness and power, but 'without' all things in accordance with His proper nature."[105] Now since the Son of God cannot be divided from the Father, it follows that even though He became incarnate among us, He remains at the right hand of the Father, for where the Father is, there also is His Word (ἔνθα γὰρ ἔστιν ὁ πατὴρ, ἐκεῖ καὶ ὁ τούτου λόγος ἐστίν).[106] This cannot but affect the space-relations of Christ, for it is in accordance with His proper nature and substance.

Finally (5), Christ is "in" us through sharing with us our bodily existence, but He is also "in" the Father through his oneness with Him.[107] But how are we to think of the relation between these two "in"'s? It is evident that in each case we have to respect the divine nature and the human nature. "As we, while receiving the Spirit do not lose the nature proper to us, so the Lord, while becoming man for our sakes, and putting on a body, was no less God (οὐδὲν ἧττον ἦν θεός), for He was not diminished by the development of the body, but rather 'deified' it and ren-

---

[103] *De decretis*, 10 (*PG*, 25.441 b). See also *De sententia Dionysii*, 9 (*PG*, 25.493 a).
[104] *Contra Arianos* II, 3 (*PG*, 26.152 c).
[105] *De decretis*, 11 (*PG*, 25.441 d). Cf. *Sermo major de fide*, 29 (*PG*, 26.1284 c): πάντα δὲ χωρεῖ ὁ θεὸς, ὑπ' οὐδενὸς δὲ οὐ χωρεῖται.
[106] *De decretis*, 11 (*PG*, 25.444 b).
[107] *De decretis*, 31 (*PG*, 25.473 c-d): *Contra Arianos* III, 22 (*PG*, 26.369 a).

dered it immortal."[108] "Deification" did not mean, of course, any change in the nature of human essence, but that without being less human we are by grace made to participate in divine Sonship.[109] The Son is of the Father and in the Father in an *absolute* sense, which we can never be.[110]

Athanasius then offers an analogical account of this relation through a discussion of Christ's prayer to the Father that *as* the Father was in Him and He was in the Father so the disciples might be one in Him. Everything turns upon the precise meaning of *as*. It cannot mean that we are to be sons of God as the Father is by nature in the Son and the Son is by nature in the Father, but it must mean according to our own nature. Therefore a *distance* (διάστασις) and a *difference* (διαφορά) are involved.[111]

The *as* signifies not identity, but an image of or a pointer to what is spoken of (ὁ δὲ λέγων καθὼς οὐ ταυτότητα δείκνυσιν, ἀλλ' εἰκόνα καὶ παράδειγμα τοῦ λεγομένου).[112] Again, in using the word *as* He signifies those who become distantly (πόρρωθεν) as He is in the Father — distantly, that is, not in place but in nature (πόρρωθεν δέ ἐστιν οὐ τόπῳ ἀλλὰ τῇ φύσει), for in *place* nothing is far from God, but only in nature are all things far from Him (ἀλλὰ μόνη τῇ φύσει πάντα μακράν ἐστιν αὐτοῦ). As I have already said, he who uses the particle *as* signifies not identity nor equality, but a pointer to what is said in the light of what is perceived (ἀλλὰ παράδειγμα τοῦ λεγομένου κατά τι θεωρούμενον).[113]

Athanasius then goes on to show through an illustration that *as* implies one thing and another (ἄλλο καὶ ἄλλο), that where a difference exists there is a certain parallel relation.[114]

We shall not be *as* the Son, nor equal to Him for we and He are different (οὐκ ἐσόμεθα ὥσπερ ὁ υἱὸς οὐδὲ ἴσοι αὐτῷ ἄλλο γὰρ καὶ ἄλλο ἐσμέν). The word *as* is applied to us inasmuch as things differing from others in nature become as they, in view of a certain reference beyond them (ἐπεὶ τὰ μὴ κατὰ φύσιν ὄντα πρὸς ἄλλο τι βλέποντα γίνεται ὥσπερ ἐκεῖνα). Wherefore the Son is simply and without any reservation in the Father, for that belongs essentially to Him by nature, but so far as we who are not like that by nature are concerned, an image and a pointer are needed (ἡμεῖς δὲ οὐκ ἔχοντες τὸ κατὰ φύσιν δεόμεθα εἰκόνος καὶ παραδείγματος) in order that He may say "As Thou art in Me and I am in Thee."[115]

---

[108]   *De decretis*, 14 (*PG*, 25-448 d).
[109]   *Contra Arianos* III, 19-20 (*PG*, 26.361-365).
[110]   *Contra Arianos* I, 56 (*PG*, 26.129 b-c); II, 62 (*PG*, 62.280 a-b); III, 22 (*PG*, 26.369 a).
[111]   *Contra Arianos* III, 20-21 (*PG*, 26.364 f.).
[112]   *Contra Arianos* III, 21 (*PG*, 26.368 c).
[113]   *Contra Arianos* III, 22 (*PG*, 26.369 b).
[114]   *Ibid.*, III, 23 (*PG* 26.369 c).
[115]   *Ibid.*, III, 23 (*PG* 26.372 b).

Παράδειγμα has been translated not as "model" or "representation" or "illustration" but as "pointer", for it is essentially an operational term in which some idea or relation is taken from our this-worldly experience and made to point beyond itself to what is quite new in order to help us get some kind of grasp upon it. The idea or relation only approaches what it indicates and does not claim to represent it. By relating παράδειγμα to εἰκών, i.e., image or likeness, Athanasius shows that he does not use it in the Platonic sense of an archetype or exemplar, nor does he equate it with the copy (or μίμημα) of the archetype. So far as the notion of imitation (μίμησις) comes into his thought, it is to speak of following Christ in the light of the pattern He has given to us.[116] But παράδειγμα refers to an image which under the impact of the divine revelation is made to point beyond its creaturely form and content to the intended reality, without however transgressing the distance or rubbing out the difference between them. It has an objective and transcendental reference, but still is no more than an instrument enabling us to get some hold on the reality revealed and not one through which we capture this reality by conceiving of it. The image fulfils its function while making clear its inadequacy, and by pointing intelligibly to what is really apprehensible although ultimately beyond our comprehension. It succeeds in that function only insofar as we can understand the παράδειγμα itself in the light of the reality it serves.[117]

In the nature of the case the παραδείγματα that we employ in theology are not those that we choose, but those that are forced upon us through the divine revelation, and which have their ultimate ground, correction, and validity in the interrelation between the Father and the incarnate Son, that is, the interrelation that bridges the χωρισμός between God and man and supplies the epistemological context and basis for all theological concepts, and therefore for our understanding of the relation between their creaturely content and the reality of God Himself. It is in Christ that the objective reality of God is intelligibly linked with creaturely and physical forms of thought, so that these forms may be adapted and given an orientation which will enable them to point out or direct our minds to what God really makes known of Himself, although in view of His infinite nature they will not be able to seize hold

---

[116] See *Contra Arianos*, III, 19 ff. (*PG* 26.361-368). There can be no imitation apart from the Spirit, for without Him we are strange and distant from God, Imitation is a reproduction through the Spirit of the libeness of Christ in us.

[117] For a fuller discussion of the Athanasian concept of παράδειγμα, see *Theology in Reconstruction*, chs. 2 and 3.

of Him as He is in Himself. The relation of transcendental reference
must remain if they are to be successful in pointing us in the direction
they intend, but that relation must also have intelligible or conceptual
content if it is not to be blind.

If we understand the *paradeigmatic image* this way and apply it to the
spatial concepts in the Nicene theology, we will have a pretty good guide
to the way in which it was able to relate the being and activity of the
Son of God to bodily places (τόπος) when He entered into our human
space (χώρα) and became man, without leaving God's "place" and without leaving the universe empty of His presence and rule. Since space is
regarded here from a central point in the creative and redemptive activity of God in Christ, the concept of space as infinite receptacle, or
as infinite substance, or as extension conceived either as the essence of
matter or as a necessity of our human apprehension, or certainly the
concept of space as the first unmoved limit of the container, all fall
away. And in their place emerges a concept of space in terms of the
relations between God and the physical universe established in creation
and incarnation. Space in this formulation is a sort of differential concept that is essentially open-ended, for it is defined in accordance with
the interaction between God and man, eternal and contingent happening.
This means that the concept of space in the Nicene Creed is relatively
closed, so to speak, on our side where it has to do with physical existence,
but is infinitely open on God's side. This is why again and again when
Byzantine art sought to express this iconically it deliberately reversed
the natural perspective of the dais upon which the figure of the incarnate,
risen, and ascended Lord was represented. Not as in Figure 1 but as in
Figure 2:

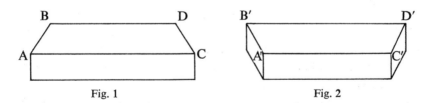

Fig. 1   Fig. 2

The Son of God become man could not be presented as one so confined
in the limits of the body that the universe was left empty of His government. He could not be represented, therefore, as captured by lines (AB
and CD), which when produced upwards met at some point in finite
space, but only within lines (A′B′ and C′D′), which when infinitely

produced never meet, for on either side they reached out into the absolute openness and eternity of transcendent God.

It must be pointed out, however, that difficulties were bound to arise, and did in fact arise, whenever the receptacle notion of space was raised from the naive popular mind to infect the pious imagination of the Church. We can see something of those results all through the iconoclastic controversies. But the most serious and persistent problems arose when the definition of place as the first unmoved limit of the container was brought back from Aristotelian physics and grafted on to Nicene theology. (Indeed, from these we are not yet free.) The rise of these difficulties is particularly clear in the thought of John of Damascus, with whom the two poles in the Nicene concept of space began to draw apart. On the one hand, he appropriated fully the Aristotelian conception defined by immediate reference to the immovable limit of the container and by ultimate reference to the Unmoved Mover, which tended to give his notion of place or space a closed or rigid character; on the other hand, however, in order to balance this he had both to develop a concept of "mental place" and to carry his theology much further in an apophatic direction than Athanasius could go, even to claiming, like Basileides, that we cannot know what God is but only what He is not. In other words, the distance that emerges with John of Damascus between the two poles of the Nicene concept tends to be so wide as to call in question the possibility of a fully conceptual connection between their creaturely content and the divine reality to which they point.[118]

John has other important and interesting things to say on the problem of spatial concepts which we cannot pursue here. Suffice it to say that as his deviation from Nicene theology was carried further in the West, especially after the middle of the twelfth century when so many of the hard-won concepts of the Fathers were replaced by Aristotelian concepts, Christian theology was set on a course of inevitable and acute conflict between its conceptions of space and those of developing modern science. A clear example of these problems can be seen in the Lutheran acceptance from the late medieval tradition of the receptacle notion of space with the consequent difficulties reflected first in the kenoticists and then in the demythologisers. In edifying contrast the Nicene conceptions have proved more fruitful and adaptable, and certainly have a much closer relation to more modern notions of space and time.

[118]   John of Damascus, *De fide orthodoxa* (*PG* 94.797 f., 850 ff., 1008 ff.).

FREE WILL (γνώμη) IN SAINT MAXIMUS THE CONFESSOR

JOHN MEYENDORFF

The doctrine of Christ's two wills, corresponding to his divine and human natures, which was the central issue in the Monothelite controversy, has often been considered incompatible with Christ understood as a single hypostasis or person. Can "nature" will? Is not the act of willing a personal act? And how can a single person have two wills? Paradoxically, Saint Maximus the Confessor, the main defender of the doctrine of the two wills, has also been accused of promoting a purely *abstract* notion of essence or nature.[1] As a matter of fact, following Leontius of Byzantium, Maximus formally sets in opposition the notion of "essence" (οὐσία) held by the "philosophers", who consider that it is a "self-hypostatic reality, not needing anything else for its existence" (αὐθυπόστατον πρᾶγμα μὴ δεόμενον ἑτέρον πρὸς σύστασιν), to the conception of the "Fathers", who recognize in it "a natural entity belonging to beings multiple and different hypostatically" (ἡ κατὰ πολλῶν καὶ διαφερόντων ταῖς ὑποστάσεσιν ὀντότης φυσική). However, as the context shows, Maximus' use of this definition of "essence" is by no means a simple return to Aristotelianism. The definition of hypostasis, which follows, precludes this: "Hypostasis", writes Maximus, "is, according to the philosophers, as an essence with (hypostatic) characteristics; according to the Fathers, it is each man in particular, being personally distinct from other men."[2] These definitions of "essence" and "hypostasis" must be further seen in the light of the Maximian notion of "energy", or "movement" (κίνησις). "We confess that nature does not exist without movement; for without movement it is no longer nature."[3] The triangle Nature-Hypostasis-Energy (or Will) is thus the

[1] G. L. Prestige, *God in Patristic Thought* (London, 1952), 278-279.
[2] *Opuscula theologica et polemica*, in J. P. Migne, *Patrologia Graeca* (hereafter *PG*), 91, col. 276 AB.
[3] *Ambiguorum Liber*, in *PG*, 91, col. 1052 B.

key to the Maximian system. The intent of this essay is to throw some light on the relation which exists, in this system, between hypostasis and will, specifically when they are viewed in connection with the concept of free will (γνώμη).

According to Maximus, the "natural will", or the "movement" of nature, is a movement towards God. It is only the hypostatic decision of Adam which changed the God-established "mode of existence" (τρόπος ὑπάρξεως) of human nature and turned it against God and therefore against nature itself. The source of man's evil is in his free, "hypostatic" decision, not in nature. The restoration of man must therefore also have a "hypostatic" source: it occurs when human nature is assumed by its Model, according to which it had been created, and which becomes the hypostasis determining its mode of existence. "Christ, being God by nature", says Maximus, "had a will naturally divine and paternal, for He had only one will with His Begetter (συνθελητὴς τοῦ ἰδίου Γεννήτορος); but being Man by nature also, he also had a naturally human will, which never opposed the will of the Father, and its acts were foreign to every imagination: for neither nature itself, not anything natural, not even free-will (γνώμη) and that which depends on it, opposes the Origin of nature, as long as it follows the norms of nature (τῷ λόγῳ συννεύει τῆς φύσεως)."[4] "Christ reestablishes nature in conformity with itself... Becoming man, he preserved the free-will (γνώμη) in impassibility and in peace with nature."[5]

The concept of free-will (γνώμη) as it occurs in these texts points to the importance of the hypostatic aspect of existence, as opposed to the natural, which is practically synonymous with "God-established". This aspect of Maximus' thought is made even clearer elsewhere. Refuting a Monothelite, who believes that Christ had only one divine-human will, Maximus first asks whether this unique will is a "natural" one. An affirmative answer would mean that Christ had a special individual "christic" nature. And if this unique will is a "gnomic" one, it cannot be characteristic of either of Christ's natures, "but only of his hypostasis, for the gnomic element individualizes the person (μόνης ἔσται τῆς αὐτοῦ χαρακτηριστικὸν ὑποστάσεως· προσώπου γὰρ ἀφοριστικὸν ὑπάρχει τὸ γνωμικόν), and Christ would have a will distinct from that of the Father and of the Spirit".[6]

Thus Monthelitism appears to Maximus as a form of Nestorianism,

---

[4] *Opuscula theologica et polemica*, in *PG*, 91, col. 77 D-80 A.
[5] *Expositio Orationis Dominicae*, in *PG*, 90, col. 877 D.
[6] *Opuscula theologica et polemica*, in *PG*, 91, col. 53 C.

since it was Nestorius who interpreted the union of two natures in Christ as a "relative" union (ἕνωσις σχετική) of two free-wills (γνῶμαι) into a single will (θέλημα), which supposes the existence of two hypostases in Christ for, as Maximus insists, free-will (γνώμη) always reflects hypostatic existence,[7] and a "gnomic" unity can only be conceived between different hypostases. Thus, Christ and the saints are united to each other "in one nature, one γνώμη and one will", when "love persuades the free-will not to oppose nature any more" and "when the law of nature is freely (γνωμικῶς) renewed through the law of grace".[8]

In his early writings, Maximus sometimes uses γνώμη as practically synonymous with θέλημα, or ἐνέργεια: thus, in speaking of divine characteristics (in Letter 6), he attributes some to the essence, and some to the "movement" or "free-will" (γνώμη) or "disposition".[9] This suggests the existence of a divine γνώμη. However, when Maximian thought and vocabulary takes final shape, γνώμη quite clearly becomes a term to designate the free-will of created hypostases, the seat of the *posse peccare*.

All modern students of Maximus emphasize that his conception of creation was aimed at refuting and overcoming Origenism. His refutation consists most notably in replacing Origen's formula Immobility – Motion – Genesis (which means that creation implied not a coming into existence of previously nonexistent beings, but a setting in motion of intellects which were eternally immobile in God) by the formula Genesis – Motion – Immobility (γένεσις – κίνησις – στάσις). By this Maximus implies that the motion of created nature starts with creation *ex nihilo*, and immobility is but an eschatological goal which is fulfilled in deification. On the anthropological level, the triad γένεσις – κίνησις – στάσις corresponds to the three forms of human existence: εἶναι – εὖ εἶναι – ἀεὶ εἶναι or Being – Well-being – Ever-being.[10]

According to Maximus, the first and the last elements of this triad are caused by God alone, who is the Creator of "being", the only Immortal One and the sole source of immortality or eternity. However, the

---

[7] *Opuscula theologica et polemica*, in PG 91, col. 192 C; cf. col. 40-45, 152 C, 268 B; *Disputatio cum Pyrrho*, in *PG*, 91, col. 329 D, 313 B.

[8] *Epistolae* 2, in *PG*, 91, col. 396 C.

[9] τὰ μὲν διὰ τὴν οὐσιάν, τὰ δὲ διὰ τὴν κίνησιν, ἤτοι γνώμην καὶ διάθεσιν (*Epistolae* 2, in *PG*, 91, col. 428 D); cf. P. Sherwood, "St. Maximus the Confessor, The Ascetic Life, The Four Centuries on Charity", Introduction, in *Ancient Christian Writers* 21 (Westminster, Md., and London, 1955), 58-60. On the chronology of Maximus' writings, see P. Sherwood, *An Annotated Date-list of the Works of Maximus the Confessor* (Rome, 1952).

[10] Cf. S. L. Epifanovič, *Prepodobnyj Maksim Ispovednik i Vizantijskoe bogoslovie* (Kiev, 1915), 55-57.

movement from "being" to "ever-being" implies man's free acceptance of God's grace: "well-being", that is the moral qualification and mode of existence of our being, depends on "our free will and motion" (τῆς ἡμετέρας γνώμης τε καὶ κινήσεως),[11] on an hypostatic or personal *choice*. "Reasonable beings", Maximus claims, "are naturally in motion by reason of being, and they strive towards the goal through free-will by reason of well-being" (πρὸς τέλος κατὰ γνώμην διὰ τὸ εὖ εἶναι).[12] Thus γνώμη is associated with the natural "motion" of nature, to which it gives a moral qualification. It is also connected with the idea of imitation or similitude of God: "God alone is good by nature, and the imitator of God alone is good by his free-will."[13] This imitation of God presupposes a synergy between freedom and grace: "The Spirit does not produce an unwilling free-will (γνώμην μὴ θέλουσαν), but it transfigures and deifies it, when it wishes so."[14]

Consequently, the sin of Adam was a catastrophe of human freedom which made a choice "against nature"; or in Maximus' words, "nature opposed itself" (πρὸς ἑαυτὴν διάστασις), and this was a possibility "according to the free-will" (κατὰ γνώμην).[15] Maximus always insists that nature as such was not involved in sin, and clearly opposes φύσις to γνώμη.[16] The result of sin was a contamination of sorts of the "natural will", which could lead to the Good only by the γνώμη. Man thus acquired a "gnomic will", which not only chooses between good and evil, but hesitates and suffers, for its decisions are blurred by "ignorance" and "imagination": it is "a sort of desire which adheres to that which is, or is believed to be, a relative good".[17]

Free-will (γνώμη), as we have seen, is then intrinsically linked with hypostatic existence. Sin, therefore, can only be a personal act, which does not corrupt nature as such. Rather it leads the created human hypostases to misuse it, and thus obliterates the true God-established relation between hypostasis and nature, depriving man of his authentic freedom.

This explains how the incarnate Logos could fully assume human nature *without assuming sin*. Sin belongs to the realm of γνώμη, and not to that

---

[11] *Ambiguorum Liber*, in *PG*, 91, col. 1116 B.
[12] *Ambiguorum Liber*, col. 1073 C.
[13] φύσει ἀγαθὸς μόνος ὁ θεός, καὶ γνώμη ἀγαθὸς μόνος ὁ θεομίμητος (*Capitum de Charitate Centuria* IV, 90, in *PG*, 90, col. 1069 C).
[14] *Quaestiones ad Thalassium*, in *PG*, 90, col. 260 CD.
[15] *Expositio Orationis Dominicae*, in *PG*, 90, col. 893 B.
[16] γνωμικῶς οἱ φυσικῶς (*Expositio Orationis Dominicae*, in *PG*, 90, col. 905 A).
[17] *Disputatio cum Pyrrho*, in *PG*, 91, col. 308 C.

of nature.[18] Christ indeed possessed a natural human will, but since the willing subject, or hypostasis, of his human nature was the Logos himself, he could in no way have had gnomic will which is the only source of sin. According to Maximus, those who attribute to Christ a gnomic will "consider him as a simple man, with a will similar to ours, ignorant, hesitant and conflicting with himself ... In the Lord's humanity, which possessed not a simple human hypostasis, but a divine one ..., there was no place for γνώμη."[19]

Thus, the spiritual life of a Christian supposes essentially a gradual transformation, in each human hypostasis, of the gnomic will into a divine and angelic γνώμη.[20] This is because our deification, i.e., "participation in divine nature", as well as the divine "condescension" which this presupposes, is incompatible with the internal conflict introduced into our nature by the devil through the γνώμη.[21] The purpose and the meaning of asceticism are to reform our γνώμη.[22] Because the true λόγος of our nature is immutable, it is the τρόπος, corrupted through free-will since the sin of Adam, which needs rebirth in Christ.

In sum, then, in making the "will" dependent upon nature, Maximus did not — as he has been accused — forget the hypostatic dimension in either Christology or anthropology. On the contrary, together with the entire Greek patristic tradition he well realized that natural existence received its qualification and "mode", in fact its very meaning, from the person or hypostasis, which is not simply an aspect of natural existence, but its very center. This conclusion gives new illustration to the apt judgement once rendered by Father Georges Florovsky on the Maximian system: "Everything will be deified, — God will be 'all in all'. But this will not be done by violence. Deification itself must be accepted and assimilated in freedom and love ... Saint Maximus has drawn this conclusion from an exact Christological doctrine on the two wills and energies ...".[23]

---

[18] Cf. *Opuscula theologica et polemica*, in *PG*, 91, col. 192 A.
[19] Ἐπὶ τοῦ ἀνθρωπίνου τοῦ κυρίου, οὐ ψιλῶς καθ' ἡμᾶς ὑποστάυτος, θεϊκῶς ..., γνώμη λέγεσθάι οὐ δύναται (*Disputatio cum Pyrrho*, in *PG*, 91, col. 308 D).
[20] *Capitum de Charitate Centuria* III, 80.
[21] *Expositio Orationis Dominicae*, in *PG*, 90, col. 901 C, 905 A.
[22] *Liber Asceticus*, in *PG*, 90 col. 953 B.
[23] G. Florovskij, *Vizantijske otcy V-VIII vv., Iz čtenij v Pravoslavnom bogoslovskom Institute v Pariže* (Paris, 1933), 227.

CHURCH-STATE RELATIONS IN THE BYZANTINE EMPIRE AS REFLECTED IN THE ROLE OF THE PATRIARCH IN THE CORONATION OF THE BYZANTINE EMPEROR

PETER CHARANIS

In Byzantium succession to the imperial throne never became automatic. A reigning emperor usually designated his successor — indeed had him enthroned — so that at the moment of his death the imperial office remained occupied, with the reins of power thus passing smoothly from the hands of the deceased to that of his successor. If this procedure did not always work out well, if at times the position of the succeeding emperor was immediately challenged so that a resort to military action was required to make it stand, it did nevertheless enable several families to retain the throne for long periods of time. There were instances, however, when the reigning emperor failed to designate his successor so that when he died the throne became vacant. In these instances the matter of designating a new emperor was either referred to the senate or settled by officers of the army, the circumstances in each instance being the decisive factor as to which group took the initiative. There was still another way whereby one became an emperor. The government of the later Roman empire has been described as absolutism tempered by the right of revolution. This observation is, of course, based on the fact that in the history of the later Roman empire there are a number of instances when a reigning emperor was challenged by a rebel, usually but not always an army officer, who succeeded in installing himself on the throne and winning acceptance as the emperor of the empire. But whatever the mode of gaining access to the throne, there were still certain forms of procedure which had to be observed, forms which gave the new occupant of the throne the aura of legitimacy, not because of the existence of specific laws, but because of the sanction of custom. One of these forms — coronation by or in the presence of the patriarch of Constantinople in an essentially religious ceremony — was, according to the view to be developed here, always obligatory.

1

The patriarch was introduced as an element in the coronation of the emperor sometime after the death of Theodosius II. W. Sickel, the first scholar to study in detail the question of imperial coronation in Byzantium, expressed the view that in 450, in connection with the accession to the throne of Marcian, the Byzantine patriarch was first called upon to crown the new emperor.[1] At first accepted by virtually every scholar, Sickel's view on this matter has, in the light of a more thorough study of Marcian's enthronement by W. Ensslin, now been generally abandoned. There is in fact a late Byzantine tradition which holds that Marcian was the first emperor to have been crowned by the patriarch, but Ensslin by a careful analysis of all sources chronologically nearest to the event concluded that it was not in connection with the enthronement of Marcian but with that of Leo I, his successor, that the Byzantine patriarch first played this coronation role.[2] Whether Marcian or Leo I was the first emperor to be crowned by the patriarch is of little importance, for the time interval between the two reigns was so short as to be insignificant in the historical evolution of the new practice. The critical question is the importance of this innovation in the domain of church-state relations in the Byzantine empire.

Sickle raised and answered this question. In his view the coronation of emperors by the patriarch had no ecclesiastical significance and consequently had no bearing on the matter of church-state relations. In performing the act of coronation, the patriarch — Sickle held — acted not in his capacity as the head of the church but as a representative of the state. Sickle's view was accepted by J. B. Bury in his essay on the "Constitution of the Later Roman Empire",[3] although two years later he apparently abandoned it. For Bury then stated: "The coronation of the Emperor Marcian and Leo I by the patriarch, with the accompanying ecclesiastical ceremony, may be said to have definitely introduced the new constitutional principle that the profession of Christianity was a

[1] W. Sickel, "Das byzantinische Krönungsrecht bis zum 10. Jahrhundert", *Byzantinische Zeitschrift* 7 (1898), 511 ff.
[2] W. Ensslin, *Zur Frage nach der ersten Kaiserkrönung durch den Patriarchan und zur Bedeutung dieses Aktes im Wahlzeremoniell* (Würzburg, 1947). Ensslin's study in complete but modified form can also be found in *Byzantinische Zeitschrift* 42 (1943/49), as reprinted in 1959, pp. 101 ff. and 369 ff.
[3] J. B. Bury, "The Constitution of the Later Roman Empire", in *Selected Essays*, ed. Harold Temperley (Cambridge, 1930), 103 ff. This essay was the Creighton Lecture, delivered in 1909 and published in 1910 by Cambridge University Press.

necessary qualification for holding the Imperial office. It also implied that the new Emperor had not only been elected by the Senate and the people, but was accepted by the Church."[4] Nevertheless, despite such protests Sickle's view generally prevailed.[5] Bury himself qualified the statement just quoted in a note stating "that coronation by the patriarch, though looked on as a matter of course, was not a constitutional *sine qua non*".[6] Moreover, in 1923 he returned to the view which he had first expressed in the "Constitution".[7]

In a study published in 1941 the present writer placed the matter of imperial coronation in Byzantium under careful scrutiny. Looking at it from various angles — as an occasion used by the patriarchs to exert definite promises from newly designated emperors; as a practice strictly adhered to and, with hardly any exceptions, sought after by every newly designated emperor, particularly by usurpers; as an act regarded by foreign potentates in the periphery of the empire as marking the acquisition of the imperial title; and, finally, as a ceremony whose ecclesiastical nature was and is self-evident — he concluded:

From whatever angle the usage of coronation is considered, it is quite evident that it was an ecclesiastical act, performed by the patriarch as the highest official of the Church. It is the clearest indication of the changed character of the empire. Christianity had transformed the Roman world and it was impossible for the constitution of the empire not to be affected by this transformation. This important step was taken in 450 when the patriarch was designated to perform the coronation ceremony. Henceforth coronation by the patriarch became an institution and, as such, a constitutional usage of the later Roman empire. By the introduction of the patriarch in the coronation ceremony of 450 the Church became an essential element in the constitutional system of the empire.[8]

At the same time this writer sought to point out that by the term "constitutional" he did not have in mind some specific document outlining the structure of the Byzantine government which was officially issued as the binding law of the land. (No such document, of course, had ever been issued.) The term was rather used in the sense that Bury understood it, i.e., as a body of principles prevalent in the custom, law, and political institutions and practices of Byzantium.

[4]   J. B. Bury, *A History of the Eastern Roman Empire from the Fall of Irene to the Accession of Basil I* (London, 1912), 39.
[5]   For some of the more important references see Peter Charanis, "Coronation and Its Constitutional Significance in the Later Roman Empire", *Byzantion* 15 (1940-1941), 49, n. 6.
[6]   Bury, *A History of the Eastern Roman Empire*, 39, n. 3.
[7]   J. B. Bury, *History of the Later Roman Empire* I (London, 1923), 11.
[8]   Charanis, 66.

Not long after the appearance of this work, Ensslin published the first installment of the study referred to above, but, owing to the war, it was not circulated in the United States until 1947 when it appeared in completed form. In this study Ensslin not only argued that the first emperor to be crowned by the patriarch was Leo I, but reiterated Sickle's view that in crowning the emperor the patriarch represented the electors rather than the Church.[9] But in a subsequent work, published posthumously, Ensslin summarized his position as follows:

To the acclamation, which was the decisive act in appointing the emperor, there was added the ceremony of coronation. The first emperor to be crowned by the Patriarch of Constantinople was Leo I (457-474); from the seventh century it became usual for the ceremony to be performed in St. Sophia. The coronation by the Western Emperors had given the Papacy the opportunity, of which full advantage had been taken, of forging from it one of the most important rights of the Church; in contrast with this, in the East the Patriarch at first acted as the representative not of the Church but of the electors, and his participation was not regarded as an essential element in making an imperial election constitutionally valid. Later, however, as the whole ceremonial took on an increasingly ecclesiastical complexion, the coronation ceremony, which always took place in the Ambo of St. Sophia, gained in significance, influenced as it was by the need of the Church for a guarantee of Orthodoxy and of her rights, and it came increasingly to be regarded as a usage sanctified by custom.[10]

With this statement Ensslin makes an important concession to those who have opposed Sickle's view, but he does not entirely free himself from that view, for as he further states: "But despite this ... the act of coronation performed by the representative of the Church still remained nothing more than an act of ecclesiastical consecration of the sovereign when he was already in full possession of the imperial power."[11]

No doubt the most thorough and detailed study of the election, proclamation, and coronation of the Byzantine emperors, a study which covers the entire chronological span of the empire, is the work of A. Christophilopoulou published in 1956.[12] Her book has been correctly

[9] Ensslin, *Zur Frage*, 23 ff.; *Byzantinische Zeitschrift*, 371.
[10] W. Ensslin, "The Government and Administration of the Byzantine Empire", in *The Cambridge Medieval History*: IV. *The Byzantine Empire*. Part II: *Government, Church, and Civilization*. Edited by J. M. Hussey (Cambridge, 1967), 3. Ensslin died on January 1, 1965, but his work had been completed by the autumn of 1961. *Ibid.*; p. VII. Cf. N. H. Baynes and H. St. L. B. Moss, eds., *Byzantium, An Introduction to East Roman Civilization* (Oxford, 1948), 270. In this latter Ensslin writes: "The Patriarch officiated at the coronation not as the representative of the Church but as a representative of the electors; and his co-operation was not regarded as essential for the legal institution of the emperor."
[11] Ensslin, "The Government ...", 3.
[12] A. Christophilopoulou, Ἐκλογή, Ἀναγόρευσις καὶ Ετέφις τοῦ Βυζαντινοῦ Αὐτοκράτορος (Athens, 1936), 237.

described as an indispensable tool for the study of these matters, though her attempt to show that in some essential respects they differed from one period to another has received unfavorable criticism.[13] Concerning the significance of the imperial coronation, Christophilopoulou generally follows the views of Sickle, although not always in a consistent manner. For instance, she claims that at least as of the enthronement of Phocas (602), the imperial coronation had taken on a religious character, which implies, of course, that now the patriarch officiated as a churchman and not as the representative of the electors. She further states (in connection with the enthronement of this same emperor) that observance of all the legal forms of the coronation required the presence of the senate and the patriarch, with the latter in his capacity as the head of the church. Elsewhere in her book, however, she categorically insists that imperial coronation was essentially a festive ceremony with no constitutional significance.[14]

In the first edition of his noted *Geschichte des byzantinischen Staates*, George Ostrogorsky expressed his views on the imperial coronation as follows:

Marcian (450-457) was indeed the first Emperor to receive the crown from the hands of the Patriarch of Constantinople. His predecessors, for all their devotion to Christianity, had been content to follow the Roman tradition and accept it from some high official or general and be raised on the shield and acclaimed by the army, the people, and the senate. The innovation of 450 is significant in the light of the powerful position which the see of Constantinople was to achieve in the very next year. From now on all Byzantine emperors were to be crowned by the Patriarch of the capital, and the coronation took on the character of a religious consecration. A religious ceremonial was thus added to the old Roman secular coronation with its military emphasis and gradually superseded the latter, and in the Middle Ages was thus regarded as the really essential act in the bestowal of the Byzantine crown.[15]

It was against this view of Ostrogorsky that Ensslin, unfamiliar with the detailed study of the same problem by the present writer, wrote the detailed study of the subject mentioned above. In a second edition of his *History*, Ostrogorsky took notice of Ensslin's observation but made no concessions on the essential points except to substitute Leo I for Marcian as the first emperor to receive the crown from the hands of the

[13]   For instance, see the review of Karajiannopoulos in *Byzantinische Zeitschrift* 50 (1957), 394-395. Christophilopoulou sought to answer this and other criticisms of her book in a subsequent publication which appeared in the *Bulletin of the Philosophical School of the University of Athens* 12 (1961-1962, 458-497) and 13 (1962-1963), 375-399.
[14]   A. Christophilopoulou, 57-58, 60-61, 65, 70, and 72.
[15]   Georg Ostrogorsky, *Geschichte des byzantinischen Staates* (Munich, 1940), 35.

patriarch.[16] He has repeated these views in the third edition, which has recently appeared in English,[17] despite the interim publication of Christophilopoulou's work of whose existence and views Ostrogorsky, of course, was aware. Thus on the important point whether the coronation of a newly-designated emperor by the patriarch was essential for his complete enthronement or merely a festive celebration with no constitutional significance there is still no agreement among scholars. The reason for this is, of course, simple. Nowhere in the sources is there any reference explicitly stating what in the constitutional set-up of the Byzantine empire was the significance, if any, of the coronation of a newly-designated emperor by the patriarch. Hence all is a matter of inference and interpretation.

2

Given this lack of explicit evidence there may never be a decisive answer to the problem of the role of the patriarch in the coronation of the emperor. Yet there *are* references in the sources whose import weighs much more heavily in favor of the coronation of a newly-designated emperor by the patriarch seen as a necessary act for his complete enthronement rather than the opposite. First of all, there are evidences of the haste with which usurpers sought to receive the crown from the patriarch. This haste can be given only one interpretation, *viz.*, that such usurpers considered their coronation by the patriarch a necessary act for the legitimization of their power. An illustration is the accession to the throne by Nicephorus I (802) as related by Theophanes. The conspirators responsible for his accession entered the Great Palace about ten o'clock on the evening of October 31. Earlier they had sent soldiers to guard the palace of Eleupherios, where the Empress Irene was spending the night. Once in the Great Palace the conspirators proclaimed Nicephorus emperor and sent emissaries to announce the news throughout the city. All of this took place before midnight. At dawn on the next day, November 1, they ordered Irene to be brought to the Great Palace, where she was put under guard, and then proceeded to the church, no doubt Saint Sophia, where Nicephorus received the crown from Patriarch

---

[16] *History of the Byzantine State*, tr. by Joan Hussey (New Brunswick, N.J., 1957), 56 and note 2.
[17] *History of the Byzantine State*, (rev. ed., tr. by Joan Hussey (New Brunswick, N.J., 1969), 61 and note 2.

Tarasius. Having been crowned, Nicephorus on the next day banished Irene to the Princes' Island in the Propontis. Obviously the haste with which the conspirators had Nicephorus duly crowned can have only one meaning, that in their opinion his enthronement was not complete until he was crowned by the patriarch. It was this coronation, one may say, that really made him emperor.[18]

Besides the haste with which usurpers sought to obtain the crown from the hands of the patriarch, another body of evidence exists which, in like manner, can be given no other interpretation than that the coronation of a newly-designated emperor by the patriarch was a necessary act for his complete enthronement. This consists of the acceptance by such emperors of conditions imposed by the patriarch in exchange for coronation. The first emperor to accept conditions imposed by the patriarch as a prerequisite for his coronation was Anastasius I (491-518). Despite the fact that with the advice of the senate he had been selected by Ariadne, widow of Emperor Zeno, and also had been accepted by the army and the people, Anastasius met the obdurate opposition of Patriarch Euphemius who suspected him of heretical views. Euphemius refused to crown the new emperor unless given a written guarantee signed by Anastasius himself that he would not change the Chalcedonian doctrine or introduce any other innovation into the church. It was not until Anastasius yielded that Euphemius performed the coronation ceremony.[19]

That Anastasius saw fit to accept the conditions imposed on him by the patriarch can only mean that he wanted very much to be crowned by him, and that he saw in such a coronation an act necessary for the completion of this enthronement. Nor is it easy to draw any other conclusion from this important incident than that coronation was an ecclesiastical act, performed by the patriarch as the highest official of the church. Had it been simply a political act performed by the patriarch as a representative of the state, there would have been no justification for Euphemius' refusal to crown the new emperor, supported as he was by the senate, the army and the people, and whose subsequent conduct shows that Anastasius had yielded to the patriarch contrary to his better judgment. This, I submit, is the only sound interpretation of the incident. No other will do; certainly not that given by Christophilopoulou,

---

[18]   Theophanes, *Chronographia*, ed. C. de Boor (Leipzig, 1883), 1: 476ff.

[19]   Peter Charanis, *Church and State in the Later Roman Empire: The Religious Policy of Anastasius I* (Madison, 1939), 10 and 12. There is a possibility that Leo I had been required to take an oath of fidelity to the "constitution" before his coronation by the patriarch. On this see H. E. del Medico, "Le Couronnement d'un empereur byzantin vu par un juif de Constantinople", *Byzantinoslavica* 16 (1955), 43-75.

who is wholly unable to fit this incident into her concept of coronation as a secular (festive) celebration without any constitutional significance.[20]

Two other examples of an emperor accepting conditions imposed upon him by the patriarch as a prerequisite for his coronation might be given: Phocas (602-610) and John I Tzimiskes (969-976). Both of these emperors came into power under questionable circumstances. Coronation by the patriarch would mean the legitimization of their position, hence their willingness to accept his conditions. This reason for their submission is not explicitly stated in the sources, but it is the only sound inference that can be drawn from such action.

Phocas came to power as a result of an army rebellion, and the accession to his banner of an important segment of the population of Constantinople. He then betook himself to the place called Hebdomon where his partisans had gathered, and sent an emissary to summon to the same place both the senate and Patriarch Cyriacus — the senate because its presence and (by implication) its consent to the proclamation of a new emperor were required if form were to be kept; the patriarch because he was needed to crown the new emperor. Cyriacus proceeded indeed to crown Phocas, but before doing so, he extracted from Phocas a declaration attesting to his orthodoxy and a promise that he would leave the church undisturbed. Afterwards the coronation ceremony took place in the Church of St. John the Baptist. The sources mark this as the elevation of Phocas to the throne, a clear indication it seems of the importance of patriarchal participation in the completion of the enthronement of the new emperor. In any event, as this writer reads the account in the sources[21] of the rise of Phocas to power he gets the definite impression that the three elements which gave legitimacy to this position were the people, the senate, and the patriarch, with the latter, of course, in his capacity as the head of the church and the official agent empowered to invest the new emperor with the principal symbol of imperial authority — the crown.

In the case of John Tzimiskes, his way to the throne was opened by the assassination of Nicephorus II Phocas, an assassination in which he was apparently implicated. Proclaimed emperor, Tzimiskes proceeded to St. Sophia as was customary to be invested with the imperial symbols. Patriarch Polyeuct, however, refused to crown him unless he first drove

---

[20] A. Christophilopoulou, 43. She questions the authenticity of this incident as reported by the sources.

[21] Theophylact Simocatta, *Historiae*, ed. C. deBoor (Leipzig, 1887), 302 ff.; *Chronicon Paschale* 1 (Bonn, 1832), 693; and Theophanas, 289.

Theophano (the wife of the murdered emperor and Tzimiskes' accomplice in the act) away from the palace, revealed the name of the actual assassin of Phocas, and repealed the laws of Nicephorus which forbade church officials to make any decisions and to name or promote anyone to ecclesiastical office without the prior consent of the emperor. Tzimiskes yielded on all points and the coronation was performed.[22] Polyeuct was acting not only in the interest of morality, but also of the church. The patriarch used the power conferred upon him by the privilege of crowning the emperor to restore certain prerogatives which had been taken from the church. This is yet another case in which it is difficult to draw any other inference than that the coronation of a newly-designated emperor was an ecclesiastical act essential for the completion of his enthronement and was performed by the patriarch in his role of the highest official of the church.

3

No doubt the most famous imperial coronation in the Middle Ages was that of Charlemagne, on Christmas day in the year 800. Still a matter of controversy is the question of who originally initiated the revival of the imperial title in the West, but there is no doubt that the papal court was very deeply involved in the whole affair.[23] The position of the Roman

---

[22]   Leo Diaconus, *Historia*, ed. C. B. Hase (Bonn, 1828), 98; John Zonaras, *Epitome historiarum*, ed. T. Büttner-Wobst (Bonn, 1897), 3:520; George Cedrenus, *Synopsis historiarium*, ed. Immanuel Bekker (Bonn, 1838-1839), II:380. By this time the regular oath required of all emperors before their coronation, the text of which appears in fourteenth century sources, was probably in use. For the origin of this oath, and an English version, see Charanis, "Coronation ...", 57-58. On this and other oaths in the Byzantine empire see N. Svoronos, "Le Serment de fidélité à l'empereur byzantine et sa signification constitutionelle", *Revue des Études Byzantines* 9 (1952), 106-142.

[23]   The literature on the subject of the coronation of Charlemagne is extensive. For the view that Charlemagne took the initiative in bringing about the event see Louis Halphen, *Charlemagne et l'empire carolingien* (Paris, 1947), 120-139, and especially 129. For the view that the papacy brought about the whole affair, see Walter Ullman, *The Growth of Papal Government in the Middle Ages: A Study in the Ideological Relations of Clerical to Lay Power* (London, 1955). The sources themselves are inconclusive, so any view must necessarily be inferential. For further commentary see Ostrogorsky, *History of the Byzantine State*, 165, n. 1. The little book of Richard E. Sullivan, *The Coronation of Charlemagne: What Did It Signify* (Boston, 1959), designed for college students, is also of use to scholars. It reproduces in English translation the principal original texts relating to this famous coronation, as well as a number of excerpts from the works of modern scholars on its meaning. Interesting also is the little book by Peter Munz, *The Origins of the Carolingian Empire* (Leicester, 1960).

church as more than a purely local organisation had by the end of the
eighth century become very insecure. It was beset by internal difficulties.
It had lost jurisdiction over Southern Italy and that part of Illyrium,
including the islands, which was still in imperial hands. Constantinople
was unfriendly. North Africa and Spain had fallen under the sway of
the Arabs. Italy was hard-pressed by the Lombards. There was no place
for the papacy to rebuild its power except in the northern Germanic
world, which was now being united, however loosely, by Charlemagne.
But more important, there could really be no church without an empire;
such had been the tradition for centuries. And the papacy knew the empire
was in the East. Moreover, that empire was unwilling to offer its protec-
tion to a pontiff whose policies it could not accept. The problem which
the Roman church faced was how to free itself from Constantinople and
yet remain within the Roman imperial tradition. With the rise of a man
as powerful as Charlemagne an attempt was made to revive the imperial
tradition in the West and to make it as much of a living force as it was
in the East. The importance of this affair for the subject of this study is
that what actually made Charlemagne emperor was his coronation by
the bishop of Rome. The question naturally arises: what in the traditions
of the Roman empire could have suggested to the pope that by crowning
Charlemagne and having him acclaimed by the congregation he would
in fact make him emperor?

A suggested answer to this question, most recently reiterated by
Dvornik, is that Leo III acted on the basis of the *Donation of Constantine*.
"Leo", writes Dvornik, "was probably influenced by the Constantinian
legend which had put under his control the three factors — army, senate
and people — which, according to the Roman constitution, elected an
Emperor."[24] That famous legend does indeed put the Roman pontiff
on a very high pedestal. In one place it says: "And to the extent of our
earthly imperial power, we (i.e., Constantine) decree that his holy Roman
church shall be honoured with veneration; and that, more than our empire and earthly throne, the most sacred seat of St. Peter shall be glorious-
ly exalted; we giving to it the imperial power, and dignity of glory, and
vigour and honour." Even stronger concessions to the papacy are revealed in the following passage:

To the holy apostles, my masters, St. Peter and St. Paul, and through them, also
to St. Sylvester ... and to all the pontiffs, his successors, who until the end of
the world shall be about to sit in the seat of St. Peter, we concede and, by this

[24] F. Dvornik, "Constantinople and Rome", *The Cambridge Medieval History.
IV. The Byzantine Empire. Part 1: Byzantium and its Neighbours*, 447.

present, do confer ... a diadem, that is the crown of our head, and at the same time the tiara; and also the shoulder band, that is, the collar that usually surrounds our imperial neck; and also the purple mantle, and crimson tunic, and all the imperial raiment; and the same rank as those presiding over the imperial cavalry; conferring also the imperial sceptors and, at the same time, the spears and standards; also the banners and different imperial ornaments, and all the advantages of our imperial position, and glory of our power.[25]

At the same time that the pontiff is so exalted, his clergy are granted the honors, powers, and privileges of senators.

The document as a whole, but particularly in the passages quoted above, has implications beyond what may have been intended by the forger. The important fact to be noted is the strictly ecclesiastical purport of the document. Whatever the honors, privileges, powers, and insignia with which the Roman pontiff is invested, he is treated throughout the document as the successor of St. Peter, an ecclesiastical officer rather than a secular ruler. Indeed in the regions over which he is designated to dominate there is no room for a secular ruler. "For", the document reads, "where the supremacy of priests and the head of the Christian religion has been established by a heavenly Ruler, it is not just that there an earthly power should have jurisdiction." What we really have in this document is two papal doctrines presented as approved by the first Christian emperor: the doctrine of the two swords formulated long before by Pope Gelasius, and the doctrine of Petrine succession. The bishop of Rome is the spiritual head of Christendom before whom even emperors should bend, but he is such by virtue of his succession from St. Peter and not because he represents a particular segment of the population of Rome. Consequently, during that solemn moment when Leo III placed the crown on the head of Charlemagne, the pope was acting, whether or not on the basis of the *Donation of Constantine*, not as the representative of any segment of the population of Rome, but strictly as a churchman, the successor of St. Peter and the holy agent through whom God was creating a new emperor.

All of this is purely Byzantine. As in Constantinople, so in Rome, coronation was an act essential to the enthronement of an emperor; as in Constantinople, so in Rome, the head of the church was the agent through whom the newly-created emperor was vested by God with his power. Quite obviously, the device of ecclesiastical coronation used by

---

[25]   This famous forgery has been consulted in the edition of C. B. Coleman, *The Treatise of Lorenzo Valla on the Donation of Constantine* (New Haven, 1922), 10-19. The wording of the passages quoted here is from the translation of E. F. Henderson, *Select Historical Documents of the Middle Ages* (London, 1905), 319-329.

the papacy to invest Charlemagne with imperial dignity had its source in Constantinople. As Duchesne put it many years ago: "It was only natural that in a ceremony which had as its aim the consecration not of a king of the Franks, but of an emperor of the Romans, the pope would be inspired by the usage in Constantinople, the only place until then where such a ceremony had been performed."[26]

4

That the patriarch represented the state in the coronation of a newly-designated emperor in Byzantium is a view which, I submit, can no longer be seriously entertained. From the outset when the head of the church was introduced into the ceremony, he acted in his capacity as a church-man and he continued that role to the very end of the empire. The cere-mony itself, although it did for a long time retain some of its original military features, became, certainly by the beginning of the seventh cen-tury, if not before, essentially religious in character.[27] Nor may one still seriously doubt the significance of the coronation act as an essential component in the complete enthronement of an emperor. Constantine XI, the last emperor who occupied the throne and the sole one who ap-parently did not receive his crown from the hands of an ecclesiastic, was

[26] *Liber Pontificalis*, ed. Louis Duchesne (Paris, 1886), 2:38. The reprint of 1955 has been used. Within the framework of the Roman empire, the act of Christmas day of the year 800 was, of course, revolutionary. But this is a matter outside the scope of this paper.

[27] For a description of the ceremony and citations to the texts see Charanis, "Coronation ...", p. 52 and note 18. To these references add: P. Schreiner, "Hochzeit und Krönung Kaiser Manuels II. im Jahre 1892", *Byzantinische Zeitschrift* 60 (1967), 70-85; and the new edition by Jean Verpeaux of Pseudo-Kodinos, *Traité des Offices* (Paris, 1966). On the role of the patriarch in the coronation of the Byzantine emperor see now also: Léon-Pierre Raybaud, *Le Gouvernement et l'Administration Centrale de l'Empire Byzantine sous les Premiers Paléologues (1258-1354)* (Paris, 1968), 47, 52, 66ff. On page 76 Raybaud writes: "Pour Sickel, le patriarche agit moins comme un prêtre que comme le représentant des corps électoraux traditionnels. Le Professeur Dölger et Treitinger ont repris, dans ses grandes lignes, la thèse de Sickel, à laquelle on peut faire un reproche majeur: le caractère religieux de l'acte du couronnement est par trop ignoré.

Par réaction, ce trait est mis en évidence dans une autre théorie, qui fait de l'Eglise le quatrième élément constitutionnel de l'empire, et dont MM. Grabar et Ostrogorsky sont les apoligistes. M. Charanis, dans un article brillant et au terme d'une analyse pénétrante, concluait dans le même sens."

On the same page Raybaud sums his own position as follows: "Le couronnement est assurément l'usage constitutionnel le plus important dans l'empire byzantine sous les premiers Paléologues."

regarded by a large segment of the people of Constantinople as having never officially become emperor.[28]

What inferences can be drawn from the significance of imperial coronation by the patriarch on the important matter of church-state relations in Byzantium? No doubt the coronation of the emperors by the patriarch did have the effect of enhancing his role in the political life of the empire. Under certain circumstances the patriarch might, as actually occurred on several occasions, require that a newly-designated emperor accept certain conditions before consenting to crown him. The increasing participation of the patriarch, sometimes decisively, in the designation of new emperors may also at least in part be attributed to the role of coronator of emperors. It is not, however, in the day-to-day interactions between church and state or in the influence that the church may have consequently obtained in the affairs of the state that the real significance of patriarchal coronation of emperors lies. It is rather in the larger, conceptual realm of Church and State.

Caesaropapism is perhaps the wrong term to describe the character of church-state relations in Byzantium. There were moments in the history of the empire when the church resisted the wishes of the state, fought hard for a cause, and in the end won. But in general the church observed the laws of the state, even those which affected its personnel and regulated its life, and relied upon the state for the enforcement of its own regulations. The idea that the state should not interfere in the affairs of the church never became rooted in Byzantium, though it was advocated by some at times. Even emperors who accepted conditions of the patriarch in order to be crowned, once enthroned, were legally free to act as they saw fit. The emperor was after all the embodiment of law, and that law applied to all segments of the population including the church. The significance of the patriarchal coronation of the emperor and the religious ceremony that accompanied it, then, lies less in the domain of practical politics than of ideas. It is one of the factors promoting and expressing the concept of the empire viewed as coterminous with Christianity, directed by two officers, each deriving his power from God, and neither conceivable apart from the other. The expression of this idea was indeed the purport of the message sent by the patriarch of Constantinople to Basil I, Grand Prince of Moscow, who seems to have viewed the Byzantine emperor with disregard.

---

[28]   Peter Charanis, "They Crown Modiolus Once More", *Byzantion* 13 (1938), 79-80. But cf. Christophilopoulou, 204 ff., who makes every effort to establish a different case.

If we, on account of our common sins, have lost cities and lands, it does not follow from this that we have to suffer disdain from Christians ... with sorrow I also learn of some words spoken by Your Nobility about my Mightiest and Holy Autocrat and Emperor. It is said that you do not allow the Metropolitan to mention in the diptychs the Holy Name of the Emperor — a thing which has never been possible before — and you say: "We have the Church, but we have no Emperor nor wish to know him." This is by no means good ... If, with the will of God, the pagans have surrounded the possessions and the land of the Emperor, *yet up to this day the Emperor has the same coronation from the Church according to the same ritual and with the same prayers; he is anointed with great consecrated oil and elected Emperor and Autocrat of the Romans, i.e., of all Christians.* If the Great Emperor, the Lord and Master of the Universe, invested with such power, has been reduced to such straits, what might not other local rulers and small princes endure ... Thus, it is by no means good, My Son, if you say that "we have the Church not the Emperor". It is impossible for Christians to have the Church, but not have the Emperor.[29]

According to this document, then, there could be no church without the emperor and, conversely, (a point made explicitly by the patriarch) there can be no emperor without the church. The emperor and the church, wrote the patriarch, "have much in the way of unity and communion and it is not possible to separate them".[30] The point to notice, however, is that the emperor was not raised above the other rulers by the territorial extent of his possessions of the power of his forces, but by his coronation and consecration *at the hands of the church.* Through that act he became the universal ruler or Christendom. That politically speaking by this time the emperor had become a mere puppet in the hands of foreign rulers did not really matter. Far more profoundly, he was still at the apex of that hierarchy of princes, who, according to another Byzantine concept, ruled Christendom.[31]

---

[29]   F. Miklosich and J. Müller, *Acta et diplomata graeca medii aevii* 2 (Vienna, 1892), 189-192. This document has been translated in part by A. A. Vasiliev, "Was Old Russia a Vassal State of Byzantium?", *Speculum* 7 (1932), 358ff. The *italics* in the passage quoted are mine.
[30]   Miklosich and Müller, 191.
[31]   On this consult G. Ostrogorsky, "Die byzantinische Staatenhierarchie", *Seminarium Kondakovianum* 8 (1936), 41-61; F. Dölger, "Die Familie der Könige in Mittelalter", *Historische Jahrbuch* 60 (1940), 397-420, reprinted in F. Dölger, *Byzanz und die Europäische Staatenwelt* (Speyer am Rhein, 1953), 34-69; A. Graber, "God and 'Family of Princes' Presided over by the Byzantine Emperor", *Harvard Slavic Studies* 2 (1954), 117-124; G. Ostrogorsky, "The Byzantine Emperor and the Hierarchical World Order", *Slavonic and East European Review* 35 (1961), 1-14.

DIE TRÄNEN DER FROMMEN IN DER GOTTESBEGEGNUNG
(Ein Beitrag zur oekumenischen Spiritualität)

WILHELM KAHLE

1

"Es war ihm aber von der Wärme des Herzens zu Gott die Gewohnheit, dass dann, wenn er dem Volke die Heiligen Bücher vorlas, die Tränen von seinen Augen wie ein Wasserstrahl waren und er in seinem Schluchzen kaum ein Wort der göttlichen Schrift aussprach."[1] Das wird von Ivan Neronov, einem der Reformer in der russischen Kirche des 17. Jahrhunderts, berichtet. Eine Zeitlang war er der Beichtvater und Protektor des Protopopen Avvakum gewesen. Solche Hinweise auf den weinenden Frommen, dessen Tränen Ausdruck der tiefen Ergriffenheit, der Rührung, der *umilenie* sind, stellen in den Berichten über Männer und Frauen in der russischen Kirche nichts Seltenes dar. Die Tränen, die sie weinen, werden nach ihren eigenen Worten und auch in denen der Berichterstatter immer als solche verstanden, die mit den Tränen, die Menschen sonst weinen, nichts gemein haben. Sie werden nicht durch menschliches Leid, durch Schmerz, Sorge um die Zukunft, durch den Abschied von einem Verstorbenen oder einfach durch eine labile Psyche bewirkt; ihre besondere Ursache ist vielmehr die vertiefte Begegnung mit Gott, seinem Worte, aber auch mit seinen Heiligen, in denen Gottes Kraft wirksam empfunden wird.

Der Protopop Avvakum gehörte auch zu denen, die oft so weinten. In seiner Lebensbeschreibung berichtet er von anderen, deren Weinen für viele sichtbar wurde. An dem Mönch Avraamij, der später in Moskau verbrannt wurde, hebt er hervor: "... er liebte es zu weinen; sogar im Gehen weinte er. Wenn er zu jemandem sprach, dann waren seine Worte

[1] N. I. Subbotin, *Materijaly dlja istorij raskola*, Bd. 1, *Žitie Grigorija Neronova, sostavlennoe posle ego smerti*, 243-305, hier 277.

sanft und flossen, wie Tränen fliessen."[2] Avraamij gehört wohl, wie aus dieser Angabe zu schliessen ist, zu denen, welchen nach den Vorstellungen der Mönchsväter und der Väter der Orthodoxie die "Gabe der Tränen" geschenkt worden war. Diese Gabe, um die man Gott bitten kann, erscheint als eine Besonderheit, nicht alle Weinenden haben sie; sie geht über das Weinen der anderen Frommen hinaus; über ihr Vorkommen wird später noch zu berichten sein.

Berichte über die Weinenden beziehen sich nicht nur auf das 17. Jahrhundert, gewiss eine Zeit besonderer religiöser Bewegtheit in der Geschichte der russischen Kirche. Aus allen Zeiten wird von solchen berichtet, deren Tränen in der Gottesbegegnung und im asketischen Tun flossen. Aus den Anfängen der russischen Kirche wird von der Gründung des Kiever Höhlenklosters berichtet: "Viele Klöster sind gegründet von Fürsten, Grossen und Reichen, aber sie sind nicht so wie die, die gegründet sind mit Tränen, Fasten, Wachen und Gebet."[3] Das ist eine Selbstaussage der Mönche des Kiever Klosters. Hier werden die Tränen mit den anderen Formen des mönchischen Lebens, mit dem Halten der Fasten, mit Nachtwachen und mit dem Gebet als ein Viertes wie selbstverständlich zusammengefügt, sie gehören zur rechten mönchischen Existenz hinzu. Diese mit durch die Tränen bestimmte mönchische Weise hat also dem Pečerskij-Monastyr' in Kiev eine andere Bedeutung gegeben, als sie etwa einem Ktitoren-Kloster zukam, das durch mancherlei Gründe verursacht entstanden sein mochte.

Von Feodosij, dem ersten hervortretenden Abt des Kiever Klosters wird berichtet, dass er sein Gebet unter Tränen sprach, indem er sich zur Erde niederwarf.[4] Tränen weinte Feodosij auch, wenn er einen der Brüder des Klosters, der recht ungeduldig war, vor sich hatte, dann erbat er für ihn Geduld.[5] Den Bettlern half er, er weinte dabei über ihr Elend.[6] So stehen schon am Anfang der Geschichte des russischen Mönchtums und der russischen Kirche die Gestalten der Weinenden. In der Vita des heiligen Fürsten Mixail Jaroslavič von Tver', gest. 1318, heisst es, dass er seine Gebete mit Tränen sprach. Von Maksim Grek erwähnt die Legende seine Demut und seine Tränen. Als er nach Russland gerufen

---

[2] A. N. Robinson, *Žizneopisanie Avvakuma i Epifanija* (Moskau, 1963), 167. In der Lebensbeschreibung des Epifanij berichtet dieser, dass beim Eintreffen der Nachrichten von den Reformen Nikons, die als ein Sakrileg verstanden wurden, die Mönche im Solovkij-Kloster stöhnten und zu weinen begannen (179).

[3] *Letopis' po Lavrent'evskomu spisku*, 3. Aufl. (St. Petersburg, 1897), 155.

[4] *Das Paterikon des Kiever Höhlenklosters*, nach der Ausgabe von D. Abramovič neu herausgegeben von Dmitrij Tschiževskij (München, 1964), 41, 50, und 71.

[5] *Loc. cit.*, 56.

[6] *Loc. cit.*, 57.

wurde, weinte er, aber auch die Mönche im Vatopaedi-Kloster, dass sie ihren guten Hirten verlieren sollten.

Von Maksim Grek wird besonders das Weinen des Nil Sorskij hervorgehoben. Ausdrücklich wird die Bitte um die Gabe der Tränen von ihm geäussert. In seinem Gebet: "Schenke mir, o Herr, das unaufhörliche Gebet im demütigen Herzen. ... gib mir, o Herrscher, Rührung und Tränen, auf dass ich über meine Sünde weine. Wahrlich, mein Herr und Wohltäter, schenke mir (Tränen), da ich sie nicht habe, auf dass mein Herz von Tränen der Liebe zu Dir erwärmt werde ...."[7] Zu der Haltung der *umilenie*, des demütigen Sicherschliessens gegenüber Gott gehören die Tränen. So ruft Nil seine Brüder auf: "Und indem wir dieser Güte und dieses unendlichen Erbarmens unseres Gottes eingedenk sind, wollen wir unser Gewissen erwärmen und Tränen und Seufzer und das übrige ausströmen lassen."[8] Die Betonung der Tränen ist nicht nur in ihrer Zeit eine Besonderheit des Nil Sorskij und seiner Schule. Dafür spricht die Tatsache, dass von seinem grossen geistigen Widersacher Iosif Volodskij Gleiches berichtet wird. Im Kloster von Volokolamsk, so berichtet Savva Černij, hörten die Tränen niemals auf, von den Augen der Mönche herabzufliessen. Dabei weinten sie nicht um der Menschen willen, vielmehr führte sie eine unaufhörliche Meditation des Todes dazu.

In späterer Zeit werden ähnliche Aussagen gemacht, so z.B. über Tixon von Zadonsk. Dabei wird ausdrücklich erwähnt, dass Tixon die Gabe der Tränen hatte. Man hörte ihn in seiner Zelle weinen und klagen, sein Weinen im Gebet war wie das eines, der seinen Freund betrauert. Einer Vision und Audition der Gottesmutter, zusammen mit den Aposteln Petrus und Paulus an ihrer Seite, die aus dem Jahre 1778 berichtet wird, folgte Zittern und ein Tränenausbruch. Ging Tixon über Land und kam er an einer Kirche vorbei, so betete er vor dem Portal, indem er niederkniete und Tränen vergoss.

Zu denen, die aus dem Geiste alter asketisch-mönchischer Traditionen lebten, gehörte im 19. Jahrhundert Ignatij Brjančaninov, 1807-1867; eine Zeitlang war er Bischof von Stavropol' gewesen. Er berichtet, dass in ihm, als er noch Soldat und Junker gewesen war, eine unbeschreibliche Sehnsucht nach Gott erwachte. Diese Sehnsucht war mit Tränen über seine bisherige geistliche Lässigkeit verbunden. Er beweinte die

---

[7] Gebet des Nil Sorskij in der Übertragung von Fairy von Lilienfeld, *Nil Sorskij und seine Schriften* (Berlin, 1963), 262-263. Vgl. aus dem gleichen Gebet: "Wer gibt meinem Haupt Wasser und meinen Augen den Quell der Tränen, auf dass ich gereue und weine und den Unflat meiner Sünden abwasche" (260).

[8] *Loc. cit.*, 279 aus dem Sendschreiben an Kassian Mavnukskij.

Stunden, die er ohne Gott verbracht hatte: "... ich gehe durch die Strassen von Petersburg im Waffenrock des Junkers, die Tränen rinnen mir aus den Augen." Er beneidete nach seinen Worten die, "die als einfache Menschen in der Kirche beten und weinen konnten, soviel die Seele nur wollte".[9]

Feofan Zatvornik, 1815-1894, war Bischof von Tambov, später von Vladimir, bevor er sich 1866 aus diesem Amte und aus der Welt zurückzog. In seinen Schriften, vor allem in seinen Briefen über das geistliche Leben übte er bedeutsamen Einfluss aus. In einem seiner seelsorgerlichen Briefe heisst es:

Es gibt ... Tränen, die von der Gnade kommen. Der Wert der Tränen bemisst sich nicht nach dem Wasser, das aus den Augen fliesst, sondern nach dem, was in der Seele bei dem Weinen und nach diesem vor sich geht. Da mir die Gnadengabe der Tränen fehlt, enthalte ich mich der Betrachtungen über sie und beschränke mich auf die Vermutung, dass die gnadenreichen Tränen mit vielen Veränderungen im Herzen zusammenhängen. Die Hauptsache ist: das Herz muss aus Dank im Feuer des Gottesgerichtes brennen, jedoch ohne Schmerz zu empfinden und verbrannt zu werden, vielmehr mit Rührung, die von der vom Throne des barmherzigen Gottes ausgehenden Hoffnung eingeflösst wird, der die Sünde richtet und sich des Sünders erbarmt. Auch dünkt es mich, dass diese Tränen am Schlusse der Mühen — nicht der äusseren, sondern der Mühen an der Reinigung des Herzens — kommen müssen, als letzte Waschung oder Spülung der Seele. Überdies: sie dauern nicht eine Stunde, nicht ein und zwei Tage, sondern Jahre (so sagt der heilige Isaak der Syrer).[10]

Die vielfachen Aussagen Feodor Dostoevskijs über die Tränen in seinen Werken, zumal in den *Brüdern Karamasov*, vor allem in den Partien, die den Starec Zosima betreffen, seien hier nur erwähnt. Die bekannte Aussage (im 4. Buche), dass jeder für alles und für alle auf Erden Schuld trage, ist von den Worten begleitet, dass jeder die Kraft

---

[9]   Vgl. Igor Smolitsch, *Leben und Lehre der Starzen*, 169, ferner derselbe, *Russisches Mönchtum* (Würzburg, 1953), 521-524.

[10]   Wiedergegeben nach der Übersetzung von Nicolai von Bubnoff, *Russische Frömmigkeit* (Wiesbaden, 1947), 110-111. Feofan fährt hier fort: "Es gibt auch — so sagt man — ein Weinen des Herzens ohne Tränen, das aber ebenso wertvoll und stark ist wie die Tränen. Letzteres ist besser für die, die mit anderen leben, welche sehen können. Alles aber ordnet der alle errettende Herr."

An anderer Stelle weist er darauf hin: "Darum können die guten Laien, die für ihr Seelenheil eifern, sich an den asketischen Schriften des Makarius, Isaak des Syrers, Johannes Klimatos, Ephraem des Syrers und anderen nicht satt lesen. Von denen aber, welchen die Belehrungen der Aufsätze fremd dünken, gilt, wie sie selbst einsehen werden: 'Sie haben den Geist Christi nicht'. Dieses Wort ist hart, aber was ist da zu tun" (*loc. cit.*, 177).

Vgl. auch in Feofans Briefen, *Was ist das geistliche Leben?* (Jordanville, 1962), 239 die Tränenlegende, die Feofan von V. A. Žukovskij (1783-1852) übernommen hat.

haben solle, die ganze Welt durch Liebe loszukaufen und mit seinen Tränen die Sünden der Welt abzuwaschen. Auch die in dem Roman eingelagerte Biographie Zosimas bietet viele Beispiele für das Weinen der göttlichen Ergriffenheit.

In die jüngste Vergangenheit hineinreichend, seien hier schliesslich noch Angaben aus den Aufzeichnungen des Priesters Aleksandr Elčaninov zitiert: "Tränen sind so wirksam, weil unser ganzes Wesen durch die Bewegung, welche sie erwecken, erschüttert wird. Durch Tränen und Leiden wird die eisige Verkrampfung des Fleisches zerbrochen und die engelgleiche Schöpfung des Geistes geboren. Die Schöpfung des Geistes wird durch Tränen, Fasten und Wachen herbeigeführt."[11] An anderer Stelle äussert er sich: "Wie sollen wir die trösten, die weinen? Indem wir mit ihnen weinen."[12] Dementsprechend sagt er: "Alle Freuden und Vergnügungen vermindern und schwächen das Leben der Seele."[13]

Das Weinen, die Tränen der Heiligen, der Mönche und der Laien haben so in allen Zeiten der Geschichte der russischen Kirche ihren legitimen Platz. Die Tränen gehören nicht nur als eine Besonderheit der Frömmigkeitsgeschichte der russischen Orthodoxie an. Ihr Vorkommen weist in die Geschichte der Frömmigkeit der gesamten Orthodoxie, der griechischen Kirche und schliesslich der alten Kirche zurück. Isaak der Syrer war hier schon in der Aussage Feofans als einer der Väter der Aussagen über die Tränen genannt worden. Mit anderen zusammen wird er auch genannt in dem grundlegenden Kapitel (VIII) des sogenannten *Ustav* des Nil Sorskij: "Über die Tränen. Wie diejenigen handeln sollen, die sie erlangen wollen."

In diesem Abschnitt führt Nil Sorskij eine ganze Reihe von Väteraussagen über die Tränen und die Gabe der Tränen an. Diese Aussagen machen deutlich, mit welcher Intensität er ihnen meditierend und betend nachgegangen ist, zugleich auch, welche Bedeutung sie im Rahmen seiner theologischen Konzeptionen und seines literarischen Nachlasses haben. Zu diesen Vätern gehören namentlich aufgeführt neben Isaak Euagrius Ponticus (unter dem Namen Neilos Sinaites), Gregor der Grosse, Johannes Klimax, Germanos von Konstantinopel, Andreas von Kreta, Symeon der neue Theologe sowie, nicht namentlich genannt, Dichter von Hymnen, die in Textteilen von Nil Sorskij zitiert werden.[14] Die Einflüsse dieser

---

[11] Es lag nur der Auszug der Zapiski in der Wiedergabe bei G. P. Fedotov, *A Treasury of Russian Spirituality* (New York, 1948) vor, hier 466.
[12] *Loc. cit.*, 423.
[13] *Loc. cit.*, 438. Vgl. ferner auch 443 und 457 sowie die Auseinandersetzung mit Isaak dem Syrer, 456-457.
[14] Vgl. die Übersetzung bei Fairy von Lilienfeld, *Nil Sorskij und seine Schriften*.

Väter, auch die anderer, bestimmten bereits von den Anfängen der russischen Kirche an deren Spiritualität und in ihren besonderen Aussagen über die Tränen das Verständnis von deren Notwendigkeit. Zeiten besonderer Reformbewegungen verstärkten oder bestätigten das, was man als eine Notwendigkeit verstehen gelernt hatte. Hier ist an die Zeit der Reformen des 17. Jahrhunderts zu denken, in der durch den Druck zahlreicher Schriften und Anthologien aus den Vätern ein grösserer Kreis als zuvor mit dem Gedankengut der mönchischen Askese, wie sie in der alten Kirche geübt wurde, in der Verbindung von Demut, Busse, Tränen und Gottesschau vertraut wurde. Einen besonders starken Einfluss übte später die Übersetzung der Philokalia von Nikodem Hagiorites durch Paisij Veličkovskij aus. Die Wiederbelebung der mönchischen Traditionen im 19. Jahrhundert, zumal im Hinblick auf die Bedeutung der Tränen, ist nicht ohne deren tiefgreifende Bedeutung verständlich. Dabei wird sichtbar, dass die Väteraussagen in ganz besonderem Masse nicht als historische, sondern als gegenwärtig gültige Aussagen verstanden werden. Die Ausführungen von Aleksandr Elčaninov über seine Lektüre Isaak des Syrers machen das deutlich. Die Gegenwärtigkeit der Väteraussagen ist aber vor allem auch durch ihre bleibende Gültigkeit im liturgischen Gebrauch gegeben. Zahlreiche Äusserungen über die Tränen finden sich in den liturgischen Formularen, in Gebeten, Hymnen und Kanones.

Es ist verständlich, dass auch in den Katechismen der Gedankenkreis von Busse und Tränen, von dem Leide um Gottes Willen einen Niederschlag gefunden hat. Besonders stark kommt das bei Petrus Mogila in der *Confessio Orthodoxa* bei der Auslegung der zweiten Seligpreisung zum Ausdruck. Es heisst hier, dass diese Seligpreisung zuerst einmal lehre, dass jene selig sind, die die ganze Zeit ihres Lebens über ihre Sünden bekümmert sind, mit welchen sie Gott und ihren Nächsten beleidigt haben und über diese ihre Sünden weinen.[15] Der orthodoxe Katechismus

---

Elf Kapitel aus den Schriften der Heiligen Väter, der sogenannte *Ustav* des Nil Sorskij, 211-255, hier 241-246. Vgl. ferner *loc. cit.*, 142.

Die Bedeutung dieser und anderer Väter für das russische Mönchtum ermisst sich auch nach dem Vorkommen der Handschriftenexemplare in den wichtigsten Klosterbibliotheken. An der Spitze stehen die Schriften von Johannes Klimax, Isaak dem Syrer, Basilios dem Grossen, nachfolgend Dionysios Aeropagita. Vgl. dazu Nikolaus von Arseniev, *Die russische Frömmigkeit* (Zürich, 1964), 117.

Vgl. auch die Häufigkeit und das Vorkommen der Väterzitate bei Nil Sorskij, zusammengestellt von Fairy von Lilienfeld, *op. cit.*, 124ff. Zur Häufigkeit des Vorkommens der Väterzitate und Erwähnungen bei Josef von Volokolamsk, vgl. Thomas Špidlik, *Joseph de Volokolamsk. Un chapitre de la spiritualité russe* (Rom, 1956), 22.

[15]   Johannes Karmiris, *Ta dogmatika kai symbolika mnemeia tes orthodoxou katholikes ekklesias* II (Athen, 1953), 656.

bezeichnet die Seligpreisungen als die erhabenste Darstellung der christlichen Vollkommenheit. In ihnen ist der Geist Christi und der der Christen dem Geiste der Welt gegenübergestellt.[16] Filaret (Drozdov) von Moskau beantwortet in seinem Katechismus die Frage in dem Abschnitt zur Busse: "Was wird von dem Bussfertigen gefordert?" — "Zerknirschung über seine Sünden, der Vorsatz, sein Leben zu bessern, der Glaube an Christum und die Hoffnung auf seine Gnade. Denn die göttliche Traurigkeit wirkt zur Seligkeit eine Reue, die Niemand gereut."[17]

Die Beziehung dieser und anderer Aussagen zu 2. Kor. 7, 10 und zu Matth. 5, 4 ist damit schon sichtbar geworden. Das "penthein" — Leidtragen, Trübsal tragen — erfährt in der russischen Orthodoxie durch die Weise der Übersetzung aus dem Griechischen eine bestimmte Prägung. Das penthein Matth. 5, 4 wird im Kirchenslavischen mit "plakati" wiedergegeben, in der Urbedeutung soviel wie "Fliessen", "Strömen", in der späteren Bedeutung "Tränen vergiessen", "Weinen". Entsprechend lautet die Übersetzung von "penthein" im Russischen auch "plakat'", "heulen", "weinen". Damit wird das Weinen selbst zum Gegenstand der Seligpreisung. In der mönchischen Nachfolge, in der die Seligpreisungen den Charakter der Weisung und Anleitung zur Vollkommenheit und der Konkretisierung des Evangeliums erhielten, wurde so das Weinen selbst zum Gott wohlgefälligen Handeln. Es ist der Schlüssel, mit dem man zur Freude bei Gott eingehen kann und zu der Gemeinschaft, die die Gläubigen in Gottes Welt nach dieser Zeit erwartet. In der Legende tritt dem Mönche Feofil im Kiever Höhlenkloster nach jahrelangem Weinen ein Engel entgegen, der ihm sagt: "Du wirst zu dem mit Freuden eingehen, der da sagte: Selig sind die Weinenden, denn sie werden getröstet."[18]

2

Die Aussagen aus dem Bereich der russischen Orthodoxie weisen zurück zu den griechischen Vätern. Über deren Aussagen zu dem Sachkomplex hat Irénée Hausherr seine umfassende Arbeit "Penthos" vorgelegt. Sie trägt die Fülle des Materials aus den Quellen in systematischer Formung

---

[16] *Orthodoxer Katechismus*, erstellt von der Orthodoxen Priesterkongregation vom Heiligen Demetrios in Thessalonike (Deutsche Übersetzung, München, 1956).
[17] *Ausführlicher christlicher Katechismus*, in Übersetzung im Anhang zur *Geschichte der Kirche Russlands* von Filaret von Černigov (Frankfurt, 1872), 353.
[18] *Paterikon des Kiever Höhlenklosters*, 161.

vor.[19] Die russisch-orthodoxen Aussagen wiesen jedoch schon über die griechischen Väter hinaus auf die biblischen Belegstellen. Es erscheint notwendig, diesen in einer kurzen Übersicht nachzugehen. Die Tränen in der Heiligen Schrift gehören zur Reue, zur Busse, zum Penthos, zu dem, was in der späteren orthodoxen Theologie die Katanyxis genannt wird. An ihnen erkennt man die rechte Busshaltung, ja, die Tränen werden in den Schriftaussagen oftmals zu einem Korrelat der Busse. Wo die Gemeinde des alten Bundes zur Umkehr aufgerufen wird und sie sich vor Gott schuldig bekennt, da zerreissen Menschen ihre Kleider, gehen in Sack und Asche und ihre Tränen sind wie Wasserfluten.[20] Umkehr, Hinkehr zu Gott ist eine Sache des innersten Menschen, er ist in seinem Herzen dabei beteiligt. Aber diese Hinwendung zu Gott ist für andere erkennbar. Das bezieht sich nicht nur auf ihre Folgen, sondern schon auf ihre gegenwärtige Äusserung, sie ist wahrnehmbar. Traurigkeit und Tränen werden notwendige äussere Zeichen der Umkehr. Auch die Trauer um den Tod eines Menschen hat ja ihre Zeichen, bis hin zu der Klage und den Tränen der Angehörigen und der Klageweiber. In diesen sichtbaren Zeichen wird die Trauer leibhaftig. Die Trennung von Menschen, die Trennung von dem Lande der Verheissung, die Trennung von der Gemeinschaft mit Gott durch eigene Vergehen haben ihre Zeichen, sie führen zu den Tränen.

Das Weinen ist dem Bereich der Erkenntnis und des Bekenntnisses der Sünden zugeordnet. Das steht in der Folge alttestamentlicher Aussagen über das Verhalten der Gottesgemeinde bei bestimmten Geschehnissen, etwa aus Anlass von Busstagen oder bei der Verlesung des Gesetzes unter dem König Josia.[21] Wichtig sind neben den Aussagen der Propheten im Alten Testament die der Busspsalmen. Als Aussagen Davids verstanden, wurden sie zum Exempel nicht nur der Haltung der Eremiten und der Frommen in der alten Kirche, sondern auch für die, die in der Welt in einem öffentlichen Amte standen. Die Busshaltung Davids, die mit dieser Haltung verbundenen Tränen führen dazu, dass nicht nur die Welt des Mönchtums, sondern die der grossen Masse der Christen in der Welt durch sie wirksam bestimmt wurde.

Besondere Bedeutung gewinnen in späterer Zeit die Weinenden im Neuen Testament. Verhaltensweisen in der Geschichte der Kirche wirken wie eine ständige Wiederholung des Weinens des Petrus, nachdem er

---

[19] Irénée Hausherr S.J., *Penthos. La doctrine de la componction dans l'orient chrétien* (Rom, 1944, Neudruck 1960).
[20] Js. 37,1; 38,3; Jer. 4,8; 6,26; 48,37; 49,3; Dan. 9,3.
[21] 2. Kön. 22,19.

seinen Herrn verleugnet hatte, noch mehr aber als eine Auslegung der Geschichte von der grossen Sünderin Luk. 7,30ff. Gerade dieser Text ist für die spätere Zeit der locus classicus. Väterzitate, Stichera und Busskanones weisen darauf hin.[22] Die Art und Weise der Gottes- und Christusbegegnung wird typologisch durch das Verhalten der weinenden Frau zu Jesu Füssen vorgebildet. Von Bedeutung sind neben den Aussagen des Psalms 126,5,6 die Aussagen der Offenbarung Joh. in ihrer Gegenüberstellung von Tränen und Leid hier und jetzt, Freude und Beseligung dort und einst. An dieser Gegenüberstellung entzündet sich vielfältig das Verständnis, dass man der Freude der Ewigkeit, in der Gott alle Tränen abwischen wird, hier weinend entgegenzuschreiten habe.[23]

Zur grössten Beispielgestalt für die Weinenden wird Christus selbst. Er weint über die Stadt Jerusalem in ihrer Unbussfertigkeit, er weint über den Tod des Lazarus.[24] Das weist die Tränen in einen neuen Gedankenkreis hinein. Zur Trauer und zum Leide über die eigenen Verfehlungen, zu den Tränen über die eigene Unwürdigkeit in der Begegnung mit Gott treten die Trauer über das Leid und die Sünden anderer hinzu. Diese Bedeutung wurde wichtig, die Tränen haben nicht nur mit der Zerstörung und Unordnung, sondern auch mit der Wiederherstellung des Menschen, der Schöpfung zu tun.[25] Solche Gedanken klingen bei Ephraem

[22] Zu den Busskanones gehört, um nur ein Beispiel herauszugreifen, der grosse Busskanon des Andreas von Kreta. Vgl. auch Kilian Kirchhoff, *Die Ostkirche betet*, Bde I-II (Münster, 1962), mit zahlreichen Einzelbeispielen, so Bd. I, 132, 137, 157, 159, 161, 162, 164, 168, 174, 176ff., und andere Stellen. Es handelt sich hier um die liturgischen Teile der Fastenwochen.

[23] Evgl. Luk. 6,21ff.; Jakobus 4,9ff.; Off. Joh. 7,17; 21,4.

[24] Evgl. Luk. 19,41; und Evgl. Joh. 11,35. Ephraem, Rede über Jesaja 26,10; "Als er über den Lazarus weinte, weinte er zugleich über alle Toten, denn er sah sein Abbild vom Tode zerbrochen und in die Verwesung weggeworfen. In seiner Güte schmerzte es ihn tief, dass er sein geliebtes Ebenbild entstellt und ins Grab geworfen, ja zum Entsetzen und zum Abscheu geworden sehen musste." Zitiert nach: *Des Heiligen Ephraem des Syrers ausgewählte Schriften*, Bd. I, in *Bibliothek der Kirchenväter*, Bd. 37, 95-103, hier 97.

[25] Vgl. R. Bultmann, Artikel "Penthos, pentheō" in *Theologisches Wörterbuch zum Neuen Testament*, Bd. 6, 40-43: "Auch im Neuen Testament bezeichnet 'penthein' die in Klagen und Tränen sich äussernde Trauer. Mehrfach ist es mit 'klaiein' verbunden." R. Bultmann stellt (42) fest, dass das Wort im Neuen Testament kein theologisch bedeutsamer Begriff sei. Er fährt (43) fort: "Die Seligpreisung der penthountes Matth. 5,4 ist aus der eschatologischen Gedankenwelt zu verstehen. Man darf die hier gemeinte Trauer nicht einseitig als die Busstrauer über die Sünden verstehen. Andererseits werden natürlich nicht Trauernde überhaupt selig gepriesen, sondern es versteht sich von selbst, dass diejenigen gemeint sind, die den leidvollen Aeon als solche durchschauen und nicht wie die 'gelōtes' (Luk. 6,25) seinen Lockungen verfallen. Ihr 'penthein' ist das Zeichen ihrer inneren Geschiedenheit von diesem Aeon und ihres Wartens auf die 'basileia tón ouranón'. Infolgedessen wird man aus dem 'penthein' die Bussklage über die Sünden auch nicht ausschliessen dürfen."

dem Syrer an; der Trauer Gottes über den durch die Sünde und den Tod
von ihm getrennten Menschen entsprechen die Tränen des seine Gottes-
ferne, seine Verlorenheit erkennenden Sünders. Christi Weise im Umgang mit Menschen wird aber auch noch in anderer Weise im Zusammenhang der Tränen gedeutet. Ephraem bemerkt, dass Jesus Tränen vergossen habe, aber dass von ihm nicht berichtet würde, dass er gelacht
habe.[26] Christus selbst gibt so das Vorbild für seine Nachfolger in der
Haltung des Ernstes, die das Lachen vermeidet und die Demut und den
Umgang mit anderen auch sinnfällig übt.[27] Besondere Anstösse gab vor
allem aus dem Munde Christi die 2. Seligpreisung, dazu das, was von
Lukas 6,21 ff. in der Feldpredigt berichtet wird.[28] Die Seligpreisung für
die, die Leid tragen, wurde zum mächtigen Aufruf, so das Heil zu erlangen. Das Leidtragen, das penthein war aber nach dem Verständnis
der Zeit Christi und dem der nachfolgenden Jahrhunderte auch Sichtbarwerden des Leides. Es schloss den Fluss der Tränen ein. Ein stilles Leidtragen ohne Tränen musste sich fragen lassen, ob nicht das Leid selbst
eingeschränkt oder der Leidende krank sei. Basilios von Caesarea entwickelte eine Psychologie der Tränen; er spricht von ihrer lösenden
Wirkung und weiss, dass Tränenlosigkeit zur schweren unheilbaren Krank-
heit führen kann.[29]

Die Aussagen über die Tränen, die Berichte über die Tränen, die man
die geistlichen Väter, die man die Frommen in Syrien, in Ägypten und
in der griechischen Lebenswelt vergiessen sah, sind so als eine Auslegung

---

[26] Ephraem der Syrer, 97. Vgl. Johannes Chrystostomos, "6. Homilie zu Evgl.
Matth.", *MPG* (= Migne, *Patrologia Series Graeca*) 57, Sp. 69. Der Hinweis hier auf
das Lachen Sarahs und des Sohnes von Noah ist mit der Bemerkung verbunden, dass
beide Personen nicht dem geforderten Gehorsam entsprachen. Johannes Chrystostomos
sagt das ausdrücklich nicht, damit er den Lachenden vernichte, sondern das Gelächter
aufhebe.

[27] Benedikt von Nursia fordert in seiner Regel von den Mönchen die Haltung der
Demut. Diese Demut, die das Leben der Mönche bestimmen soll, ist wie eine von der
Erde zum Himmel aufgerichtete Leiter, Gott weist ihr die Richtung. Zur Demut gehört
nach Benedikt, dass der Mensch nicht gerne zum Lachen bereit sei. Das Lachen ist
Sache der Toren, Christus steht demgegenüber als die wahre Weisheit. Die 12. Stufe
der Demut, die Benedikt aufweist, fordert, nicht nur im Herzen demütig zu sein,
sondern auch äusserlich in der Körperhaltung diese Demut zu bekunden. Das geschieht
durch Neigung des Kopfes und durch den niedergeschlagenen Blick.
Vgl. Johannes Chrysostomos, "6. Homilie zu Evgl. Matth.", *MPG* 57, Sp. 69:
"Wenn du so weinst, wirst du ein Nachfolger (mimetes, imitator) des Herrn. Denn er
selbst hat geweint, sowohl über Lazarus, als auch über die Stadt ..."

[28] Johannes Chrysostomos "15. Homilie zu Evgl. Matth.", *MPG* 57, Sp. 225
bezeichnet diese Seligpreisung als "entole (praeceptum)", die der "didaskalos
(magisterium)" aller Philosophie ist.

[29] Basilios von Caesarea, *Homilie über die Danksagung*, *MPG* 31, Sp. 217-237, hier
Sp. 228-229.

der Aussagen der Heiligen Schrift zu verstehen. Es lässt sich hier nur in einigen Exempeln aufzeigen, in welchen Zusammenhängen das Reden von den Tränen steht. Die *Apophtegmata patrum* geben einen Einblick in die Führung von Mönchen durch ihre geistlichen Väter. Immer wieder wird von diesen die Wichtigkeit des Penthos betont, es ist Gott wohlgefällige Trauer, ist Zerknirschung über den Stand, in dem man sich befindet. Antonios fordert auf, dass man ein zerknirschtes Herz habe, weine und im Herzen seufze.[30] Der Abbas Arsenios wird nach seinem Tode gepriesen, dass er sich in diesem Leben beweint habe. Wer sich hier nicht selbst beweint, wird in der Ewigkeit ständig weinen; sei es also hier freiwillig oder dort in der Ewigkeit wegen der Qualen für die Übeltäter: "Es ist unmöglich, nicht zu weinen."[31] Gelasios ruft zum geduldigen Bleiben im Kellion auf und zugleich dazu, dass man seine Sünden beweine.[32] Gottesfurcht, Demut, Askese in der Nahrungsaufnahme und das Penthos werden als Anweisung für das rechte mönchische Leben nebeneinandergestellt.[33] In einer noch umfangreicheren Zusammenstellung der von einem Novizen verlangten Tugenden — sie wird dem Johannes Kolobos zugeschrieben — fehlt das Weinen ebenso wenig.[34] Die göttliche Traurigkeit hat eine doppelte Bedeutung, lehrt der Abbas Poimen, sie wirkt Neues und sie behütet zugleich.[35] Im Gespräch der zwölf Anachoreten trägt einer nach dem anderen seine Erfahrungen zusammen. Der letzte entfaltet die Vision und Audition des jüngsten Gerichts. Er hat das Weinen der Verlorenen gehört. Nun beweint er selbst das Menschengeschlecht.

Wie die anderen Räume der Christenheit, so hat auch Syrien seine Glaubensstreiter und Helden der Frömmigkeit; das ist einer der Gründe, der Theodoret von Kyrrhos seine "Geschichte der Gottesliebe" schreiben liess. In Italien folgte ihm über ein Jahrhundert später in dem Anliegen, auch die dort vorhandenen Gestalten christlicher Askese und Demut aufzuzeigen, Gregor der Grosse in seinen "Dialogen". In beiden Darstellungen erscheinen die Gestalten der Weinenden. Julian Sabbas

---

[30] *Apophtegmata patrum*, in *MPG* 65, Nr. 33, Sp. 85.
[31] *Apophtegmata patrum*, Nr. 41, Sp. 105.
[32] *Apophtegmata patrum*, Nr. 6, Sp. 153.
[33] *Apophtegmata patrum*, Nr. 34, Sp. 216.
[34] *Apophtegmata patrum*, Nr. 6, Sp. 172.
[35] *Apophtegmata patrum*, Nr. 39, Sp. 332. Poimen bezeichnet die göttliche Traurigkeit als den Anfang des neuen Lebens Nr. 69, Sp. 337. Poimen, Nr. 119, Sp. 353: "Wer von seinen Sünden gereinigt sein will, der kauft sich los durch Tränen. Und der Tugenden erlangen will, der erkauft sie durch Tränen. Denn das Weinen ist der Weg, den die Schrift und die Väter uns überliefert haben, wenn sie sagen: weinet. Ausser diesem gibt es nämlich keinen anderen Weg."

benetzt den trockenen Boden mit seinen in den Sand rinnenden Tränen,
Gott verwandelt diese Tränen in eine Wasserquelle, die dem verdur-
stenden Begleiter Asterios den Durst stillt.[36] Auch Markianos, Domnina
und Symeon Stylites — den Gewaltigen, das grosse Wunder des Erd-
kreises nennt ihn Theodoret — gehörten zu denen, die ihre Gebete weinend verrichteten.[37]

In der Geschichte der orthodoxen Kirchen, aber auch in denen der
Nestorianer und der Monophysiten reisst nun die Kette der Aussagen über
das tränenreiche Penthos nicht ab. Nach den Anfängen in Ägypten, in
Syrien und Palästina, in der griechisch sprechenden Welt wurden sie in
den Kirchen der slawischen Völker und in der Kirche der Rumänen fort-
geführt. Zu denen, die besonders aussagekräftig waren, gehörten Basilios
von Caesarea, Ephraem der Syrer, Euagrius Ponticus, Johannes Chrysostomos, Diadochos von Photike, Johannes Klimax, Johannes von
Damaskus, Symeon der neue Theologe, Niketas Stethates.

Die Fülle der Bilder, mit denen die Tränen charakterisiert werden,
ist ein Zeichen dafür, in welchem Masse die Tränen bei den Vätern auch
Gegenstand der Meditation gewesen sind. Die Tränen erwecken die Seele,
die tot war, zu neuem Leben. Die Tränen reinigen und erneuern das
entstellte Ebenbild Gottes, die Seele als den Wesenskern des Menschen.
In den Bereich dieser Aussagen gehört der Aufruf Ephraems, so, wie man
über einen Toten weine, über die eigene tote Seele zu klagen; jene Tränen
über einen Toten vermöchten nicht, ihn zu erwecken, diese aber seien
imstande, der Seele neues Leben einzuflössen.[38] Die Ströme der unaufhör-
lich vergossenen Tränen sind wie Gewässer, aus denen eine starke innere
Freude geschöpft wird — so sagt es Johannes Chrysostomos.[39] Andererseits kann er die Tränen auch mit einem starken Regenguss vergleichen,
durch den die Luft gereinigt wird. Wie solchem Regenguss die Klarheit
der Luft folgt, so ist die Folge der Tränen heitere Stille.[40] Euagrius Ponticus ruft auf, die Gabe der Tränen zu erbitten, um durch die in ihnen
sichtbar werdende Reue die Härte des Herzens zu erweichen.[41]

Der Charakterisierung des toten, des harten, des beschmutzten Herzens
gesellt sich die Bezeichnung des unruhevollen, brennenden und begierigen

---

[36]   Theodoret von Kyrrhos, *Historia religiosa*, MPG 82, Sp. 1312-1313.
[37]   Theodoret, *MPG* 82, Sp. 1323-1340 zu Markianos, Sp. 1491-1496 zu Domnina,
Sp. 1464 ff. zu Symeon Stylites.
[38]   Ephraem, 100.
[39]   Johannes Chrysostomos, "6. Homilie, Kap. 5 zum Evg. Matth.", MPG 57,
Sp. 67-68.
[40]   *Loc. cit.*, Sp. 69-70.
[41]   Euagrius Ponticus in *Kleine Philokalie*, hrsg. Matthias Dietz und Igor Smolitsch
(Zürich/Köln, 1956), 34.

Herzens hinzu. Die Tränenströme vermögen die begierlichen Brände des Herzens zu löschen.[42] Es weinen die, die zu Christus gefunden haben, sie weinen noch mehr deshalb, weil die Tränen ihnen in der Unruhe eine Erquickung sind. Der Weg des Gotteskämpfers ist von der Sorge begleitet, von Gott wirklich geliebt zu sein, er ist mit Tränen ohne Schmerzen übergossen.[43]

Von besonderer Intensität sind die Aussagen des Johannes Klimax in seiner Paradiesleiter. Im dieser Schrift (7. Gradus) entfaltet er in einer Fülle von Aussagen die Bedeutung der Tränen für den, der sich dem Gottesreiche nähern will. Dem Wasser der Taufe für die Neugeborenen stellt er die Tränen gleichsam als ein zweites Taufwasser für die, die in Schuld gefangen sind, gegenüber.[44] Diesem auch bei anderen vorkommenden Gedanken ist das häufig anzutreffende Bild von der Bedeutung der Tränen als einem Reinigungsbade zugehörig; die Tränen waschen die Sünde ab. Zur Erleuchtung des Herzens gehören sie mit hinzu, so sagt es Isaak der Syrer. Wenn die Gnade die Augen eines Menschen zu öffnen beginnt, dass sie das Wesen der Dinge zu sehen vermögen, dann beginnen die Augen auch Tränen zu vergiessen.[45] Der Schüler Symeons des neuen Theologen, Niketas Stethatos, bringt die Tränen in die Beziehung zu der Welt des Lichtes, die die Seele schauen darf. Die Schau des Lichtes bewirkt, dass die Augen unter der Leuchtkraft des Heiligen Geistes eine Flut von Tränen vergiessen.[46]

3

Wie es eine Tradition der Tränen und der Aussagen über sie in den Kirchen des Ostens gegeben hat, so auch eine im Westen. Zu ihren Bezeugern gehören Tertullian, Ambrosius, Augustin, Gregor der Grosse, Bernhard von Clairvaux, Franziskus von Assisi. Sie bestimmten den mächtigen Strom dieser Tradition der sichtbaren Zerknirschung und Busse; er wurde noch durch die während der Bilderstreitigkeiten aus dem Osten in den Westen geflohenen Mönche verstärkt. Der Weg führte weiter in die Mystik des Hochmittelalters. Im Spanien des 16. Jahrhunderts ist

---

[42] Johannes von Damaskus, *Theotokion der orthodoxen Liturgie.*
[43] Diadochus von Photike in *Kleine Philokalie*, 55 und 57.
[44] Johannes Klimax, Gradus 7: "Peri tou charopoiou penthous", *MPG* 88, Sp. 801-816.
[45] Vgl. Nikolaus von Arseniev, *Die russische Frömmigkeit* (Zürich, 1964), 115 zu Homilie 56.
[46] Niketas Stethatos in *Kleine Philokalie*, 116-117.

später eine besondere Wiederbelebung dieser Vorstellungen in zwei bestimmenden Gestalten festzustellen; es sind Ignatius von Loyola und Johannes vom Kreuz. Von jedem dieser beiden sind in verschiedenen Richtungen neue Anstösse ausgegangen.

Tertullian beschreibt die Praxis der öffentlichen Busse. Sie ist begleitet von den Zeichen Sack und Asche, von der Nahrungsaskese, von einem betrübten Geist und von den Gebeten, die durch Tränen und Seufzen verstärkt sind. "Dies alles tut die öffentliche Busse, um die Sinnesänderung erkennbar zu machen."[47] Ambrosius von Mailand fordert, dass der Sünder die Vergebung mit Tränen und Seufzen erbittet, dass dabei auch die anderen für den einzelnen Sünder ihre Tränen vergiessen. Die äussere Haltung der Büssenden richtet sich auch bei ihm nach dem Vorbilde der grossen Sünderin. Ambrosius kennt solche Büsser, in deren Gesicht die Tränenströme tiefe und scharfe Linien gezogen haben.[48] Hieronymos spricht von der Jakobsleiter, von der Heilige stürzen, aber auch Sünder emporsteigen können; diese gelangen bis zur obersten Sprosse, wenn sie ihre Vergehen durch die Tränen der Busse abwaschen.[49]

Einer der bedeutendsten Zeugen für die Tränen ist Augustin. In der Auseinandersetzung mit dem Neuplatonismus im 7. Buch der Konfessionen spricht er aus, dass dessen Schriften nicht die Tränen des Bussbekenntnisses, nicht den zerknirschten Geist, nicht das zerschlagene und demütige Herz kennen. Augustin schildert (im 8. Buche, Kap. XII) die ungewöhnliche Bewegung seiner Seele, wie diese Bewegung sie in einen Strom von Tränen auflöste und es ihn wie ein Sturm durchfuhr. Das steht in Verbindung mit seinem Bekehrungserlebnis im Garten.[50] Von seinen letzten Lebenstagen wird berichtet, dass er Tränen der Busse über sein bisheriges Leben vergoss. Wegweisung waren ihm dabei die Busspsalmen, die er sich an das Krankenlager bringen liess. Augustins Bekenntnisse sind zum prägenden Beispiel für das Selbstverständnis und das Gottesverständnis der Menschen in der Kirche des Westens geworden. An ihre Aussagen knüpfen spätere an, entfalten sie in ihren eigenen Erlebnissen und den Anweisungen für andere.

Zu ihnen gehört Gregor der Grosse. In der *Regula pastoralis* fordert er, dass die Sünden nicht nur aufgegeben werden müssen, sondern auch

---

[47] Tertulliani Opera I, Opera catholica in *Corpus Christianorum*, "De paenitentia", Kap. IX, 4, 336.

[48] Ambrosius, "De paenitentia", Opera pars VII, I, 16; *CSEL* (= *Corpus scriptorum ecclesiasticorum latinorum*), Bd. 73, 160-161.

[49] *Eusebii Hieronymi Epistulae*, pars II, Ep. 118 (7,2) *Ad Julianum Exhortatoria*, in *CSEL*, Bd. 55, 444-445.

[50] *Confessiones*, Lib. VII, *CSEL*, Bd. 33, Kap. 27, 168. *Ibid.*, Lib. VIII, Kap. 12, 193.

zu beklagen sind. Zu ihrer endlichen Vergebung gehört hinzu, dass sie durch die Tränen getilgt werden.[51] Das Pauluswort 1. Kor. 6,10, dass die Korinther abgewaschen und geheiligt seien, deutet Gregor als das Abwaschen von der Sünde. So kann er sagen, dass die Busse durch schmerzliche Tränen den Sünder abwäscht und reinigt. Die Priester ruft er auf, ihr Verhalten so einzurichten, dass die Glieder der Gemeinde ohne Hemmungen zu ihnen ihre Zuflucht nehmen und im tröstenden Zuspruch der Priester unter Gebet und Tränen sich wieder reinwaschen können.[52]

Gregors Äusserungen bestimmten in starkem Masse die Praxis der nachfolgenden Jahrhunderte und des Mittelalters. Die monastische Renaissance, die im 10. Jahrhundert begann, führte zu einem Höhepunkt im Leben und Werk Bernhards von Clairvaux. Die Tränen der Busse, die Christus- und Brautmystik, vereinigen sich in seinem Leben und in seinen Predigten. Bernhard greift (im Sermon 3 zum Hohen Liede) wiederum auf das Beispiel der grossen Sünderin zurück.[53]

Das Erbe Bernhards wirkte sich bedeutsam aus. Der persönliche Charakter der Frömmigkeit zeichnet sich auch bei Franziskus von Assisi ab. In den Legenden und Viten zu dessen Leben wird häufig von den Tränen des Heiligen und seiner Brüder berichtet. Aufschlussreich ist hierbei der Legendenkranz der Fioretti, da er aus der Sicht der Frömmigkeit des Volkes das Leben des Franziskus nachzeichnet. Eindrucksvoll ist vor allem der Bericht über das Generalkapitel des Ordens in Santa Maria degli Angeli. Er schildert das Bild der 5000 versammelten Brüder, die in der Ebene zusammensitzen, "alle mit Reden von Gott beschäftigt, im Gebet, in Tränen, in Übungen der Liebe und so still und bescheiden, dass man gar kein lautes Treiben und keinen Lärm vernahm ...".[54]

---

[51] *Regula Pastoralis* III, Kap. 30, *MPL* (= Migne, *Patrologia Series Latina*) 77, Sp. 111-112. Gregor vergleicht hier einen Übeltäter mit einem Schreiber. Hat dieser aufgehört zu schreiben, so ist damit das von ihm Geschriebene noch nicht ausgelöscht. Entsprechend ist die Unterlassung neuer Sünden nicht das letzte, die alten müssen durch die Tränen der Busse gelöscht werden, wie ein Schreiber Geschriebenes auslöscht.

[52] *Regula Pastoralis* II, Kap. 5, *MPL* 77, Sp. 33. Eine Verdinglichung und Vergröberung des Verständnisses der Tränen ist bei Gregor festzustellen, wenn er, wie es auch schon bei Theodoret zu sehen ist, eine massive Wundergeschichte in der Vita Benedikts von Nursia berichtet. Danach hielt Benedikts Schwester Scholastika ihren Bruder anlässlich eines Besuches fest, indem sie Tränen vergoss, die sogleich ganze Regenströme und ein Unwetter zur Folge hatten. Das nötigte ihn zu bleiben. — Dialogorum liber secundus (*MPL* 66, Sp. 194-196). Aus dem Buche der Dialoge zitiert auch Nil Sorskij (*MPL* 77, Sp. 300-301) in der vorliegenden Arbeit Anm. 14.

[53] Bernard von Clairvaux, Sermo 3 in *Cantica Canticorum*, *MPL* 183, Sp. 794-796.

[54] "Blütenkranz des Heiligen Franziskus von Assisi", in der Übersetzung von Otto Frhr. von Taube, Kap. XVIII, 689 in Henry Thode, *Franz von Assisi* (Wien, 1924). Vgl. dort auch 668, 675, und 702.

Von anderen Heiligen jener Zeit wird gleiches berichtet. Von Elisabeth von Thüringen heisst es, dass sie umso mehr weinte, je glücklicher sie sich fühlte, ihre Tränen seien wie aus einer ruhigen und verborgenen Quelle geflossen, ohne die Anmut ihrer Züge zu verändern. Entsprechendes gilt für Gestalten der sogenannten deutschen Mystik. Tränen begleiteten die Visionen Heinrich Seuses. Es drängte ihn zu weinen, seine Tränen waren auch mit der Vorfreude auf künftige Gotteserfahrungen verbunden.[55]

In der spätmittelalterlichen Mystik sind im Hinblick auf die Aussagen über die Tränen Veränderungen festzustellen. Im Gefüge der Gesamtsicht treten nun andere Momente stärker hervor. Sie sind mit einer Spiritualisierung früherer Motive verbunden. Im Mittelpunkt stehen jetzt die Demut in der Nachfolge, die geistliche Armut. Der Fromme hält sich in der Zucht und überlässt sich nicht törichter Freude in der Nachfolge Christi. So sagt es Thomas à Kempis im XXI. Stück "Von der Reue des Herzens".[56] Der Frankfurter lehrt, dass da, wo Christus und seine wahren Nachfolger sind, notwendig eine wahre, gründliche Demütigkeit und ein niedergedrücktes und beharrendes Gemüt, dazu das Innere voll heimlichen verborgenen Jammers und Leidens sei.[57]

Die grossen Visionäre der abendländischen wie der östlichen Christenheit kennen neben den Tränen der Busse auch die Tränen, die aus der Spannung zwischen visionärer Erhebung und nachvisionärer Wirklichkeit ihres Lebens und ihrer Umwelt entstehen. Bei den Ekstatikern ist auch die eigentliche Gabe der Tränen vorhanden gewesen.[58] Diese Tränengabe hat charismatischen Charakter, sie gehört dem schon in der mystischen Gottesgemeinschaft lebenden Menschen zu, der von der Sehnsucht nach dem Paradiese, der göttlichen Welt erfüllt ist.[59]

[55]   In der 1966 in Düsseldorf erschienenen Ausgabe *Deutsche mystische Schriften* des Heinrich Seuse charakterisiert der Herausgeber im Schlussregister die "Tränen" als "Ausdruck tiefer Ergriffenheit". Das trifft die Sachlage; die Tränen Seuses sind ein Ausdruck gesteigerter Bewegtheit, sie erscheinen in einer anderen Bedeutung als die der Mönchsväter des Ostens.

[56]   Thomas Hemerken à Kempis, *De imitatione Christi*, Liber I, XXI in *Opera omnia*, ed. M. J. Pohl, Bd. II, 39-41; ferner hier im gleichen Bande, 414-415, Kap. XII, "De elevatione mentis", und "Oratio de lacrimosa contritione peccatorum".

[57]   Der Frankfurter, *Eine deutsche Theologie*, übertragen von Joseph Bernhart, München O.J. (1947), Kap. XXVI, 185-187.

[58]   Vgl. *Dictionnaire catholique de Théologie*, Tome V 2 "Extase", Sp. 1877; dort ferner Tome XIV 2 "Symeon le nouveau théologien", Spalte 2950ff.

[59]   Hierher gehört auch die Legende der heiligen Odila; sie berichtet, dass die Heilige ihre Augen ausgeweint habe. Vgl. auch *Missale Romanum*, Messgebete "pro petitione lacrimarum", Orationes diversae, n. 21.

Vgl. ferner *Enchiridion asceticum*, 5. Aufl. (Freiburg, 1958), Hrsg. M. J. Rouet de Journel und J. Dutilleul, Angaben zu Athanasius Nr. 224, zu Cassianus Nr. 821, zu Nilus Nr. 875, zu Isaak von Ninive Nr. 1004. Rob. Bellarmin, *De gemitu columbae*

4

In den Kirchen der Reformation ist mehr als in den anderen christlichen Konfessionen eine Differenzierung der dogmatischen Aussagen vom Glaubensleben und von der tradierten Frömmigkeit eingetreten; die Wege der systematischen Lehraussagen und des Habitus der Frömmigkeit sind im Protestantismus zudem immer weiter auseinandergegangen. Die reformatorische Wendung gegen die traditionellen Weisen der Askese, gegen die Veräusserlichung der Gebräuche, gegen die "Möncherei" liess für den Gegenstand dieser Darstellung wenig Raum, zumal wenn man das Gewicht der Freude an der Rechtfertigung im reformatorischen Sinne in Erwägung zieht. Dennoch würde man in der Meinung fehlgehen, anzunehmen, dass die Tradition der Tränen im Protestantismus abgebrochen wäre. In der sich entfaltenden Andachtsliteratur des 17. und 18. Jahrhunderts, in den Biographien von Männern und Frauen des Pietismus, in den Gesangbüchern wie den Gebetbüchern der evangelischen Frommen findet sich eine Fülle von Aussagen, die deutlich machen, wie sehr Reue, Busse, letztlich die gesamte Hinwendung zu Gott in enger Verbindung zu Tränen gesehen werden. Hinter den theologisch-systematischen Aussagen, die mit der asketischen Haltung des östlichen und westlichen Mönchtums und der traditionellen Volksfrömmigkeit nichts gemein haben, lebt vielfach doch eine Frömmigkeit, die tief in der Tradition der alten und mittelalterlichen Christenheit verwurzelt ist.[60]

(Regensburg, 1920).

Vgl. dazu auch den Kommentar in der kommentierten Ausgabe der *Regula Benedicti* in *MPL* 66, Sp. 331. Er betrifft die Forderung Nr. 58 (entsprechend *CSEL* 75, 32), seine früheren Sünden täglich unter Tränen und Seufzen im Gebete vor Gott zu bekennen. Da nicht allen die Gabe der Tränen gegeben sei, sei hier für jene von Benedikt das allen mögliche Seufzen hinzugenannt worden. Vgl. ferner Otto Zöckler, *Askese und Mönchtum*, Bd. I (Frankfurt/M., 1897) Literaturangaben, 268, ferner 279 ff.; M. Lot-Borodin, Le mystère du don des larmes" in *Orient chrétien — Vie spirituelle*, tome XLVIII, 65-110 (1936); B. Steidle, "Die Tränen, ein mystisches Problem im alten Mönchtum" in *Benediktinische Monatsschrift*, Bd. 20 (1938), 181 ff.; Bd. 21 (1939), 236 ff.

[60] Im Folgenden sei eine Beschränkung auf die Feststellungen vorgenommen, die für den Bereich des deutschen Protestantismus gelten. Für den Gesamtprotestantismus trifft bei dessen starken inneren Kommunikationen, zum Teil jedoch zeitlich verschoben, Ähnliches zu. Als ein Beispiel von vielen seien John Bunyans Äusserungen in seiner Selbstdarstellung "Überreiche Gnade für der Sünder grössesten" herausgegriffen: "Von allen Zähren sind die, welche durch das Blut Christi hervorgerufen werden, die schönsten, und von allen Freuden ist am seligsten die, welche mit Trauer um Christus sich mischt. O, es ist ein heilsam Ding, vor Gott auf unseren Knien zu liegen mit Christus in unseren Armen." John Bunyan, *Überreiche Gnade für die Sünder grössesten*, in der Übersetzung von Emanuel Hirsch (Berlin, 1966), 131.

Die Reformation hatte nach ihrer Bedeutung für die Frömmigkeitsgeschichte zwei Züge. Der eine war der der Auflösung eines mönchisch
bestimmten Lebensideals, der Wendung gegen die mittelalterlichen Formen der Askese. Der andere Zug umschloss die Forderung, dass das
Leben der Christen eine einzige Busse sein solle. Das vertiefte Sünder- und
Bussbewusstsein in den reformatorischen Kirchen konnte dabei an
Äusserungen und Ausprägungen der Frömmigkeit des Mittelalters an-
knüpfen, in denen die Demut vor Gott, die Forderung, dass der Christ
immer von der Busse bestimmt sein solle, als grundlegend angesehen wurde, ohne dass damit schon die Gedanken von Verdienst und Lohn und
ausdrücklich die Werkgerechtigkeit verbunden waren. Viele Aussagen,
etwa bei Johann Arndt, lassen sich auf Äusserungen mittelalterlicher
Mystik, Christusliebe und Christusnachfolge zurückführen. Zunehmend
konnten deshalb auch Menschen wie Bernhard von Clairvaux, Franziskus
von Assisi, Thomas à Kempis und der Anonymus der *Theologia deutsch*
in die Reihe der *testes veritatis* mit einbezogen werden. Ja, die Auseinandersetzung mit der römisch-katholischen Kirche im Streit um die
historische Kontinuität führte sogar dazu, die grossen Beispielgestalten
der alten Kirche und der Kirche des Mittelalters verstärkt hervorzu-
heben, soweit diese nicht durch Aussagen, die der Rechtfertigungslehre
widersprachen, oder durch kirchenpolitische Entscheidungen zu der
besonderen Entwicklung der Papstkirche beigetragen hatten, soweit sie
nicht als Scholastiker aristotelische Philosophie und christliche Theologie
verbunden hatten, sondern schlicht als Beispiele der Frömmigkeit gelebt
und gewirkt hatten.[61]

Bei Johann Arndt sind die Einflüsse mittelalterlichen mystischen Gutes

---

[61] Im Umbruch der Reformation blieben die Formeln der dogmatischen Aussagen
erhalten, auch wenn ihre Inhalte tiefgehende Wandlungen erfuhren. Erhalten blieben
vielfach auch Inhalte und Formen der Frömmigkeitsübung. Im Spannungsbereich von
Rechtfertigung und Heiligung, von Rechtfertigung und guten Werken, von den nun
als korrekt geltenden theologischen Aussagen und dem Glaubensleben der einzelnen
konnte sehr bald älteres Gut einen bedeutenden Platz einnehmen. Diese Entwicklung
wurde durch eine umfangreiche Editionsarbeit, die vor allem die griechischen Kirchenväter und auch die Mönchsväter erfasste, wesentlich unterstützt. Von der Herausgabe
der *Theologia deutsch* durch Martin Luther in der Frühzeit seines Wirkens über die
Ausgabe der *Vitae patrum* von Georg Major, noch 1544 durch Luther mit veranlasst,
über die Aufnahme mittelalterlichen mystischen Gutes bei Johann Arndt, über die
Makarius-Ausgabe Gottfried Arnolds, über die *Historie der Wiedergeborenen* von
Joh. H. Reitz, die *Auserlesenen Lebensbeschreibungen heiliger Seelen* von Gerhard
Tersteegen führt ein breiter, vielfältig begangener Weg in den Ekklektizismus des
späteren Pietismus aller Schattierungen, in die Erweckungszeit und das Leben von
Gemeinschaftskreisen. Dieser Weg ist ständig durch persönliche und literarische
Begegnungen mit Katholiken, mit katholischem und noch älterem Erbe bestimmt
worden.

deutlich und hinreichend dargelegt worden.[62] Das wirkt sich auch auf seine Äusserungen über die Tränen in dem Zusammenhang von Reue und Busse aus. Für ihn ist bestimmend: "Und wenn ein Mensch soviel Tränen vergösse, soviel Wasser im Meer ist: so wäre er doch nicht wert des himmlischen Trostes; denn es ist lauter unverdiente Gnade."[63] In diesen Grenzen, die durch die Ablehnung des frommen Werkes und durch die Betonung der Gnade gesetzt sind, — sie galten ja auch für viele der Weinenden in früherer Zeit — haben die Tränen ihre Bedeutung. "Maria Magdalena ist die weinende Seele des Menschen."[64] "Die Tränen sind das rechte geheiligte Weihwasser, auf dass im Glauben und in Kraft des Blutes die geistlichen Israeliten gewaschen und gereinigt werden."[65] "Der Tränentrank ist aus der zarten Weintraube der andächtigen Herzen gepresst."[66] So betet Johann Arndt mit Jeremia 8,23: "Lass meine Augen Tränenquellen werden." Das ist die biblische Formulierung der Bitte um die Gabe der Tränen. Mehrfach, gerade auch im Zusammenhang mit dieser Bitte hebt Johann Arndt die Bedeutung der göttlichen Traurigkeit für den Weg des Christen hervor.[67]

In dem Kapitel "Was Busse tun heisse und wie sie geschehen müsse, und wie uns Gottes Güte zur Busse leite" (2. Buch, Kapitel 9), legte Johann Arndt das Wort des Propheten Joel 2,12 zu Grunde.[68] Seine Ausführungen sind eine Entfaltung dieses Wortes. Im nächsten Kapitel "Von vier Eigenschaften der wahren Busse" (2. Buch, Kapitel 10), erläutert Johann Arndt Psalm 102,10.

Die Gedanken und Vorstellungen Johann Arndts haben nicht nur an-

---

[62] Ernst Benz hat in seiner Arbeit *Die protestantische Thebais* (Wiesbaden, 1963), auf die Beziehungen des Pietismus zu der Tradition der Wüstenväter, vor allem auf die erneuten Einflüsse Makarius' des Ägypters auf protestantische Strömungen im 17. und 18. Jahrhundert, verursacht durch die Übersetzungen seiner Homilien, hingewiesen, ferner auf die Einflüsse, die von Thomas à Kempis und dessen Weltfluchtvorstellungen ausgingen (51 ff.).
Das Frömmigkeitsideal des Thomas à Kempis stellt bereits eine Spiritualisierung der ursprünglichen Aussagen von dem Leben in der Wüste dar. Dieses Leben wird in das "Kämmerlein", in die Abgeschiedenheit von den anderen transponiert. Ebenso sichtbar wird eine erneute Spiritualisierung des Thomas in der Wiedergabe bei Johann Arndt, der die Zelle, von der Thomas spricht, durch die Übersetzung in das "Gewissen" verwandelt (Benz, 53).
[63] Johann Arndt, *Vier Bücher vom wahren Christentum*, 10. Aufl. (Halle, 1751), 79.
[64] *Loc. cit.*, 80.
[65] *Ibid.*
[66] *Loc. cit.*, 84.
[67] *Loc. cit.*, 83; ferner auch aus dem dem Werke beigefügten "Paradiesgärtlein", 153.
[68] Joel 2,12: "So spricht der Herr: Bekehret euch zu mir von ganzem Herzen, mit Fasten, Weinen und mit Klagen. Zerreisset eure Herzen und nicht eure Kleider ..." Arndt, 242; vgl. auch 244.

dere bestimmt, das Verhältnis ist vielmehr wechselseitig. Die Frömmigkeit Johann Arndts entsprach der weiter Kreise der Frommen. Das liess
diese immer wieder nach seinem Andachtsbuche und nach anderen
greifen, die dem seinen verwandt waren. Zu diesen Andachtsbüchern
gehörten auch die von Benjamin Schmolck, 1672-1737. Unter ihnen
wurde neben den zahlreichen von ihm gedichteten Liedern das eine mit
dem Titel "Der mit rechtschaffenem Herzen zu seinem Jesu sich nahende
Sünder" besonders geschätzt. In der Vorrede dieses Buches heisst es:

Die Reue muss also recht schaffen seyn, jedoch nicht knechtisch. Sie entsteht
aus der Betrachtung der Gerechtigkeit Gottes, die den Sündern den Fluch drohet,
weil verflucht syn soll, wer nicht alle Worte des Gesetzes erfüllet, dass er
darnach thue, 5. Mose 27,26. Ist sie aber einmahl in die Flamme gesetzt, so
wird die Gluth durch das Oel der Barmhertzigkeit Gottes vermehret und
erhalten. Petrus empfande ohnfehlbar nach der entsetzlichen Verläugnung
seines Heylandes, die Pfeile der Gerechtigkeit Gottes in seinem Gewissen. Er
war mehr erschrocken als betrübet. Als ihn aber Jesus liebreich anblickte, da
fing er erstlich an bitterlich zu weinen, weil er sahe, dass er den betrübet, der
ihn und je so herzlich geliebet ... Es weinet also ein rechtschaffener bussfertiger
Sünder über seine Sünde mehr aus Liebe zu seinem beleidigten himmlischen
Vater als aus Erschreckniss vor der Strafe eines eifrigen Gottes. Die Furcht ist
wie Moses Stab, die bey vielen Zweiflern den Feltz des Hertzens aufreisset, und
Löcher schmeist, durch welche aber hernach sich die Liebe in milde Fluthen
ergiesset, 4. Mose 20,8. Doch je mehr die salzigen und bittern Gewässer der
Reue fallen, desto häufiger laufen die Ströme des lebendigen Wassers zusammen,
die von dem Leibe des Heylands fliessen, Joh. 7,38 ...[69]

Das Halle August Hermann Franckes wurde in seiner Zeit das "singen-
de Halle" genannt. Unter den von August Hermann Francke Geprägten
werden Tränen geweint, im Lied- und Andachtsgut hat das Weinen dieser
Frommen seinen eigenen Platz. Nikolaus von Zinzendorf singt in einem
seiner Lieder: "Ich weinte eine See". In einem seiner in Amerika entstandenen Lieder heisst es: "Kein einigs zähr und thränelein, o Vater!
soll inzwischen aus deinem thränen-püchlein, wo du's gezehlt, ent-

---

[69]   Benjamin Schmolck, *Der mit rechtschaffenem Hertzen zu seinem Jesu sich nahende
Sünder*. Vermehrte Auflage (Chemnitz, 1780), Vorrede Blatt 3.
   Bemerkenswert ganz im Sinne der Alten erscheint in dem vorliegenden Zitat die
Aussage, dass die Tränen nicht aus der Furcht vor der Strafe, sondern aus Liebe zu
Gott geweint werden. Wichtig erscheint auch die Beziehung zwischen den Tränen als
den salzigen und bittern Gewässern der Reue zu den göttlichen Strömen lebendigen
Wassers, die von Jesus Christus ausgehen.
   Ein Kuriosum, aber als solches aufschlussreich für die Verbreitung dieses Schmolck'-
schen Andachtsbuches, ist die Klage des Herausgebers der vorliegenden Ausgabe, dass
zahlreiche nicht zulässige Abdrucke des Buches vorgenommen worden wären. Vorrede
Blatt 6.

wischen."[70] Zu den eigentlichen Schülern des Hallenser Pietismus gehörte Carl Heinrich von Bogatzky, 1690-1774. In seinen Aussagen zu
Matth. 5,4 innerhalb seines Andachtsbuches *Güldenes Schatzkästlein*
werden die Vorstellungen über Sünde, Busse und Tränen ebenfalls sichtbar. Die aufrechten Christen zeichnet göttliche Traurigkeit aus; sie führt
von eigener Gerechtigkeit und allem falschen Trost weg. Christen sind
um ihrer Sünden willen traurig und niedergeschlagen. Wer diese Traurigkeit nicht empfindet, "der ist auch noch ein unbussfertiger, unseliger
Mensch".[71]

Bei Carl Heinrich von Bogatzky ist nicht nur in den hier angeführten
Zitaten, sondern auch in seinem Liedgut eine gewisse Spiritualisierung
festzustellen; die Tränen werden stärker zum Bilde, zum Synonym für
die wahre Reue des Herzens. Auch bei Gerhard Tersteegen wird Ähnliches deutlich, die Sublimierung der Tränen zur Haltung des sich demütig
Beugenden.[72] Die Bitte, dass die Augen Tränenquellen sein möchten, wie
sie bei Joh. Arndt und seinen Nachfolgern in der Andachtsliteratur so
häufig getan wird, ist formal gewiss die Bitte um die Gabe der Tränen.
Doch hat diese Bitte gegenüber der Bitte um die Tränengabe, wie sie
die Mönchsväter und die orthodoxen Väter getan haben, einen anderen
Charakter. Sie wird mehr und mehr zu einer Gleichnisaussage für die
Bitte um die wahre Reue und Busse, sie steht für die Bitte um die völlige
Hingabe des Sünders an seinen Heiland. Die barocke Häufung der Bild-
aussagen im 17. und noch im 18. Jahrhundert kann nicht darüber hin-
wegtäuschen, dass die Inhalte begannen, sich zu verschieben.[73]

Im protestantischen Bereich erscheint der Pietismus, auch in seinen
verschiedenen Ausläufern, als ein Versuch, wenngleich schon in spirituali-

---

[70] Bei John Joseph Stoudt, *Pennsylvanian German Poetry*, zitiert nach Ernst Benz,
Die protestantische Thebais, 112. Vgl. ferner E. Beyreuther, *Der junge Zinzendorf*
(Marburg/L., 1957), 233; ferner ders., *Zinzendorf und die sich allhier beisammen finden*
(Marburg/L., 1959), 202 und 204.
[71] *Güldenes Schatz-Kästlein der Kinder Gottes*, 61. Aufl. (Halle, 1892), 237. Es heisst
hier u.a. in dieser Erklärung: "Wenn man in der Busse seine Armut, sein sündiges
Elend erkennet, so ist das zweite Stück, dass man auch darüber Reue und Leid träget
und eine göttliche Traurigkeit hat: denn unter dieser göttlichen Reue und Traurigkeit,
oder Seelenangst, wird uns Sünde und Welt vergället, das böse harte Herz angegriffen,
niedergeschlagen, gebrochen, erweicht, gebessert und verändert ..."
Aus einer Auslegung von Psalm 56,9 und 126,5.6: "beuget dich dein Elend, und du
musst kämpfen, flehen und weinen; denke, es ist lauter Samen auf die Ewigkeit, da
soll kein Thränlein und Seufzer verloren seyn, denn Gott hat sie alle gezählt" (98).
[72] *Geistliche und erbauliche Briefe über das inwendige Leben und wahre Wesen des
Christenthums*, 2. Bd., 4. Teil (Solingen, 1775), 14.
[73] Vgl. Erich Seeberg, "Zur Frage der Mystik" in *Menschwerdung und Geschichte*
(Stuttgart, 1938), 98-137; hier vor allem 103 ff.

sierter Form, Verhaltensweisen der wahren Christen in Abgrenzung von
den lauen Christen, den Weltkindern, festzuhalten. Hinter dieser Gegenüberstellung wirken Vorstellungen aus alten Tagen der Christenheit nach.
Sie bewogen die Christen der alten Kirche und der auf deren Traditionen
beharrenden Kirchen, einen anderen Weg als die "Welt", den des Eremiten, des Mönches, des nur seinem Gotte lebenden Frommen zu gehen.
Die Forderung des Busskampfes, die Fixierung der Bekehrung, der Durchbruch zum Glauben, die Wiedergeburt, die Bestimmung dessen, was er-
laubt ist, das Festlegen dessen, was man trägt und wie man sich hält, das
alles knüpft an die in den Anfängen der Christenheit bereits entwickelten
Topoi und die Vorbilder der Frommen an.

Es ist aber festzustellen, dass das Weinen nunmehr an einzelne Daten
und Geschehnisse gebunden wird. Die Tränen begleiten die Reue, die
Beichte als die Vorbereitung zur eucharistischen Gemeinschaft mit
Christus. Das gilt für die, die schon ganze Christen sind. Für die anderen
gilt, dass die Tränen den Akt der Umkehr, der Wende der Bekehrung
zum Christenleben begleiten. Wie die Gebete, die als "Reu- und Busstränen" bezeichnet sind, mit dem Hinweis auf die Tränen in den Andachts-
und Gebetsformularen ihren Platz haben, so bieten andererseits die
Historien, die Eigenberichte von der Bekehrung, von der Übergabe des
Herzens zahlreiche Beispiele für diese Bindung der Tränen an ein be-
stimmtes Datum. Nicht nur der Bericht, den August Hermann Francke
von seinem Durchbruch zum wahren Glauben gegeben hat, auch die
Berichte zahlreicher anderer stellen dar, wie sich die Tränen mit der
Erschütterung des Sünders über seine Sünde und die Annahme durch
Christus verbinden.

Im Zuge der Entwicklung des Protestantismus im Laufe des 18. Jahrhunderts erschien immer mehr den Beobachtern, die von aussen die
Erscheinungen von Reue, Busse und Tränen wahrnahmen, die Gesamt-
erscheinung des Pietismus als exaltiert. Das Vordringen stoischen Ge-
dankenguts im 18. Jahrhundert, die Betonung der Ratio liessen die
Empfindungen kühler werden, die Urteile schärfer; sie führten unter den
Gebildeten weitgehend zu einer Abkehr von der Prägung, wie sie Halle
und Herrnhut geschaffen hatten. So wurde aus Eruptionen Fluss, aus
leidenschaftlichem Aufbruch wurde Sentimentalität.[74] Nun verschwindet

---

[74] Max Wieser, *Der sentimentale Mensch* (Gotha/Stuttgart, 1924), schildert diese
Übergänge anhand der Entwicklung Gellerts nach seinen Tagebüchern. Zur Psychologie des Sentimentalen äussert Wieser im gleichen Zusammenhang: "Sein Wohl-
gefallen an der Selbstzergliederung der eigenen Seele in ihren Schmerzempfindungen
und Lustgefühlen ist lediglich eine Verflachung des Mystizismus. ... In dieser Psychologie des Weltschmerzes löst sich das mittelalterliche Beichtwesen auf."

geistiges Gut nicht einfach. Es wirkt, wenngleich nicht mehr in der Kraft der ersten Stunde, weiter, vielleicht nur in der Tradierung des sprachlichen Guts. Je stärker seine Kraft war, umso stärker ist auch die nachwirkende Prägung im Sprachgebrauch.

Über die klassischen Andachtsbücher mit ihren zahlreichen Auflagen war schon gesprochen worden. Eine Bewahrung im Sprach- und Denkgut zeigt sich auch in den Gesangbüchern, doch ist wahrzunehmen, dass hier mit fortschreitender Zeit ebenfalls eine Reduzierung dieser Aussagen eintrat. Im alten Quandtschen Gesangbuch finden sich noch zahlreiche Lieder, in denen der Sünder seine Vergehen beweint.[75] Auch im Gesangbuch der Kirche der altpreussischen Union, vom Jahre 1829, dem ersten dieser Kirche nach ihrer Gründung, finden sich noch zahlreiche Einzelbeispiele. Diese Beispiele gehören nach ihrer Herkunft weitgehend dem ausgehenden 17. und dem 18. Jahrhundert an.[76] Weit geringer ist die Zahl der Aussagen über die Tränen in dem gegenwärtig in Gebrauch befindlichen *Evangelischen Kirchen-Gesangbuch* der Evangelischen Kirche in Deutschland.

Doch haben sich nicht nur im Andachts- und Gesangbuchgut Reste jener Busshaltung des Protestantismus aus dem 17. und 18. Jahrhundert erhalten, es hat auch kleine Gruppen im Bereich des deutschen Protestantismus gegeben, bei denen die Bedeutung der Tränen noch im 19. Jahrhundert, ja bis hinein in die Gegenwart betont wurde. So hatten sich in Ostpreussen in den im 19. Jahrhundert entstandenen Gebetsvereinen Züge einer solchen Frömmigkeit der Tränen erhalten.[77] Bedingt durch

---

[75] *Altes Quandtsches Gesangbuch*, Jubiläumsausgabe (Gelsenkirchen, 1953), herausgegeben von den westdeutschen Gebetsvereinen. Zu den Dichtern dieser Lieder gehören u.a. Joh. Hermann Schein, D. Derschau, G. Schirmer, Barth. Ringwaldt, Ludwig Oehlert, Luise Henriette Kurf. von Brandenburg, Benjamin Schmoll und Erdmann Neumeister. Vgl. die Lieder vor allem unter der Rubrik "Katechismuslieder von der Busse und Bekehrung", Nr. 218,4; 219,2.4; 220,3; 221,1; 226,4; 227,4; 230,3; 232,5.6; 233,4; 239,4; 244; und 247,2.
[76]   In dem Bussliede, "An dir allein, an dir hab' ich gesündigt" (Nr. 385,2) heisst es: "Dir ist mein Flehen, mein Seufzen nicht verborgen/ Und meine Tränen sind vor dir." In einem anderen der Lieder (Nr. 395,2.3) heisst es: "Herr, du wollest meiner schonen,/ Sündlich bin ich ja geboren,/ Habe Herr dein Bild verloren;/ Wo ist Rettung nun zu finden/ Aus dem schnöden Joch der Sünden?/ Sieh mich hier zu deinen Füssen/ Zähren bitter Reu vergiessen;/ Heil und Hilfe kommt mir Armen/ Nur aus göttlichem Erbarmen./ Mit Maria Magdalenen/ Dank' ich dir, o Herr, mit Tränen;/ Will wie Petrus heilsam weinen,/ Mich aufs Neu mit dir vereinen ..." In dem Passionsliede, "Seht, welch ein Mensch is das" (Nr. 198,3) heisst es: "Seht, welch ein Mensch is das!/ Ja, opfert Tränenfluten!/ Denn eure Blutschuld macht/ Des Heilands Herz verbluten."
[77]   Vgl. *Statuten des ostpreussisch-evangelischen Gebetsvereins*, hrsg. von Ch. Kukat (Tilsit, 1908), 105, und 124. Das Mitteilungsblatt der gegenwärtig noch bestehenden Gruppen ist der "Friedensbote".

die Auswanderung vieler Mitglieder dieser Vereine, die weitgehend der masurischen und litauischen Volksgruppe angehörten, ist es auch zur Gründung solcher Vereine vor allem im Ruhrgebiet gekommen. Zu den besonderen Äusserungen dieser Gruppen und ihrer ostpreussischen Heimat gehörte das bewegte und vielfach im Weinen sich äussernde Reagieren auf die Verkündigung des Wortes Gottes. Tränen, in abgemilderter Form auch Seufzen, galten als die dem Bussruf angemessene Weise, wie sich die Angesprochenen verhielten.[78] Es wäre nicht zutreffend, dieses Verhalten auf Züge einer besonderen slavischen Religiosität zurückzuführen. Für diese Erscheinungen war vielmehr die Bewahrung des Gutes des älteren Pietismus bestimmend. Noch gegenwärtig werden in dem Mitteilungsblatt dieser Gebetsvereine im Ruhrgebiet Andachten aus der Zeit des Frühpietismus, ja auch Ausschnitte aus Tauler-Predigten als jetzt gültige Andachten gedruckt. Auch das hier bereits erwähnte Quandt'sche Gesangbuch ist durch die Vereinigung dieser Gebetsvereine neu aufgelegt worden.[79]

5

In den vorausgegangenen Darlegungen sind von den Anfängen der Kirche an Theologen zusammen genannt, die sich in vielem recht unterscheiden. Ihre Zusammenfügung hier will durchaus keine Harmonisierung bedeuten. Die Gemeinschaft eines christlichen Erbes, das sie ein jeder auf seine Weise betonten und pflegten, mag dennoch angetan sein, Verbindendes zwischen den oft unterschiedlichen Positionen der Genannten in den Blick zu bekommen. Es gibt nun auch, wie es eine Traditionsfolge der Bejahung der Tränen gegeben hat, aus dem gleichen Kreise eine Reihe kritischer Anmerkungen zum Missbrauch der Tränen. Fragen haben bereits die Kirchenväter an diejenigen gerichtet, denen das Weinen zu einem festen Habitus christlicher Existenz geworden war, ohne dass dem eine hinreichende Spiritualität entsprochen hätte.

Basilios warnt die, die gerne weinen, die Tränen, die Christus selbst vergossen hat, nicht zur Entschuldigung ihrer Labilität oder Leiden-

---

[78] Ähnliche Erscheinungen hat es im 19. Jahrhundert unter den von Herrnhut geprägten Esten und Letten in den damaligen Ostseeprovinzen Russlands gegeben. Dabei äusserte sich die innere Haltung der Busse in einer bestimmten Haltung des Kopfes, sogar beim Gespräche mit anderen. Vgl. zur Tradition einer besonderen Körperhaltung *Regula S. Benedicti* in *CSEL* 75, 50-51, "De humilitate"; hier wird in der 12. Stufe gefordert, das Haupt geneigt zu halten und die Augen niederzuschlagen.
[79] Vgl. oben Anm. 76.

schaftlichkeit zu missbrauchen. Er kennt die Gefahren in weicheren Naturen, dass eigene Empfindsamkeit sich des Schutzes der Frömmigkeit bedient.[80] Auch Johannes Chrysostomos stellt die wahren Tränen den falschen gegenüber. Diese werden zur Demonstration vergossen und um von anderen Lob zu erhalten, nur jene aber beziehen sich auf die echte Reue.[81] Die Gefahr, dass die Tränen als ein gutes Werk verstanden werden können, berechenbar mit der Aussicht auf den Lohn Gottes, sieht auch das Paterikon des Kiever Höhlen-Klosters. Einem solchen Missverständnis wehrte bereits in den Anfängen des russischen Mönchtums die schon erwähnte Erzählung vom Mönche Feofil. Er hatte die Tränen in einem Glase gesammelt, die er über seinen Gebeten geweint hatte. Da trat, so berichtet die Legende, ein Engel vor ihn und sagte ihm: "Du hast gut gebetet, aber weshalb treibst du Eitelkeit mit deinen Tränen?" Er hielt ihm ein anderes Gefäss, dass einen wohlriechenden Duft ausströmte, mit den Worten entgegen, dies seien die Tränen, die Feofil nicht gesammelt habe, die er aber bei seinen Gebeten abgewischt hatte oder die auch einfach auf die Erde gefallen waren; sie habe Gott selbst gesammelt.[82] Gefahren und Missbrauch kennt in der russischen Kirche auch im 19. Jahrhundert der Metropolit Filaret (Drozdov) von Moskau. In seinem Katechismus merkt er in der Erklärung der 2. Seligpreisung an: "Warum ist diese Verheissung (getröstet zu werden) dem Gebot, Leid zu tragen, hinzugefügt?" Seine Antwort lautet: "Damit die Trauer und die Kümmernis über die Sünden nicht zur Verzweiflung ausarte."[83]

Kritische Anmerkungen über Art und Weise des Vergiessens der Tränen hat es auch in der abendländischen Kirche gegeben. Bernhard von Clairvaux äussert sich in der Schrift "Über die verschiedenen Grade

---

[80] Basilios von Caesarea, *Predigt über die Danksagung* in *MPG* 31, Kap. 6, Sp. 217-237; hier Sp. 229-234.

[81] "6. Homilie zu Evgl. Matth.", *MPG* 57, Sp. 69.

[82] *Paterikon des Kiever Höhlen-Klosters*, 160-161. Dass Gott die Tränen zählt und ihm das Urteil über deren Wert zukommt, ist ein Gedanke, der zu den verschiedensten Zeiten ausgesprochen wurde. Im Liedgut des Protestantismus drückt das Paul Gerhardt aus: "Wie dirs und anderen oft ergehet,/ Ist ihm wahrlich nicht verborgen;/ Er sieht und kennet aus der Höhe/ Der betrübten Herzen Sorgen./ Er zählt den Lauf der heissen Tränen/ Und fasst zuhauf all unser Sehnen./ Gib dich zufrieden!" (*Evangelisches Kirchen-Gesangbuch*, Nr. 295,3). Angesichts möglicher Verzweiflung in der Reue ruft Paul Gerhardt zur Fröhlichkeit auf gegen Sorgen, Grämen, Pein. In seinem Weihnachtsliede "Ich steh an deiner Krippe hier" spricht er es aus: "Wann oft mein Herz vor Kummer weint/ Und keinen Trost kann finden,/ Rufst du mir zu: ich bin dein Freund,/ Ein Tilger deiner Sünden./ Was trauerst du, oh Bruder mein?/ Du sollst ja guter Dinge sein,/ Ich sühne deine Schuld" (*Ibid.*, Nr. 28,5). Vgl. auch die folgende Anmerkung.

[83] *Ausführlicher christlicher Katechismus*, 369-370.

der Demut und des Hochmuts", dass es einen — den neunten — Grad des Hochmuts gebe, bei dem der Mensch seine Sünden beweine, aber dabei übertreibe und in den Anklagen gegen sich selbst masslos werde.[84] Es mag mit diesem einen Beispiel aus der Kirche des Westens sein Bewenden haben. Die Bussmahnungen, die Hinweise auf die rechte Art der Busse, die ja zahlreich sind, betreffen ebenso auch das Verhalten derer, die Busstränen vergiessen. Das gilt auch für den Protestantismus schon vom Reformationsjahrhunderte an.

Ein gesetzliches Verständnis des Weges zum Heile, ein Biblizismus, der in der Nacheiferung biblischer Vorbilder seinen Ausdruck fand, waren die Voraussetzungen der Tränen in der Geschichte der Christenheit. Übertreibungen und Masslosigkeit bestimmten später vielfach das Weinen der Frommen. Doch wirkten darauf zunehmend auch die Veränderungen ein, die ungeachtet der Stellung des einzelnen in der Entwicklung der Christenheit eintraten. Zur Haltung des Penthos und den damit verbundenen Tränen gehörte die mönchisch-asketische Existenz als der eigentliche Lebensgrund. Die spätere Betonung des Koenobiums war dazu angetan, wie anderes auch das Weinen zu regulieren, d.h. aber es in seinen Äusserungen zu verändern.[85] Die Umsetzung spiritueller Erfahrungen aus Stille und Abgeschiedenheit ist in ihren Schwierigkeiten frühzeitig von den Vätern selbst erkannt worden. Gleichfalls führte die Umsetzung mönchischer Traditionen in das Leben der grossen Stadtgemeinden zu Schwierigkeiten. Johannes Chrysostomos und Theodoret von Kyrrhos riefen neben anderen dazu auf, die geistlichen Erfahrungen des Mönchtums in das religiöse Leben der Laien in den Städten hineinzutragen, doch wurden die Spannungen bei dieser Übertragung schnell sichtbar.[86]

---

[84] Bernhard von Clairvaux, *Tractatus de gradibus humilitatis et superbiae*, Kap. XVIII, "De nono gradu superbiae qui est confessio simulata", in *MPG* 182, Sp. 966-967.

[85] Die Väter der Kirche, zumal die Mönchsväter, die die Bedeutung der Tränen und gar die Gabe der Tränen betont haben, gehörten nach dem Grundtypus, auch wo sie als Äbte oder als Bischöfe amtierten, den Anachoreten, den Eremiten, den Mönchen strenger Observanz an. Ihre Frömmigkeit war Individualfrömmigkeit, sie war das Ergebnis langer und tiefgehender Erfahrungen in Stille und Einsamkeit. Die Übertragung ihrer Erfahrungen auf einen grösseren Kreis von Schülern, von Ratsuchenden musste notwendig bei diesen zu einem Formalismus führen, auch und gerade, wo man sich bemühte, dem Vorbild des geistlichen Vaters nachzueifern.

[86] Der Lebensweg des Johannes Chrysostomos unterstreicht das bei seinen Kämpfen gegen die Sünden der Zeit. So handelt es sich bei dem Aufruf, in der Welt so zu leben wie in der Einsamkeit, um die Angabe eines fernen Zieles. Es kam dahin, dass der weinende Einsiedler und Mönch in seiner Leid- und Busshaltung die Idealgestalt, das Vorbild für die grosse Masse der anderen Christen wurde; er allein näherte sich den von Christus selig gepriesenen Vollkommenheiten an.

Es wird nützlich sein, die Aussagen über die Tränen der Frommen, über die Gabe der Tränen noch einmal in ihren historischen Zusammenhängen zu skizzieren. Die Aussagen des Alten und Neuen Testaments, das Verhalten der Frommen in der Heiligen Schrift sind die hinreichende Grundlage für alle späteren Erscheinungen; sie wurden zur Anregung, zum Typos für die Frommen der alten und neueren Kirche. Die grossen Asketen lebten in ihrem Kampfe um Errettung und Bewahrung der Seele, in ihrem Ringen um die Christus- und Gottesgemeinschaft in leibhaftiger Schriftauslegung und Aufnahme der grossen Beispiele in der Schrift; sie entwickelten dies auf verschiedene, oft sich übersteigernde Weise. Ihre Tränen waren nicht Ausdruck empfindsamer Stimmung, sie stellten vielmehr die Realisierung, das Sichtbarwerden des Penthos dar. Das hat in der Übersetzung von Matth. 5,4 aus dem Griechischen in das Kirchenslavische einen bezeichnenden Ausdruck gefunden.

Die Spiritualität des Ostens hat auch die des Westens bestimmt. Benedikt von Nursia und Gregor der Grosse legen dafür Zeugnis ab. Umgekehrt gewannen die Aussagen Gregors in seinen Dialogen, die der Papst Zacharias ins Griechische übersetzte, Einfluss auf die Frömmigkeitsgeschichte des Ostens. So wirkte Gregor in die Askese und Theologie des Nil Sorskij hinein, er wird zu einem der Kronzeugen von dessen Penthos-Verständnis. Wie durch die Kirche des Ostens zieht sich auch durch die des Abendlandes eine nicht abreissende Folge der Aussagen über die Tränen der Frommen. Ihren besonderen Niederschlag fanden sie im Mönchtum und in den von diesem besonders bestimmten Kreisen der Laien. Die Übung der Frömmigkeit im Katholizismus des 16. und 17. Jahrhunderts lässt Steigerungen des Verständnisses von der Bedeutung der Tränen sichtbar werden. Einflussreich waren in einer Zeit, die durch den Buchdruck ganz andere Aussagemöglichkeiten erhielt, die Editionen der Kirchenväter des Ostens, der Mystiker und Asketen. Elemente mittelalterlicher Frömmigkeit wirkten ebenso wie diese Editionen in der protestantischen Mystik eines Johann Arndt und seiner Nachfolger auf das Luthertum ein. Sie erfuhren eine besondere Steigerung ihrer Auswirkungen in der Theologie und Frömmigkeit des Pietismus.

Ähnliches gilt für den Bereich der orthodoxen Kirchen. Die Ausgabe der Philokalia durch Nikodem Hagiorites, deren Übersetzung in das Kirchenslavische durch Paisij Veličkovskij, in die russische Sprache durch Feofan Zatvornik waren ein erneuter Anstoss, die in dieser Sammlung enthaltenen zahlreichen Äusserungen der orthodoxen Väter über Busse, Penthos und Tränen — gewiss nicht nur über diese allein — in das 19. und 20. Jahrhundert hineinzunehmen. Die starke Bedeutung der

Tränen, wie sie in der russischen Orthodoxie in dieser Zeit sichtbar wurde, legt davon Zeugnis ab.

Die Aussagen über die Tränen haben in der Geschichte der christlichen Frömmigkeit einen grösseren Raum eingenommen, als dies für die Gegenwart zutrifft. Das gilt nicht nur für den Protestantismus, für den diese Feststellung bereits gemacht worden war, sondern ebenso für den Katholizismus und die Orthodoxie. Die Haltung des in der göttlichen Traurigkeit Lebenden, des um Christi und um seiner eigenen und anderer Sünden willen Weinenden ist immer mit einer Ablehnung und scharfen Kritik der "Welt" verbunden gewesen. Wo sich diese Sicht der Welt aber änderte, vollzogen sich auch Änderungen in der Askese und in der Spiritualität.[87] Der Fluss der Tränen, der einmal mächtig strömte, bestimmte mit seinen Grundwassern auch die, die selbst nicht die Gabe der Tränen erbaten oder besassen. Dieser Fluss ist heute zu einem kaum wahrnehmbaren Rinnsal geworden.

Wo an die Stelle des um Gott und seine Seele ringenden Gotteskämpfers, des *podvižnik*, der nur sich selbst und andere in Frage stellende Skeptiker tritt, entfallen die Voraussetzungen der Tränen in der Busse, die Tränen für die anderen und die Tränen, die aus dem Jubel über die erlebte Gottesbegegnung hervorkommen. Wo sich die Rechtfertigung des Sünders in die Rechtfertigung Gottes verwandelt, dass dieser Rede und Antwort zu stehen habe, tritt ein weitergreifender Wandel ein, entfallen die göttliche Traurigkeit und die tränenreiche Reue, die Frucht bringt. Wo an die Stelle des Menschen, der in seinem Sündersein als tot verstanden wird, der Tod Gottes tritt, ist für die Weise, wie die Väter fragten, bekannten und weinten, kein Raum mehr. Der Weg dieser Entwicklung kann hier auch nicht andeutungsweise skizziert werden.

Der heute vielfach ausgesprochenen Forderung nach einer oekumenischen Theologie, die die Grenzen der Konfessionen zu überwinden habe, muss sich notwendig eine andere Forderung hinzugesellen. Diese muss die Aufgabe umschliessen, neben der Untersuchung der dogmatischen Lehrsätze der Kirchen eine oekumenische Bestandsaufnahme der christlichen Frömmigkeit und ihrer Äusserungen in Geschichte und Gegenwart durchzuführen. Als ein Beitrag dazu seien die vorliegenden

---

[87] Ein anderes Verständnis des 1. Artikels des Glaubensbekenntnisses, der Aufgaben des Frommen in dieser Welt veränderte und bestimmte die am Sündersein, an Christus und an seiner Nachfolge, an der Teilhabe an der jenseitigen Welt orientierte Haltung der Christen. Bei einer verstärkten Betonung der Würde und Freiheit des Menschen in seinen natürlichen Gaben trat folgerichtig der Gedanken- und Vorstellungskreis von Reue, Busse, göttlicher Traurigkeit und der Tränen um Gottes Willen zurück.

Darlegungen zu verstehen. Es hat in der Geschichte der Tränen der Frommen an Übersteigerungen, an Verzerrungen nicht gefehlt. Doch war die Existenz dieser Tränen nicht nur eine jener Absonderlichkeiten, an denen die Geschichte der Christenheit reich ist. In dem, was Christen im Mönchtum, was Heilige und Ekstatiker, was Fromme in den verschiedenen Konfessionen bei diesen Tränen bewegt hat, war immer Grundlegendes wirksam. In der Veränderung christlicher Formen und Verhaltensweisen gilt es auch künftig, nach dem Grundlegenden und Unaufgebbaren zu fragen.

SOPHIA — VISIONEN DES WESTENS

ERNST BENZ

Im Jahre 1932 hat Georges Florovsky in Sofia (!) eine Abhandlung über die Verehrung der Sophia-Weisheit Gottes in Byzanz und in Russland veröffentlicht.[1] Dieser Aufsatz hat wesentlich dazu beigetragen, die etwas wirren Diskussionen über die Himmlische Sophia, die durch die von Vladimir Solov'ev berichteten Visionen der himmlischen Sophia und seiner aus ihr abgeleiteten Sophien-Lehre hervorgerufen waren, mit konkreten Anschauungen über die ikonographische Tradition der Darstellung der Hl. Sophia und über ihre liturgische Verwendung in der orthodoxen Kirche zu erfüllen. Die nach den Ereignissen der bolschewistischen Revolution in Westeuropa einsetzende romantische Schwärmerei für die orthodoxe Kirche, die häufig dazu führte, dass die geistvollen Spekulationen von Religionsphilosophen der russischen Emigration als orthodoxe Kirchenlehren ausgegeben wurden, hat gerade die Lehre von der himmlischen Sophia im Bewusstsein der europäischen Gebildeten, die sich mit den modernen Entwicklungen der christlichen Religionsphilosophie befassten, als etwas besonders "Russisches" erscheinen lassen. Darüber ist die schlichte Tatsache etwas in Vergessenheit geraten, dass die Gestalt der himmlischen Sophia eine Gestalt ist, die von Anfang der Kirchengeschichte an in der Gesamtüberlieferung der christlichen Theologie eine bedeutsame Rolle gespielt hat und die auch

---

[1] George Florovskij, "Von der Verehrung der Sophia-Weisheit in Byzanz und Russland", in: *Arbeiten des V. Kongresses der russischen akademischen Organisation im Ausland*, Teil I (Sofia, 1932), 495 ff. (russisch); weitere Literatur zur ostkirchlichen Sophienlehre: A. Nikolsky, "Sophia — die Weisheit Gottes", in: *Zeitschrift der Archäologie und Geschichte*, Bd. XVII (St. Petersburg, 1906) (russisch); A. Ammann, "Darstellung und Deutung der Sophia im vorpetrinischen Russland", in: *Orientalia Christiana Periodica* IV, N. I-II (Rom, 1938); zuletzt zusammenfassend: L. Zander, "Die Weisheit Gottes im russischen Glauben und Denken", in: *Kerygma und Dogma*, 2. Jg. Heft 1, 1-53.

der religiösen Erfahrung und dem religiösen Bewusstsein des christlichen Abendlandes ständig gegenwärtig war. Allerdings hat sich die Sophiologie des Westens anders entwickelt, als dies auf dem Boden der östlich-orthodoxen Kirche der Fall war — wobei die russisch-orthodoxe Kirche in keiner Weise isoliert betrachtet werden darf, sondern im Rahmen des Gesamtzusammenhanges der verschiedenen orthodoxen Kirchen gesehen werden muss, die ja das Erbe der alten byzantinischen Kirche weiter-geführt haben.

Die himmlische Sophia erscheint bereits in der spätjüdischen Über-lieferung als eine weibliche himmlische Gestalt neben Gott und hat im kanonischen Schrifttum und in den Apokryphen des Alten Testaments ihren Ausdruck in den Sprüchen Salomos, in Jesus Sirach, im Baruchbuch und in der Weisheit Salomos gefunden. Traditionellerweise wird diese Gestalt religionsgeschichtlich in die Kategorie der "Hypostasen" einge-ordnet, die wie die Engel Zwischenwesen zwischen Gott und der Welt sind und die sein Wirken auf die Welt vermitteln. Wilhelm Bousset[2] had diese Hypostasen als "Zwitterbildungen eines kindlichen zur vollen Abstrak-tion noch unfähigen Denkens" bezeichnet und betrachtet sie als "Mittel, polytheistische Neigungen der Volksreligion zu überwinden, den Glauben an göttliche Wesen umzugestalten, dadurch, dass man sie zwar beibe-hielt, aber Gott entschieden unterordnete oder in seinem Wesen als seine Eigenschaften untergehen liess". Als die in der Religionsgeschichte des Judentums am meisten ausgebildete Vorstellung dieser Art führt Bousset die Weisheit Gottes an, die er als eine Hypostase der weltdurchwaltenden, schöpferischen, Gesetz gebenden Vernunft Gottes versteht. Die Gestalt der himmlischen Weisheit wäre demnach das klassische Beispiel einer solchen "Zwitterform des kindlichen Denkens", das der vollen Abstrak-tion noch nicht fähig ist und dessen theologische Reflexion noch im Mytho-logischen stecken geblieben ist.

Diese Deutung wird indes dem Phänomen in keiner Weise gerecht. Am Anfang der Sophiologie steht nicht eine Reflexion, sondern eine visionäre Begegnung mit der Gestalt der himmlischen Weisheit, die von den durch ihre Epiphanie Betroffenen als eine himmlische Frauengestalt mit allen numinosen Schauern geschaut wird. Diese Gestalt ist nicht Produkt der Reflexion, vielmehr ist umgekehrt die Weisheitslehre der Versuch der reflektierenden Auslegung einer visionären Erfahrung. Dieser visionäre Ursprung der Sophiologie erklärt auch den eigentümlichen Vorrang des bildhaften vor dem begrifflichen Denken innerhalb der Sophiologie. Die

---

[2] Wilhelm Bousset, *Die Religion des Judentums im späthellenitischen Zeitalter* (Tübingen, 1926), 343.

"Zwitterbildung" ist nicht das Produkt der Unfähigkeit des Denkens zur vollen Abstraktion, sondern die typische und in der ganzen Geschichte der Vision sich wiederholende Folge der Unmöglichkeit einer adäquaten sprachlichen Deutung der visionären Erfahrung: diese sieht sich häufig genötigt, sich eher der Bilder, als der Begriffe zu bedienen, um das Unsagbare auszudrücken, da die Bilder mehrdimensional sind, mehr Ober- und Untertöne haben, und assoziationsreicher sind als die Begriffe. Die Begegnung mit der Gestalt der himmlischen Sophia muss so überwältigend gewesen sein, dass sie sich sogar gegen den traditionellen Patriarchalismus der jüdischen Gesetzesreligion und ihren strengen Monotheismus durchsetzte. Die himmlische Weisheit ist die einzige weibliche Gestalt, die in der spätjüdischen Frömmigkeit und Theologie Anerkennung fand.

Das erstaunliche an der Weisheitsliteratur des Spätjudentums ist die Tatsache, dass die himmlische Sophia darin gerade nicht, wie Bousset behauptet, als Mittelwesen zwischen Gott und der Welt steht, sondern als eine Gestalt neben Gott, die ähnlich wie der göttliche Logos auf die Seite Gottes und nicht auf die Seite der Kreatur gehört und nicht Geschöpf, sondern Gehilfin Gottes bei der Schöpfung ist.

Die Entwicklung der Sophiologie in der christlichen Kirche kann hier nicht einmal andeutungsweise dargestellt werden; entscheidend ist, dass die Sophiologie älter ist als die Mariologie und dass erst im Zuge der nachmaligen Verbreitung der Verehrung der Gottesmutter in der byzantinischen Kirche eine Verbindung zwischen der Gestalt der himmlischen Sophia und der Gottesmutter hergestellt wurde - wobei die bereits entwickelte Lehre von der Himmlischen Sophia als himmlischer Gestalt zu der Entwicklung der Mariologie und der Verbreitung der kultischen Verehrung der Gottesmutter und der kirchlichen Liturgie beigetragen hat. Allerdings hat sich dann die Entwicklung im Bereich der östlich-orthodoxen und der römisch-katholischen Kirche des Westens verschieden vollgezogen. Im Westen hat die Mariologie von Anfang an so stark dominiert, dass sie neben sich eine eigene Sophiologie nicht hat aufkommen lassen. In der östlich-orthodoxen Kirche hat sich die Sophienlehre noch länger als eine selbständige Lehre gehalten und ist nicht von der Mariologie aufgesogen worden.

Bezeichnenderweise ist aber auch im Westen die Sophiologie in einem Bereich erhalten geblieben, in dem immer starke Einwirkungen ostkirchlicher Theologie und Frömmigkeit lebendig waren — in der deutschen Mystik, die ohne den ständigen Zustrom der mystischen Literatur, z.B. des Dionysios Areopagita, und der östlichen Mönchsväter wie Makarios nicht verständlich ist.

Bezeichnenderweise erhält die Sophienlehre auch im Westen ihre
Nahrung und Inspiration nicht durch die theologische Reflexion, sondern
durch Visionen, durch Erfahrungen der Epiphanie der himmlischen
Gestalt selbst. Da diese Visionen der himmlischen Sophia in der modernen religionsphilosophischen Diskussion geradezu als ein Monopol der
orthodoxen Theologie oder gar ein Monopol Solov'evs dargestellt werden,
sei hier die Traditionskette der östlichen Sophien-Visionen — sozusagen
zur Rettung ihrer Ökumenizität — durch eine Darstellung von Epipha-
nien der Sophia im Westen ergänzt.

1

Das eindruckvollste visionäre Bild der himmlischen Weisheit im Bereich
der mittelalterlichen deutschen Mystik findet sich bei Heinrich Seuse
(± 1366). Zur Eigentümlichkeit seiner Mystik gehört es, dass nicht die
Person Christi in dem schulmässigen Verständnis der dogmatischen
Christologie seiner Zeit, sondern die Gestalt der himmlischen Weisheit
den Gegenstand seiner Andacht, seines Heilsstrebens, seines Erkenntnis-
triebes, seiner religiösen Anschauung und seiner Liebe bildet. Diese Gestalt ist bei ihm ebensowenig mit der Gestalt Christi wie mit der Gestalt der
Gottesmutter identisch, sie hat noch einen durchaus selbstständigen
Charakter. Sie hat deutlich androgyne Züge, erscheint bald als himmlischer Jüngling, bald als himmlische Jungfrau. Vor allem aber umfasst
sie in sich die gesamte himmlische und irdische Welt. Das Universum in
seiner ursprünglichen Form, wie es aus der Hand Gottes hervorging, ist
in ihr mitenthalten. Gott und die Welt sind in ihr noch miteinander
verbunden; sie umfasst mit Gott gleichzeitig die Welt in Gott, wie sie
durch Christus ihre Erneuerung und Vollkommenheit findet.

Seuse hat eine tief ergreifende Beschreibung der himmlischen Weisheit
gegeben. Er berichtet, wie er über das 24. Kapitel des Jesus Sirach medi-
tierte, das eine Beschreibung der Gestalt der himmlischen Weisheit enthält, und wie ihm über der Meditation dieser Stelle die Gestalt der Weisheit selbst erschien:

Sie schwebte hoch über ihm in einem Thron aus Wolken, sie leuchtete wie der
Morgenstern und schien wie die blinkende Sonne; ihre Krone war Ewigkeit,
ihr Gewand war Seligkeit, ihre Worte waren Süssigkeit und ihre Umarmung
war aller Lust Befriedigung. Sie war fern und nah, hoch und niedrig, sie war
gegenwärtig und doch verborgen. Sie liess mit sich umgehen und doch konnte
niemand sie greifen. Sie reichte über den obersten Rand des höchsten Himmels

und berührte den tiefsten Grund des Abgrunds. Sie zerteilte sich von einem
Ende bis zum anderen gewaltig und richtete alle Dinge fröhlich aus. Wenn er
jetzt meinte, eine schöne Jungfrau zu haben, plötzlich fand er einen stolzen
Jüngling. Bisweilen gebärdete sie sich als eine weise Meisterin, bisweilen hielt
sie sich wie eine stattliche Geliebte. Sie beugte sich liebreich zu ihm und
grüsste ihn gar freundlich und sprach gütig zu ihm: "Praebe, fili, cor tuum
mihi (Spr. 23,26) — Gib mir dein Herz mein Sohn!" Er fiel ihr zu Füssen und
dankte ihr herzlich aus demütigem Grunde. — Soviel ward ihm zuteil und
diesmal sollte ihm nicht mehr werden.[3]

2

Nach Seuse hat wohl Jakob Boehme die umfassendste Lehre von der
himmlischen Sophia entwickelt, die die Grundlage sowohl seiner Kos-
mologie, Anthropologie wie seiner Auffassung von der Heilsgeschichte
bildet. Die himmlische Weisheit ist bei ihm die Gestalt, in der sich der
überschwengliche, transzendente Wille Gottes in eine leibhafte Form
fasst und zur Offenbarung, Darstellung und Verwirklichung seiner selbst
kommt.[4] Jakob Boehme hat nicht nur eine Lehre von der himmlischen
Sophia dargelegt, sondern er hat sie auch gesehen. Er hat zwar keinen
eigentlichen Visionsbericht über eine Erscheinung der himmlischen Sophia
überliefert, aber an einigen der zahlreichen Stellen, an denen er über sie
spricht, lässt er deutlich erkennen, dass hier ein persönliches visionäres
Erlebnis zugrunde liegt. Dies ist vor allem in seiner Schrift "Von wahrer
Busse" der Fall, wo sich ein Gespräch der Seele mit der Jungfrau Sophia
findet. Auch hier ist die Brautmystik die Grundlage des Verhältnisses
zwischen Gott und Mensch, aber gegenüber der traditionellen Christus-
mystik mit veränderten Vorzeichen: die Seele ist der Bräutigam, die
himmlische Sophia die Braut.

Der Titel deutet bereits das Moment der persönlichen Erfahrung an:
*Die Pforte des Paradiesischen Rosengartens/ niemand als Christi Kinder
verstanden/ welche diese erkannt haben.* Boehme schreibt dort:

Wan sich der Eckstein Christus mit dem verblichenen Bilde des Menschen in
seiner herzlichen Beehrung und Busse beweget/ so erscheinet Jungfrau Sophia
in der Bewegung des Geistes Christi/ in dem verblichenen Bilde von der Seele
in ihrem Jungfräulichen Schmucke: vor welcher sich die Seele in ihrer Unreinig-
keit entsetzt, dass alle ihre Sünden erst in ihr aufwachen/ und vor ihr erschrecken

---

[3] H. Seuse, *Deutsche Schriften*, hrsg. v Karl Bihlmeyer (Stuttgart, 1907), K. III, 11 ff.
[4] Siehe darüber ausführlicher bei Ernst Benz, *Der vollkommene Mensch nach Jakob
Boehme* (Stuttgart, 1932), 21 ff.; und *Adam, der Mythos vom Urmenschen* (Otto Wilh.
Barth-Verlag, München Planegg, 1955).

und zittern. Denn alda gehet das Gericht über die Sünde der Seelen an/ dass sie auch wohl in ihrer Unwürdigkeit zurücke weichet/ und sich vor ihrem schönen Buhlen schämet/ in sich gehet/ und sich vernichtiget/ als ganz unwürdig ein solches Kleinod geschmecket haben/ und sonst niemanden wissende. Aber die edle Sophia nahet sich in der Selen-Essenz, und küsset sie freundlich/ und tingiret mit ihren Liebe-Strahlen das finster Feuer der Seelen/ und durchscheinet die Sele mit ihrem Liebes-Kusse: So springet die Sele in ihrem Leibe vor grossen Freuden/ in Kraft der Jungfräulichen Liebe auf/ triumphieret/ und lobet den grossen Gott kraft der edlen Sophia.[5]

Kann man deutlicher sein mit Anspielungen auf ein persönlicheres Erlebnis, als wenn man sagt: die bräutliche Verbindung der Sophia mit der Seele werde nur "von den Unsern verstanden/ so dieses Kleinod geschmecket haben und sonst Niemanden wissende"? So spricht nur jemand, der selbst "geschmecket" hat, der selbst ein "Wissender" geworden ist. Auch der Hinweis auf das "Springen" der Seele "vor grosser Freude" erinnert ja unmittelbar an ähnliche Aussagen Eckarts und Seuses über das Gefühl des "Springens" der Seele in ihrem Leib bei der Begegnung mit der himmlischen Weisheit.

3

Die meisten Elemente der Sophienlehre Jakob Boehmes kehren in den sophiologischen Hymnen Gottfried Arnolds, zum Teil in der von Boehme selbst geschaffenen Terminologie wieder. Die typische sprachliche Formulierung lässt aber deutlich erkennen, dass es sich bei Arnold nicht einfach um eine sprachliche Anleihe bei Jakob Boehme handelt, sondern dass bei ihm selbst eine erlebnishafte Teilhabe an dieser ganzen Form der bildhaften spekulativen Anschauung vorliegt, die sich nicht nur in der Sphäre der Reflexion abspielt, sondern die in einer reichen Variation von Affekten, Empfindungen und Stimmungen abläuft, die von der tiefsten Verzweiflung bis hin zur höchsten Verzückung den typischen Charakter der Erfahrung im Affektbereich der Liebesmystik tragen.

Dies gilt nun vor allem für das Werk, das bereits im Titel den besonderen Typus seiner Mystik zum Ausdruck bringt: "Das Geheimnis der göttlichen Sophia". Seine Mystik ist Sophienmystik, Sophiologie. Ohne Zweifel greift er in dieser Sophiologie die älteren Traditionen der Sophienlehre der deutschen Mystik auf, die ja vor allem auf Jakob Boehme und

---

[5] Jakob Boehme, "Von wahrer Busse", in: *Die Pforte des Paradiesischen Rosengartens/ niemand als Christi Kinder verstanden/ welche diese erkannt haben*, 1. Buch, c. 45, Gichtelsche Ausgabe, Bd. I, col. 1648f.

seine Schule zurückgehen und die ihre noch tieferen Wurzeln in der Mystik Seuses, einer ausgesprochenen Weisheitsmystik haben. Gottfried Arnold war mit dem Jakob-Boehme-Kreis persönlich verbunden durch seine Zugehörigkeit zum deutschen Zweig der englischen Philadelphen, das heisst, jener englischen Boehmeschüler, die ihr geistliches Oberhaupt in der Mystikerin und Visionärin Jane Leade und in den beiden anderen bedeutenden Mystikern Thomas Bromley und John Pordage hatten. Ebenso war er mit der Gruppe von Boehmeschülern verbunden, die sich um Johann Georg Gichtel scharten, der die berühmte Gesamtausgabe der Werke Jakob Boehmes veranstaltet hatte und seinerseits als Oberhaupt einer mystischen Sekte, der sogenannten "Engelsbrüder", eine Sophienmystik verkündete.[6]

So sehr die spekulative Ausdeutung der Gestalt der Sophia bei Gottfried Arnold im einzelnen durch eine jahrhundertelange Tradition bestimmt ist, die ihm als dem Historiker der mystischen Theologie sehr wohl bekannt ist, so sehr ist sie doch bei ihm in einer persönlichen mystischen Erfahrung begründet. Dies geht bereits aus den zahlreichen Andeutungen seiner Einführung hervor. Dort legt Arnold dar, dass der Mensch eine innere Beziehung zur himmlischen Sophia zunächst durch ein stilles Aufhören und leises Hinhören erhält. Ist der Geist des Menschen dann ins Inwendige eingekehrt, dann spürt er in seinem Herzen das Lockende und Ziehende der Sophia, die schliesslich in ihm eine nicht zu löschende Feuerbrunst entzündet. "Vor allen dingen wisse und glaube, o mensch, dass diese edle Sophia nicht fern von dir/ sonder fast näher als du dir selbst/ seyn wolle und könne/ wo du sie nicht vertreibest". Die Sophia meldet sich im Herzen durch ein geheimnisvolles Sich-regen, Sich-erinnern und Rufen der Seele, das kein Mensch leugnen oder austilgen kann.

Denn es ist nichts anders/ als ein sanffter und lieblicher Hauch und einspruch in die seele/ die ihr unversehens und ungesucht geschiehet/ wenn sie etwa inwendig stille ist. Ja es ist eine so subtile und gelinde Einrede/ dass sich auch mit dem geringsten Ausbruch der groben natur in worten oder werken/ ja auch durch Gedanken/ die sonst an sich nicht böss seyn möchten, kann gedämpffet werden.[7]

Die Berechtigung oder Nichtberechtigung des inneren Rufens der Sophia hat entscheidende Folgen für das ganze menschliche Leben. Von Jugend

---

[6] Johann Georg Gichtel, *Realencyklopädie*, 3. Ausg. VI, 657ff., *Allgemeine Deutsche Biographie* IX, 147ff.; v. Harless, *Jakob Boehme und die Alchimisten* (1882); C. B. Hylkema, *Reformateurs* II (1902), 409ff.; Erich Seeberg, *Gottfried Arnold* (1923), 364ff. Die "Engelsbrüder" haben ihren Namen von Matth. 22,30: "In der Auferstehung werden sie weder freien noch sich freien lassen, sondern sie sind gleich wie die Engel Gottes im Himmel." Der Name hebt bereits die Ehelosigkeit hervor.
[7] Vorrede 51 §2 und 53 §11.

an geschieht ihre verborgene Einsprache, und ihr Besuch hält so lange an, als der Mensch ihr nicht widersteht. Öffnet sich der Mensch, so erscheint die himmlische Weisheit der Seele zunächst in dem Bilde einer ehrwürdigen und liebreichen Mutter (S. 99, nach Jesus Sirach 15, 2); und zwar so lange, bis die menschliche Natur gebändigt und neu geformt ist. Wenn sich die Seele dann als treu und gehorsam erwiesen und die Liebe der Sophia durch einen harten Kampf gegen die Sünde erkämpft hat, so verwandelt diese ihre ernsthafte Gestalt in die Gestalt einer anmutigen Jungfrau und wird zur Braut.

Hiermit deutet Arnold dem aufmerksamen Leser die erlebnishafte Grundlage seiner eigenen Sophienmystik an. So zurückhaltend Arnold über seine eigenen geistlichen Erfahrungen spricht, so hat er doch an einer Stelle deutlich erkennen lassen, dass ihm eine persönliche visionäre Begegnung mit der himmlischen Jungfrau zuteil wurde, die von allergrösster Bedeutung für das Gesamtverständnis seiner Mystik und Sophiologie ist und die allen seinen theologischen und spekulativen Aussagen eine besonders persönliche Färbung verleiht. Es handelt sich um die visionäre Erfahrung einer nächtlichen Stunde — um eine Vision der himmlischen Sophia, den "Bericht einer Nachtbegebenheit".[8]

Parallel zu diesem "Bericht einer Nachtbegebenheit" ist ein anderes Gedicht, dessen Vorbericht in etwas kürzerer Form dieselbe Szene vom Kuss der Sophia schildert, die er in der "Nachtbegebenheit" beschrieb.[9]

Daran anschliessend wird in Gestalt eines Dialogs zwischen der göttlichen Weisheit und ihrem Liebhaber der ganze Heilsweg des Menschen im Lichte der Sophiologie geschildert, wobei die himmlische Sophia von ihrem Liebhaber, den sie mit Worten wie "liebster Buhl' und Schatz", "Verlobter meiner Liebe", "mein edler Bräutigam" anredet, auch seine ganze und ungeteilte Liebe und Hingabe verlangt.

Dementsprechend antwortet ihr Geliebter mit einem Treugelöbnis, in dem er ihr mit der Anrede "schönster Ehegemahl, holdseligster Gespiele" die Treue und ungeteilte Hingabe gelobt:

> Ich will dein eigen sein und alles opfern dir
> mir nichts mehr wollen selbst, noch suchen, noch begehren

---

[8] "Bericht von einer nacht-begebenheit", in: Gottfried Arnold, *Neue Göttliche Liebes-Funcken und Ausbrechende Liebes-Flammen/ in fortgesetzten Beschreibungen der grossen Liebe GOttes in CHristo JESU/ dargestellet in: Das Geheimnis der göttlichen Sophia CXII*, 293 ff.

[9] *Vertrauliche Unterredung der göttlichen weissheit mit einem zu ihr gezogenen menschen: nach der beschreibung eines liebhabers dieser H. Jungfrau. Poetische Lob- und Liebes-Sprüche von der Ewigen Weissheit/ nach Anleitung Des Hohenlieds Salomonis: Nebenst dessen neuen Übersetzung und Beystimmung der Alten*, ausgefertigt von Gottfried Arnold, in: Das "Geheimnis der göttlichen Sophia", LXVIII, 1000.

als was du durch mich willst;
dein bin ich im Leben
dir bleib ich ergeben
und weiche nun nimmer,
mein anderes Ich.[10]

Das Gedicht über die "Nachtbegebenheit" trägt alle Zeichen einer spontanen visionären Erfahrung. Die Vision entspringt, wie häufig in der visionären Erfahrung, einem Gebet, das "in tiefer Nacht" dem Herzen Arnolds entsteigt: "Das Jesus doch in mir gewurzelt ewig bleibe!" Die Vision erfolgt als Erfüllung eines Gebetes "im Augenblick". Vor seinen geistlichen Augen erscheint die göttliche Weisheit. Die Erscheinung der himmlischen Sophia ist ganz individuell und bestätigt so den Charakter der spontanen visionären Erfahrung. Dass sie "nicht in hohem Glanze, den sie sonst oft bei Menschen zu brauchen pflegt", erscheint, deutet darauf hin, dass Arnold von anderen Erscheinungen der himmlischen Sophia weiss, die ihm teils aus den biblischen Urkunden, teils aus Berichten anderer Liebhaber der himmlischen Weisheit bekannt sind; dabei ist wohl an Jakob Boehme und Gichtel zu denken. Vielleicht hat er auch die Vision der Weisheit vor Augen, die Seuse beschreibt. Dort heisst es: "Sie leuchtete wie der Morgenstern und schien wie die blinkende Sonne" (s. oben S. 122). Die Erscheinung der Weisheit, die ihm zuteil wird, ist nicht von so hohem Glanze umgeben, wie er sich vorgestellt hat, sie ist aber eine Frauengestalt, "die grösser als ein Mensch ist", "von Schönheit funkelnd ganz", "gleichzeitig liebreizend und ehrwürdig". In ihm mischen sich inbrünstige Liebe und jubelnde Freude mit dem Gefühl der Ehrerbietung und dem Bewusstsein der Unwürdigkeit. In seiner feinen Psychologie bemerkt Arnold, dass die Spontaneität seiner inbrünstigen Liebe durch die Ehrerbietung gehindert wurde. Er wagt nicht, diese himmlische Gestalt, die den Gegenstand seiner Sehnsucht bildet, zu umfassen und zu küssen. Die Ehrerbietung zwingt ihn zu tiefer Demut, zum Bekenntnis seiner Unwürdigkeit und zur Bitte um Gnade. Die Geliebte steht vor ihm als die Fürstin, vor der er im Staub liegt und angesichts seiner Unwürdigkeit zweifelt, ob er in ihrer Gegenwart überhaupt zu reden würdig sei. Die Geste der Zuneigung geht nicht von ihm, sondern von der Jungfrau Sophia aus, sie neigt sich zu ihm, umfasst ihn, legt ihren linken Arm an seine Rechte, zieht ihn an sich und küsst ihn. Jetzt erst wagt er, seine Augen zu ihr zu erheben; er sieht ihr liebliches Antlitz unmittelbar vor sich und empfindet diesen Akt der Vereinigung als eine unfassbare Erhöhung. "Wie wenn ein König sein Gemahl zum Bettler

---

[10] *Loc. cit.*, LXXXIII und III, 106.

schicket, so war mir, als mein Gott die Weisheit zu mir sandt".

Die Weisheit selbst wird von ihm bei der ersten Erwähnung ihrers Namens als "Gottesbraut" bezeichnet. In ihrer Zuwendung zu ihm und in dem Kuss erweist sie sich als seine Braut. Damit ist auf das Verhältnis des Gläubigen zur himmlischen Sophia die ganze Liebesmystik des Hohen Liedes übertragen, das auch die Bilder für die Beschreibung seiner Begegnung mit der himmlischen Sophia liefert und das ja mit dem Vers beginnt: "Er küsse mich mit dem Kuss seines Mundes" (Hohelied 1,2).

Auch der christologische Aspekt tritt hier deutlich hervor. Das Motto zu Beginn dieses Gedichtes: "Woher kommt mir das, dass die Mutter meines HErrn zu mir komme?" stammt aus dem Grusswort der Elisabeth an die sie besuchende Maria (Luk 1,43). Dieses Wort von der "Mutter meines Herrn" ist hier vor Gottfried Arnold nicht auf die Maria, sondern auf die himmlische Sophia bezogen. Die traditionelle mariologische Deutung dieses Wortes ist hier also ins Sophiologische zurückübersetzt. Dahinter steht die Sophiologie Jakob Boehmes, die das Zustandekommen der Menschwerdung so deutet, dass sich die Menschwerdung des Sohnes Gottes durch die der Jungfrau Maria innewohnende himmlische Sophia vollzieht. Nach Jakob Boehme hat sich in der Jungfrau Maria die Verbindung der menschlichen Natur mit der himmlischen Sophia wiederum vollgezogen, die nach dem Fall Adams abgerissen war. In Maria findet die Erneuerung der ersten Ehe zwischen Mensch und Sophia statt: Sophia, die von Adam floh, als sich dieser von Gott abwandte, geht in Maria wieder in die menschliche Natur ein und eröffnet damit dem Sohn den Weg zu seiner Fasslichkeit im Fleische.[11]

Diese persönliche nächtliche Begegnung mit der himmlischen Sophia hat die ganze Dichtung Arnolds geprägt, die die himmlische Sophia zum Gegenstand hat und die er in seinem Werk "Das Geheimnis der göttlichen Sophia oder Weissheit" und in dem angehängten Werk "Neue göttliche Liebes-Funken und Ausbrechende Liebes-Flammen in CHristo JESU dargestellt" zusammengefasst hat.

In diesen Gedichten entfalten sich auch zahlreiche andere Aspekte der Sophiologie, wie sie Jakob Boehme entwickelt hatte, vor allem der kosmologische Aspekt, der in dem eschatologischen Aspekt wiederkehrt. Die Weisheit, in der Gott das Urbild der Welt und des Weltzieles erschaut, ist auch die Gestalt, in der sich die von Gott ins Dasein gerufene Schöpfung im vollendeten Gottesreich erfüllt.

---

[11] Ernst Benz, *Der vollkommene Mensch nach Jakob Boehme* (Kohlhammer, Stuttgart, 1937), c. IX, "Sophia und Menschwerdung Christi (Sophia und Maria)", 101-110.

Auch bei Gottfried Arnold is durchweg der androgyne Aspekt der Sophiologie aufrechterhalten: Die Sophia ist das ursprüngliche Gottesbild im Menschen, die ursprüngliche himmlische Braut Adams, die in ihm wohnt und sich mit ihm zu der ursprünglichen mann-weiblichen Ganzheit der "imago dei" verbindet, die ihn aber in dem Augenblick verlässt und zu Gott zurückkehrt, in dem Adam seine Augen von dem Urbild, nämlich Gott, abwendet und auf die Kreatur in ihrem Für-Sich-Sein ohne Gott richtet und aus dem ewigen Tag der göttlichen Schöpfung zum ersten Mal in einen Schlaf versinkt. Die Erschaffung der Eva aus seiner Seite erscheint auch bei Gottfried Arnold nur als ein irdischer Ersatz für die himmlische Sophia, und auch Gottfried Arnold lässt keine Zweifel darüber aufkommen, dass die ursprüngliche androgyne Integrität des Menschen nur erreicht werden kann, wenn er sich von seiner irdischen Eva wiederum zur himmlischen Sophia wendet.[12]

4.

GOTT reisst mir die scheinbarste liebe hinweg/
  Die seine kan hindern/
  Und mercklich vermindern/
So ich zu der weissheit im innersten heg.
  Da muss ich so rein
  und eyfferig seyn/
Dass ich mir sonst keine verlobte zuleg.

5.

Die eyffersucht meiner vertrauten ist gross/
  Sie machet zu schande
  auch ehliche bande/
Und leidet kein sterblich gemahl in dem schos:
  Nur jungfrau muss seyn/
  Was geht in sie ein/
Von fremder und eigener liebe gantz blos.

6.

Doch kan mir der wechsel nicht hinderlich seyn/
  Wenn jene ich fasse/

---

[12] Gottfried Arnold, *Poetische Lob- und Liebes-Sprüche/ von der Ewigen Weissheit/ nach Anleitung des Hohenlieds Salomonis: Nebenst dessen neuen Übersetzung und Beystimmung der Alten*, in: "Das Geheimnis der göttlichen Sophia", LXVIII, 1000.

Und alles verlasse/
Damit ich sie hab und geniesse allein.
Mir bringet die ehr/
Viel tausendmal mehr/
Als alle wollüste mit trieglichem schein.

Es wäre interessant, die Auswirkung der Sophiologie des radikalen, separatistischen Pietismus auf den kirchlichen Pietismus zu verfolgen, in dem die Sophiologie gleichfalls gelegentlich eine Rolle spielt. So war der Begründer der lutherischen Mission in Trankebar, Bartholomaeus Ziegenbalg, bereits während seines Theologie-Studiums an der Theologischen Fakultät der Universität Halle durch den Umgang mit seinen pietistischen Lehrern und Kommilitonen mit der Lehre von der Himmlischen Sophia vertraut. Er trat seine Ausreise von Kopenhagen an die Koromandel-Küste von Ostindien auf einem dänischen Schiff namens Princessa Sophia Hedwiga an, das am 30. Nov. 1705 zur grossen Fahrt auslief. In seinen täglichen "exercitia pietatis" richtete er seine Meditation auf den Schiffnamen "Sophia" und sann über die göttliche Weisheit nach. In der Vorrede zu seiner Schrift über die Himmlische Weisheit, die 1710 in Leipzig erschien und die die Frucht seiner Meditationen war, sagt er, dass ihm diese Betrachtungen "eine grosse Gemüthsruhe gewährt hatten, so dass weder das Sausen des Windes noch das Brausen der aufgeregten Wellen, noch das Lärmen und Schreien der Schiffsleute mich in meinen Gedanken stören konnte, sondern dass ich mich mit Gottes Beistand stets in einem solchen Zustand erhalten konnte, dass ich zu beiden, zum Leben und zum Sterben bereit war".

Diese Schrift hat Ziegenbalg allerdings erst in Indien zum Abschluss bringen können. Er hat sie der dänischen Prinzessin Sophia Hedwig gewidmet. Diese Erstlingsarbeit Ziegenbalgs ist im Druck zugänglich unter dem Titel: "Allgemeine Schule der wahren Weisheit, darinnen einem jeden Menschen aus Gottes Wort und eigener Erfahrung (!) gezeigt wird, wie und auf was für Weise man diejenige Weisheit in dieser Welt suchen, finden und erlangen soll, welche uns Menschen sowohl zeitlich und ewig beseligen kann. Geschrieben auf dem grossen Weltmeer in einem Schiff Sophia genannt von Barth. Ziegenbalg".

Wie sehr ihm auf seiner Reise die Gestalt der himmlischen Weisheit gegenwärtig war, bezeugt auch der Brief, den er vom Cabo de bona Esperanca den 30. April 1706 an seinen verehrten Hallenser Lehrer August Hermann Francke schrieb, in dem es heisst: "Sind auch aus der bisherigen Führung in unsern Herzen ganz gewiss versichert, dass Gott hinfort ebenfalls mit seiner himmlischen Weisheit und kräftigen Wirkung seines

Heiligen Geistes bei uns sein werden und uns grosse Freudigkeit verleihen, den Geruch seiner Erkenntnis allenthalben, wo wir auch hinkommen möchten, sowohl unter den Heiden, als auch den hin und her zerstreueten und in der Irre gehenden Christen offenbar zu machen".[13]

4

Die Sophienlehre Jakob Boehmes hat eine ausserordentlich intensive Verbreitung in den verschiedenen theosophischen Schulen gefunden, die im Kreis der Schüler Jakob Boehmes entstanden sind. Eine charakteristische Form hat sie bei dem Schüler Boehmes angenommen, der als der Herausgeber seiner gesammelten Werke bekannt geworden ist, bei Johann Georg Gichtel. In Regensburg 1638 geboren, zeigte er schon in seiner Jugend eine auffällige visionäre Begabung. Nach einem Studium der Theologie, Geschichte und Jurisprudenz befreundete er sich 1664 als Rechtsanwalt mit Justinianus von Welz, dem Begründer der protestantischen Heidenmission, und ging mit ihm in die Niederlande, um ihn auf sein überseeisches Missionsfeld in Guayana zu begleiten, blieb aber dann zur Werbung für dieses Missionswerk in der Heimat zurück. In den Niederlanden schloss er sich dem Kreis der Schüler Jakob Boehmes an, die in Amsterdam eine Freistatt gefunden hatten. Dort wurde er nach verschiedenen Konflikten mit anderen Vorkämpfern eines mystischen Spiritualismus Oberhaupt einer eigenen Sekte der "Engelsbrüder", die einen radikalen Separatismus von allem institutionellen Kirchentum predigte.

Im Mittelpunkt der Verkündigung Gichtels, die literarisch vor allem in seinen theosophischen Niederschriften vorliegt,[14] steht die Lehre von der himmlischen Jungfrau Sophia. Seine Briefe enthalten zahlreiche Bekenntnisse, aus denen hervorgeht, dass auch seine Sophiologie nicht eine intellektuell übernommene Lehre darstellt, sondern auf mehrere Erscheinungen der Gestalt der himmlischen Sophia zurückgeht. Diese visionären Erfahrungen dominieren in einer so eindeutigen Weise, dass sie für ihn den Grundtypus der Heilserfahrung des Menschen darstellen. Die Heilserfahrung ist bei ihm als Verlöbnis des geistigen Menschen mit der jungfräulichen Sophia verstanden. Dementsprechend ist bei ihm die Ehelosigkeit nicht nur Voraussetzung der eigenen Heilserfahrung, son-

---

[13] Arno Lehmann, *Es begann in Trankenbar* (Berlin, 1955), 14,16.
[14] Hgg. von Gottfried Arnold in 2 Bänden 1701, dann unter dem Titel: *Theosophia Practica*, hgg. von Johann Wilhelm Ueberfeld (1722).

dern er verlangt sie auch von seinen Anhängern, die dem von ihm ge-
gründeten Orden der "Engelsbrüder" angehören. Die Bemühung um
eine kompromisslose Aufrechterhaltung dieses Ideals bei sich und bei
anderen hat einen grossen Teil seiner geistlichen Kämpfe ausgemacht,
wie aus seinem geistlichen Briefwechsel hervorgeht. In diesem Briefwechsel
bemüht sich Gichtel immer wieder, Freunde, von denen er erfährt, dass
sie einer irdischen Eva und einer weltlichen Eheschliessung zuneigen,
vor diesem Schritt zu warnen und weist dabei auf sein eigenes Vorbild
hin. So schreibt er zum Beispiel:

Ich habe mich auch lange geübet, und manche Versuchung durchpassiert, ehe
mir meine liebste Sophia ist vermählet worden: und nun ich gebunden bin, kan
ich nicht brechen, und mich mit dem Welt-Geist in Verlöbniss einlassen: Ich
muss GOtt die Ehre geben, und Ihn allein anbäten, welches die Reichen dieser
Welt nicht verstehen.[15]

Gichtel hat diese asketische Forderung als die wörtliche Erfüllung des
höchsten Gebotes Jesu verstanden: "Es sind etliche verschnitten, die sich
selbst verschnitten haben um des Himmelreiches willen. Wer es fassen
kann, der fasse es!"[16]

Hierin stecket die Ursache, dass der enge Weg zwar von vielen gesuchet, von
wenigen aber gefunden wird, weil wir Sophiam im Weibe suchen, und nicht in
JEsu, der gantz deutlich lehret: wer nicht verläugnet Vater, Mutter, Brüder,
Weib, Kinder, Güter, kan mein Lehr-Jünger nicht seyn. Und eben um des
Himmelreiches willen habe ich mich beschidten, und die mir 10 gantzen Jahre
nachgestellte Mariage verläugnet, auch mit Sophia eher nicht in empfindliche
Gemeindschaft durchbrechen mögen, bis ich Schulrecht gethan, und mein Hertz
unzetheilet meinem Bräutigam ergeben... Wir müssen uns nur untersuchen, ob
wir nach unserem ersten Paradies-Bild hungern; Hoc Opus Hic Labor; der
Cherub mit seinem zweyschneidigen Schwert lässet noch Mann noch Weib ins
Paradies, es müssen nur Jungfrauen seyn, und wird ein mächtiger Ernst erordert,
durch dieses Schwert Cherubs zu dringen; wer nicht mit der Armathur Christi angetan, und ohne Unterlass im Gebät streitet, wird wenig fördern; ich habs
durch GOttes Beystand erreicht bereits 44 Jahre, und kans bezeugen ... Die
töhrichten Jungfrauen schlafen, und denken nicht ans Öel, wollen auch nicht
aufwachen, bis des Bräutigams Stimme erschallen wird, dann wirds zu spät
seyn.[17]

Von hier aus wird auch Gichtels heftige Auseinandersetzung mit Gottfried Arnold verständlich. Gottfried Arnold hat sich in seiner radikalen
spiritualistischen Epoche dem Kreise der englischen Philadelphen
angeschlossen, die durch einen regelmässigen Sendboten namens Ditt-

---

[15]   Im 53. Brief.
[16]   Matth. 19,12.
[17]   Brief 134.

mar mit den deutschen Brüdern verkehrten, und stand auch in einer engen Beziehung zu dem Gichtel'schen Kreise. Wie oben angeführt (S. 129), hat er aufgrund seiner eigenen Visionen die asketischen Forderungen Gichtels geteilt, dass die Ehe mit der himmlischen Sophia jede irdische Mariage ausschliesse. Um so grösser war das Entsetzen Gichtels, als sich Gottfried Arnold im Zusammenhang mit einer inneren Selbstkorrektur seines radikalen Spiritualismus 1701 mit Anna Maria Sprögel, der Tochter des Johann Heinrich Sprögel und der Susanne Sprögel, verheiratete, die die Häupter eines mystischen spiritualistischen Pietistenkreises in Quedlinburg waren und in deren Haus Gottfried Arnold als Hauslehrer tätig war. Gichtel hat Gottfried Arnold diese Verehelichung nie verziehen und hat darin einen Verrat Gottfried Arnolds an seiner ersten Braut, der Sophia, erblickt, obwohl Arnold zunächst offenbar die Absicht geäussert oder den Eindruck erweckt hatte, er wolle um der Sophia willen eine rein geschwisterliche Ehe mit seiner angetrauten Gattin führen. Aber die Ehe mit der "Schwester" entwickelte sich zu einer Ehe im Fleisch und war mit Kindern gesegnet. Gichtel hat sich mit einer boshaften Bemerkung über Gottfried Arnold gerächt: "Herr Arnold hat uns zwar nachzufolgen sich beflissen, und eine Schwester zum Weibe genommen; allein weil sie nicht überwunden und die Matrix in den Tod geführt, hat er auch nicht bestehen können, und ist in Kinder verfallen".[18]

Zahlreiche Andeutungen Gichtels lassen erkennen, dass bei ihm eine Reihe visionärer Erfahrungen vorliegt, die im Laufe seines Lebens eingetreten sein müssen und in denen er eine progressive Vereinigung mit der Gestalt der himmlischen Weisheit erfahren hat. Gichtel selbst wird nicht müde, diese Erfahrungen als einen Prozess zu schildern, der sich über sein ganzes Leben hinzieht und nach immer neuen Krisen und Versuchungen zu immer tieferen Formen der Begegnung führt. So schreibt er darüber ganz allgemein: "Sophia ist mir zwar frühe erschienen, und hat mir ihre Treue, Hülfe und Beystand zugesaget; es liefen aber wol in die 30 Jahre hin, ehe meine Seele und Gemüt confirmiert, und besänftiget ist worden, wie ernstlich ich auch im Streit stund, und den Versucher abschlug".[19]

Er weist ausdrücklich darauf hin, dass nicht weltlicher Ehrgeiz ihn veranlasst habe, seine Botschaft von der himmlischen Sophia anderen zu verkünden, sondern dass ihn die überwältigende Erfahrung der Begegnung

---

[18] Brief 134.
[19] Im 122. Brief.

mit ihr genötigt habe, andere Seelen zu suchen, um ihnen davon mitteilen und sie zu derselben Form der Heilserfahrung führen zu können.

Nun war meine Intention nicht mit einigen Menschen Kundschaft zu machen, sondern ich spielte kindlich mit der Sophia in ihren Wundern, denn sie zeigte mir ein Mysterium nach dem anderen, so wol in der inneren als äusseren Natur geöffnet, und dadurch überaus inbrünstig und feurig in der Natur gemacht, dass weil ich allein nicht satt von Lobsingen werden kunte, einfältig im Hertzen gewünschet, Dass GOtt andere verliebte Hertzen zu diesem Spiel führen und ziehen wolte, damit mein Lobgesang vermehret werden möchte.[20]

Hier bekundet sich der echte Ursprung einer mystischen Gemeinschaftsbildung, da das mystische Erlebnis einerseits zur Kommunikation nötigt, andererseits aber den missionarischen Impuls enthält, andere zu einer gleichartigen Erfahrung hinzuführen.

Es entspricht dem überwältigenden und intimen Charakter seiner Visionen der Begegnung mit der himmlischen Sophia, wenn er von dem entscheidenden Erlebnis in seinen Briefen meist nur in Andeutungen spricht. Nur an einigen Stellen lüftet er den Schleier und macht nähere Angaben über dieses Erlebnis. So schreibt er z.B.:

Wir haben die Braut im Geiste gesehen, und ihre Stimme gehöret, auch wohl bemerket, dass solche in viel andere sich ausgehallet, und zu uns mit Schaaren gezogen hat, welche auch, ehe wir noch eines mit ihnen gesprochen, erwecket und angezündet worden, also bald alles verkauft, ausgetheilet und sich ernstig in ihrer Werbung angestellt. Sie waren aber nicht alle weise Jungfrauen und der Eigenheit abgestorben: da sich die himmlische Sophia dem natürlichen Leben entzogen, zu prüfen, ob sie vom Himmel-Brot JEsu im Glauben essen, und GOtt oder ihren Händen trauen wolten, wichen sie wieder nach Aegypten und liessen das Gebät und Glauben fahren ... Wollen wir der himmlischen Sophia wahrer Bräutigam seyn, und ihrer Beywohnung im Geiste allezeit geniessen, so müssen wir einen gantz demütigen, kindlichen, einfältigen Willen gegen sie und untereinander haben, einander lieben, und für einander streiten und unser Leben stellen ...[21]

Auch hier wird deutlich, wie die visionäre Erfahrung selbst zur Gemeinschaftsbildung führt, diese dann aber auch eine Reihe von Konflikten in sich birgt, die nicht zuletzt durch die Ausschliesslichkeitsforderung des Ehegelübdes mit der himmlischen Sophia und die radikale Forderung des Zölibats verursacht sind.

Wohl am ausführlichsten hat Gichtel über seine Sophienerlebnisse im Zusammenhang mit einer allgemeinen Schilderung des Verhältnisses der himmlischen Sophia zu ihren Liebhabern berichtet, eine Schilderung, in

[20] Im 109. Brief.
[21] Im 81. Brief.

der er unter seinen Freunden für die Hingabe an die himmlische Sophia
wirbt. Dort gibt er eine Art biographischer Zusammenfassung der einzelnen Phasen seines eigenen Verhaltens zur Jungfrau Sophia:

So trauet auch die Jungfrau sich nicht so leicht in ihrer Buhler Armen, sondern
wil Leib, Seel und Geist zum Pfande haben, und solches nicht allein, sondern
ein treues standhaftes Hertz, das weder in Lieb noch Leid weichet, und lieber
das Leben als ihre Lieb fahren lässet. Ew. L. weis selbst dass leichter Treue
zugesaget: auch nimmts unsere himmlische Sophia gar bereitwillig an, küsset,
hertzet und umarmet ihren lieben Buhler und verlorenen Limbum gantz innig;
aber ihr Perl vertrauet sie keinem, der nicht seine Ichheit völlig abgestorben,
und lässet keinen in ihren Armen ruhen, der nicht ein Ritter des Teufels oder
des eigenen Willens worden, und allerley Proben bestanden hat, welches nicht
eines Jahres Werk, sondern in ihrem Belieben stehet, wie lang sie wil ... Ich
hab zwar auch viel geliebt, nicht zwar aus mir selbsten, sondern aus Gnade
dessen, der meine und aller Menschen Seele liebet. Verstunde aber im Grunde
nicht, was doch GOtt mit mir vorhatte, dass er mich, der ich doch im gutem
Wohlstande äusserlich stunde, Kutschen und Pferde hatte, in solche Torheit
vor aller Welt gestecket, und selbst meiner eigenen Vernunft zum Narren
gemacht hat, von allen Mitteln berauben, und aus meinem Vaterland bannen
und exuliren lassen, hernach doch wieder zu Wien am Käyserlichen Hof, auch
anderer Chur- und Fürsten zu weit höheren Dignitäten nöthigen, und mit
Erbschaften und reichen Weibern lange Jahre versuchen lassen. Und als mir
im Jahre 1673 die himmlische Jungfrau Sophia von Angesicht zu Angesicht
erschienen, und Mund zu Mund Treue zugesaget, auch viel Hertzen wider
meinen Willen, und ohne mein eigen Suchen, der ich gar verborgen gelebet, zu
mir gezogen, dennoch in greulicher Verwirrung, Zerstreuung und gäntzlicher
Verlassung von aller Creatur gesetzet, dass es geschienen, als wäre GOtt selbst
mit Ihm uneins, und wollte zum Lügner werden. Bis ich endlich mich des
natürlichen Lebens verwogen und erwehlet hab lieber zu sterben, als zu weichen,
da sich das Blatt gewendet, und ich lernen müssen, dass wir zwar Treue
zusagen in guten Tagen, aber auch in bösen vest halten müssen.[22]

5

Gichtel und seine Gemeinde der "Engelsbrüder" haben wenige Spuren in
der deutschen und niederländischen Frömmigkeitsgeschichte hinterlassen.
Bezeichnenderweise finden sich einige späte Nachwirkungen bei Michael
Hahn,[23] der 1758-1819 lebte und in Sindelfingen, wo er schliesslich auf

---

[22] Im 80. Brief.
[23] Über Michael Hahn s. Gottlob Lang, *Michael Hahn, Einführung in seine Gedanken-*
welt mit einer Auswahl aus seinen Werken (Stuttgart, 1922); Joh. Mich. Hahn, *Kurze*
Darstellung seines Lebens und seiner Lehre (Stuttgart, 2. Ausg., 1952) bei der M. Hahn-
schen Gemeinschaft in Stuttgart, Paulinenstr. 21; W. F. Stroh, *Die Lehre des würtem-*
bergischen Theosophen Joh. Mich. Hahn systematisch entwickelt und in Auszügen aus

dem Schloss der Herzogin Franziska einen Zufluchtsort fand, eine eigene Gemeinde gründete, die sich im Anschluss an seine theosophischen Erbauungsschriften um ihn scharte und bis zum heutigen Tage noch existiert. Auch bei ihm äussert sich eine voll entfaltete Sophiologie, die mit der Forderung der völligen Ehelosigkeit als der Voraussetzung einer Vermählung mit der himmlischen Sophia verknüpft ist. Hahn berichtet selbst zwar nicht von einer Vision der himmlischen Sophia, doch lassen, ähnlich wie bei Gichtel, viele Andeutungen seiner Schriften erkennen, dass auch für ihn, der in vielen anderen Fällen eine visionäre Begabung bekundet, Erlebnisse visionärer Art die Grundlage seiner Sophiologie bildeten.

Ein letzter Vertreter der Sophiologie ist dann Johann Jakob Wirtz (1778-1858), der Stifter der Nazarenergemeinde, der seine geistlichen Erfahrungen in einer Selbstbiographie[24] und in Gestalt von Eingebungen, Visionen und Weisungen in seinen "Zeugnissen und Erfahrungen des Geistes" niedergelegt hat.[25] Für ihn, den protestantischen pietistischen Seidenweber in Basel, ist charakteristisch, dass sich die Sophienlehre, die schon bei Jakob Boehme mariologische Züge aufweist, in eine voll entwickelte Mariologie verwandelt. Der protestantische Pietist Wirtz hat mit innerster Überzeugung die leibliche Himmelfahrt der Maria verkündet, fast ein Jahrhundert, bevor sie in der römischen Kirche zum verpflichtenden Dogma erhoben wurde.

Auch in der protestantischen Tradition der Sophiologie hat also schliesslich die Mariologie die Selbständigkeit der sophiologischen Erfahrung und Theologie zu Fall gebracht und hat diese in einen Bestandteil der Mariologie selbst verwandelt.

---

seinen Schriften dargestellt (Stuttgart, 1859); Ernst Benz, "Die Sympathie der Dinge", in: *Eranos-Jahrb.* 24 (1955), 176 ff.

[24] Biographie von Johann Wirtz, *Ein Zeugnis der Nazarener-Gemeinde von der Entwicklung des Reiches Gottes auf Erden* (Barmen, 1862).

[25] Biographie von Johann Wirtz, 2 Bände (Barmen, 1863-1866).

PROTESTANTISMUS UND ORTHODOXIE IM GESPRÄCH

ROBERT STUPPERICH

Unseren Zeitgenossen will es oft scheinen, als sei erst das zwanzigste
Jahrhundert dazu berufen, Brücken zwischen den Kirchen und Konfessionen zu schlagen. Vielfach ist es selbst den Theologen aus dem Ge-
dächtnis entschwunden, dass, wenn vergangene Zeiten es auch erheblich
schwerer hatten, Entfernungen zu überwinden und vor allem von ihrem
festgefügten konfessionellen Bewusstsein her Wege zu anderen christlichen Kirchen und Gemeinschaften einzuschlagen, Versuche dazu niemals
unterlassen wurden. Die Kirchengeschichte spricht eine deutliche Sprache.
Wenn aber in ihren Darstellungen diese Versuche konfessioneller Begegnung nicht besonders laut angeklungen sind, so hängt es oft daran, dass
die historischen Vorarbeiten noch immer nicht weit genug gediehen sind.
Selbst in der Geschichte der ökumenischen Bewegung konnten diese
Ereignisse nur unvollständig berücksichtigt und teilweise überhaupt nicht
herangezogen werden.[1] In Archiven und Bibliotheken liegt aber noch viel
unverwertetes Material, das unsere Anschauung von den Bestrebungen
und Bemühungen vergangener Jahrhunderte zu verdeutlichen geeignet
ist. Ja, selbst die in verschiedenen Sprachen vorliegenden Quellen sind oft
unbeobachtet und daher auch unwirksam geblieben. Es fehlt immer noch
an Quellenpublikationen, vor allem was das osteuropäische Gebiet an-
langt. Dabei darf von vornherein betont werden, dass die Religionsgespräche, die dort gehalten wurden, und die Schriften, die dort erschienen
sind, keineswegs immer der Polemik dienten, sondern ebenso vom Ge-
sichtspunkt der Irenik und der Verständigung zu betrachten sind.
   Es bleibt nicht nur historisch interessant, dass sich die Reformatoren

---

[1] Rouse/Neill, *Geschichte der ökumenischen Bewegung* I, 2. Aufl. (1963), 231 ff.; dazu
R. Stupperich, *Wege der Verständigung zwischen dem Protestantismus und der
russischen Orthodoxie*, Ostdeutsche Wissenschaft VII (1960), 229-248; ders., *Ökumeni-
scher Brückenschlag zur Russ.-orth. Kirche im 19. Jh.*, *ibid.*, Bd. XI (1964), 156-180;
L. Müller, *Orthodoxie und Protestantismus* (Una Sancta, 1966), 46 ff.

von Anfang an bemüht haben, mit der östlichen Kirche Verbindungen anzuknüpfen, es ist auch für die Fortführung des damals begonnenen Gespräches nicht unwesentlich, den Gang der früheren Gespräche zu kennen und die bereits behandelte Thematik zu verfolgen. Es könnte sein, dass aus diesen in früheren Jahrhunderten geführten Gesprächen manches noch für die Gegenwart wichtig wäre. Auf dieser Grundlage könnte vieles besser erörtert und ein tieferes Verständnis der Gemeinsamkeit und der Verschiedenheit gewonnen werden.

1

Die reformatorische Voraussetzung, mit der alten Kirche auf gleichem Boden zu stehen, führte zu der Folgerung, dass es nicht schwer sein müsse, zu einer Verständigung mit der Kirche des Ostens kommen zu können, die die altkirchliche Grundlage festgehalten habe. Für Melanchthon und seine Schüler lag es nahe, die Annäherung zuerst bei den Griechen zu suchen und mit ihnen ein Gespräch zu beginnen. Bemerkenswert ist die Tatsache, dass der in Siebenbürgen als Nachfolger des Johannes Honterus tätige Melanchthon-Schüler Valentin Wagner bereits 1544 in seiner κατήχησις den Versuch unternahm, die Griechen in Kronstadt, aber auch im ganzen Griechentum anzusprechen und mit ihnen ein Gespräch anzubahnen,[2] wie es einige Jahre später Melanchthon beim Patriarchen von Konstantinopel auch versuchte. Leider besitzen wir kein Exemplar der 1. Ausgabe der κατήχησις mehr; die 2. Auflage von 1550 zeigt uns, welche Fragen Wagner in den Vordergrund stellte und wie er in dieser Schrift argumentierte. Es handelt sich um ein umfangreiches Werk von 26 Bogen, gewählt ist der Weg der Unterweisung, wie er dem Pädagogen angemessen erschien. Melanchthon und Camerarius rühmten dieses Werk.

Bezeichnenderweise hat Melanchthon selbst nicht denselben Weg beschritten, eine neue Denkschrift zu verfassen, sondern übersetzte die CA ins Griechische, schickte also ein "amtlich" beglaubigtes Schriftstück an den Patriarchen, von dem er eine Anerkennung erhoffte.[3] Melanchthons pädagogisches Geschick und sein Einfühlungsvermögen drücken sich dabei sehr deutlich aus. Nicht nur, dass er in der griechischen Fassung die historischen Bemerkungen erheblich erweiterte, er unternahm es, nach-

---

[2] Bela Holl, *Die erste Ausgabe der* κατήχησις *Valentin Wagners* (Magyar Konyus-szemle 38/9162), 293-302.
[3] Vgl. E. Benz, *Wittenberg und Byzanz* (1949), 6ff. Der griechische Text der CA wird demnächst als Heft 8 in den *Quellenheften zur ostdeutschen und osteuropäischen Kirchengeschichte* in einer Neuausgabe erscheinen.

dem er die östliche Liturgie gründlich studiert hatte, die Terminologie derselben ins Bekenntnis einzutragen und auf diese Weise die CA den Griechen verständlicher und vertrauter zu machen. Als gründlicher Kenner der Patristik war Melanchthon sich bewusst, dass es keinen Sinn hatte, mit den Griechen über die Rechtfertigung zu sprechen, da sie die paulinische Auffassung weniger betonten und sich fast ausschliesslich an die johanneische Erlösungslehre hielten. Die *Confessio Augustana* "variatissima" hat daher in Art. IV die Rechtfertigung durch die den Griechen geläufigen Begriffe Erlösung und Wiedergeburt umschrieben.

Auch der Brief Melanchthons[4] an den Patriarchen Joasaph von Konstantinopel vom 25.9.1559, der der griechischen Augustana als Beilage beigegeben war, bringt die Motive des Magisters deutlich hervor. Ihm lag es daran, das Gemeinsame zu betonen: Heilige Schrift, altkirchliches Dogma und Lehre der Kirchenväter. Er nennt als Zeugen Irenäus, Athanasius, Basilius, Gregor von Nazianz, Epiphanius und Theodoret. Ebenso betont er die Ablehnung der alten Irrlehren und der lateinischen Neuerungen.

Wir wissen freilich nicht, ob die CA damals in die rechten Hände gelangt ist. Vermutlich war das nicht der Fall. Der erste Verständigungsversuch ist daher als erfolglos anzusehen.

Leider sind die ersten mit viel Verständnis gewonnenen Gesichtspunkte für ein orthodox-protestantisches Gespräch zunächst nicht weiter angewandt worden. In den späteren bekannten Gesprächsversuchen der Tübinger Theologen mit dem Patriarchen Jeremias II. von Konstantinopel[5] ist die vorsichtige, dem biblischen Sprachgebrauch angeglichene Sprache Melanchthons durch die Sprache der beginnenden lutherischen Orthodoxie abgelöst. Selbst die erste Absage des Patriarchen hat die Tübinger keines Besseren belehrt. Sie sprechen zu Griechen so, wie sie untereinander reden, ohne auf die besondere theologische Lage der Griechen einzugehen.

Schon die ersten Versuche des 16. Jh.s, die mehrfach dargestellt sind, hätten, wenn sie besser beachtet und vollständiger behandelt worden wären, für das sich allmählich weiterhinziehende Gespräch mehr austragen können. Die Beschäftigung mit der geschichtlichen Überlieferung hätte zeigen können, dass im frühen 16. Jahrhundert der Protestantismus

---

[4] *CR* IX (1922); vgl. Benz, 59 ff.

[5] *Acta et Scripta theologorum Wirtembergensium et patriarchae Hieremiae* (Wittenberg, 1584), 143 ff., teilweise deutsche Übers. *Wort und Mysterium* hrsg. v. Kirchl. Aussenamt, (1958); vgl. dazu die Kritik von E. Benz, *Tübingen und Byzanz*, Zeitschrift f. Religions- und Geistesgeschichte (1962), 368 ff.

einen besseren Zugang zum Gespräch mit der Orthodoxie hatte als die folgende Zeit. Die bessere Kenntnis der Patristik vermittelte Gesprächs-partnern eine gute Ausgangsbasis. Die Schüler Melanchthons dagegen wollten die eigenen Anschauungen den Orthodoxen ohne Vermittlung und Verständigung nahebringen. Die Thematik hatten die Tübinger gewählt, ohne die Motivation Melanchthons zu beachten; sie haben den Patriarchen genötigt, auf ihre Position einzugehen, d.h. zur CA Stellung zu nehmen, und durften sich nicht wundern, dass dieser nun seine eigene Position herausstrich.

In diesem Briefwechsel (1573-1581) zwischen den Tübingern und Patri-arch Jeremias II. geht es um Glauben und Kirche. Die Antwort des Patriarchen ist charakteristisch. Der Tübinger Auslegung der CA stellt er die Auslegung der Kirchenväter entgegen, wobei er sich vornehmlich auf Chrysostomus, auf den Areopagiten und auf die Kanones der ökume-nischen Synoden beruft. Damit wird das Thema der Tradition aufge-nommen; dabei will es den Griechen nicht in den Sinn — auch stossen sie sich daran —, dass die Protestanten trotz ihres Anschlusses an die früheste Kirche die westliche Überlieferung festhalten und den Zusatz des filioque im Bekenntnis stehen lassen. Würde ihnen die Apologie zugleich mit der CA vorgelegt worden sein, hätten sie die starke Berufung auf die grie-chischen Väter wohltuend empfunden und in dieser Hinsicht keinen Mangel gesehen.

Die Rechtfertigungslehre Luthers konnten die Griechen nicht aufneh-men. Das eigentliche Anliegen der Reformation ist daher von ihnen auch nicht gesehen worden, zumal sie von ihrer Anthropologie her keinen Zu-gang zu ihr hatten und die paulinische Theologie nicht in gleichem Masse betonten. Die Theologie des Römerbriefes und die abendländischen Fol-gerungen in ihrer Satisfactions-und Rechtfertigungslehre werden als "juridistisch" bezeichnet. Die Menschwerdung bedeute bereits Eintreten Christi für den Menschen. Das Schauen Christi sei schon Erlösung, die den Menschen zum Erfüllen des Willens Gottes befähigt.

Zugänglich war den Griechen die Lutherische Sakramentslehre, beson-ders die Abendmahlslehre, obwohl sie seit den Unionskonzilien von Lyon (1273) und Florenz (1439) gerade in dieser Beziehung bereits latinisierende Auffassungen vertraten. Die altkirchliche Auffassung von der μεταβολή war stellenweise der lateinischen Wandlungslehre (μετουδίωεις) gewichen. Auch die im 12. Jahrhundert im Westen festgelegte Siebenzahl der Sakramente war schon bei den Griechen üblich geworden. Nur im äußeren Brauchtum war die alte eigene Auffassung noch gültig.

Patriarch Jeremias II. hatte gesehen, daß die ihm vorgelegte Thematik erhebliche Unterschiede in der Denkweise und in einzelnen Lehren zeigte, insbesondere was die Geltung der Tradition, die Auffassung von den guten Werken und von den Sakramenten betraf. Als er auf der Reise nach Moskau seinen letzten Brief nach Tübingen schrieb, meinte er, den Dialog nicht weiter fortsetzen zu sollen. Ein Nebeneinander kam für ihn nicht in Frage. Er konnte sich nur eine Lösung der Kirchenfrage denken: "Wir wollen euch aufnehmen, wenn ihr die Lehren der griechischen Kirche und die Kanones der sieben ökumenischen Konzilien anerkennt ... Dann werden die zwei Kirchen eine sein.'

Während die Wittenberger und Tübinger Versuche, das Gespräch mit der Orthodoxie in Gang zu bringen, von deutschen Voraussetzungen ausgingen, ist das interkonfessionelle Gespräch mit den Griechen im 17. Jahrhundert von anderen Positionen aus erfolgt und hat auch einen anderen Charakter angenommen. Bemerkenswert bleibt in diesem Zusammenhang vor allem die Gestalt des Ökumenischen Patriarchen Kyrill Loukaris. Dieser stammte aus dem damals venezianischen Kreta, studierte in Padua, wo ihm die abendländische Theologie bekannt wurde. Dazu kamen seine späteren Bekanntschaften mit Niederländern in Alexandrien und Konstantinopel. Vorher muß Kyrill Loukaris während seines Aufenthaltes in Ostrog (Polen) 1596-1602 die polnischen Protestanten kennengelernt haben. In dieser Zeit wurde die Wilnaer Konföderation von 1599 abgeschlossen. Möglichkeiten eines Zusammengehens der Orthodoxen und Protestanten im katholischen Raum zeichneten sich ab und sagten eine Verständigung voraus. In welchem Mass Kyrill mit dem Protestantismus in dieser Zeit bekannt wurde, bleibt ungewiss. Von Gesprächen bzw. Verhandlungen mit den Protestanten ist aus dieser Zeit nichts bekannt.[6] Im Jahre 1612 rechtfertigt er sich gegenüber dem Patriarchen Timotheos, als sei er ein λουτερανός.

Wenn er als Patriarch die stärkere Anwendung der Predigt fordert, wenn er sich für eine neugriechische Bibelübersetzung einsetzt (gedruckt in Genf 1638) und sich schliesslich in seinem Bekenntnis (Genf 1629) an protestantische Ausdrucksformeln anschliesst, dann ist darin die Erkenntnis niedergelegt, dass Orthodoxie und Protestantismus viel Gemeinsames besitzen und besitzen müssen, falls ihre Prinzipien echt sind und in rechter Weise befolgt werden. Dieses Ergebnis wird mehr durch persönliche Gespräche als durch Lektüre erzielt sein.

Leider sind wir nicht in der Lage, das Werk des Kyrill Loukaris voll abzuschätzen. Weder liegen uns seine Briefe vor, die er nach Moskau

---

[6] Vgl. K. Roozemond, *Notes marginales de Cyrille Lucaris dans un exemplaire du grand catechisme de Bellarmin* ('s-Gravenhage, 1963), Einl.

geschrieben hat, noch sind seine Beziehungen nach Genf und zu den holländischen Reformierten voll geklärt. Seine Briefe an seinen holländischen Freund David de Willem sind teilweise erhalten,[7] aber sie stammen aus der Frühzeit des Patriarchen. Nachweislich kannte Kyrill schon früh Calvins *Institutio*, ohne damit zum Calvinisten geworden zu sein. Wenn ihn später der holländische Resident in Konstantinopel, Cornelis Haga, dazu überredete, sein Bekenntnis in vulgärem Griechisch zu schreiben, so ist, wie K. Rozemond mit Recht hervorhebt, seine theologische Entwicklung zu wenig bekannt, als dass ein Pauschalurteil darüber abgegeben werden könnte. Die Schrift, lateinisch in Genf gedruckt, trägt eine Widmung an Cornelis Haga. Wie alle griechischen Theologen, so hat Kyrill Loukaris grosses religionsphilosophisches Interesse, das ihn über die Providentia nachdenken und von dieser Seite aus sich mit dem Calvinismus berühren lässt.

Das eine ist deutlich, der Patriarch war ein theologisch gebildeter Mann, der sich das abendländische Denken angeeignet hatte und darum in der Lage war, ein überkonfessionelles Gespräch zu führen. Aus den in Genf vorhandenen Archivalien wird sich ein deutlicheres Bild vielleicht noch ergeben.

Zu einem Gespräch im eigentlichen Sinne hatte Kyrills Ὁμολογία keinen Anlass gegeben, wenn sie auch durch solche ausgelöst wurde. Im Orient hatte sie Widerspruch geweckt und eine gegenteilige Wirkung erzielt, nämlich die Annäherung an römische Auffassungen. Die λατινόφρονες erzielten noch mehr. Während die bisher genannten Versuche nur private Unternehmungen waren, teils allerdings auch zu einer grösseren Diskussion führten und die öffentliche Meinung bestimmten, ja sogar die kirchliche Auffassung sich in bestimmter Weise verfestigen liessen, führte der Gegensatz nicht nur zur Abfassung der *Confessio Orthodoxa* des Petrus Mogila, sondern zu den Verhandlungen auf den Synoden in Jassy 1642 und in Jerusalem. Des weiteren ist auch über die von Metrophanes Kritopulos geführten Gespräche und seine auf Betreiben der Helmstädter Theologen verfasste Ὁμολογία (1652) zu berichten, die ebenso eine Privatschrift ist. Beachtlich ist, dass auch für diesen, der in England und Deutschland studiert hat, entsprechend der religionsphilosophischen Neigung der Griechen und der damaligen geistigen Situation die Gottesfrage und besonders die Frage der Prädestination (Kap. 4)

---

[7] E. Legrand, *Bibliothèque hellénique*, Bd. 4 (1896), 313-329. Etwa 130 Briefe des Patriarchen Kyrill Loukaris sind noch unveröffentlicht, darunter ca. 30 an den Zaren Mixail Fedorovič. Vgl. G. Hofmann, *Patriarch Kyrill Lukaris. Einfluss abendländischer Schriften auf seine Predigten*, Orient. christ. period. VII (1941), 261.

wichtig geworden ist. Zeitlich dem Bekenntnis des Kyrill Loukaris na-
hestehend, nimmt die Schrift des Metrophanes eine vorsichtigere Position ein. In einer der altkirchlichen Auffassung näherkommenden Betrachtung über die Kirche und über die sieben Mysterien (Kap.
5) weiss
er das Wesen der orthodoxen Lehre besser gegenüber den römischen
Einflüssen abzugrenzen. Die sieben Mysterien werden in altkirchlicher
Weise von ihm unterschieden in drei wesentliche (Taufe, Eucharistie und
Busse) und vier dem kirchlichen Brauchtum zuzurechnende. Metrophanes
nimmt Stellung zur Tauffrage seiner Zeit ebenso wie er die altkirchliche
Position in der Eucharistie festhält. Die Art der μεταβολή ist ἄγνωστος
und ἀνερμήνευτος. Mit Recht wird selbst von orthodoxen Verfassern
zugegeben, dass diese Erklärung aufschlussreicher und deutlicher, ja
dem Wesen der orthodoxen Kirchenlehre entsprechender ist, als das Bekenntnis des Petrus Mogila mit seinen oft latinisierenden Deutungen.[8]

2

Als im 16. Jh. Auswanderer aus Polen/Litauen und Gefangene aus Livland
nach Moskau gelangten und ihren evangelischen Glauben vertraten, kam
es teils zu Gesprächen, teils zu Konversionen und antilutherischer
Polemik. Die Fremdgläubigen waren meist Lutheraner, bisweilen auch
Antitrinitarier. Bei dem Kreise, der im Jahre 1553 in Moskau vor das
geistliche Gericht gestellt wurde, scheint das letztere der Fall gewesen zu
sein.[9] Auch Einheimische unterlagen hin und wieder ihrem Einfluss.

Dass Ivan IV. über den lutherischen Glauben orientiert war, geht keineswegs auf Lektüre, sondern auf persönliche Gespräche zurück. Ob er
solche mit dem Pastor Mag. Wettermann aus Dorpat oder anderen
livländischen Gefangenen wirklich geführt hat, ist nicht zu erweisen. Er
hatte einen Dolmetscher Hans Caspar, auf dessen Urteil er viel gab.
Paul Oderborn schreibt über diesen in seiner *Vita Joannis Basilidis*
(Wittenberg 1585), er berichtet auch von konfessionellen Gesprächen:
"uns werfen sie Sektiererei vor, während sie selbst ständig von der östlichen Orthodoxie abweichen". Aber diese privaten Gespräche verschwin-

---

[8] Vgl. W. Gass, *Symbolik der griechischen Kirche* (1872); E. Hammerschmidt, *Die
Kirche in der Bekenntnisschrift des Metrophanes Kritopoulos*, Kirche im Osten 6
(Göttingen, 1963), 9-15.
[9] Vgl. I. Sokolov, *Otnošenija protestantizma k Rossii* (Moskau, 1880), 58 ff. N. A.
Kazakova i Ja. S. Lur'e, *Antifeodal'nye eretičeskie dviženija na Rusi XIV-načala
XVI veka* (Moskau-Leningrad, 1955).

den völlig hinter den grossen offiziellen Religionsgesprächen, die Ivan IV.
in Moskau mit dem Senior der böhmischen Brüder in Polen, Jan Rokyta,
geführt hatte.

Ključevskij ist der Meinung, Ivan hätte selbständig, auf Grund seiner
grossen Belesenheit in der Hl. Schrift, in den Kirchenvätern und anderen
theologischen Büchern die entscheidenden Streitpunkte herausgestellt
und seinen Kontrahenten aufgefordert, *vol'no i smelo* (frei und tapfer)
zu reden. Dieses Gespräch drehte sich um das Schriftverständnis und die
Cognitio pristinae religionis. Nach Meinung Rokytas sei der Zar durch
seine (Rokytas) stärkeren Argumente überwunden worden, so dass er
hätte schweigen müssen. Die Antwort hatte der Zar ihm schriftlich geben
lassen.[10] In seinen Darlegungen spielen die äusseren Bräuche die grösste
Rolle. Lediglich an einer Stelle, wo er vom Glaubensbegriff und vom
Verhältnis von Glauben und Werken spricht, polemisiert er gegen das
lutherische *Sola fide* und betont Jac. 2.

Die Heiratspolitik des Hauses Romanov brachte neue Probleme auf,
die zunächst im 17. Jh. nicht unüberwindlich erschienen.

Bereits 1602 waren neue Religionsgespräche eingeleitet, als Herzog
Hans von Holstein nach Moskau kam. Sein plötzlicher Tod unterbrach
die Verhandlungen. Moskau hatte gemerkt, dass die russische Kirche
nicht ausreichend zu einem derartigen Gespräch vorbereitet sei und liess
den Priester Ivan Nasedka die lutherische Position gründlich studieren.
Dieser hielt sich 1623 in Dänemark auf und wurde dann der kontrovers-
theologische Berater des Patriarchen von Moskau.[11]

Das Religionsgespräch in Moskau 1644/45 zwischen dem Grafen Waldemar und dem Patriarchen Joseph ist um der sprachlichen Schwierigkeiten willen schriftlich geführt worden.[12] Es konnte nicht verhandelt
werden, sondern es wurden Streitschriften gewechselt. Jede Denkschrift
musste erst übersetzt werden. Es entstanden dadurch nicht nur grosse
Unterbrechungen, sondern auch viele Missverständnisse. Der Patriarch
sprach in seinem Sendschreiben vom 22.4.1644 aus, dass die Lutheraner
den christlichen Glauben nicht in allem hielten; teils seien es noch Ab-
weichungen der römischen Kirche, teils aber eigene der Reformation,
durch die sie sich von der Orthodoxie schieden. Selbst wollten sie die

---

[10]   L. Müller, *Die Kritik am Protestantismus in der russischen Theologie* (1951), 23 ff.
Die ältere Auffassung bei S. Solov'ev, *Russkaja istorija*, Bd. 9, 313 ff. und V. Ključevskij,
Kurs russkoj istorii, Bd. 2, 193; A. Golubcev, *Pamjatniki prenij o vere, vozniksix po
delu koroleviča Val'demara* (Moskau, 1891).
[11]   L. Müller, 35 ff.
12   *Ibid.*, 43 ff.

Bräuche wie die Lehre so bewahren, wie sie sie übernommen hatten. Daher sei eine orthodoxe Taufe für Waldemar keine Wiedertaufe. Der Prinz antwortete, er hätte nicht vermutet, dass seine christliche Taufe angezweifelt werden würde. Er würde dabei bleiben. Beständigkeit ist eine Gabe des Hl. Geistes, nicht etwa Eigensinn. Den Glauben wechseln sei keine geringe Sache; er wolle seinem Gott treu sein und nehme keine fremde Religion an. Er bestehe darauf, dass er in Dingen der Religion nur anzunehmen brauche, "was in der Hl. Bibel als Gottes eigenes Wort zu finden ist". Er würde sonst wider Gottes Gebot und wider sein Gewissen handeln. Neben der Hl. Schrift hätten sie auch die altkirchlichen Symbole und die Schriften der Kirchenväter. Letztere liessen sie gelten, soweit sie mit der Hl. Schrift übereinstimmten. "Diese sind zwar gut, aber ihnen ist nicht weiter zu glauben, als sie mit der Bibel übereinstimmten."

3

Wie bei den Griechen, so hat sich auch bei den Russen das Gespräch der Konfessionen und sein Charakter völlig geändert, als die orthodoxen Theologen dazu übergingen, selbst den Protestantismus in seinen Heimatländern zu studieren. Wie Zar Peter selbst bereit war, im Auslande mit Vertretern anderer Kirchen über Glaubensfragen zu sprechen, so haben sich auch russische Theologen seitdem dazu bestimmen lassen. Im Jahre 1706 wollte der in russischen Diensten stehende General Freiherr von Eberstadt ein Religionsgespräch veranstalten, an dem von lutherischer Seite der Kirchenrat Cyprian aus Gotha, von russisch-orthodoxer Seite aber der Kiever Akademie-Präfekt Feofan Prokopovič teilnehmen sollten. Infolge des Krieges kam das Gespräch nicht zustande. In Feofans theologischem System fällt manches auf; nicht nur die Betonung der *sola scriptura*, der die Tradition untergeordnet ist, sondern vor allem die breite Darstellung der Rechtfertigungslehre, was sonst in der orthodoxen Theologie nicht üblich ist. Wir wissen, dass er einst für seinen Schüler einen *Tractatus de justificatione* in zwei Tagen niedergeschrieben hat. Er konnte überzeugt sein, dass dieser Entwurf nicht unwidersprochen bleiben würde. Ihm lag aber so viel an dieser Lehre, dass er seine Zeitgenossen getrost herausforderte. Schon vor diesem Traktat hatte er einen anderen geschrieben und zwar in russischer Sprache "O neudobonosnom zakonnom ige" (1712), in dem er die paulinischen Gedanken vom Gesetz aus dem Galaterbrief entwickelte. Als er nach Petersburg berufen wurde, begann er 1716 als Prediger zu wirken. Seine Predigten sind uns erhalten. Seine Leitgedanken können ebenso seinem Buch *O blaženstvax* (Erklärungen der Seligpreisungen Christi), 1723, entnommen werden. Feofan musste in Petersburg vieles sehen, was ihm nicht gefiel. Wenn die Welt sich in Gottlosigkeit stürzt, schreibt er aus der neuen Residenz nach Kiev, dann will sie als heilig angesehen werden. Am meisten nimmt sie Anstoss am Evangelium, an der Rechtfertigungslehre! Mochten aber seine Gegner in den ausgefahrenen Geleisen gehen, er selbst hielt sich für berufen, das Gegenteil zu sagen, und er tat es auch: "breviter et clare contrarium demonstro, si id ipsum plumbeae mentes capere valeant."[13]

Die Gegner schwiegen nicht, sie behaupteten, das Buch *Von den Seligpreisungen*, das der Zar gelesen und gebilligt hatte, sei ganz lutherisch. Dieses Urteil ist auch später wiederholt worden, jedoch ohne Nachweis. Dass Feofan die Grundlagen seiner Kirche verlassen hätte, ist aber unannehmbar. Dass er bei seiner Auseinandersetzung sich aus Protest selbst zum anderen Bekenntnis[14] habe leiten lassen, davon kann keine Rede sein. Feofan drückt in seiner Verkündigung nur seine Nähe zum Evangelium aus.

Zu konfessionellen Gesprächen im heutigen Sinne kam es nicht, wohl aber zu freundschaftlichem Gedankenaustausch. Niemand hat diesen Tatbestand so klar gesehen und so deutlich zum Ausdruck gebracht, wie der Jenenser Professor J. Fr. Buddeus, der mit Prokopovič im Briefwechsel stand und mit ihm zu einer weitgehenden Verständigung gelangt war.[15]

Buddeus schrieb am 29.3.1729 an Prokopovič, wie gross die Unterschiede zwischen ihren Kirchen auch seien, das Gemeinsame sei grösser; beide Kirchen ständen auf dem Grunde der Hl. Schrift, und sie führten beide den Menschen dazu, dass er im Vertrauen auf Gott und die in Christus geschehene Erlösung gottselig in der Welt lebe.

Die Berliner Akademie der Wissenschaften hatte sich durch ihren Präsidenten Leibniz bestimmen lassen, sich auf das Thema des evangelisch-orthodoxen Gesprächs einzustellen. Ihre Mitglieder Heineccius in Halle und Leonhard Fritsch in Berlin haben sich eingehend mit den Vor-

---

[13] Epistolae Th. Prokopowicz (Moskau, 1776), Ep. 6,21.
[14] Vgl. P. Verxovskij, *Učreždenie duxovnoj Kollegii i duxovnyj reglament* (Rostov/Don, 1916).
[15] R. Stupperich, *Feofan Prokopovič und Joh. Fr. Buddeus*, Zeitschrift für osteuropäische Geschichte (1935), 341 ff.; E. Winter, *Halle und die deutsche Russlandkunde im 18. Jahrhundert* (Berlin, 1952).

fragen einer gemeinsamen Verhandlung beschäftigt. Aber zu einem theologischen Gespräch ist es trotzdem nicht gekommen.

Im 18. Jh. erregte der Unterricht lutherischer Prinzessinnen, die den Zarenthron besteigen sollten und vorher zur Orthodoxie übertraten, ein gewisses Aufsehen.[16] Als Simeon Todorskij die Prinzessin Sophie von Anhalt-Zerbst (Katharina II.) unterrichtete, legte er dem Unterricht gleicherweise Luthers *Kleinen Katechismus* und die *Confessio Orthodoxa* des Petrus Mogila zugrunde. Der fromme Metropolit, der in Halle studiert hatte, stellte selbst die Übereinstimmung der Konfessionen fest. Das war ein praktischer Eklektizismus, der den Schwierigkeiten aus dem Wege ging.

Als in der folgenden Generation Erzbischof Platon (Levšin) vor derselben Aufgabe stand, legte er seine eigene Glaubenslehre zugrunde, die in deutscher Sprache 1770 in Riga gedruckt wurde. Auch er betonte die geringen Differenzen zwischen Orthodoxie und Protestantismus. Hier war der Zweck bestimmend, aber auch der Zeitgeist, der für konfessionelle Verschiedenheiten keinen Sinn hatte, der viel eher bereit war, das Verbindende überall zu sehen. Die regierenden Häupter, die in ihrem Briefwechsel auf diese Fragen eingingen (Katharina II., Friedrich d. Gr. und die Landgräfin Amalie von Hessen) sprachen nur witzelnd von den theologischen 'Spitzfindigkeiten', "worüber auf Ehre jeder anständige Mensch in Unkenntnis bleiben kann" (Friedrich d. Gr.). Auch im Zeitalter der Erweckung und der Romantik sind private Gespräche an der Tagesordnung. In der Aera Hegels beschäftigt sich die russische geistige Welt wieder stärker mit konfessionellen Fragen. In Xomjakovs Darlegungen über das Wesen der Konfessionen begegnen wir auch positiven Wertungen des Protestantismus. Von der Reformation spricht er als vom "reinigenden Gewitter". Das Wort Gottes sieht er als den Blitz an, der Flammen des Glaubes und der Liebe ausgelöst habe. Weiter rühmt Xomjakov die protestantische Freiheit, die sich mit dem orthodoxen Freiheitsverständnis berührt. Andererseits wiederholt er wieder die alten Vorwürfe, dass der Protestantismus rationalistisch sei, dass er mit der Tradition wertvolles Gut preisgebe, ja dass er infolgedessen keine Kirche mehr sei. In dieser Richtung folgen ihm Kireevskij und Samarin. Während im Kreise Xomjakovs kein protestantischer Partner zugegen war, ist von besonderem Interesse das konfessionelle Gespräch im Hause der Grossfürstin Elena Pavlovna, deren Hofdame Edith von Rahden mit Jurij Samarin disputierte. Die in der Schweiz begonnenen Gespräche wurden

---

[16]   R. Stupperich, *Zur Heiratspolitik des russischen Herrscherhauses im 18. Jahrhundert* (Kyrios, 1941), 214-239.

brieflich fortgesetzt. Während Samarin auf orthodoxer Seite die Kirche betont, stellt er den Protestantismus als Summe von isolierten Einzelnen dar. Der Protestant hat nach seiner Auffassung die Einheit des Glaubens verloren und diesen Mangel durch die Wissenschaft ersetzt. Dabei kommen der menschliche Wille und die christliche Liebe zu kurz. Edith von Rahden betonte dagegen die persönliche Christuserfahrung, die für sie das entscheidende Faktum im Leben ist. Schliesslich hat dann Samarin am 20.11.1869 bekannt: "Nous sommes au fond de la même Eglise".[17]

In solch tiefergreifender Weite wie in diesem Briefwechsel ist das konfessionelle Gespräch weder im 19. noch im beginnenden 20. Jh. sonst irgendwo geführt worden. Meistens wurde es gemieden, wie Zander in seinem Buch *Einheit ohne Vereinigung* von der Petersburger Gesellschaft um die Jahrhundertwende berichtet.[18]

4

Stellen wir in 4 Jahrhunderten nur private Unternehmungen fest, Gespräche unter vier Augen, selten öffentliche Dispute, die gelegentlich durch Austausch von Streitschriften ersetzt werden, so änderte sich das Bild im letzten halben Jahrhundert. Die Tatsache, dass das Interesse an der Orthodoxie so stark zunahm, hing mit dem Schicksal der Russ.-orth. Kirche und mit dem schweren Los zahlreicher ihrer Glieder zusammen, die über die ganze Welt verstreut wurden. In gewisser Weise stellten auch die aus ihrer kleinasiatischen Heimat ausgesiedelten Griechen, die ebenso in aller Welt neue Wohnsitze suchten, neue Gesprächspartner.

Diese Gespräche, die in den 20er Jahren zwischen Protestanten und Orthodoxen zu verzeichnen sind, — vielfach entstanden sie auf karitativer Basis —, sind zwar nicht mehr ganz privat. In Berlin stand der Zentralausschuss für Innere Mission dahinter. Aber diese Unternehmen hatten noch lange nicht den offiziellen Charakter, wie die nach dem 2. Weltkrieg. Hier kann auf das Vorbild der Anglikanischen Kirche hingewiesen werden. Diese hatte seit fast 100 Jahren solche Bemühungen gezeigt und hat in den Bestrebungen, zur Interkommunion mit der orthodoxen Kirche von Rumänien und mit dem Patriarchat von Konstantinopel zu kommen, Erfolge gehabt. Solche Bemühungen, auf dem Wege theologischer Konferenzen zur Verständigung zu kommen, gehen auch weiter.

---

[17] *La correspondance entre G. Samarin et la baronesse E. de Rahden*, 2. Auflage (1894).
[18] L. A. Zander, *Einheit ohne Vereinigung* (Stuttgart, 1959), 401.

Auf deutscher Seite wurden sie mehrfach mit dem Patriarchat von Moskau durchgeführt und werden nunmehr mit dem Ökumenischen Patriarchat eingeleitet.

Die zuletzt genannten Konferenzen werden im Unterschied zu den Gesprächen früherer Zeiten von offiziellen kirchlichen Delegationen durchgeführt. Sie werden verantwortlich von den betreffenden Kirchen getragen. Hier geht es nicht mehr um mehr oder weniger private Meinungen, sondern um Ansichten und Lehren der Kirchen. Das ist gegenüber früheren Versuchen ein Fortschritt. Die Ergebnisse haben einen verbindlichen Charakter und werden von den Kirchen zur Kenntnis genommen.

Das Wichtigste in sachlicher Hinsicht ist die Auswahl der Thematik. Von den im Druck erschienenen Referaten, *Communiqués* und *Resumées* der Verhandlungen, die als Arnoldshain I-IV bezeichnet werden, obwohl nur das erste Gespräch in Arnoldshain, die drei weiteren in Zagorsk, Höchst und Leningrad stattgefunden haben, gewinnt man den Eindruck, dass die Thematik in starkem Masse von seiten der evangelischen Leitung vorgeschlagen und nur in geringem Masse von orthodoxer Seite mitbestimmt wurde. Dabei ist der Wunschzettel, den Professor Parijskij aus Leningrad 1956 in Bonn vorgelegt hat, in starkem Masse berücksichtigt worden. Erklärlicherweise wurde die Lutherische Rechtfertigungslehre als der *articulus stantis et cadentis ecclesiae,* der den orthodoxen Teilnehmern meist unverständlich ist, auf deren Wunsch in den Vordergrund gestellt, während die andere Seite anfangs Fragen wie Schrift und Tradition geklärt haben wollte. Da die Voraussetzungen theologischer Art verschieden sind, angefangen von der Anthropologie, wird immer wieder bei der neutestamentlichen Heilslehre eingesetzt, wobei im Ergebnis jeweils die stärkere Betonung der paulinischen bzw. johanneischen Lehre herausspringt. Immerhin ist hier vom neutestamentlichen Ausgangspunkt her die grösste Aussicht der Verständigung gegeben, obwohl der patristische Kommentar wieder manche Verschiedenheit aufdeckt. Die Thematik braucht trotzdem nicht gleichbleibend zu sein. Wenn die genannten Gespräche von beiden Seiten als eine Einheit verstanden werden, so ist doch nicht zu bezweifeln, dass sich von Mal zu Mal ein grösseres Verständnis für die Gegenseite erschliesst.

Als Aufgabe der Gespräche wurde von deutscher Seite einmal die Orientierung, zum anderen die Zurkenntnisnahme der "gegenseitigen theologischen Entwicklung seit Abbruch der Beziehungen" bezeichnet. Statt "Abbruch" könnte ebenso "seit der Anknüpfung neuer Verbindungen" gesagt werden. Es ist klar, dass auf diesem Gebiet ein grosser

"theologischer Nachholbedarf" besteht. Die Gespräche sollten nicht nur
"exemplarisch" sein, sie müssen Möglichkeiten eröffnen.[19]

Auf Einzelheiten dieser Gespräche kann in unserem Zusammenhang
nicht eingegangen werden. Die Thematik ist erklärlicherweise weit.
Einen ähnlichen Verlauf wie der russisch-deutsche Dialog nahm auch der
der Russisch-orthodoxen mit der Finnisch-lutherischen Kirche. Die Zu-
sammenkünfte fanden in grösseren Abständen in Helsinki statt.

In diesem Bericht müssen auch die Kontakte erwähnt werden, die
zwischen dem Ökumenischen Patriarchen und der Evangelischen Kirche
in Deutschland bestehen. Diese haben dazu geführt, dass ein erstes
theologisches Gespräch im Phanar im März 1969 stattfand, in dem das
Hauptthema "Der Heilige Geist und die Kirche" behandelt wurde.[20]
Ein zweites Gespräch, das der Christologie gewidmet sein soll, steht
bevor. Die Erörterungen des 16. Jahrhunderts sind bei der Neuan-
knüpfung des theologischen Gesprächs bewusst erwähnt worden, obwohl
sie auf einer neuen Grundlage erfolgten und alle Missverständnisse nicht
fortleben lassen wollen.

Bei Verhandlungen zwischen Altkatholiken und russischen Orthodoxen
war für die Einigung von russischer Seite gefordert worden: Anerkennung
1. aller orthodoxen Dogmen und 2. des sakramentalen Priestertums.
Angesichts dieser Forderung, auf die der Protestantismus niemals eingehen kann, hat Ludolf Müller die Frage gestellt, ob es dann überhaupt
einen Sinn hätte, noch weiter zu verhandeln.[21] Er hat diese Frage trotzdem bejaht in der Annahme, dass im Gespräch sich manche Position
klären und das Verständnis ein anderes wird. Gerade wenn wir bedenken,
dass der Geist der Orthodoxie dem Protestantismus verwandt ist, wird
die Möglichkeit der Verständigung bejaht werden müssen. Dabei braucht
man kein Optimist zu sein. Der Weg der konfessionellen Verständigung
ist ein weiter und langwieriger Weg. Das vor Augen stehende Ziel ist
aber klar und kann denjenigen, die ihm mit vollem Ernst zustreben,
nicht entschwinden. Selbst wenn die Annäherung nur gering erscheinen
sollte und vor allem vielen, die mit Eifer daran arbeiten, zu langsam
geht, soll sie darum weder gering geachtet noch vernachlässigt werden.
Die Losung, die Patriarch Athenagoras ausgegeben hat, zuerst in den

---

[19]   Vgl. H. Schaeder, *Der deutsch-russische Dialog* (Zeitwende/Die neue Furche, 1967),
421-425. Die Berichte über Arnoldshain I-IV sind erschienen als Studienhefte 3-6,
hrsg. vom Aussenamt der EKiD im Luther-Verlag (Witten, 1961, 1964, 1967 und 1970).
[20]   Vgl. *Dialog des Glaubens und der Liebe*. Theologisches Gespräch zwischen dem
Ökumenischen Patriarchat von Konstantinopel und der EKiD 1969 (11. Beiheft zur
Ökumenischen Rundschau) (Stuttgart, 1970).
[21]   Vgl. L. Müller, *Orthodoxie und Protestantismus* in "Una Sancta" (1966), 53.

Dialog der Liebe einzutreten, um dann die Fragen des theologischen Verständnisses aufzunehmen, wird daher der einzig richtige und gangbare Weg sein. Im Gespräch der Konfessionen kommt auch manches auf die Personen an, die daran beteiligt sind. Sie sollten zwar ihren Standpunkt vertreten und nicht verwischen, aber sie sollen auch Geduld haben und vor allem nicht das ausschliessliche Recht für sich in Anspruch nehmen. An dieser Stelle wird der Segen nicht ausbleiben und für beide Seiten sich aus dem *mutuum colloquium* eine *consolatio fratrum* ergeben.

THE BRITISH NON-JURORS AND THE
RUSSIAN CHURCH

STEVEN RUNCIMAN

Of the various attempts made in the seventeenth and early eighteenth centuries to bring about closer union between the Orthodox and the Anglican Churches, the final and most protracted efforts were those made by two high ecclesiastics from the Patriarchate of Alexandria, Arsenios, Metropolitan of the Thebaid, and the Archimandrite Gennadios, and by leaders of the Non-Juring clergy in England and of the Episcopalian Church of Scotland. These negotiations were remarkable (1) because the Orthodox protagonists were dealing with unofficial elements in the Anglican Church, and (2) because both sides were anxious to involve the Orthodox Church of Russia.

The story of the negotiations is known to us almost entirely from English sources. There seems to be no reference to these discussions in Orthodox sources either at Constantinople or in Russia, except for the correspondence of Arsenios with his friend Chrysanthos, Patriarch of Jerusalem.[1] The letters exchanged between the British Non-Jurors, the Orthodox visitors, and the Patriarchate of Constantinople, with all the theological and ecclesiological details, are fully recorded by the leading Non-Juror, Thomas Brett. This manuscript, written in the hand of Brett's colleague, Alexander Jolly, later Bishop of Moray, was first published in 1845 in Lathbury's *History of the Non-Jurors* and republished in a fuller version in 1868 in Williams' *The Orthodox Church of the East in the XVIIIth Century*.[2] But parts of the story are not very clear, even though a little

---

[1] For Arsenios' correspondence see M. Constantinides, *The Greek Orthodox Church in London* (Oxford, 1933), 9-10.

[2] T. Lathbury, *History of the Non-Jurors* (London, 1845), 309-361. G. Williams, *The Orthodox Church of the East in the XVIIIth Century* (London, 1868), is entirely concerned with these negotiations. Some minor corrections to Williams' narrative are given in J. H. Overton, *The Non-Jurors: Their Lives, Principles and Writings* (London, 1902), 451 ff.

more light is thrown by the unpublished records of the Russian Church in London.[3]

Arsenios and Gennadios had come to London in the summer of 1714 in order to raise funds for the Patriarchate of Alexandria. The Patriarch, Samuel Capasoulis, had been obliged to raise vast sums in order to outbid an attempt by Cosmas, Archbishop of Sinai, to replace him on the throne, and as a result he was 30,000 dollars in debt. The prelates, who arrived accompanied by four deacons, a reader, and a cook, did not have a very easy or successful time. Arsenios did write in glowing terms to Chrysanthos of Jerusalem to say with what honour and respect he and Gennadios were treated. But in fact the Russian Church records report that they were at first suspected of being Roman Catholic spies, owing to a rumour put about, it was thought, by the Jesuits, and they had some difficulty in clearing themselves of the charge.[4] Arsenios and Gennadios were saved by making friends with Humphrey Wanley, the antiquary, who had recently retired from the post of Secretary to the Society for the Promotion of Christian Knowledge, and who was in a position to guarantee their respectability. Although Wanley's friendship may have promoted their acceptance, the money which they were able to raise was meagre. Bishop Robinson of London gave them 200 pounds out of Queen Anne's Bounty, and King George I added another 100 pounds. Robinson promised a further 100 pounds to be given to them when they should announce their departure from England.[5] This does not suggest that they were greatly welcomed by the Anglican establishment.

Meanwhile Arsenios busied himself on a more useful project. Nearly forty years earlier Joseph Georgirenes, Metropolitan of Samos, had succeeded in founding a Greek church in London, with the help of Henry Compton, then Bishop of London. But the church had been short-lived, owing to the hostility and, it must be confessed, the somewhat sharp practice of the Vicar of St. Martins-in-the-Fields in whose parish the church was situated. This was the era of Titus Oates and the Popish Plot. And in the militantly Protestant atmosphere prevalent in London at the time, the rich Orthodox ritual and the icons hanging in the church seemed suspiciously Papistical.[6] Now the growing Greek community

---

[3] I am deeply indebted to Mr. Igor Vinogradoff for having supplied me with a transcript, in Russian, of the relevant material from the unpublished Records of the Russian Church in London.

[4] Williams, lx-lxi; Constantinides, *loc. cit.*; and Records of the Russian Church in London which tell of the prelates' difficulties.

[5] Williams, *loc. cit.*

[6] A full and admirable account of the first Greek church in London, situated in

in London was more badly in need of a church than ever before. In 1717, Tsar Peter of Russia paused in Holland on his return from a state visit to Paris. Whether on his own initiative or as a result of instructions received from the East, Arsenios had previously been in touch with the Tsar, who had sent him 500 rubles. Arsenios, who had recently reported to Jerusalem that two members of Parliament had promised him help with the foundation of a Greek church, now chose to cross to Holland where he met and persuaded the Tsar to finance the building of a church in London and to give it his patronage. (The Tsar was at the moment on amicable terms with the British Government.) In this way the church was given a semi-diplomatic status which enabled it to survive. The first priest was Archimandrite Gennadios. When in 1731 a permanent Russian Embassy was established in London it became the official Embassy church, though it continued for several more decades to be served by Greek priests.[7]

Arsenios made contact with the Non-Jurors a year before his interview with Peter in Holland; and the first proposals of the Non-Jurors for establishing inter-communion between their body, which they claimed to represent the authentic Church in Britain, were sent off with his help to Constantinople in the spring of 1717.[8] That autumn a letter, dated 8 October and signed by the leading Non-Jurors, was sent to the Tsar. After referring to his well-known interest in unionist movements, it asked for his help. It seems safe to assume that the letter was written on Arsenios' advice, as a result of his interview in which he had tried to interest Peter in the projected union. The Tsar appears to have sent back a friendly but non-committal answer.[9]

The letter of the Non-Jurors seems to have been taken to Russia by the hand of Arsenios' attendant, the Pro-Syncellos James, who had followed the Tsar there presumably to arrange for a visit by Arsenios to the Russian Court. Here again it is uncertain whether this proposed visit was the result of instructions from the East or whether Arsenios was acting on his own initiative. When he departed from London is unknown, but by 1721 he was living in St. Petersburg. Before Arsenios'

Hog Lane (now St. Martin's Lane), is given in the Greater London Council, *Survey of London* XXXIII (London, 1966), 278-287. This is based on Georgirenes' own manuscript, from the Public Record Office, the Journal of the House of Lords, the Westminster Public Library, the Historical Manuscripts Commission collection, the Bodleian, and other sources.

[7]   Records of the Russian Church in London.

[8]   Williams, 3-11.

[9]   Lathbury, 318-319; Williams, 12-14.

departure, he arranged that the Patriarch's reply to the proposals of the Non-Jurors be sent to him for transmission to them. The result now was that though the Patriarch dated his letter 12 April (O.S.), 1718, it was not until the autumn of 1721 that the letter, with a covering note from Arsenios, dated 18 August, 1721, reached London also by the hand of James the Pro-Syncellos.[10]

The patriarchal reply, though polite in tone, was unyielding on various matters of theology so that some of the Non-Jurors felt that it was useless to continue with the negotiations. But Brett and his friends were determined to try again. They wrote a treatise explaining their viewpoint in greater detail. This document, dated 29 May, 1722, was sent in multi-copy to Arsenios with the request that he give copies to the Tsar and to the Synod of the Russian Church. Other letters asking for co-operation, dated 30 May, were sent directly to the Synod and to the Imperial Grand Chancellor, Count Golovkin (whom they called Galowskin). The Pro-Syncellos once again acted as courier, and on 9 September wrote to announce his safe arrival in Russia. Three months later, on 9 December, Arsenios wrote London that their letter had been forwarded to the Patriarch and copies had been delivered to the Russian addressees, who expressed favourable interest. For once he was not indulging in wishful thinking. In February, 1723, the Archbishop of Novgorod wrote in the name of the Russian Synod to invite the Non-Jurors to send two of their number to Russia for fuller discussions.[11]

Since the Russian Church, because of the abolition of the Muscovite Patriarchate, was now entirely dependent on the Tsar, it is relevant to ask why did Peter consider the negotiations worth pursuing? The answer lies in the political situation at the time. For some years Peter had been on very bad terms with the British Government; but as British trade was most important to Russia, Britain being Russia's best customer, he was always at pains to maintain, even if a little clumsily, that his quarrel was not with the British people but with King George I in his role of Elector of Hanover. Peter probably shared with other European statesmen, such as Alberoni, the belief that the Jacobites were a far stronger force in Britain than in fact they were. His Scottish physician, Robert Erskine, had considerable influence over him and was often visited by Jacobite relations and friends, such as Sir Harry Stirling. Erskine him-

[10]   Lathbury, 319-335; Williams, 15-83.
[11]   Lathbury, 346-347; Williams, 134-135. For Archbishop Fiodosij Ianovskij of Novgorod, who was Senior Vice-President of the Russian Synod, see I. Smolitsch, *Geschichte des Russischen Kirche* I (Leiden, 1964), 121-123, and 223.

self had in the past been a useful ally to British representatives and was a good friend of Admiral Norris, the commander of the British fleet in the Baltic, and, despite rumours to the contrary, always himself kept clear of Jacobite intrigues. But Erskine's visitors could well have persuaded the Tsar that they represented a considerable section of British opinion; and Peter was aware that the Non-Jurors were essentially anti-Hanoverian in their sympathies. By encouraging the Non-Jurors, Tsar Peter clearly believed that he would be able to show sympathy to an important group in British religious circles while at the same time embarrassing King George's government.[12]

Unfortunately the Non-Jurors were not able to do what was required of them. They had kept all their negotiations secret — it would have been asking for trouble if any of their leading members were known to be intending a visit to Russia. Consequently they hoped that a secret journey might be arranged, and wrote to Arsenios to ask him to allow his cousin, Bartholomew Cassano, who was still in England, to accompany their delegates as interpreter. But the months passed: and it became ever clearer that it was going to be very difficult to find delegates willing and able to go on such a mission. In July, 1724, they wrote to Arsenios to apologize to him and to the Russian Synod for the delay.[13]

It is probable that the Non-Jurors had already begun to despair of the negotiations. They had just received from Constantinople a copy of the *Confession of Dositheus*, with a letter signed by each of the Orthodox Patriarchs stating that the *Confession* contained his considered beliefs and that there could be no further discussion on theological issues. As the *Confession* contained clear statements in favour of the two main points that the Non-Jurors could not accept without modification, transubstantiation and the honour to be paid to saints and icons, it was hard to see how negotiations could proceed further. Even so the Non-Jurors still hoped that under Peter's influence the Russian Church might be less intransigent. But then there came the news that Peter had died

---

[12]   For Anglo-Russian relations at the time, see L. A. Nikoforow, *Russisch-Englische Beziehungen unter Peter I*, trans. W. Müller (Weimar, 1954), which includes a summary of the Russian state documents (cf. especially pp. 245 ff. and 303 ff.). For the part played by Robert Erskine and by the Jacobites, see E. Schuyler, *Peter the Great, Emperor of Russia* II (London, 1884), 377-379, 387, and 519 ff.; also J. F. Chance, *George I and the Northern War*, especially 93, 165-166, 269, and 285-286; and "George I and Peter the Great After the Peace of Nystad", *English Historical Review* XXVI (1911), 278 ff. None of the sources used by these authors makes any mention of ecclesiastical negotiations; and I am not aware of any Russian ecclesiastical sources that do mention them.

[13]   Lathbury, 350-352.

in January, 1725. New to power, his successor, his widow Catherine, was in no position to pursue a policy that might lead to international complications. The Russian Synod showed no further interest.[14]

About the same time Thomas Payne, the Levant Company's chaplain at Constantinople, learnt from the Patriarchate of these negotiations and reported his information to Archbishop Wake of Canterbury. In September, 1725, the Archbishop had occasion to write to Chrysanthos of Jerusalem to thank him for sending a copy of Adam Zoernikoff's work on the Dual Procession to the University of Oxford; at the same time, knowing the Patriarch to be a friend of Arsenios, he added a stern paragraph pointing out that Arsenios and his colleagues had been intriguing with a small and schismatic group in Britain which in no way represented the Anglican Church. He promised that his "faithful presbyter, Thomas Payne", would inform the Patriarch of the true position in England.[15]

The Eastern Patriarchs had in fact never been greatly interested in the negotiations. At no time had they been willing to make any compromise to oblige the Non-Jurors. The almost complete silence that followed from Russia after the overtures of the Non-Jurors in 1722 made it clear that the Russian interest had been purely political and inspired by the Tsar's government. Arsenios seems to have returned to Egypt under a cloud, though we may hope that he brought with him some money for the Patriarchate of Alexandria. All that he had achieved was to reestablish a Greek church in London; but this church, discreetly financed from Russian sources, kept so quiet that practically nothing is known of it. His intrigues with the Non-Jurors had not been helpful for Anglican-Orthodox relations. The general temper of the Anglican Church in the eighteenth century was not sympathetic to the creed and the ritual of Orthodoxy; and the episode only served to strengthen its prejudices against what the Anglicans regarded as the superstitions of the East. It was only the Episcopalian Church of Scotland which maintained any interest in Orthodoxy;[16] but that body was in no position to suggest any further ecclesiastical connections with the Patriarchates. The entrance of the Russian Church into the negotiations had been futile, though

---

[14] Lathbury, 355-356; Williams, pp. xxxvii-xxxviii.
[15] Williams, pp. xxxviii-xxxix.
[16] Mr. Scott-Charles, the Librarian of the Aberdeen & Orkney Diocesan Library, has had the kindness to inform me of two Scottish bishops of the time, Rattray and Abernethy Drummond, who were in touch with Orthodox Eastern ecclesiastics, but whose papers are in private hands and inaccessible. The Scottish Episcopalian Church has always shown a considerable sympathy with Orthodox theology, as its Prayer Book of 1929 bears witness.

in the long run it may have served some use in drawing Anglican attention to that great Church. For when in the nineteenth century there were new attempts to bring Anglicanism and Orthodoxy closer together, it was towards Russia that Anglican protagonists made their first advances.

ÉGLISE DE PIERRE, ÉGLISE DE PAUL, ÉGLISE DE JEAN
DESTIN D'UN THÈME OECUMÉNIQUE

YVES M.-J. CONGAR, O.P.

La *Courte Relation sur l'Antéchrist* (1900) est le dernier écrit de Vladimir Solov'ev.[1] A cette époque et depuis dix ou onze ans, Solov'ev se voyait déçu dans son rêve de libre théocratie. Il avait dessiné le programme d'une union du prophétisme, qu'avait exalté l'Ancien Testament, du sacerdoce, qui avait dominé l'Occident catholique, et de la royauté vivante dans les empereurs orthodoxes de Byzance, puis de Russie.[2] Il avait songé à une union de l'Orthodoxie et du Catholicisme, dans *La Russie et l'Eglise universelle* (1882). Les difficultés étaient venues. Il voyait monter les périls du matérialisme, du moralisme adogmatique (L. Tolstoj), du démonisme du surhomme nietzschéen. Il ne croyait plus à la réalisation de l'idéal théocratique dans les limites de l'histoire. Une vision apocalyptique et eschatologique s'imposait à son esprit, comme jadis aux Juifs de l'époque exilique. Dans son dernier écrit, il imaginait qu'un moine, Pansophius, avait laissé un récit anticipé des événements catastrophiques de la fin.

Un surhomme avait fondé un empire universel de paix et de prospérité. La chrétienté était réduite à 45 millions de fidèles. La papauté avait trouvé refuge à Saint-Pétersburg et s'était purifiée de ses prétentions de puissance, tandis que ce qui restait du protestantisme s'était guéri de sa négativité critique. L'empereur avait réuni un concile au cours duquel il voulait se faire proclamer le maître également de la religion. Y prenaient

---

[1] Nous suivons la traduction française d'E. Tavernier, ami de Solov'ev, in *Trois Entretiens* (Paris, 1916), 171-217. Etude du thème chez Solov'ev: B. Schultze, *Vladimir Soloviev e i tre principi nella Chiesa*, in *La Civilta Cattolica*, anno 101 (1950), III, 37-52. Du même encore, *Die Schau der Kirche bei Nicolai Berdiajew*, in *Orientalia christ. Anal.* 116 (Rome, 1938), 189-195, *Drei Principien in der Kirche*.

[2] Voir *Le peuple juif et le peuple chrétien* (1884); *La question slave* (1884); *L'histoire et l'avenir de la Théocratie* (1er volume seul paru) (1885-1887). Déjà en 1877, dans *Les trois forces*, il avait vu la vocation de la Russie dans l'union ou la synthèse des forces religieuses dispersées, la séparation ou la dissociation lui apparaissant comme le plus grand mal.

part le pape Pierre II, le starec Jean, le professeur Ernst Pauli, représentant et typifiant les trois grandes branches du christianisme. Le pape et le starec s'opposant à la prétention de l'imposteur tombaient foudroyés. Mais Ernst Pauli reprenait leur profession de foi, la signait en leur nom et emportait leurs corps, comme des reliques, dans le désert de Jéricho. Là, ils revenaient à la vie et les trois, Pierre, Jean et Paul s'embrassaient et s'unissaient peu avant le retour du Fils de l'homme au devant duquel ils conduisaient le petit troupeau demeuré fidèle et définitivement réuni.

La personne de l'imposteur, la localisation de la réunion dans la région du jeûne et des tentations du Christ, évoquent irrésistiblement la Légende du Grand Inquisiteur. Nous allons voir que Solov'ev a pu mettre en œuvre d'autres réminiscences. Il a eu aussi, sinon des imitateurs, du moins des successeurs. D. S. Merežkovskij participait sans doute au courant libéral de la critique néotestamentaire, dans une ligne modernisante. Il annonçait une nouvelle Eglise, non plus de Pierre ou de Jean, mais vraiment universelle, une Eglise de l'amour et de la liberté, où se fondraient les formes actuelles du christianisme, orthodoxe, catholique et protestante.[3] Par contre ce fut un slavophile authentique, Allemand de naissance et Letton d'adoption, W. Schubart, qui, en 1938, reprit l'inspiration de Dostoevskij et de Solov'ev; il annonçait un âge de Jean, messianique, où seraient dépassés l'homme gothique, médiéval, et l'homme prométhéen moderne.[4] L'homme russe, porteur de ce messianisme johannique, riche d'intériorité et d'amour, une fois libéré de l'athéisme bolchévique, apporterait à l'Europe ce souffle qui renouvellerait le monde.

Des rêves d'un dépassement et d'une synthèse de Pierre, de Paul et de Jean, ont été exprimés parfois dans les débuts du Mouvement oecuménique: ainsi par l'archevêque luthérien d'Upsal Nathan Söderblom et par son disciple le professeur Friedrich Heiler.[5] Même un auteur juif comme Franz Rosenzweig pensait alors que l'Eglise de Pierre, où il voyait l'Eglise de l'Amour, et celle de Paul, qui est l'Eglise de la foi, appelaient le complément d'une Eglise de l'Espérance, qu'il attribuait à

---

[3] Cf. *Actes du Congrès religioso-philosophique de Pétrograd* (Pétrograd, 1906); cf. M. Jugie, *Theologia dogmatica Christian. Oriental.*, T. IV (Paris, 1931), 481.

[4] *Europa und die Seele des Ostens*. Version fr. *L'Europe et l'âme de l'Orient*. Trad. D. Moyrand et N. Nicolski (Paris, 1949).

[5] Nathan Söderblom exprimait cette idée, non sans quelque inspiration syncrétiste, dans le discours de clôture de la Conférence de "Life and Work" à Stokholm, 1925. Cf. *The Stockholm Conference* (1925), ed. G. K. A. Bell, 741; *Le Christianisme social* (oct.-nov. 1925), 1125 et Fr. Heiler, *Evangelische Katholizität* (*Ges. Aufsätze*, I) (Munich, 1926), 249, 258 s., 310-311.

Jean mais dont le principe était selon lui porté par le peuple juif.[6] Ces
mêmes rêves avaient déjà hanté plus d'un esprit au XIXe siècle.

M. D. Stremoukov pense que Solov'ev a pu tenir de K. Golovin l'idée
de typifier les trois formes majeures de christianisme en la personne des
Apôtres Pierre, Paul et Jean.[7] Il ajoute avec raison que l'idée était d'ailleurs peu originale. On la trouve en effet développée chez Schelling, et
peut-être même, avant lui, esquissée chez Fichte.[8] Or l'influence de
Schelling sur la pensée russe du XIXe siècle, et singulièrement sur celle
des Slavophiles, est un fait bien connu.[9] L'époque aimait les interpréta-
tions et les constructions philosophiques de l'histoire, usant du procédé
de typification. Dans la 37e leçon de sa *Philosophie der Offenbarung*
(1842)[10] Schelling aborde l'interprétation de la Réforme. Pierre est celui
qui donne la loi, il est le principe stable. Paul est le mouvement, la
dialectique, la science. Il a été le premier protestant, par sa résistance à
une autorité illimitée de Pierre: le chapître II des Galates est la *Magna
Charta* du protestantisme. L'Eglise véritable ne consiste dans aucune de
ces deux formes telles quelles mais, à partir du fondement posé en Pierre,
elle s'avance, par le moyen de Paul, vers sa fin qui est de devenir une
Eglise de Jean.[11] Catholicisme et protestantisme ne sont que des formes
de transition de l'unique Eglise véritable, qui doit advenir.

Ces idées connurent un assez grand succès.[12] Elles trouvaient un certain

[6] Fr. Rosenzweig, *Der Stern der Erlösung* (Francfort, 1921). F. Fuchs (in *Rev. des
Jeunes*, 25-I-1927, p. 181) signale une vision messianique analogue chez Hans
Ehrenberg.

[7] *Vladimir Soloviev et son œuvre messianique* (= *Public. de la Fac. des Lettres de
l'Univ. de Strasbourg*, 69) (Paris, 1935), 291, n. 51.

[8] Dans les fragments d'un écrit de l'hiver 1806-1807 (*Die Republik der Deutschen zu
Anfang des zwei-u.-zwanzigsten Jahrhunderts unter ihrem funften Reichsvogte: Sämtl.
Werke*, Bd. VII), Fichte projetait une Constitution qui, reconnaissant les trois
Confessions, en admettait une nouvelle à laquelle se rallieraient tous les esprits libres
et qui, avec le temps, deviendrait la religion nationale; elle s'appellerait celle des
"chrétiens universels": cf. S. Léon, *Fichte et son temps*, T. II, 2e partie (Paris, 1927),
84-85.

[9] Cf. W. Setschkareff, *Schellings Einfluss in der russischen Literatur der 20er u. 30er
Jahre des XIX. Jahrhunderts* (Leipzig, 1939); A. Gratieux, *A. S. Khomiakov et le
Mouvement slavophile*, I, *Les hommes* (= *Unam Sanctam*, 5) (Paris, 1939), 71.

[10] Schelling, *Sämtliche Werke*, II. Abteilg., IV. Bd. (2. Hälfte, 1858), 298-344.

[11] "Hätte ich in unserer Zeit eine Kirche zu bauen, ich würde sie dem hl. Johannes
widmen. Aber früher oder später wird sie gebaut werden, die die drei Apostelfürsten,
Petrus, Paulus, Johannes vereinigt, da die letzte Potenz die frühere nicht aufhebt oder
ausschliesst, sondern sie verklärend in sich aufnimmt. Diese würde dann das wahre
Pantheon der christlichen Kirchengeschichte sein." Schelling, *Sämtliche Werke*.

[12] On les trouvera discutées encore à notre époque, du point de vue de la dualité
catholicisme-protestantisme, par L. Lambinet, *Das Wesen des katholisch-protestan-
tischen Gegensatzes. Ein Beitrag zum gegenseitigen Verstehen*, Geleitwort v. R. Grosche

parallélisme dans les vues de F. Ch. Baur sur l'enchaînement des textes et des thèmes dans la littérature néotestamentaire.[13] Bien sûr, Baur venait d'un tout autre horizon, il opérait avec des schèmes hégéliens. On ne peut faire avec lui qu'un rapprochement. Par contre, on trouvera dans Döllinger toute une documentation groupant les noms, aujourd'hui assez oubliés, d'hommes politiques ou d'hommes d'Eglise allemands qui, dans les années 1848-1858, se sont référés au thème de Pierre, Paul et Jean comme signifiant trois moments successifs dont le dernier serait une *Zukunftkirche* johannique.[14] Il cite ainsi les professeurs Piper à la Diète de Stuttgart en 1857, Merz,[15] Ullmann,[16] et enfin le ministre de l'instruction publique et des Cultes de Prusse, von Bethmann Hollweg, en 1858. "Aux apôtres Pierre et Paul, qui ont eu l'un et l'autre leur temps dans l'histoire de l'Eglise, doit succéder Jean", déclarait celui-ci. C'est le thème schellingien. Döllinger était plus sobre. Il préconisait une réforme des catholiques et des protestants, mais finalement une union de tous dans une Eglise catholique rénovée. Il faisait une place aux Eglises orthodoxes, sans les comprendre dedans. Mais il est notable qu'assez souvent, à cette époque, on pense au catholicisme et au protestantisme, peu à l'Orthodoxie. Tel est encore le cas du pasteur L. Stählin qui, au lendemain du premier concile du Vatican et dans le climat des idées unioniques de Döllinger, reprenait, en les modifiant quelque peu, les idées de Schelling.[17] C'était de l'unionisme, ce n'était pas encore l'Oecuménisme. L'idée de Schelling avait également plu au Père Hecker quand, avant sa conversion, il aspirait à servir la réalisation du règne de Dieu. A travers Schelling chez qui les Slavophiles avaient déjà vu une approche de l'Orthodoxie,

---

(Einsiedeln-Köln, 1946), 137 s.; discussion de Schelling et de Erwin Reiser dans *Die Kirche des Kreuzes u. das deutsche Schicksal* (München, 1934), et dans *Die christl. Botschaft im Wandel der Epochen* (München, 1935, et qui), 160 s., y ajoute une discussion des vues de F. Heiler.

[13]   Bauer voyait l'histoire du christianisme primitif sous le signe de l'opposition entre un judéo-christianisme pétrinien et un pagano-christianisme paulinien, qui était surmontée dans le johannisme. Ou encore la tendance de Matthieu, puis celle de Luc, synthétisée en Jean (préparé par Marc). Dans l'histoire de l'Eglise, Baur distinguait la période d'avant la Réforme (âge d'auto-affirmation de l'Eglise), celle d'après la Réforme (négation: l'Eglise se perd dans le monde), et l'âge présent, "die dritte höhere Zeit der Kirche". Cf. K. Barth, *Die protestantische Theologie im 19. Jahrhundert* (Zollikon-Zurich, 1947), 456.

[14]   J. J. I. Döllinger, *L'Eglise et les Eglises*, trad. fr. A. Bayle (Paris, 1862), 348-351. L'ouvrage est de 1861. Signalons la réaction de M. J. Scheeben, *Die Hl.-Geist-oder-Johannes-Kirche nach Döllinger*, in *Pastoral Blätter* 2 (1872), Regensburg.

[15]   *Armut und Christentum*, 88.

[16]   *Wesen des Christentums* (Hambourg, 1849).

[17]   L. Stählin, *Katholizismus und Protestantismus. Darstellung und Erläuterung der kirchengeschichtlichen Ansicht Schellings* (Augsburg, 1873).

Hecker avait compris l'idéal de la *Sobornost'*.[18]

Schelling lui-même avait indiqué une source de son idée:[19] le célèbre Abbé calabrais du XIIe siècle Joachim de Flore († 1202): les idées joachimites connaissaient alors une certaine faveur dans le climat du mythe du progrès répandu depuis la fin du XVIIIe siècle.[20] La pensée de Joachim est essentiellement typologique et symbolique. Or les symboles n'étant pas une définition mais un signe de la réalité, ils sont susceptibles de s'appliquer, sous différents angles, à des réalités diverses. C'est pourquoi, chez Joachim, ils se chevauchent sans pourtant se contredire, mais également sans qu'on puisse exposer sa pensée selon une logique linéaire simple.

C'est en méditant sur l'Apocalypse que Joachim a perçu le principe de tout son système. Il ne s'agit pas seulement pour lui d'une concordance typologique entre l'Ancien et le Nouveau Testament, telle qu'on en trouvait une dans toute l'éxégèse patristique et médiévale. Selon lui, l'Evangile lui-même est annonciateur, et la concordance se poursuit entre l'Ancien et le Nouveau Testament d'un côté, l'histoire de l'Eglise de l'autre. C'est ainsi que Joachim parvient à son idée de trois âges rapportés respectivement au Père, au Fils et au Saint-Esprit: le Nouveau Testament lui-même est prophétique; le Christ cèdera la place au Saint-Esprit. Le deuxième âge de cette économie trinitaire, qui va de l'Incarnation jusqu'en 1260, connaît déjà une typologie de Pierre et de Jean, sous la forme de l'Eglise d'Occident, représentée en Pierre et Jean-Baptiste, et de l'Eglise d'Orient, représentée en Jean l'Evangéliste et la Vierge Marie.[21] Joachim connaissait l'Eglise grecque: il était en contact avec elle dans le sud de la Péninsule; plusieurs de ses thèmes, en théologie trinitaire par exemple, se ressentent d'une influence grecque. Joachim avait pour les Grecs de l'affection et de l'estime, ce qui ne l'empêchait pas de les critiquer, de les considérer comme séparés de l'Eglise romaine et devant revenir à son

---

[18]   Voir *La vie du Père Hecker*, par N. Elliott, trad. fr. (Paris, 1897), 70; Ch. Maignen-*Le Père Hecker est-il un saint?* (Paris, 1898), 167.

[19]   Schelling, *Sämtliche Werke*, II. Abteilg., IV. Bd. (2. Hälfte, 1858), 298 n.

[20]   Lessing s'y était référé dans *Die Erziehung des Menschengeschlechts* (1780). Selon lui, le tort de Joachim avait été d'annoncer l'âge de l'esprit comme prochain, alors qu'il se réalise lentement.

[21]   "Voluit Deus esse duplicem Ecclesiam, Orientalem scilicet atque Occidentalem, ut, misso Petro summo pontifice ad occidentalem Ecclesiam, confirmaret in ea ecclesias, ticum seu sacerdotalem ordinem quem designat Ioannes (le Baptiste), et misso Ioanne evangelista, castitatis speculo, ad Ecclesiam orientalem, confirmaret in ea virginalem et castam religionem quam designat Maria. Siquidem ut magisterium oraedicationis Romae, ita doctrina monasticae atque eremeticae professionis in Ecclesia orientali noscitur accepisse exordium": *Tractatus super quatuor Evangelia* (ed. E. Buonaiuti, Rome, 1930), 33; comp. 38, 1.12; 178-179; 232; 281.

unité.[22] Joachim lui-même était absolument loyal à l'égard de l'autorité papale, et il avait à la Curie, non seulement de solides appuis, mais des admirateurs et une réelle influence.

Une autre typologie de Pierre et de Jean s'ajoute chez Joachim à la précédente. Elle ne se situe plus dans le cadre du deuxième âge, mais dans le rapport entre le deuxième, âge du Fils, et le troisième, âge du Saint-Esprit. Elle se rattache à une tradition bien connue en Occident depuis S. Augustin, voyant en Pierre le type de la vie active et en Jean celui de la vie contemplative. Augustin se demandait d'abord comment apprécier la situation respective de Pierre, qui aimait le Christ plus que les autres disciples, et de Jean, que le Christ aimait plus que les autres.[23] Augustin traite la question avec une délicatesse et une profondeur que ne trahissent ni son style ni sa rhétorique. La question se résoud si l'on voit en Pierre la figure de la vie active ou de l'Eglise en tant qu'elle lutte ici-bas contre le péché et le mal pour s'en libérer; en Jean, par contre, la figure de la contemplation qui commence bien ici-bas, mais durera au-delà du temps présent et même s'épanouira pleinement dans l'éternité:[24] de même, pour lui, Marthe et Marie représentent deux grandes orientations de vie qui se partagent le même homme. C'est une même et unique Eglise qu'Augustin voit représentée en Pierre et Jean, une même Eglise qui existe à la fois sur terre dans les difficultés, et au ciel dans la paix. Augustin dit expressément que les deux apôtres sont à la fois ce que signifie Pierre et ce que signifie Jean.[25] On a cependant volontiers retenu de son admirable texte, non seulement la représentation de l'action et de la contemplation respectivement par Pierre et par Jean, mais l'idée que la première cesserait alors que la seconde durerait et même s'épanouirait pleinement quand le temps de la première serait passé.

C'est dans cette ligne que se situe Joachim, mais en changeant profondément la pensée de S. Augustin. Pour lui comme pour l'évêque d'Hippone, Pierre et Jean représentent respectivement la vie active et la

---

[22]   Cf. P. Fournier, *Etudes sur Joachim de Flore et ses doctrines* (Paris, 1909), 27 et 29, n. 2. Cette étude est évidemment dépassée. La bibliographie sur Joachim, qui s'accroît d'année en année, est énorme. Nous n'avons pas à l'indiquer ici. Exposé très documenté de l'interprétation scripturaire de l'Abbé calabrais dans H. de Lubac, *Exégèse médiévale. Les quatre sens de l'Ecriture* II/1 (= *Théologie*, 42) (Paris, 1961), 437-558. Sur l'attitude de Joachim à l'égard de l'Eglise grecque, p. 475.

[23]   *Tractatus CXXIV in Ioannis Evang.* 4 (PL 35, col. 1971-1972).

[24]   *Tractatus CXXIV in Ioannis Evang.* 5, col. 1972-1975.

[25]   *Tractatus CXXIV in Ioannis Evang.* 7, col. 1975-1976: "Nemo tamen istos insignes apostolos separet. Et in eo quod significabat Petrus, ambo erant; et in eo quod significabat Ioannes, ambo futuri erant (...) Nec ipsi soli, sed universa hoc facit Ecclesia sponsa Christi ..." etc.

vie contemplative, mais celle-ci est dite devoir durer après celle-là, cela signifie, pour Joachim, la succession du troisième au second. Ce sera l'Eglise de l'Esprit, dans laquelle les *pii sacerdotes* ou *pii pastores*, dont Pierre aura été le chef, feront place aux *boni claustrales, boni eremitae*, dans la ligne de Jean.[26] Cela ne signifie pas que les structures de l'Eglise que l'on aura connues dans le deuxième âge seront totalement abolies: pour Joachim, à la différence des Spirituels qui se réclameront de lui au XIIIe siècle, la papauté existera encore dans l'âge de l'Esprit, mais ce sera une papauté elle-même spirituelle, comme tout sera spirituel, en particulier l'intelligence des choses. A cela se rattache l'attente d'un *papa angelicus*, dont l'idée et l'espérance ont continué de s'exprimer jusqu'à nos jours.[27]

L'idée d'attribuer la présence de Jean à l'Orient et celle de Pierre à l'Occident ou du moins à Rome répondait trop bien à la nature des choses pour n'avoir jamais été exprimée avant Joachim. Le témoignage le plus remarquable à cet égard est sans doute celui du concile d'Aix-la-Chapelle en 836, parce qu'il fait une place également au troisième "Grand", à savoir à Paul, auquel il ne peut assigner un lieu particulier.[28] Le problème de la part respective de Pierre et de Jean dans l'autorité de l'Eglise romaine s'est trouvé posé à divers moments de l'histoire.[29] Celui de la position de l'apôtre Jean vis-à-vis de Pierre avait été parfois évoqué et il le sera encore après Joachim par les grands docteurs du XIIIe siècle:[30] il a une incontestable portée ecclésiologique. Il a préoccupé tout près de nous encore le Père Sergej Bulgakov.[31] Ce n'est pas exactement

---

[26] H. de Lubac, 455. Cf. Joachim, *Liber introductorius in Apocalypsim* (Venise, 1527), c. 9, fol. 12, et c. 19, fol. 17, "De vita activa designata in Petro et de contemplativa designata in Ioanne"; *Tractatus super quator Evang.*, éd. citée, 121; *Expos. in Apocalypsim*, pars IV, c. 14: ed. Venise 1527, fol. 17ᵛ-19ʳ, 48ʳ-50ᵛ, 62ʳ-63ᵛ, 170; *Liber concordiae* (Venise, 1519), fol. 18ʳ, 109ᵛ; *Liber figurarum* (dont nous admettons l'authenticité): cf. L. Tondelli, *Il libro delle Figure dell'Abate Gioachino da Fiore* I (Torino, 2e éd., 1953), 49 s., 156 s., et 164, 166; II, Tavole, tabl. IV, 1; V, VI et XX.
[27] Cf. Fr. Baethgen, *Der Engelpapst* (Halle, 1933), 38, 81 s.; Fr. Heiler, *Der Katholizismus, seine Idee u. seine Erscheinung* (München, 1923), 324-340; id., *Altkirche Autonomie und päpstlicher Zentralismus* (München, 1941), 386-393.
[28] Per beatum videlicet Petrum apostolorum principem in occiduis, per beatum vero Johannem apostolum et evangelistam in Orientis, id est Asiae, partibus, per beatum etiam Paulus in tota generaliter mundi latitudine fundata ...": *Mon. Germ. Hist. Concilia* II, 733.
[29] Voir Y.-M. Congar, *Saint Paul et l'autorité de l'Eglise romaine d'après la Tradition* (= *Acta Studiorum Paulinorum. Congressus internationalis catholicus*) (Rome, 1961), 491-516.
[30] Voir appendice en fin du présent article.
[31] Sergej Bulgakov, *Svv. Petr i Ioann, dva pervoapostola* (Paris, YMCA Press, 1926), 91 pages.

notre thème qui se trouve abordé là. Nous en rapprochons, par contre, avec Innocent III et Grégoire IX, chez lesquels il n'est pas téméraire de soupçonner une réminiscence de Joachim.

Le texte d'Innocent III se situe à l'un des moments les plus sombres des relations entre l'Orient et l'Occident, celui de la quatrième croisade et de la prise de Constantinople par les croisés. Le pape qui n'a pas approuvé cette action, prend acte du fait accompli: il mesure ce qu'il croit en être les avantages et les possibilités. Il y voit une occasion de rétablir l'unité. C'est dans cet état d'esprit qu'il écrit aux évêques, abbés et clercs de l'armée des croisés.[32] Il développe une argumentation subtile et serrée tout à la fois, à partir des personnages typiques de Marie Madeleine, qui représente la Synagogue, Pierre qui est le principe romain d'unité, et Jean, qui figure le peuple grec.[33] Paul n'intervient pas dans cette typologie. Notons en passant le sens assez remarquable qu'a le pape du génie romain d'unité et de commandement et du sens johannique et oriental de la pluralité des Eglises de Dieu. Pierre et Jean courent tous deux au sépulcre (Jean 20, 4): ils ont reçu l'un et l'autre l'annonce de Marie Madeleine, c'est à dire de la Synagogue. Mais Jean court plus vite: les Grecs ont reçu l'Evangile les premiers et ont compris d'abord "*humanitas Christi mysteria*", mais "*nisi forte per pauci*", il n'ont pas parfaitement pénétré le mystère de sa divinité; c'est pourquoi Jean voit les bandelettes qui entouraient le corps et, à part, enroulé (non déployé), le suaire qui recouvrait la tête.[34] Pierre, par contre ... A partir de là, Innocent développe toute une théologie trinitaire à la lumière de l'amour des divines Personnes les unes pour les autres, ce qui l'amène à justifier le *Filioque*. Il conclut qu'un jour, prochain croit-il sans doute en raison des événements, Jean "*videbit quod Petrus viderat et credet quod credit Ecclesia Latinorum, ut amodo simul ambulent in domo domini cum consensu*".[35] Marie Madeleine, qui reste pour l'instant en dehors, croira aussi à la fin.[36]

La lettre de Grégoire IX dont il nous faut dire un mot, se situe dans

---

[32] *Reg.* VII, 154, le 13 novembre 1204: Potthast 2324; PL 215, col. 456 s.

[33] "Sicut per Mariam Magdalenam Judaeorum intelligitur Synagoga, ita per Petrum qui ad Latinos est specialiter destinatus, et apud eos Romae sepulturam accepit, populus intelligitur Latinorum. Graecorum vero populus per Joannem, qui missus est ad Graecos, Ephesi tandem in Domino requievit. Petrus unam construxit Ecclesiam, videlicet Ecclesiarum omnium unum caput. Unde Dominus dixit ei: "*Tu es Petrus ...* (Mt. 16). Joannes autem in Asia plures Ecclesias stabilivit, tamquam unius capitis multa membra" (*Reg.* VII, col. 457 B).

[34] *Reg.* VII, col. 458 A.

[35] *Reg.* VII, col. 459 D.

[36] *Reg.* VII, col. 459 D-460 A.

la suite des efforts entrepris pour convaincre les Grecs sous l'impulsion à la fois de l'empereur grec Jean III Vataztes et de la papauté. Une ambassade pontificale composée de deux franciscains (Haymon de Faversham, Rodolphe de Reims) et de deux dominicains (Pierre de Cézanne et Hugues) fut envoyée à Constantinople en 1233.[37] Grégoire IX le recommandait par la lettre qui nous intéresse, adressée au patriarche Germain II.[38] Le pape compare d'abord le schisme grec au schisme des dix tribus du Nord, auxquelles Dieu a donné cependant les grands prophètes Elie et Elisée ... Puis le pape fait une application assez inattendue de l'épisode de Jean et de Pierre courant au sépulcre au matin de Pâques, à la célébration eucharistique, soit avec du pain fermenté, soit avec du pain azyme. Par un curieux renversement de la perspective qui nous est plus coutumière, le pape rattachait le mode grec de célébrer à la passibilité propre à l'Incarnation, celui des latins à la glorification pascale ... Les deux rites peuvent se réclamer d'un apôtre: les Grecs de Jean, les Latins de Pierre.[39] Mais de toute façon, après la transsubstantiation, il n'est plus question de pain levé ou de pain azyme, mais seulement du Pain vivant! Et Grégoire de conclure: "Utinam et tu tandem aliquando iuniorem discipulus qui vidit et credidit, secutus introeas: ut omnibus, nobiscum vere psallas illud Davidicum: *Ecce quam bonum et quam iucundum habitare fratres in unum!*"[40]

La position de Grégoire IX était intéressante: sur un point qui avait suscité des controverses sans issue, il professait que les deux positions étaient légitimes et qu'elles pouvaient se réclamer des Apôtres. Lors de la conférence de Nymphaion (27 mars au 8 mai 1234), la question des azymes fut abordée. De part et d'autre dominaient une attitude plutôt polémique et une certaine méfiance. Les Grecs ne voulaient rien concéder, mais le passage de la lettre du pape sur la dualité de tradition apostolique

---

[37] Voir M. Roncaglia, *Les Frères Mineurs et l'Eglise grecque orthodoxe au XIIIe siècle* (1231-1274) (Le Caire, 1954), 43 s.

[38] *Epist. Cum iuxta testimonium veritatis* du 17 ou 18 mai 1233: Potthast 9198. Texte dans Mansi, *Concil. ampl. Coll.*, XXIII, col. 59-62 ou *Bullarium Romanum*, éd. Turin, T. III, pp. 471-473. La version grecque se trouve dans Wadding, *Annales Minorum*, Quaracchi, T. II, pp. 362-267. Nous citons d'après Mansi.

[39] "Graecus ad fidem cum discipulo iuniore praecurrens et tantae gratiae non ingratus, illius dignationis qua Deus miseriae compassus humanae homo voluit esse possibilis, eligens quotidie reminisci, hostiam constituit offerri fermentatem (...) Latinus vero cum Petro secutus litterae monumentum, de qua procedit spiritualis sensus, prior introivit et linteamenta posita, que sacrosanctum corpus, quod ecclesiam signat, involverant, separatumque sudarium quod fuerat super caput, aspexit, sacramentum glorificati corporis celebrare mirificentius in azymis sinceritatis elegit. Sed uterque panis ... (Mansi, XXIII, col. 60 E-61 A).

[40] Mansi, XXIII, col. 62 A.

les intéressait et ils demandèrent avec insistance quel en était le sens. Les Latins renvoyèrent au pape lui-même le soin de s'expliquer, puis se lassèrent, s'énervèrent et finirent par reprendre contre les Grecs tous leurs griefs ....[41]

Qu'on nous permette de conclure, sans esprit de confessionalisme, dans une perspective romaine. Rome est le lieu du martyre et de la tombe de Pierre, du martyre et de la tombe de Paul, du martyre enfin de Jean, si l'on donne créance au témoignage de Tertullien qui affirme cette triple apostolicité de l'Eglise romaine.[42] Tout chrétien admettra que les trois apôtres représentent bien les éléments essentiels de l'Eglise: principe et autorité, verbe et apostolat, amour et vision. Bien sûr il faut se garder d'un romantisme imaginatif et sentimental. Un bon moyen pour cela est précisément de garder unis ces trois principes (Schelling parlait de "*Potenzen*"). L'idée d'une Eglise de Jean qui ne serait pas aussi de Pierre serait une chimère inconsistante.[43]

Rome, c'est la papauté. Or, avec un accent d'intense conviction spirituelle, Sa Sainteté Paul VI a plusieurs fois exprimé la conscience douloureuse qu'il avait d'être ou de sembler être l'obstacle majeur, le "*stumbling block*" sur la route de l'unité.[44] Il y a à cela des raisons doctrinales, ecclésiologiques, dont nous ne voulons pas sousestimer l'importance. L'étude de l'histoire nous a cependant appris que les idées sont liées à des situations, à des modalités concrètes d'existence. A cet égard, le visage que la papauté a présenté, grosso modo, entre S. Grégoire le Grand et Léon XIII ou Jean XXIII, a eu sa très large part dans l'opposition, non seulement sentimentale, parfois même passionnelle ("*Antirömische Affekt*"), mais ecclésiologique, suscitée par la papauté du côté orthodoxe ou du côté protestant: Jean et Paul n'ont pas reconnu Pierre.

Mais voici que Pierre est devenu Jean et qu'il s'est fait Paul aujourd'hui. Avec Jean XXIII, le pape est apparu comme un père oecuménique possi-

---

[41] Relation des légats (sur laquelle cf. M. Roncaglia, 47-51). Après avoir cité le passage de la lettre de Grégoire IX, les Grecs remarquent: "Ex his verbis videtur nobis quod dominus papa velit annuere duas traditiones. Quaerimus igitur a vobis si haec est fides vestra, quod in illis discipulis significentur duae traditiones in sacramento Graecorum et Latinorum?" (Mansi, XXIII, col. 295 E-296 A).

[42] *De Praescriptione*, 36, 3.

[43] Schelling le reconnaissait. On le reconnaissait même dans le milieu de la "Hochkirche" allemande: cf. Schaefer, *Apostolat und apostolische Sukzession in der Urkirche*, in *Die Hochkirche* 13 (août, 1931), 261-266, et Fr. Heiler in *Oekumenische Einheit* (1949), 30.

[44] Ainsi dans l'encyclique *Ecclesiam suam* du 6 août 1964 (*Acta Apost. Sedis*, 56, 656); Allocution du 28 avril 1967 aux membres du Secrétariat pour l'Unité: *Document. cathol.* (1967), col. 870.

ble. Avec Paul VI, en un style plus calculé, intellectuellement plus appuyé, il apparaît comme "expert en humanité"; il prononce des paroles, accomplit des gestes, prend des initiatives qui ne trompent pas. Il sait tirer les conséquences et payer le prix du "dialogue de charité" repris avec l'Orient dans l'humilité et la sincérité. Un style nouveau exprime une conversion profonde.

Nous ne voulons pas dire, nous ne pensons pas, que tout doive revenir à Pierre: les chrétiens de Jean et de Paul ont reçu des charismes trop précieux, des prophètes trop éminents — comme les tribus du Nord — pour que nous n'attendions pas grandement d'elles. L'oecuménisme est autre chose que le pur unionisme. Il semble que, dans une perspective oecuménique authentique, le rêve de Schelling, débarrassé d'un romantisme imaginatif et sentimental facile, ait un élément de vérité. Il pourrait agir comme un "mythe", au sens que Georges Sorel donnait à ce mot, celui d'une grande image expressive et motrice ... A envisager les ecclésiologies des trois grands groupes de chrétiens, on peut constater qu'à partir du XIe siècle, mais surtout au début du XIVe, l'ecclésiologie catholique a mis en œuvre la catégorie de *potestas*. Dans la mesure où elle a été dominée par l'affirmation de la primauté papale, cette *potestas* a été celle de la juridiction. Luther s'est élevé contre une telle ecclésiologie. Il a voulu rétablir une primauté de l'idée de la communauté. Pour lui, toute *potestas* était de ce monde: idée dans laquelle on peut soupçonner quelque influence de Marsile Padoue. Mais surtout Luther a affirmé qu'il n'existait qu'une seule *potestas*, une seule autorité, celle de la Parole de Dieu, et que tout se déduisait d'elle. Si nous ne nous trompons, la théologie orthodoxe déduirait plutôt la *potestas* du sacrement. Nous aurions ainsi trois affirmations qui comportent évidemment toutes trois une part imprescriptible de vérité. Et nous pourrions chercher une nouvelle formulation de l'idée de Schelling et de Solov'ev dans la ligne Autorité de Gouvernement, Parole, Sacrement.

On voit par là que le grand problème reste celui de l'ecclésiologie. Vatican II a certainement, à cet égard, ouvert des perspectives d'une valeur oecuménique dont on ne peut mesurer la portée. Il a, de multiples manières, dénoncé le juridisme dans la façon d'aborder la réalité "Eglise". Celle-ci n'est pas d'abord une "société", bien qu'elle en soit effectivement une; elle se comprend d'abord comme "mystère", dans la ligne du sens que Saint Paul donne à ce mot. Tout est ainsi recentré vers le haut, sur le Christ et son Saint-Esprit. L'Eglise est le "sacrement", c'est-à-dire le signe et l'instrument de l'achèvement de la création en Dieu, tel qu'il peut résulter de l'envoi du Verbe et du Saint-Esprit au sein de notre histoire. Dès lors aussi, quand on considère cette Eglise en elle-même, la première valeur que l'on affirme[45] est celle de la qualité commune de l'existence chrétienne constitutive du peuple de Dieu sous sa nouvelle et définitive Disposition de l'Alliance. On rencontre une ontologie de grâce à base sacramentelle et charismatique. L'affirmation de l'autorité (*potestas*) ne vient qu'ensuite et elle se présente sous le signe du *service* de cette communauté des hommes rassemblés par le Christ et son Saint-Esprit.[46] De même, lorsqu'il s'agit des rapports entre "l'Eglise" et le temporel,[47] ces rapports ne sont pas formulés, comme jadis, en termes d'un pouvoir et d'une autorité concurrentiels, mais en termes de mission et de service. Du reste, l'autorité issue des Apôtres est elle-même communautaire ou collégiale, et elle est également constituée par une ontologie sacramentelle de grâce (sacramentalité de la consécration épiscopale par laquelle on devient d'abord membre du collège et qui est radicalement la forme concrète de la succession apostolique).

Il y a donc, dans l'ecclésiologie de Vatican II, une approche très substantielle du Sacrement et de la Communauté comme valeurs fondamentales. Mais cette même ecclésiologie s'oppose à une réduction de tout au Sacrement et à la communauté. L'autorité apostolique instituée par Jésus-Christ est bien ordonnée à la célébration des sacrements, et elle est bien elle-même sacramentelle. Cependant elle a aussi une source extra-sacramentelle propre : précisément l'institution du Seigneur (Cf. Mat. 16, 16-19 ; 18, 19 ; 28, 18-20). On ne peut donc pas réduire purement et simplement l'élément d'autorité (*potestas*) à l'élément sacramentel, pas plus qu'à la valeur Communauté. Il reste une dualité : Pierre et Jean, selon la typologie que nous exposons ici. Cette dualité, quand elle s'applique à la fonction pétrienne telle que celle-ci s'affirme dans la tradition romaine, demeure, nous le savons, l'une des difficultés majeures entre l'Orthodoxie et le Catholicisme. Comment peut-il exister une telle autorité qui ne dérive pas d'un sacrement?

Il nous semble certain que les développements médiévaux tels surtout qu'ils se sont formulés dans le cadre et dans le climat d'une rivalité entre la papauté et les principats séculiers, ont porté l'opposition à un point extrême, que tout, aujourd'hui, nous invite à réviser : ainsi dans la formule d'Augustin d'Ancone (Agostino Trionfo: début du XIVe s.): "*Papa est nomen iuridictionis.*" Ici, la fonction papale était expressément détachée

---

[45]   *Lumen gentium*, ch. II.
[46]   *Lumen gentium*, ch. III.
[47]   Constitution Pastorale *Gaudium et Spes*.

de la qualité d'évêque de Rome! Nous avons sérieusement commencé de dénoncer et de dépasser cet unilatérisme. Jean XXIII a sans cesse lié sa fonction de père oecuménique et de pasteur de l'Eglise de Rome. La théologie travaille dans le même sens. Il y a encore cependant beaucoup à faire pour débarrasser cette théologie des séquelles d'une histoire séculaire, caractéristique du moyen âge occidental, au cours de laquelle l'ecclésiologie s'est développée dans le cadre et le climat d'une lutte entre les "deux pouvoirs", l'Eglise et l'Etat.

Il y a également beaucoup à faire pour que toutes les déclarations de la Constitution dogmatique *Dei verbum* passent dans la chair vivante de l'Eglise catholique et même dans sa conscience théologique:

Ce magistère n'est pas au-dessus de la Parole de Dieu mais il la sert, n'enseignant que ce qui fut transmis, puisque par mandat de Dieu, avec l'assistance de l'Esprit-Saint, il écoute cette Parole avec amour, la garde saintement et l'expose aussi avec fidélité, et puise en cet unique dépôt de la foi tout ce qu'il propose à croire comme étant révélé par Dieu (n. 10).

Il faut donc que toute la prédication ecclésiastique, comme la religion chrétienne elle-même, soit nourrie et régie par la Sainte Ecriture ... La force et la puissance que recèle la parole de Dieu sont si grandes qu'elles constituent, pour l'Eglise, son point d'appui et sa vigueur, et, pour les enfants de l'Eglise, la force de leur foi, la nourriture de leur âme, la source pure et permanente de leur vie spirituelle. Dès lors ces mots s'appliquent parfaitement à la Sainte Ecriture: "Elle est vivante donc et efficace, la parole de Dieu" (Héb. 4, 12), "qui a le pouvoir d'édifier et de donner l'héritage avec tous les sanctifiés". (Actes 20, 32; 1 Thess. 2, 13); (n. 21).

Il n'y a donc pas d'autonomie de l'autorité, dans l'Eglise, ni d'autonomie du sacrement, par rapport à la Parole. Mais on ne peut réduire toute autorité, non plus que l'efficacité sacramentelle, à la Parole (tel est le sens de l'affirmation de "l'*opus operatum*" au concile de Trente). Jésus n'a pas posé *seulement* la Parole pour faire des hommes un peuple qui soit Peuple de Dieu et Corps du Christ. Il a aussi disposé le sacrement et le charisme d'un ministère doué d'autorité. Si donc on voulait reprendre l'idée de Schelling et de Solov'ev comme une typification de l'autorité du ministère, du Sacrement et de la Parole, ce devrait être moins pour conclure à un dépassement de Pierre et de Paul en Jean, que pour inviter à approfondir l'implication et la complémentation mutuelles des trois éléments, en dépassant des unilatéralismes dont l'existence, hélas, n'est pas toute imaginaire. N'est-ce pas la visée même d'une théologie vraiment oecuménique?

APPENDICE

Situation respective de Jean et de Pierre selon quelques théologiens
du moyen âge occidental.

Les symboles, nous l'avons vus, peuvent recevoir des significations diverses. Tandis que, pour Ambroise Autpert, moine écrivant vers 766, Jean
était la figure de l'Eglise,[48] pour un auteur irlandais anonyme du VIIe
ou VIIIe siècle, Marie et Jean, au pied de la croix, représentaient respectivement "Ecclesium et principatum!"[49] Ce n'est pourtant pas sous cet
aspect qu'on a traditionnellement vu S. Jean, surtout quand la question
était posée de sa situation vis-à-vis de S. Pierre. Nous avons vu comment
S. Augustin concevait les choses. Pierre était la vie terrestre de lutte
contre la mal, Jean la vie de contemplation qui doit remplir l'éternité.
Dans ces conditions, on peut comprendre que Pierre ait aimé le Christ
plus que les autres, tandis que Jean fut aimé du Christ plus que les autres:
"hoc per Petrum significatum est plus amantem, sed minus amatum:
quia minus nos amat Christus miseros quam beatos."[50] La raison paraîtra
sans doute contestable à un lecteur de Nygren …

S. Bède (†735) reste strictement dans la ligne de S. Augustin: comme
celui-ci, il voit en Pierre et Jean une figure des deux vies, comme lui il
n'omet pas d'affirmer que les deux apôtres ont excellé dans l'une et dans
l'autre.[51]

Rupert de Deutz, mort en 1135, traite la question d'une façon originale:
il la résoud par analogie avec ce qui nous est dit de Jacob qui, ayant une
prédilection d'affection humaine, charnelle, pour Joseph, n'a pas laissé,
par obéissance à la volonté de Dieu, et à son plan de salut, d'attribuer
la bénédiction royale à Juda.[52] Ainsi la prédilection d'amitié humaine

---

[48]   *In Apocalypsim: Maxima Bibl. vet Patrum* (Lyon, 1677), T. XIII, col. 440 D-411 A.
[49]   Commentaire sur les Evangiles, édité sous le nom de S. Jérôme dans PL 30, 588.
[50]   *Tract.* CXXXIV in *Ioannis Evang.*, 6: PL 35, 1975.
[51]   *Homil.* I, 8 (PL 94, 45-49: cf. 47 C et 48 B).
[52]   "Cum tali amoris privilegio diligeret (Petrus) eum (Christum), non tamen huic, sed
Petro, specialiter dixit: *Tu es Petrus* … (Mt. 16, 18)"; Rupert évoque alors la prédilection de Jacob pour Joseph: "non tamen huic sed Judae benedictionem regalem dedit:
Non auferetur … (Genèse 49, 10). Quare? Videlicet quia in dandis benedictionibus non
suam sed Dei voluntatem facere debuit, non carnis affectu, sed Spiritus instructum
sequi dignum fuit. Hoc illi pene simile est. Siquidem dominus noster cum omnes
discipulos et praecipue Petrum amore spiritus vel mentis diligeret, hunc Ioannem
quodam cordis amore velut homo hominem diligens, non tamen caeteris in apostolatu
praeferre voluit (…) Igitur in ordine vel dignitate apostolatus beatus ille Simon
Bar-Iona, cui primo non caro et sanguis sed Pater qui in caelis revelavit, primatum
gerere et claves regni coelorum accipere meruit, hic autem discipulus velut ille dilectus

que Jésus a eue pour Jean ne l'a pas empêché d'attribuer le primat à Pierre "in ordine vel dignitate apostolatus".

Au XIIe siècle encore, un Godefroid d'Admont († 1165) voit en Pierre et Jean le type des deux vies; il insiste sur le privilège qu'a eu Jean de reposer sur la poitrine de Jésus.[53] Anselme de Havelberg († 1158), Prémontré, archevêque de Magdebourg, qui nous a conservé une si précieuse relation des conférences tenues à Constantinople avec Nisetas et Nicomédie, applique la typologie de Pierre et de Jean au débat alors institué entre moines et clercs réguliers.[54] Pierre est le type de ces derniers ("Ordo canonicus"), Jean des premiers. Jean est plus aimé, il, est "quietis et theoriae assuetior"; Pierre aime davantage, il est "ministerio verbi paratior". Les deux ordres se précèdent l'un l'autre tour à tour, comme Jean a précédé Pierre pour arriver au tombeau, dans lequel Pierre est entré le premier.

C'est à la façon augustinienne de poser la question que nous revenons avec la Scolastique: la première Scolastique — Prévostin de Crémone par exemple[55] — et celle des grands: Bonaventure et Thomas d'Aquin, morts tous deux en 1274. L'Ecriture, d'un côté, témoigne que Pierre aimait le Christ plus que les autres (cf. Jean 21, 15s.), d'un autre elle appelle Jean "le disciple que Jésus chérissait" (Jean 21, 20). Cela pose une question: qui a été le meilleur, lequel a été le plus aimé de Dieu finalement?

Bonaventure répond:[56] le Christ aimait Pierre davantage, encore qu'il

---

Joseph partem non parvam extra fratres suos consecutus est de thesauro patris de Spiritu intellectus, qui vere iucunditatem et exultationem super eum thesaurisavit" (Rupert développe ensuite ce qu'est cette "gratia intellectus"): *De Trinitate et operibus eius. De Spiritu Sancto*, IV, 10, PL 167, 1681.

On a noté, au XIIe siècle, un accroissement du culte de S. Jean l'Evangéliste: cf. H. Preuss, *Johannes in den Jahrhunderten* (Gütersloh, 1939), surtout pp. 16 s.; G. Schreiber, *Die Prämonstratenser und der Kult des Johannes Evangelist*, in *Zeitschr. f. kathol. Theol.* 65 (1941), 1-31; id., *Mittelalterliche Passionsmystik u. Frömmigkeit*, in *Theol. Quartalsch.* 122 (1941), 32-44 et 107-123.

[53] *Homil.*, XII, in festo S. Ioannis Evang., PL 174, 671.

[54] *Liber de ordine canonicorum*, c. 34, PL 188, 1113-1114; c. 35, 1114-1116, où on lit, col. 1145 A: "per Ioannem agnoscendi studium et theoriae munus, quod ordine prius est, significari. In Petro vero, ministerium verbi exprimi"; c. 36, col. 1116-1117.

[55] Prévostin, dans sa *Summa theologica* (lib. III, fin: Paris, B.N. lat. 14526, fol. 48 d) pose la question de savoir: "Utrum Dominus magis dilexit minus diligentem."

[56] Cf. III *Sent.* d. 32, a. unic., q. 6 (ed. Quarrachi III, 706-708); comp. *Com. in Luc*, c. 22, n. 11 (VII, p. 543a: "Misit autem Petrum et Joannem tanquam duos qui erant inter alios magis principales: unus tanquam magis diligens, alter tanquam magis dilectus"); *Com. in Ioan.*, c. 21, n. 51, VI, p. 528b. Nous suivons H. Berresheim, *Christus als Haupt der Kirche nach dem hl. Bonaventura. Ein Beitrag zur Theol. der Kirche* (Bonn, 1939), 343-344.

ait donné à Jean de plus grands témoignages d'affection. A Pierre, qui aimait avec plus de ferveur et était aimé avec plus de force, Jésus a remis la "cura pastoralis" de toute l'Eglise; à Jean qui aimait avec plus de tendresse, "suavius", et qui était aimé avec une note plus marquée d'intimité, "familiarius", il a confié sa mère. Marie est éminemment l'Eglise: elle est la perfection du mystère de l'Eglise en son intériorité spirituelle. Pierre qui est la vie active reçoit la charge pastorale, qui suppose un particulier déploiement de l'amour de Dieu en amour du prochain. Nous pouvons noter en plus que S. Bonaventure a gardé, de Joachim de Flore, l'idée d'une perfection croissante dans le temps de l'histoire du salut: S. François est pour lui l'homme eschatologique. Mais Bonaventure se distingue de Joachim en ce que pour lui cette croissance se réalise dans le temps de l'Evangile, ouvert par l'Incarnation, et que toute la vie de l'Eglise se déroule dans le temps eschatologique.[57]

Thomas d'Aquin traite aussi notre question, rapidement dans son commentaire des Sentences,[58] plus à fond dans son commentaire sur l'Evangile de Jean et dans la Somme.[59] Dans le commentaire, plus développé, Thomas d'Aquin indique d'abord trois raisons pour lesquelles le Christ a aimé Jean d'une plus spéciale dilection: pour son intelligence plus pénétrante, pour sa pureté, à cause de sa jeunesse. Mais comment cette prédilection a-t-elle été possible, alors que, d'après l'Ecriture (Prov. 8, 17), Dieu aime ceux qui l'aiment et qu'à cet égard, Pierre devrait être plus aimé, ayant lui-même aimé davantage? Thomas expose et discute les diverses réponses proposées. Il écarte la facile distribution de mérites consistant à dire que Jean, davantage aimé, aurait été plus heureux, et Pierre, davantage aimant, aurait été meilleur. Il faut aller plus profond et rejoindre l'explication augustinienne par référence à la vie contempla-

---

[57] Cf. J. Ratzinger, *Die Geschichtstheologie des hl. Bonaventura* (Munich et Zurich, 1959), 51 (S. François, homme eschatologique), 106, 115-116 et 119, n. 40.

[58] III *Sent.* d. 31, q. 2, sol. 3: "Petrus plus dilexit Christum dilectione, quae ab ipso in membra diffunditur: sed Joannes plus dilexit dilectione, quae in Christo sistit; et ideo Petro Dominus commisit cura membrorum; Joanni autem curam matris, quae ad personam eius specialius spectabat. Unde et Petrus a Christo plus diligebatur quantum ad affectum interiorem, quia donum maioris caritatis erat ei tunc collatum. Sed Joannes plus diligebatur quantum ad signa exteriora familiaritatis; et hoc propter quattoor causas. Primo, quia per Joannem significatur vita contemplativa, quae familiorem habet Deum, quamvis activa sit fructuosior, quae significatur in Petro. Secundo propter aetatem, quia iuvenis erat. Tertio propter castitatem. Quarto propter ingenitam mansuetudinem."

[59] Dans la *Catena aurea* sur S. Jean (en 1268), S. Thomas fait de longs extraits des *Tractatus in Ioannis Evang.* de S. Augustin (c. 21, n. 3) auxquels il ajoute des textes de Theophylacte de S. Jean Chrystostome. Voir ensuite *Sum theol.* I^a q. 20, a. 4, ad 3 (1267-1268) et *Com. in Ev. Ioannis*, c. 21, lectio 5, n. 2 (en 1272).

tive et à la vie active. De nouveau, Thomas écarte une explication qu'on pourrait rattacher à Rupert de Deutz, consistant à distinguer dans le Christ ses sentiments spontanés d'homme et ceux qu'il aurait éprouvés par conformité à la volonté divine: on ne peut supposer dans le Christ aucun décalage entre sa volonté d'homme et sa volonté de Dieu ... Mieux vaut dire que Dieu a aimé chacun des deux Apôtres selon la grâce qu'il voulait pour chacun: Pierre pour le rendre davantage aimant, Jean pour le rendre d'intelligence plus pénétrante. Quant aux mérites respectifs de chacun, Dieu seul peut les peser: tel est le dernier mot dans la *Somme*. Mais certains disent, ajoute S. Thomas, que Pierre aurait plus aimé le Christ dans ses membres, c'est pourquoi Jésus lui a confié l'Eglise, Jean l'aurait davantage aimé en lui-même, c'est pourquoi il a reçu le soin de la Mère du Seigneur. Une dernière explication revient au niveau humain et psychologique: Pierre aurait eu plus d'amour au plan de la promptitude et de la ferveur, Jean aurait été plus aimé au plan des témoignages plus personnels d'affection ...

Les grands Scolastiques ne semblent guère avoir envisagé la question de Pierre et de Jean dans une perspective véritablement ecclésiologique. L'étude mériterait d'être faite. On devrait profiter pour cela des réflexions du Père Sergej Bulgakov, qui a revendiqué, à côté d'une primauté de Pierre, une certaine primauté de Jean, que celui-ci avait exercée sur les Eglises d'Asie au point de vue du gouvernement, à savoir dans l'ordre prophétique.[60]

---

[60]   Cf. supra note 31.

AN ORTHODOX VIEW OF
MODERN TRENDS IN EVANGELISM

N. A. NISSIOTIS

The understanding and practice of evangelism is one of the most interesting subjects of church life and theology today, because it is here that the main streams of contemporary theology converge; it is also here that the main difficulties of presenting the Christian message to modern man become apparent. That is why evangelism is today both a main theological issue and an acute practical problem. This paper seeks to set out a critique and a contribution to the present debate on modern trends in evangelism.

1. CONTEMPORARY TRENDS

Traditional theologies seem to be unable to provide the framework for a renewed action in common as the heart of the ecumenical movement,[1] and radical theologies in trying to repair this lack cannot reach a satisfactory consensus which meets with the approval of all church traditions. The Churches seem to be divided more because of their different concepts of evangelism and their different evangelistic practices than because of their confessional disagreement. In most cases the debate and disagreement about the nature of evangelism cut across all the Confessions and exist in each separate confession, especially among members of the Western Churches.

There are, however, some encouraging signs of consensus, sometimes as silent recognition of facts imposed on the Church as a whole by the

---

[1] If there is at the moment a crisis within the ecumenical movement, it is due to a large extent to the fact that, though almost all of the Churches have accepted the central and crucial importance of this subject for study and action in common — in spite of their very diversified approach to it — they are unable to agree on the theological presuppositions and therefore cannot advance in putting it into practice. Thus the whole evangelistic basis of the ecumenical movement is threatened.

rise of secularism and other modern movements, which produce a deeper understanding of the challenges of evangelism and a new evangelistic and missionary attitude on the part of the Churches in the modern world. There is a certain amount of agreement that lack of faith cannot be located principally in the so-called non-Christian areas of the world, which were in the past regarded as fields of mission. Unbelief exists equally in all parts of the world and the Church is in a diaspora situation everywhere. This consensus leads to the abolishment of the distinction between mission and evangelism, between professional missionaries and the rest of the members of the Church. We are continuously reading and hearing that everybody everywhere is called to be an evangelist and to share with others in the ongoing, saving, and renewing action of God, by his personal witness to Christ in his daily professional life and through his involvement in the changing society. Evangelism in this sense is first and foremost the presence, service, and witness of Christians, through their involvement in the transformation of the world for the sake of humanity. It is through an honest and frank dialogue on the truth that evangelism with the non-Christian, the Marxist, the Agnostic, the Jew, the Hindu, the Muslim, begins. Dialogue and service are the new points of contact with the non-converted. With him we can search for the truth in an existential way and with him we can share in the difficulties of the human condition. Mission is not primarily a numerical increase in the members of the Church. Its purpose is not to convert or proselytize people from the error of another religion to the Church; it is rather to struggle, together with the non-Christian, about truth as God has revealed it. Evangelism in this sense is a presence of the Church in solidarity with men, helping them to discern the signs of the times by explaining what our time means in reference to the final end, thus inviting all men to share in the action of God in history.

This approach to evangelism, however, raises several questions. Such thought and action conceive and operate solely on an anthropocentric basis and in the service of the development and evolution of humanity, without taking into account the proclamation of God's redeeming act and the need for individual transformation. Thus the central and important element in mission runs the risk of becoming only the standpoint in which a man is caught in modern society, and the set of experiences, images, human expectations and aspirations, as well as the evil powers operating in them, are not discerned. The risk is that one builds with these data a theology of evangelism which is only a theology of human solidarity. The final result can be that Christians should attempt to work out a theology of mission without reference to God.

A new concept of evangelism which rightly negates the static, quantitative, space-dimension of "mission" should not fall into the other extreme of effacing from the *kerygma* its vital starting point: "repent and believe". By equating mission and evangelism with presence and service in the world through involvement in it, one should not neglect the distinction between the *kerygma* and the solidarity of Christians with the world and its problems. It is certainly a sign of progress that the Churches today are beginning to use "mission", "evangelism", and "*diakonia*" as synonyms; but this can lead to a humanistic syncretism if proclamation is then identified with service in the name of the incognito Christ. Between proclamation and service lies the need for conversion to God. Proclamation is the heart of evangelism and is addressed to all men, while conversion represents the conscious answer of man before the revealed personal God.

It also marks great progress for a theology of mission within an ecumenical perspective to accept the existence of strikingly different types of evangelism, with a rich variety of applications in the form of the Christian Gospel, respecting different human conditions and cultures. However, it is risky to profess on this basis that one can speak of Buddhist, or Hindu, or Muslim or even secular Christianity in the same way as one speaks of Catholic, Protestant, or Western and Eastern Christianity. Again one should rejoice that the past exclusiveness of the Christian message with regard to other religions has today been replaced by dialogue on an equal footing between Christian and non-Christian. In India, for instance, the Christian-Hindu dialogue is part of the Indian ecumenical movement. But in this dialogue the uniqueness of Christ and His Cross (and not the wisdom of Christians or of a certain culture) should remain the corner-stone of the *kerygma*. It is in Christ's person that a Christian evangelist can include the non-Christian partner of the dialogue in the effort to search further with him for the truth. In such a dialogue Christians are definitely not wiser, from the human point of view, nor do they really know more about the final wisdom than their partners in the dialogue. But they witness to God, acting in Christ. He is the third partner in all kinds of dialogue about truth, for He knows, or better, He is the truth; and He will be revealed as such through the Spirit during the dialogue, *if* a Christian does not profess himself, his culture, and "his service" to humanity, but *is* a living witness of the Gospel in true repentance and humility, which place him on an equal footing with the non-Christian.

2. A THEOLOGY OF EVANGELISM
OR A THEOLOGY OF COMMUNICATION?

At the base of the problems indicated above is the ongoing debate about
a theology of evangelism which raises the question of what constitutes the
essence of the Gospel itself.[2] It seems to me that often we no longer work
with a clear understanding of what the Gospel is. Our discussion no longer
centres around the way, i.e., the methods and the means, or the "how"
of proclaiming the Gospel in a pluralistic, polyformic, and rapidly changing world, but it raises the question of the "what", the content of evangelism for the world. The problem involved is that of a radically new interpretation of the Christian message to a world in revolution which is
seeking perfect manhood as a God-given task in Christ. This is precisely
where the study of evangelism becomes so difficult and, at the same time,
exciting and decisive for the life and mission of the Churches. This subject
cannot be or become simply an academic discussion. A theology of
evangelism appears to be a reflection on the historic facts and world
realities which confront Christians as humans in all their daily pre-
occupations and dealings, and which claim from them a radically new
type of theological thinking. An honest confrontation with this theology
is not merely an intellectual exercise; it is a way of renewing ourselves
so that we can perform our task better and understand the Gospel
better, and thus help others to become living witnesses of the Gospel
where they are and where they work. Struggling with the problems raised
by a radical theology of evangelism can reveal to us the limited way in
which we share God's work. It can lead to a realization that many Christian
communities have fallen into inertia and are faithless to their own calling
as bearers of the apostolic *kerygma*, because they have not been committed to the realities of life. It is therefore possible that through this
confrontation with some of the new trends in evangelism a new impetus
for action can be created in us.

Although one must admit that the extremisms of the new trends in
modern missiology with their prosecularist attitude shake others from
their procelestial beatitude, for the sake of evangelism, and in order to
avoid extremist positions, one must dispute honestly some of the positions
maintained in current missiologies. Can a "theology of evangelism" exist
only as a "theology of communication"? I mean by this latter term that
theological thinking which replaces reflection on the salvation proclaimed

[2]   This is due to some extremist positions which make the humanist framework and
the political and social involvement of the Churches in the modern world appear to be
the only decisive factor and criterion of the Christian presence.

by the Church in Christ by a study of the human condition and those acts which promote human welfare, justice, and peace. This theology works on the assumption that secularized man finds salvation in the human context alone, and it therefore rejects all kinds of metaphysics and cannot understand anything of salvation by the intervention of a personal God. Human activism, on the one hand, and the intellectual *"non possumus"* of modern man in matters of faith, on the other, become the point of departure for a theology able to involve the evangelist, without proclamation of the Word itself, in the realities of life and in solidarity with all men. The witness and presence of Christ are equated in this view with the humanistic attitude in general, on the assumption that Christ's humanity implies His active and saving presence in all human realities. The evangelist is to witness to Christ simply by sharing actively in His presence. Consequently, the ongoing situation in the world is the element that really shapes evangelism, and not the direct proclamation of the Gospel, which is considered a theory held by doubtful traditions and church institutions.

There can of course be no missionary activity which is not concerned with humanity. But one should beware of accepting a new, one-sided, anthropocentric interpretation of Christianity which minimizes the judgement of God in history and forgets that the Word of God is not only and primarily communication *with* the world, but also communication *to* the world of something new. The Word of God has an element of discontinuity in its own essence when it is communicated to the world. It can never be absolutely at home in human conditions. Evangelism cannot, therefore, be identified simply with a sharing of the evangelist in human progress and development by improving the standards of human welfare, justice, and peace. It is right that a theology of communication should try to accommodate the Gospel. This effort is legitimate and necessary, but it becomes one-sided when it tries to restrict the Word to current, temporary, and local situations. Then it risks depriving the Word of its "otherness" with regard to human conditions and achievements. If this happens, its power for cutting across all human realities, for renewing man and calling all people back to repentance, risks being lost.

It is true that evangelism must be based on a theology of communication, but the latter should remain part of the theology of the Word and of the Good News. A theology of communication on its own runs the risk of becoming a human monologue, containing in itself its own criteria. One does not evangelize only by accepting the implications of the Gospel for the *humanum*. One evangelizes primarily by focusing human activity on God's appeal to man to choose in full freedom between Him and the powers and principalities operating in history. That is why a dialogue between the Christian faith and absolute ideologies or other living faiths is possible only if it includes a reciprocal witness to truth; otherwise, at least for the Christian evangelist, it is not an authentic and honest dialogue undertaken in love. Evangelism must always be the result of love in Christ who is the truth. This implies that evangelism results from the love of Christ for all men and is undertaken in full fidelity to Him who is the truth. This does not mean a show of superiority or a judgement on the non-Christian by the evangelist. God's presence judges both the evangelist and the non-Christian.

Therefore a common involvement with the non-Christian, for the sake of humanity, or simple dialogue without proclamation is not the whole of evangelism. The main dimension of evangelism is the communication of the Gospel itself as well as the discernment of the times. This an evangelist has to do in either a direct or an indirect way, before he involves himself in social action or in a dialogue. In a dialogue with a non-Christian it is wrong and misleading to eliminate the crucial element of evangelism, namely proclamation of the Gospel, simply to facilitate a dialogue "on equal footing" or from a wrong understanding of Christian humility. For a Christian "equal footing" and "true humility" mean to bear witness to the foolishness of the Gospel out of love for the others and a desire that they may be saved. This foolishness must remain as the foolishness of the Gospel in the eyes of the non-believing world; otherwise this "humility" and "equal footing" may camouflage an evangelism which is trying to be what it is not. This element of "show" is more marked in the prosecularist evangelism than in the evangelism which is faithful to Christ, even though the latter may appear to be an egoistic and absolutist evangelism which impedes dialogue because it presents an impossible truth.

Of course, a dialogue must follow certain stages and must respect the other's possibilities of understanding, his ways of thinking, his different cultural background, and his general existential situation. An evangelist should never cause a shock in his partner's life. But on the other hand one has to pass through the scandal of faith in order to become mature and able to accept what from the human point of view is the "impossible" element of the Gospel. A theology of the Word can never avoid this paradox, which frustrates the human mind. That is why it cannot become only a theology of communication by dropping this impossible element and operating simply in an anthropocentric framework.

3. CHRIST AND HIS CHURCH

These criticisms of some of the radical prosecularist trends in the contemporary theology of evangelism may seem to bear little resemblance to the positions maintained by the so-called conservative evangelicals. However, I think that today we are beginning to realize that this debate cuts across confessional barriers. The opposition between, on the one hand, a theology of the Word, based directly on the biblical message and the personal experience of the Gospel within the sacramental, historical community of faith, and, on the other hand, a theology of communication, with its strong emphasis on the *humanum* and the social involvement of the Churches, is to be found in almost all Churches today.

There may be similarities between some conservative evangelicals and some Orthodox when they take positions in opposition to the prosecularist theologians, yet there is a great difference between the Orthodox and the conservative evangelical attitude. This difference consists in that in any kind of evangelistic theology an Orthodox would begin from a sound ecclesiology; that is from the Church as the focus, means, and sign of the regathering of the whole world into fellowship with God, the historical, visible, and institutional Church, which cannot be separated from the event in Christ. This strong ecclesial basis, which is a *sine qua non* for the Orthodox understanding and practice of evangelism, is lacking, though in different ways and for different reasons, from both the radical and the conservative evangelical theology of the non-Orthodox Churches (and also in the works of certain radical Roman Catholic theologians).

In the eyes of an Orthodox observer the reason for these non-ecclesial attitudes is to be found in a mistrust of the institutional aspects of the Church as a whole, namely as a universal reality and essentially necessary element in evangelism. Behind this mistrust lie three elements held in common by conservative evangelicals and radical prosecularists: (1) Both sharply question authority in the Church, considering it only on the human basis without reference to its charismatic, pastoral foundation, and as an expression of the essence of the ecclesial community in the Holy Spirit. (2) Both betray a limited understanding of the evangelistic task of the Church, because they are only concerned with the Church's external, sociological, human character. In this sense the prosecularist speaks of the need to secularize the Church by identifying her with her function of serving the *humanum* in contemporary world realities, while the conservative evangelicals, though in many different ways, regard the

Church as an organization which is secondary to the main truth of the conversion and renewal of the individual. (3) Both betray a non-Trinitarian Christology, which is the main reason for their lack of a genuine understanding of the ecclesiological basis of evangelism. For most of the prosecularist evangelists and socio-theologians, Christ tends to become an isolated principle for a generalized positive interpretation of the *humanum*. This attitude forgets that it is the Logos who took flesh and not vice-versa. His humanity does not exist in the same dialectic way between good and evil as does ours; it is the concrete humanity of Jesus of Nazareth, which has a unique purpose, and is sanctified and purified by the Spirit through a concrete process in time and space. This means that the communication of the effects of the humanity of Jesus for humanity in general cannot be so easily generalized. It has to be the result of a communication of the same Spirit in a definite historical context to a converted person who experienced the decision of faith within and through the Body of Christ. The cosmic dimension of Christology is not a conclusion of the generalized Christ-principle and His humanity. It is the immediate reality of the historical Church, the *Ecclesia* of God, as the microcosm of the whole Creation, redeemed through Christ and in the Spirit for a distinctive fellowship with the Trinitarian God. There are concrete signs within this new world-wide community, which is supra-cultural and supra-national, and they are recognized in its message to the whole world, and are centred on the visible signs of restored communion with God. On the other hand, the conservative evangelical, although he very rightly insists on the need for personal conversion and emphasizes the fundamental elements of evangelism, is inclined to disregard the role of the ecclesial reality of faith and the return to God in the Church. This is again due to a unilateral Christology, in the sense that the individual is in Christ through a direct personal relationship and in virtue of a personal experience of return to Him. For an Orthodox this direct relationship with Christ is not possible without the reality of a continuous Pentecost, i.e., the existence of the apostolic community, membership in which is a *sine qua non* for conversion, namely for understanding and focusing evangelism in the secular world. Of course, there are conservative evangelical communities like the Pentecostals or the Quakers which do profess this continuous Pentecostal event; but in most cases they also run the risk of neglecting, in their evangelism, the historical signs of the ecclesial community, which are the result of a well-applied Christology. Thus both the prosecularists and the conservative evangelicals risk evangelizing either on the basis of a generalized christomonism, which seeks its justification only in the social realm of church activism, or on the basis of a pneumatomonism, which is founded solely on individual experience. .

This attitude of reserve on the part of an Orthodox to those trends in contemporary evangelism which lack ecclesiological presuppositions is equally present for an evangelism based only on the Bible. In the Eastern Churches belief is not in Christ and in the Bible, but in Christ through the Bible, and thus inevitably in the Church. In the same way, the Bible is not preached and persons are not converted "to the Bible" but rather through it, in the Church, to God. In this sense, it seems to me that the Orthodox theory and practice of evangelism has been, and is, the commentary of the biblical understanding of conversion as it is expounded by Irenaeus as "a return to the *Ecclesia* of God".[3] Ecclesial conversion does not mean that the Church is the final end of every evangelistic act. One must understand here the "Church of God" in the right theological perspective, namely "of God" to whom and to whose Kingdom one is converted, where God, His Kingdom, and His *Ecclesia* are not separated, but are kept in unbroken continuity and inner organic relationship. Return to the Kingdom and to God is impossible without the ecclesial reality in all places and at all times from Pentecost up to the present day. The Church is both the bearer *and* the sign of God's coming Kingdom in history. She is the unique means of evangelism of and for conversion to God, with the clear, distinctive elements of her sacramental life and her preaching ministry of the Word of God. The Church is neither a sacred purpose in herself, nor a simple human organization, but rather the channel for Christ's grace in the fellowship of the Spirit, existing out of, in, and for the love of God the Father. As such she cannot be separated either from her origin in God or from her purpose in God. In the Spirit she passes continuously from her human aspect to her decisive and central role in the divine economy by incorporating the people of God into the Body of Christ. She is, therefore, neither confining the Spirit of God to her institutional organization seen as a sociological unit, nor imprisoning the individual by human authority clothed with false sacralism. The Orthodox will never understand these approaches to the Church, and the problematics involved, because they see in the Church the new, transfigured fellowship of men, concretely in time and space, as prefiguring and representing the world-wide potentially all-inclusive human race. There are no limitations to the grace of God, but, within this

---

[3] *Adversus haereses*, 16.3.

limitless grace, the Church represents the *new* action of God in Christ, through the Spirit, as an act of redeeming and of regathering all people into One fellowship. This is happening totally anew in and for the whole world after Pentecost, and in virtue of Christ's sacrifice. The institutional problematic of the Church betrays a negation of her origin and purpose in God, because it neglects to see God's distinctive action in history, which reunites and regathers all men into One communion. The Church, therefore, is not directly present everywhere and is not identical with all human activities, nor is she present only in the "pure individuals", nor is she an end in herself. In a real theology of evangelism she has to remain as the dynamic, new, life-giving point of departure for the proclamation of the Good News and as a distinctive corporate reality in the world, sanctified by the Spirit and structured as the Body of Christ here and now.

The purpose of my observations is less to criticize the modern trends in evangelism than to contribute to them the conviction that real evangelism is impossible without an ecclesial basis. Following the remarkable developments that have taken place in ecumenical relationships, confrontation through constructive criticism is now necessary. The present debate on contemporary trends in the theology of evangelism is certain to enrich the Orthodox Church also, but it is perhaps her role in this always to draw attention to the importance of the ecclesial, communal perspective of theological thought and Christian action. In this regard, although the two main trends expounded above often appear to be very anti-ecclesial, they themselves are in fact new ecclesial forms of evangelistic action in a new context, because without ecclesial presuppositions there is no possibility of mission, evangelism, conversion, or social involvement. The ecclesial dimension is by the very nature of the Gospel inherent in all our acts and visions. We have, simply, to agree on what we mean when we speak of the Church in reference to evangelism and social action. The Orthodox maintain in this debate, as in all situations, that one must not minimize the God-given charismatic community of faith, which is the key manifestation of the Will of God for the world and goes beyond human failure and sin. In the final analysis I am convinced that our difference does not lie so much, and only, in the importance or non-importance of the ecclesial aspect of evangelism but rather in our understanding of what the Church is, as the channel of Grace, namely the way we relate Christ and the Holy Spirit with the historical Church.

If this be the case, then the Orthodox contribution centres on total commitment to the Body of Christ, as the primary reality of the presence of God in history transcending all confessionalisms and provincialisms. It is not sufficient to speak of Christ's presence or of conversion to Christ, or of Christ's truths, or of the presence of Christ in the world. We can only do this if we present it together with the reality of His Body, the elect people of God, called out of the world in order to be sent into it anew as bearers of the message of this new and distinctive reality of the Body. It is not sufficient to preach Christ alone, lest he become the intellectualistic, monistic principle of an individual faith. Christ must be preached within His historical reality, His Body in the Spirit, without which there is neither Christ nor the Gospel. Outside the context of the Church evangelism remains a humanism or a temporary psychological enthusiasm.

The time is now propitious, after these years of collaboration between the Churches in the West and the Orthodox, to focus our evangelism on the reality and service of the Una Sancta, together overcoming all kinds of sectarianism. This will open new horizons in evangelism and mission. We shall never experience, in its full depth, the purpose of our common calling in the growing ecumenical fellowship of the Churches, unless we all recapture the reality of the One Body whose unique message we bear all together from within the One fellowship to the world. The unity we seek has nothing to do with a universalistic structure to give evangelists more power for the sake of a more powerful evangelistic campaign; it is the essence of the multifold Christian mission everywhere. Witness is in unity and unity is in witness, if the essence of the Gospel message is reconciliation with God and the regathering of all people into His One Body. Schisms, diversities of theological interpretations and forms, and opposition to Church authorities should not be allowed to confuse the central issue of evangelism: "return to the *Ecclesia* of God".

In this context, it should be easy to understand why the first Orthodox ecumenical pioneers, under the leadership of distinguished writers like Father Georges Florovsky, insisted on the central importance of commitment to the One Church in all thoughts and acts connected with a theology of evangelism. Of our contemporary ecumenical teachers, Professor Florovsky in particular has always tried to be christocentric and ecclesial at one and the same time. As concerns the social Gospel movement he has warned us that "the doctrine of the Church is in danger of becoming a kind of charismatic sociology",[4] while in the case of pro-

---

[4] "Christ and His Church: Suggestions and Comments", *L'Eglise et les Eglises*, Etudes et travaux sur l'Unité chrétienne offerts à Dom Lambert Beauduin (Belgium, édition de Chevetogne, 1954), 159.

secularist generalized Christology he has said: "the true history of man is not a political history, with its utopian claims and illusions but a history of the Spirit ... Christ is ever abiding in His Body, which is the Church and in her the *Heilsgeschichte* is effectively continued and is still going on".[5] For him Christ and His Church cannot be separated for even a moment. Today, within the new trends in a theology for evangelism, Father Florovsky's christocentric-ecclesial theology well voices the constructive contribution which the Orthodox would make for the sake of the appropriate realization of our common calling within the one missionary apostolic Church, which is for and at the service of the whole world.

---

[5] "Predicament of the Christian Historian", *Religion and Culture: Essays in Honor of Paul Tillich*, ed. by Walter Leibrecht (New York, 1959), 166.

LA LEVÉE DES ANATHÈMES DE 1054 (7 DÉCEMBRE 1965) ET SA SIGNIFICATION DANS LA CONJONCTURE OECUMÉNIQUE CONTEMPORAINE

C. J. DUMONT, O.P.

Le geste historique accompli simultanément à Rome et à Istanbul, le 7 décembre 1965, par le Pape Paul VI et le Patriarche oecuménique Athénagoras 1er est dû à une initiative de ce dernier. Il se situe dans la ligne d'une politique hardie et persévérante de rapprochement fraternel entre toutes les confessions chrétiennes que s'est tracé l'actuel patriarche de Constantinople, en fidélité — il ne faut jamais l'oublier — aux initiatives prises déjà dans ce domaine par le trône oecuménique dès le début de ce siècle.[1] Ce serait mal comprendre ce geste que de l'isoler des très nombreuses démarches qu'a entreprises ou auxquelles s'est résolument prêtée l'Eglise de Constantinople, soit dans le cadre des mouvements de "Foi et Constitution" ou du "Christianisme pratique", soit dans celui du "Conseil oecuménique des Eglises" depuis sa fondation en 1948, soit, en marge de ce dernier, dans les rapports bilatéraux amorcés déjà vers la même époque mais envisagés d'une manière plus organique en conséquence des trois conférences pan-orthodoxes de Rhodes.[2] Sans aucun doute, l'importance de l'Eglise catholique romaine et de l'Eglise orthodoxe ne pouvait manquer de donner à ce geste un relief que n'offraient pas les rencontres diverses au sein ou en marge des organismes que nous venons de citer. Aux données historiques très précises auxquelles ce geste se référait, vient s'ajouter le fait que le fâcheux incident de 1054

---

[1] Rappelons les lettres encycliques du patriarche Joachim III et de son synode aux chefs des Eglises autocéphales (12 juin 1902 et 25 mai 1904) et celle de l'Eglise de Constantinople à toutes les Eglises du monde (en janvier 1920). Ces lettres et la réponse qu'y a donnée le patriarcat de Moscou ont été publiées en traduction française dans *Istina* II (1955), 78-96.

[2] Il s'agit principalement des rencontres théologiques bilatérales avec des délégations d'Eglises de la communion anglicane et d'Eglises vieilles-catholiques de l'Union d'Utrecht, décidées lors de la 3e conférence pan-orthodoxe de Rhodes (1964). Il existe également des rapports entre le patriarcat oecuménique et l'Eglise luthérienne d'Allemagne (EKD).

était demeuré présent dans toutes les mémoires. Depuis la tragique séparation causée par cet incident, les deux fractions de la chrétienté demeurées en communion respectivement avec les sièges de Rome et de Constantinople, ont conservé chacune une cohésion, et en conséquence, une personnalité très marquée qui favorisait la conservation de ce souvenir. Si important qu'ait donc été et que demeure ce geste accompli par bienveillance mutuelle le 7 décembre 1965, ce serait, pensons-nous trahir les intentions profondes du patriarche Athénagoras que de l'isoler d'un contexte plus largement oecuménique en dehors duquel il ne pourrait recevoir qu'un éclairage partiel et en partie fallacieux.

1. LE CHEMIN FRAYÉ PAR LA RENCONTRE DE JÉRUSALEM
(6 janvier 1964)

Que l'idée de démarches positives capables de favoriser un rapprochement effectif entre l'Eglise orthodoxe et l'Eglise romaine ait été, dès son accession au trône oecuménique, une des idées maîtresses hantant la pensée et le cœur du patriarche Athénagoras, c'est ce qui suffirait à prouver l'élan avec lequel il salua l'avènement sur le siège de Rome du cardinal Roncalli, devenu le pape Jean XXIII. Connaissant l'intérêt prêté par celui-ci à la grande cause de la réunion des chrétiens mais principalement à la réconciliation de l'Eglise orthodoxe et de l'Eglise romaine, il salua son élection avec une grande joie, je dirais même avec une grande ferveur. Il appliqua même au nouveau pape les paroles par lesquelles l'évangéliste saint Jean désignait le Baptiste-précurseur: "Il y eut un homme envoyé de Dieu, qui s'appelait Jean." (Jean 1, 6). A ses yeux, Jean XXIII — que vingt ans de séjour en milieu orthodoxe avaient familiarisé avec la mentalité et les coutumes de l'Eglise d'Orient — était appelé par Dieu à "préparer les voies" menant à la réconciliation de tous les chrétiens. Dès ce moment, Athénagoras 1er ne manqua pas une occasion de déclarer son grand désir d'aller rendre visite au nouveau pape. C'était à lui-même, disait-il, titulaire du second siège de la chrétienté, de se rendre près de celui qui en occupait le premier siège.[3] L'expression de ce désir fut,

---

[3] Certains se sont étonnés, bien à tort, de cette reconnaissance de Rome comme premier siège de la chrétienté. L'Eglise orthodoxe n'a jamais mis en question cette donnée de la tradition la plus primitive de l'Eglise indivise même depuis qu'elle conteste le sens que cette primauté a pris dans l'Eglise catholique-romaine depuis la séparation du XIe siècle. Mais c'est aussi tout à fait à tort que certains milieux catholiques-romains ont vu dans une telle déclaration une disposition à accepter la primauté romaine de juridiction telle qu'elle est actuellement définie et exercée par le pontife romain.

naturellement, entendue à Rome, et Jean XXIII n'était pas homme à refuser de saisir une si favorable occasion de renouer des rapports de bonne fraternité avec l'Eglise orthodoxe.

Cependant bien des obstacles s'opposaient à la réalisation de ce souhait. Au premier plan se posait une question de protocole. A l'expression de son désir, Athénagoras avait joint la formulation d'une condition: il se rendrait volontiers à Rome, pourvu que le pape soit disposé à lui rendre ensuite sa visite, Ceci posait à l'entourage du pape un bien grand problème: il n'était pas dans les usages reçus que le pape rendît la moindre visite, quelle que soit l'importance ou la dignité du personnage — fût-il chef d'état — venu le visiter; pouvait-on faire une exception en faveur d'un dignitaire ecclésiastique, représentant, de surcroît, une Eglise en rupture de communion depuis neuf siècles avec le siège de Rome? D'ailleurs en 1965, les papes n'avaient pas encore rompu avec la tradition qui les retenait prisonniers volontaires du Vatican depuis qu'un pouvoir politique italien s'était emparé des Etats-Pontificaux. Les accords du Latran, signés entre le pape Pie XI et le gouvernement italien représenté par Benito Mussolini le 11 février 1929, avaient bien rendue officielle une paix rétablie depuis longtemps entre les deux pouvoirs, et supprimé ainsi le motif de cette réclusion volontaire. Mais ni le pape Pie XI ni le pape Pie XII n'avaient enfreint la coutume si ce n'est pour se rendre à leur villégiature de Castelgandolfo. Si hardi que devait se montrer par la suite le pape Jean XXIII dans ce domaine (et bien plus encore Paul VI), on n'osait pas encore envisager alors une innovation aussi considérable qu'un voyage à Istanbul qui eût posé, d'ailleurs, bien des problèmes politiques.

Il y avait cependant des accommodements possibles: ne pourrait-on pas recevoir le patriarche dans quelque somptueux appartement du palais pontifical où le pape lui rendrait sa visite? Cette solution fut effectivement envisagée, mais il y avait aussi des obstacles du côté orthodoxe. S'il occupe bien, par ordre traditionnel de préséance, le premier des sièges patriarcaux de l'Eglise orthodoxe, le patriarche oecuménique ne se voit reconnaître aucune primauté de juridiction sur les autres Eglises-sœurs ou sur l'ensemble qu'elles forment. A quel titre voulait-il accomplir son voyage à Rome? Au titre de représentant de l'Eglise orthodoxe? Dans ce cas, il fallait, en toute hypothèse, qu'il en reçût le mandat de toutes les Eglises autocéphales et le moins qu'on puisse dire c'est que celles-ci ne semblaient aucunement disposées à le lui donner. A titre personnel? Mais un tel voyage serait demeuré sans portée; il eût d'ailleurs rencontré sans aucun doute le désaveu des autres Eglises orthodoxes en raison du risque de confusion qu'une telle démarche n'aurait pas manqué d'entraîner: comment, dans l'esprit des fidèles orthodoxes, le titulaire d'une si haute charge pourrait-il encore agir à titre personnel en une matière aussi grave de rapports ecclésiastiques? Les événements que nous avons vécus récemment nous font apparaître ces considérations comme appartenant à un autre âge, si rapides sont aujourd'hui les évolutions dans ce domaine. Nous verrons cependant qu'il en reste encore quelques vestiges et qu'il ne faut pas trop se hâter de considérer ces obstacles comme périmés.

L'annonce d'un prochain pèlerinage du pape Paul VI à Jérusalem devait soudain offrir une possibilité à la réalisation du désir de rencontre que le patriarche Athénagoras n'avait cessé de déclarer. Plus question de visite à rendre, du moins de Rome à Constantinople. Et qui pourrait faire grief au patriarche oecuménique de se rendre en pèlerinage lui-même aux Lieux-Saints et de choisir pour cela la même date que le pape de Rome? Rapidement les contacts furent pris et un programme de rencontre soigneusement élaboré par entente entre les deux parties, programme qui sauvegardait le caractère de pèlerinage du voyage entrepris par les deux prélats ainsi que la nature purement personnelle et fraternelle de leur rencontre.[4]

Il est sûr qu'entre la date de l'avènement de Jean XXIII (28 octobre 1958) et ce 6 janvier mémorable de 1964 ou Paul VI et Athénagoras se donnèrent l'accolade près du tombeau du Christ, de grands événements s'étaient produits à Rome: le second concile du Vatican avait tenu ses deux premières sessions. Son intention déclarée de renouveau, son ouverture oecuménique, l'accueil fait aux observateurs non-catholiques (parmi lesquels hélas seule, des Eglises orthodoxes, l'Eglise patriarcale russe était officiellement représentée), tout cela avait déjà singulièrement modifié le climat des rapports entre l'Eglise catholique romaine et les Eglises ou communautés qui ne sont pas en pleine communion avec le siège de Rome. Dans l'ordre doctrinal, les premiers jalons posés par le concile pour dégager l'enseignement de l'Eglise romaine d'une conception trop étroite et trop juridique de l'Eglise, permettaient à la rencontre de prendre une signification plus profonde que celle d'une manifestation de bonne volonté réciproque. Les cadeaux qui furent échangés n'avaient pas été choisis au hasard. Ils témoignaient d'une reconnaissance réciproque de la structure

---

[4] Une autre circonstance favorable consistait dans le fait que le pape devait rencontrer à Jérusalem d'autres patriarches orthodoxes ou orientaux et tout d'abord le patriarche de Jérusalem, chef de l'Eglise locale. Cela enlevait à la rencontre avec Athénagoras son caractère de singularité.

hiérarchique sacramentelle toujours présente et vivante dans ces deux fractions de la chrétienté.[5] Bien que jusque là purement symbolique, ce geste mutuel permettait qu'un premier pas soit franchi sur la voie de la réconciliation. Il rendait en outre évident que, au-delà de la néfaste théologie de la Contre réforme et du durcissement de l'attitude orthodoxe qui devait en résulter, et en dépit de tous les dissentiments qui les tiennent éloignées de la pleine communion de la vie sacramentelle, l'Eglise orthodoxe et l'Eglise catholique romaine restent deux parties de l'unique Eglise du Christ, momentanément en contestation sur un nombre minime de questions concernant la foi et la discipline de l'Eglise. Mais n'anticipons pas.

En dehors des échanges officiels de salutations, d'adresses, de discours, rien n'a transpiré du colloque prolongé que le pape et le patriarche ont eu en tête-à-tête, hors de la présence de leurs suites respectives. Du texte de la déclaration commune qui a accompagné la levée des anathèmes, à la fin de l'année suivante, on peut cependant déduire qu'ils y ont pris comme un engagement de ne pas laisser sans lendemain cette première rencontre. Le patriarche Athénagoras ne devait pas tarder à mettre à profit les bonnes dispositions de son interlocuteur. Soucieux avant tout de sortir d'un œcuménisme limité aux bonnes paroles et d'en venir enfin à une politique de rapprochement marquée par des actes réalisant, de manière progressive, ce rapprochement, sa première pensée comme sa première étape fut de proposer qu'il soit procédé à l'élimination du grand obstacle que constitue, sur la voie de la réconciliation, le souvenir des pénibles incidents de 1054. Le légat du pape, le cardinal Humbert de Moyenmoutier, déposa alors en effet sur l'autel de Sainte-Sophie une bulle excommuniant nommément le patriarche de Constantinople et deux autres personnages impliqués dans le conflit qu'il avait pour mission de tenter de régler.

Depuis la rencontre de Jérusalem les envoyés du trône œcuménique avaient retrouvé le chemin de Rome. Les facilités et la rapidité des communications permettaient des échanges fréquents et personnels. Le Secrétariat pour l'Unité, créé par le pape Jean XXIII à l'occasion du Concile, offrait un partenaire valable — et particulièrement ouvert et bienveillant — à la Commission constituée près du synode constantinopolitain pour les relations entre le trône œcuménique et les Eglises ou corps ecclésiasti-

---

[5] Le pape Paul VI fit don au patriarche Athénagoras 1er d'un calice comme gage déjà d'une certaine participation au sacrifice eucharistique célébré par le patriarche. De son côté celui-ci a offert au pape un encolpion, insigne de la dignité épiscopale et a tenu à l'imposer lui-même au pontife romain.

ques non-orthodoxes. Quand l'un ou l'autre des membres de cette commission se déplaçait en Europe occidentale pour prendre part à quelque réunion tenue dans le cadre du Conseil œcuménique des Eglises, il en profitait pour passer par Rome où il était assuré de recevoir le meilleur accueil soit auprès du Secrétariat pour l'Unité, soit même auprès du pape en personne. Ainsi s'explique qu'ait pu être proposée et mûrir tranquillement l'idée mise en avant par le patriarche. La proposition fut d'emblée reconnue par le pape Paul VI comme méritant d'être soigneusement étudiée et comme susceptible d'être menée à bonne fin. L'étude entreprise conduisait à des conclusions favorables, tant pour le fond, que pour la forme à adopter.

2. LES COMMISSIONS AU TRAVAIL

A Istanbul, l'étude du projet fut confiée à une commission composée du métropolite Méliton, alors métropolite d'Héliopolis, et de Thyra, aujourd'hui métropolite de Chalcédoine; du métropolite de Myre, Chrysostome, professeur à l'Ecole supérieure de théologie de Halki; de l'archimandrite Gabriel, premier secrétaire (protosyncelle) du patriarcat, aujourd'hui métropolite; de M. Anastassiadés, professeur de droit canonique à l'Ecole théologique de Halki; et du Rév. Père Paul Evamghélos, grand archidiacre.

A Rome, le pape Paul VI désigna comme membres de la commission: Son Excellence Mgr. J. Willebrands, secrétaire du Secrétariat pour l'Unité; Mgr. Michel Maccarone professeur d'histoire ecclésiastique à l'Université du Latran; le Rév. Père Alphonso Raes, préfet de la bibliothèque vaticane, ancien président de l'Institut Pontifical Oriental de Rome; le Rév. Père Christophe Dumont, directeur du centre d'Etudes "Istina" de Paris; le Rév. Père Alphonse Stickler, canoniste, recteur de l'Université pontificale salésienne de Rome. Le Rév. Père Duprey, sous-secrétaire du Secrétariat pour l'Unité en sa section orientale, devait faire office de secrétaire.

C'est du 7 novembre 1965 qu'est datée la nomination par le pape Paul VI de la commission romaine. Dès le 10 novembre — il ne fallait pas perdre de temps car des deux côtés l'on souhaitait que la démarche commune projetée pût avoir lieu avant la fin très proche du concile — put être remis aux membres de la commission romaine un premier schéma directeur rédigé par l'un d'eux, proposant les grandes lignes selon lesquelles une *Déclaration commune* pourrait être signée par le pape et par le patriarche. Ce premier projet fut discuté, pour le fond et certains détails de rédaction, lors d'une première réunion de la commission, le 12 novembre. On porta un soin très attentif à l'exactitude des expressions évoquant les événements de 1054; on nota en particulier, que les excommunications réciproques n'avaient été portées que sur quelques personnalités déterminées: d'une part les légats, d'autre part le patriarche Michel, l'évêque Léon d'Ochrida et le secrétaire du patriarche, Constantin. Les termes de la bulle d'excommunication "et tous ceux qui les suivent dans les dites erreurs et présomptions" sont eux-mêmes limitatifs; et ne tous cas ils ne visent pas l'Eglise de Constantinople comme telle dont le même document loue pour sa piété l'empereur (dont il était important de se conserver les bonnes grâces), le clergé, le Sénat et le peuple de la "très chrétienne et orthodoxe cité de Constantinople".

De même la bulle synodale ne visait que les trois légats: le cardinal Humbert; Pierre, archevêque d'Amalfi et le diacre Frédéric, chancelier de l'Eglise romaine; ce sont eux, en effet, qui avaient collectivement pris la responsabilité de l'excommunication déposée sur l'autel de Sainte-Sophie.

Il était de toute première importance que l'acte dont on se disposait à effacer les traces fût très exactement défini, d'autant plus que dans l'opinion courante cet acte continuait à passer pour une excommunication réciproque des deux Eglises elles-mêmes.

Moyennant les quelques modifications que cette discussion appela, un premier projet de rédaction de la déclaration commune envisagée fut soumis à la commission lors de sa réunion du 15 novembre. N'y furent apportées par la commission que des modifications de détail. Ce texte devait être proposé comme base de discussion à la commission orthodoxe qui, durant ce temps, élaborait de son côté un projet analogue. L'accord devait être obtenu au cours d'une réunion commune des deux commissions qui se tint à Istanbul les 22 et 23 novembre 1965. Entre temps, le projet élaboré par la commission catholique avait pu être soumis à l'approbation du pape. C'est naturellement au titre de base de discussion que Paul VI l'approuva, se réservant de donner son agrément au projet définitif qui devait résulter des travaux de la commission mixte.

Celle-ci tint à Istanbul quatre séances: deux le lundi 22, deux le mardi 23. La commission orthodoxe qui avait pu avoir connaissance du projet élaboré par la commission catholique avant l'arrivée de celle-ci à Istanbul,[6]

---

[6] Ce texte fut porté à Istanbul par le Rev. Père André Scrima présent à Rome pour assister, avec la bénédiction du patriarche, aux sessions conciliaires. Il prit part aux travaux de la commission mixte en qualité de secrétaire.

se déclara d'emblée prête à recevoir comme base de discussion ce projet où elle avait reconnu, "parfois jusque dans les expressions mêmes" un exposé de ses propres vues. Ceci facilita grandement le travail ultérieur. Il s'agissait toutefois de préciser la rédaction de certains passages et surtout de déterminer d'un commun accord le contenu de ce qui devait être le point central de la discussion.

Une première proposition fut faite par la commission orthodoxe. En effet, une simple déclaration commune ne pouvait suffire à l'accomplissement du geste que l'on se proposait. Quel que puisse être, pensait-elle, le retentissement d'une telle déclaration, celle-ci ne pouvait avoir valeur canonique dans aucune des deux Eglises puisque signée de part et d'autre par une autorité non reconnue. Il fallait donc, outre cette déclaration, qu'un acte propre de chaque Eglise effectuât, au sein même de cette Eglise, cela même qu'exprimerait la déclaration commune. La commission orthodoxe envisageait que ce soit, pour l'Eglise patriarcale, un *"Tomos"* synodal dont le texte avait déjà été préparé. Elle demandait à la délégation catholique que le pape de Rome procédât à un acte correspondant conforme aux usages de l'Eglise romaine. Après avoir reçu de la commission orthodoxe des explications plus détaillées sur ce point, la commission catholique se déclara disposée à soumettre au pape Paul VI le vœu exprimé et à le recommander de manière favorable à son attention.

Si ce premier point ne nécessita pas de longues discussions, il en alla autrement quand, des formes de procédure, on passa à l'examen du fond même de la question. La difficulté venait ici des conceptions sensiblement différentes, en Orient et en Occident, du sens juridique et théologique des sanctions canoniques d'excommunication. Selon le droit de l'Eglise romaine, l'excommunication, peine médicinale, s'éteint d'elle-même par la mort de celui qui en a été frappé: dans cette perspective, lever une excommunication quelconque 900 ans après la mort des intéressés devait paraître dépourvu non seulement de signification, mais même de portée. Du côté catholique on tenait absolument à ce que l'acte que l'on était, d'un commun accord, résolu à accomplir ne donnât pas le moindre prétexte à être considéré comme vide de sens. Aux yeux de la tradition canonique orientale, au contraire, une levée posthume d'un anathème pouvait paraître possible, étant donné que le souvenir en pèse toujours sur la mémoire du défunt qui a été frappé. L'exposé minutieux et circonstancié de ces deux points de vue demanda un certain temps. On tomba cependant assez facilement d'accord sur la nécessité de maintenir une parfaite parité entre les mesures à prendre de part et d'autre. En conséquence une formule fut mise au point, qui devait assurer à ces mesures le même effet pratique sans entrer dans les particularités des conceptions et usages canoniques propres à chaque Eglise. Ce qui était un obstacle à la réconciliation, c'était moins, en effet, les sentences passées que le souvenir qui en était demeuré ainsi que le malaise persistant qui en était résulté. Après donc qu'au nom des deux parties eussent été exprimés dans la déclaration commune le regret des torts que, de part et d'autre, on avait pu avoir dans les fâcheux incidents de 1054, et le pardon réciproque qui en était accordé, le "souvenir" de ces incidents et des excommunications elles-mêmes fut déclaré "enlevé de la mémoire de l'Eglise".

Un autre point devait encore retenir l'attention des deux délégations; mais comme il en avait été tenu soigneusement compte dans le projet de rédaction adopté comme base de travail, il ne présenta aucune difficulté. Il s'agissait bien de marquer que l'acte que l'on allait accomplir, s'il engageait l'Eglise catholique romaine dans sa totalité, ne pouvait engager, du côté orthodoxe, que la seule Eglise de Constantinople. En effet, le patriarcat oecuménique n'a d'autorité juridique sur aucune des Eglises autocéphales, ni sur l'ensemble des Eglises orthodoxes. S'il était vrai que les excommunications de 1054 avaient été portées par le seul siège de Constantinople et, à ce titre, pouvaient faire de sa part l'objet de "remise" ou d'oubli, cette mesure se trouverait sans portée pour les autres Eglises sœurs jusqu'à ce qu'elles la fassent leur: le texte que l'on préparait ne devait fournir occasion à aucune confusion sur ce point. A plus forte raison, devait-on prendre garde de ne pas parler à cet égard de l'ensemble de l'Eglise orthodoxe au nom de laquelle le patriarcat oecuménique n'avait pas qualité pour agir.

Un autre point encore était apparu d'une grande importance. Il fallait replacer ce geste bilatéral dans le contexte plus général du mouvement oecuménique en faveur duquel l'Eglise orthodoxe, mais particulièrement le trône oecuménique, avaient toujours témoigné un vif intérêt. Il fallait prévenir toute susceptibilité possible de la part du Conseil oecuménique des Eglises que l'on sentait quelque peu inquiet à la vue du rapprochement accompli entre le siège de Rome et celui de Constantinople, rapprochement amorcé depuis de longues années mais devenu spectaculaire depuis la réunion du second concile du Vatican. Il fallait enfin éviter le risque que l'acte de levée des excommunications — cette expression s'est conservée dans la presse et dans l'opinion, bien que, nous venons de le voir, elle ne soit pas canoniquement exacte — ne puisse être interprétée comme mettant fin par lui-même à l'état de schisme qui tient les deux Eglises, catholique-romaine et orthodoxe, éloignées de la pleine communion de vie sacramentelle. Ces deux derniers aspects du problème étaient d'ailleurs quelque peu connexes. Là encore, le projet de déclaration en avait tenu compte et l'échange de vues put se borner au choix des expressions les plus heureuses pour éviter les deux inconvénients redoutés.

Le texte officiel de la déclaration devant être à la fois le texte grec et le français, il était particulièrement important que les termes employés dans les deux langues se correspondent aussi exactement que possible, jusque dans leurs nuances. Cette difficulté philologique donna à la commission mixte quelque souci, mais l'on parvint à s'entendre sans grande difficulté.

Ces deux journées de travail, — d'un travail effectué dans les conditions psychologiques des plus favorables non seulement parce que le principe de l'acte à accomplir était acquis de part et d'autre, mais parce que la plupart des membres des deux délégations se connaissaient de longue date et que leurs rapports étaient faits de confiance et d'amitié — permirent donc de mettre au point le texte de la *Déclaration commune* que nous ne croyons pas inopportun de reproduire ici, afin que la mémoire s'en conserve plus fidèlement.

3. TEXTE DE LA *DÉCLARATION COMMUNE*

1. Pénétrés de reconnaissance envers Dieu pour la faveur que, dans sa miséricorde, il leur a faite de se rencontrer fraternellement aux lieux sacrés où, par la mort et la résurrection du Seigneur Jésus, a été consommé le mystère de notre salut et, par l'effusion du Saint-Esprit, a été donné naissance à l'Eglise, le pape Paul VI et le patriarche Athénagoras 1er n'ont pas perdu de vue le dessein qu'ils ont conçu, dès lors, chacun pour sa part, de ne rien omettre désormais des gestes qu'inspire la charité et qui puissent faciliter le développement des rapports fraternels ainsi amorcés entre l'Eglise catholique romaine et l'Eglise orthodoxe de Constantinople. Ils sont persuadés de répondre ainsi à l'appel de la grâce divine qui porte aujourd'hui l'Eglise catholique romaine et l'Eglise orthodoxe ainsi que tous les chrétiens à surmonter leurs différends afin d'être à nouveau "un" comme le Seigneur Jésus l'a demandé pour eux à son Père.
2. Parmi les obstacles qui se trouvent sur le chemin du développement de ces rapports fraternels de confiance et d'estime, figure le souvenir des décisions, actes et incidents pénibles qui ont abouti en 1054 à la sentence d'excommunication portée contre le patriarche Michel Cérulaire et deux autres personnalités par les légats du siège romain, conduits par le cardinal Humbert, légats qui furent eux-mêmes ensuite l'objet d'une sentence analogue de la part du patriarche et du synode constantinopolitain.
3. On ne peut faire que ces événements n'aient pas été ce qu'ils ont été dans cette période particulièrement troublée de l'histoire. Mais aujourd'hui qu'un jugement plus serein et plus équitable a été porté sur eux, il importe de reconnaître les excès dont ils ont été entachés et qui ont amené ultérieurment

des conséquences dépassant, autant que nous pouvons en juger, les intentions et les prévisions de leurs auteurs dont les censures portaient sur les personnes visées et non sur les Eglises, et n'entendaient pas rompre la communion ecclésiastique entre les sièges de Rome et de Constantinople.

4. C'est pourquoi le pape Paul VI et le patriarche Athénagoras 1er en son synode, certains d'exprimer le désir commun de justice et le sentiment unanime de charité de leurs fidèles et se rappelant le précepte du Seigneur: "Quand tu présentes ton offrande à l'autel, si là tu te souviens d'un grief que ton frère a contre toi, laisse là ton offrande devant l'autel et va d'abord te réconcilier avec ton frère." (Mt. 5, 23-24), déclarent d'un commun accord:

(a) Regretter les paroles offensantes, les reproches sans fondement et les gestes condamnables qui, de part et d'autre, ont marqué ou accompagné les tristes événements de cette époque;

(b) Regretter également et enlever de la mémoire et du milieu de l'Eglise les sentences d'excommunication qui les ont suivis, et dont le souvenir opère jusqu'à nos jours comme un obstacle au rapprochement dans la charité, et les vouer à l'oubli;

(c) Déplorer, enfin, les fâcheux précédents et les événements ultérieurs qui, sous l'influence de divers facteurs, parmi lesquels l'incompréhension et la méfiance mutuelles, ont finalement conduit à la rupture effective de la communion ecclésiastique.

5. Ce geste de justice et de pardon réciproque, le pape Paul VI et le patriarche Athénagoras 1er avec son synode sont conscients qu'il ne peut suffire à mettre fin aux différends, anciens ou plus récents, qui subsistent entre l'Eglise catholique romaine et l'Eglise orthodoxe et qui, par l'action du Saint-Esprit, seront surmontés grâce à la purification des cœurs, au regret des torts historiques ainsi qu'à une volonté efficace de parvenir à une intelligence et à une expression commune de la foi apostolique et de ses exigences.

En accomplissant ce geste, cependant, ils espèrent qu'il sera agréé de Dieu, prompt à nous pardonner lorsque nous nous pardonnons les uns les autres, et apprécié par le monde chrétien tout entier, mais surtout par l'ensemble de l'Eglise catholique-romaine et par l'Eglise orthodoxe, comme l'expression d'une sincère volonté réciproque de réconciliation et comme une invitation à poursuivre, dans un esprit de confiance, d'estime et de charité mutuelles, le dialogue qui les amènera, Dieu aidant, à vivre de nouveau, pour le grand bien des âmes et l'avènement du règne de Dieu, dans la communion de foi, de concorde fraternelle et de vie sacramentelle qui exista au cours du premier millénaire de la vie de l'Eglise.

(Suivent les signatures:)
PAUL VI, pape; ATHENAGORAS 1er, patriarche.

4. COMMENTAIRE DE LA *DÉCLARATION COMMUNE*

Ce texte appelle quelques remarques qui corroboreront ce que nous avons déjà dit à son sujet. Le premier paragraphe constitue un préambule. Il commence par une action de grâces, selon la coutume recommandée par l'usage même de saint Paul: *"Primum gratias ago"* (Rom. 1, 8), l'objet de cette action de grâces est la rencontre de Jérusalem dont l'importance ne vient pas du concours de foules qu'elle a provoqué, mais du caractère sacré des lieux où elle s'est accomplie, ces lieux où s'est consommé le mystère de notre salut par le double événement de la mort et de la résurrection du Seigneur et où, par l'effusion de l'Esprit-Saint au jour de la Pentecôte, l'Eglise a pris naissance. On a veillé à faire mention à la fois de la mort et de la résurrection du Christ, ce à quoi tiennent à juste titre la tradition et la théologie orthodoxes. C'est là un point sur lequel la théologie catholique s'est longtemps montrée trop peu attentive mais dont elle a, dans un passé récent, de nouveau compris toute l'importance. En mentionnant l'effusion du Saint-Esprit à la Pentecôte, qui fut l'acte de naissance de l'Eglise, on situait d'emblée dans sa véritable perspective le geste que l'on allait accomplir et on en soulignait la véritable portée: c'était un acte de nature ecclésiale devant affecter la réalité même de l'Eglise. En même temps se trouvait ainsi formulée une évocation trinitaire, conforme aux usages traditionnels tant de l'Eglise d'Orient que de l'Eglise d'Occident.

Le geste réciproque de levée des excommunications se trouve ensuite rattaché à un dessein conçu à la fois par le patriarche oecuménique et par le pape de Rome depuis cette rencontre historique. Il n'est pas dit qu'ils ont pris alors, ensemble, la résolution ici mentionnée; il y a là une réserve imposée par le fait que rien n'a transpiré officiellement du tête-à-tête des deux prélats, mais seulement que cette résolution résulte de cet entretien. Toutefois cette affirmation présentée ici de façon générale a une portée qui dépasse le geste accompli à Istanbul le 7 décembre 1965. La suite des événements devait d'ailleurs prouver qu'il s'agit bien là d'une disposition d'esprit permanente appelée à produire encore d'autres effets.

La fin du paragraphe marque la conviction qu'ont les deux prélats d'agir en fidélité à l'appel de Dieu, mais un appel qui, s'il concerne le rapprochement entre l'Eglise catholique et l'Eglise orthodoxe, porte également sur l'effort mutuel de réconciliation de tous les chrétiens. L'acte que l'on se dispose à faire ne doit donc pas être interprété comme visant exclusivement la ré-union souhaitable entre les deux Eglises, mais comme se situant dans le contexte plus vaste d'une réconciliation générale à laquelle, loin de paraître comme un obstacle, il entend être une première contribution.

Les deux paragraphes suivants situent d'une manière très précise les faits qui vont être l'objet de la mesure à laquelle on veut procéder. Ces faits sont présentés comme un obstacle majeur rencontré par les deux

Eglises sur le chemin menant à leur pleine réconciliation. Plus que ces faits eux-mêmes — désormais ensevelis dans le passé — c'est le souvenir qui en demeure qui constitue cet obstacle. Mais déjà est précisée la substance de ce qui, alors, a suscité par son souvenir l'obstacle toujours présent : une excommunication réciproque portée de part et d'autre à l'encontre de trois personnalités. Le passé est irréformable, on ne peut malheureusement pas faire que ce qui a été n'ait pas été. Mais déjà, cependant, les progrès de l'histoire ont permis d'apprécier les faits selon le jugement "plus serein et plus équitable" qu'elle a permis de porter sur eux. Ce jugement, s'il n'a pas fait apparaître que les mesures prises alors aient été sans aucun fondement, a conduit à reconnaître les excès qui, de part et d'autre, les ont entachées. Il a aussi fait ressortir les funestes conséquences qui s'en sont suivies, en particulier la rupture de communion entre ces deux fractions de la chrétienté. Cette rupture ne se trouvait ni visée, ni accomplie par l'acte même des excommunications, mais celui-ci devait y conduire. Le texte de la déclaration commune se garde d'affirmer catégoriquement qu'une telle rupture n'a pas été, en fin de compte, le but visé par les auteurs des censures ; cela relève, en effet, des intentions secrètes dont Dieu seul a connaissance et reste juge. Il affirme toutefois que "pour autant que nous puissions en juger" — de tels conflits étaient plus ou moins monnaie courante durant le premier millénaire entre les deux premiers sièges de la chrétienté, sans avoir jamais mené à une rupture définitive et l'on pouvait assez naturellement croire qu'il en serait de même cette fois — les conséquences qui en ont résulté ont dépassé "les intentions et les prévisions" de ceux qui en ont posé les causes. Ces nuances révèlent le minutieux souci apporté à ne rien affirmer dans la déclaration qui puisse être contesté à l'avenir.

De tous, le quatrième paragraphe est le plus important. Il constitue, en effet, le geste accompli qu'il veut exprimer dans toute sa précision. C'est d'abord le motif, très évangélique, qui inspire le pape et le patriarche *en son synode*. Notons, au passage, que cette dernière précision s'imposait car si, en droit canonique latin le pape se trouvait habilité à agir seul, le patriarche ne le pouvait que mandaté par son synode. Il est vrai qu'en procédant à la promulgation de cette déclaration au cours d'une session du second concile de Vatican, le pape témoignait de sa volonté ferme d'agir en union étroite avec l'ensemble de l'épiscopat de l'Eglise catholique romaine, et ceci est d'une très grande portée ; mais il n'était pas tenu juridiquement à le faire. Le motif évangélique est précisé par la citation de Mt. 5, 23–24, qui fait du pardon mutuel des offenses et de la réconciliation entre frères une des conditions d'un culte agréable à Dieu. Il y a là un lien d'une grande portée théologique qui constitue un des axes de tout l'effort œcuménique. Il va de soi qu'il a une portée tout à fait générale et qu'en le citant, le pape de Rome comme le patriarche œcuménique s'engagent implicitement à s'en souvenir pour d'autres circonstances du passé et pour d'éventuelles situations analogues dans l'avenir.

Vient ensuite, en trois points, la substance du geste réciproque. C'est d'abord un regret commun des excès qui ont affecté "cette période particulièrement troublée de l'histoire", événements qui ont culminé dans le refus opposé aux légats pontificaux à leur demande d'audience auprès du patriarche. Notons toutefois que, dès 1053, des faits regrettables avaient incité le pape Léon IX à envoyer une délégation à Constantinople pour mettre fin de façon amiable à des incidents — paroles offensantes (regrettables, parce qu'offensantes bien que constituant parfois des reproches justifiés), des reproches sans fondement (s'ajoutant bien fâcheusement aux reproches fondés), auxquels vinrent s'ajouter des gestes condamnables tels que la fermeture des églises latines de la grande cité, le fait de fouler aux pieds les hosties consacrées par les prêtres latins, en protestation contre l'usage des azymes, et finalement le dépôt sur l'autel de Sainte-Sophie, par les légats, de leur bulle d'excommunication du patriarche. Il s'agit là de faits qui ont "marqué ou accompagné les tristes événements de cette époque". Exprimé en commun, à propos de faits où se trouvait engagée dans le passé la responsabilité des deux parties, ce regret prend valeur de demande et d'accord réciproque de pardon, ainsi qu'il sera explicitement mentionné plus loin.

Puis vient la considération des sentences d'excommunication ellesmêmes. Nous avons dit plus haut pourquoi l'on en était venu à ne pas parler formellement d'une "levée" ou d'une "remise" de ces excommunications, nous n'y reviendrons pas. La première disposition exprimée est de les "regretter" c'est-à-dire que l'on voudrait — si la chose était possible — faire qu'elles n'aient pas existé. Mais, les choses ayant été ce qu'elles ont été, on entend, du moins, en effacer le souvenir de la "mémoire" de l'Eglise. La "mémoire de l'Eglise" est une notion riche de la théologie orthodoxe, liée à une notion fort saine de la tradition, expérience accumulée de l'Eglise et toujours présente et vivante dans sa réalité actuelle. Il faut donc prêter à cette expression un sens non pas seulement psychologique mais ontologique. Ce sens ontologique se trouve d'ailleurs souligné et renforcé par l'apposition de l'expression: "et du milieu de l'Eglise": par le présent acte, ces sentences d'excommunication doivent être considérées comme n'existant plus au sein de l'Eglise, comme ne figurant plus sur ses registres ni dans ses archives, de telle sorte qu'elles ne puissent plus opérer non seulement en vertu du souvenir qu'on en conservait, mais encore en raison de l'impossibilité d'en tirer désormais un argument pour une hostilité réciproque entre les deux Eglises. On voit dans quel sens et de quelle façon a pu être résolue après mûre discussion la difficulté signalée plus haut et qui consistait dans une conception différente, en Orient et en Occident, de la notion même d'excommunication et de sa portée.

Le troisième alinéa de ce même paragraphe étend l'expression du regret — le mot "déplorer" a été choisi comme plus fort encore que "regretter"— à tous les faits antérieurs ou postérieurs aux événement de 1054 et qui, tout autant sinon plus que les excommunications mutuelles, ont conduit, dans la suite, à la rupture complète de communion ecclésiastique. Il importait, en effet, de joindre ici comme cause de cette rupture, aussi bien tout ce qui s'était passé avant 1054 (et qui avait motivé l'envoi de la légation pontificale à Constantinople) que ce qui s'était passé ensuite, cristallisant les oppositions, durcissant les positions, monnayant l'amertume réciproque engendrée par ces funestes incidents. Est également mentionnée l'influence des divers facteurs responsables de l'aggravation des rapports d'hostilité réciproque. Si ces facteurs sont mentionnés, c'est qu'ils continuent d'être agissants et engendrent les mêmes conséquences fâcheuses qu'ils ont toujours provoquées. Ce sont "l'incompréhension et la méfiance mutuelles". Cette mention est un discret mais pressant appel à se départir de ces regrettables dispositions qui constituent autant d'obstacles permanents à la voie de la réconciliation.

Le cinquième paragraphe limite la portée du geste que l'on vient d'accomplir. Certains pourraient en effet penser — et cette opinion erronée n'a pas manqué d'être répandue par certains organes de presse dès avant et plus encore après la promulgation de l'acte — que les excommunications une fois enlevées, se trouvait par là même rétablie la pleine communion entre les deux Eglises. Il importait de rappeler que, juridiquement, ces excommunications n'ayant pas visé les Eglises elles-mêmes mais quelques-unes seulement de leurs personnalités, le fait de les effacer ne pouvait constituer en lui-même une réconciliation parfaite entre les deux Eglises. Il fallait rappeler aussi que, de toute manière, l'acte accompli n'engageait du côté orthodoxe que le patriarcat de Constantinople et non les autres Eglises autocéphales ni l'Eglise orthodoxe dans son ensemble sur laquelle le patriarcat oecuménique n'a aucune juridiction au sens propre. C'est pourquoi il est dit: "Ce geste de justice et de pardon réciproque" — il ne s'agit pas, en effet, d'un simple pardon mais d'un pardon qui s'accompagne d'un acte de justice consistant dans la reconnaissance des torts mutuels, — "le pape Paul VI et le patriarche Athénagoras 1er avec son synode sont conscients qu'il ne peut suffire à mettre fin aux différends, anciens ou plus récents, qui subsistent entre l'Eglise catholique et l'Eglise orthodoxe". Comme il se devait, c'est ici l'Eglise orthodoxe comme telle et dans son ensemble qui est mentionnée. Il est bien évident que le geste accompli se situe dans le cadre de ce que la troisième conférence pan-orthodoxe de Rhodes appelle le "dialogue de la charité". Il ne concerne — à plus forte raison ne tranche — aucun différend doctrinal ou dogmati-que, même ceux qui étaient déjà explicitement ou implicitement liés aux événements de 1054, comme, par exemple, la toujours épineuse question du *Filioque*. Il reste, parmi les traditions héritées du passé, des différends en matière disciplinaire (comme la question du divorce) même si la plupart des querelles qui, dans ce domaine, ont tellement agité les Latins et les Grecs, paraissent aujourd'hui aux uns et aux autres périmées. Mais il y a aussi des différends "plus récents", tels que les définitions dogmatiques du 1er concile du Vatican sur la primauté et l'infaillibilité de l'évêque de Rome, la proclamation des dogmes de l'Immaculée-conception (8 décembre 1854) et de l'Assomption (1950) de la Vierge Marie.

La déclaration ne veut cependant pas rester sur cette évocation des difficultés et tient à formuler des paroles d'espoir. Cet espoir ne peut se fonder que sur l'action de l'Esprit-Saint opérant la "purification des coeurs". Mais il suppose que l'on soit, de part et d'autre, soucieux d'étendre "le regret des torts historiques" au-delà de ceux qui ont marqué les événements visés par la présente démarche. On sent, sous-jacente à cette remarque, la difficile question des Eglises dites "uniates". Il faut, d'autre part, que l'on dépasse le plan des velléités et des bonnes et pieuses inten-tions dont on dit que l'enfer est pavé. Est nécessaire, en effet, une "volonté efficace", c'est-à-dire une volonté soucieuse de porter à bonne fin ce qu'elle entreprend. Or, ce qu'elle doit entreprendre, c'est "de parvenir à une intelligence et à une expression communes de la foi apostolique et de ses exigences". Il s'agit bien, en effet, des conditions essentielles d'un rétablissement de la pleine communion: une "intelligence commune" en matière doctrinale, en ce qui concerne la foi et la structure hiérarchique sacramentelle de l'Eglise. Si, dans "l'expression" de ces données de foi comprises dans un même et unique sens, une certaine pluralité a été reconnue par le concile comme légitime, du moins faut-il que la légitimité de ces expressions diverses pour signifier une même vérité soit reconnue en commun. Mais de quelle foi s'agit-il? La précision ici donnée est fort importante: il s'agit de la foi apostolique et de ses exigences. C'est ce qu'il y a de proprement apostolique dans la foi professée par chacune des deux Eglises, orthodoxe et catholique, qu'il s'agit de discerner en commun en la purifiant des soustractions que par négligence on y aurait opérées, ou des additions insuffisamment contrôlées qu'au cours des siècles on aurait pu y joindre. Ainsi se trouve bien posé le problème oecuménique dans son ensemble tel que le conçoit l'Eglise orthodoxe, point de vue entièrement acceptable par l'Eglise catholique romaine bien que, en matière oecuménique, cette dernière ait jusqu'ici semblé accorder plus d'importance au problème de la "catholicité" qu'à celui de l'apostolicité.

Le dernier alinéa de ce cinquième paragraphe se présente comme une conclusion replaçant à nouveau l'acte accompli dans le contexte plus général de l'effort oecuménique, contexte dans lequel il souhaite prendre valeur d'exemple et d'invitation à poursuivre, d'une volonté ferme, l'effort de réconciliation mutuelle. Ce qui est en question, d'ailleurs, c'est "le plus grand bien des âmes" et "l'avènement du règne de Dieu".

Une dernière ligne évoque, enfin, comme un but à atteindre "la pleine communion de foi, de concorde fraternelle et de vie sacramentelle qui exista" entre nos deux Eglises "au cours du premier millénaire de la vie de l'Eglise". On aura remarqué l'expression "au cours de" qui, mieux que le mot "durant" évoque une période où, si la pleine communion a été fréquente, elle a cependant subi des interruptions nombreuses et parfois prolongées.

5. L'ACCUEIL FAIT AU GESTE ACCOMPLI

Dans leur déclaration commune, le pape Paul VI et le patriarche Athénagoras 1er avaient exprimé leur conviction qu'en agissant comme ils le faisaient ils exprimaient "le désir commun de justice et le sentiment unanime de charité de leurs fidèles". L'enthousiasme qui, de la part de ces derniers accompagnait la proclamation solennelle de cet acte de bienveillance mutuelle tant à la cathédrale du Fanar devant une foule très dense et tous les membres du saint-synode qu'à Saint-Pierre de Rome en présence des Pères conciliaires et d'un concours énorme de peuple, suffirait à prouver qu'ils ont, en effet, été les très fidèles interprètes de leurs troupeaux respectifs. Sauf de très rares dissonances dans certains organes de la presse grecque, on peut assurer que partout, dans le monde, l'opinion reçut l'événement avec une très profonde satisfaction.

Sur le plan officiel, toutefois, il y eut, de la part des Eglises autocéphales, un souci manifeste de souligner que l'acte accompli par le siège de

Constantinople n'engageait que lui seul. Cette réaction était normale et s'accompagnait d'ailleurs, dans la plupart des cas, de témoignages de satisfaction à l'égard des bonnes intentions qui, de part et d'autre, avaient inspiré la démarche. Certains, cependant, regrettèrent que le trône oecuménique n'ait pas consulté les Eglises-sœurs avant de procéder à ce geste. En effet ce ne fut que fort peu de jours avant qu'il ne soit accompli que ces Eglises furent informées de ce qui se préparait; et une information n'est pas une consultation. Le délai qui demeurait était d'ailleurs trop court pour que le sentiment, que ces Eglises eussent pu souhaiter exprimer, pût efficacement parvenir à Istanbul, d'autant plus que les textes préparés eux-mêmes, dont nous avons dit qu'ils n'avaient été mis au point qu'à la dernière minute, ne leur avaient pas été communiqués. Ce serait sans doute se faire une vue trop optimiste des choses que de penser qu'il n'en est pas résulté quelque amertume à l'endroit du siège oecuménique de la part de maintes Eglises-sœurs. Celles-ci ne pouvaient oublier qu'elles avaient été aussi peu informées et consultées à la veille de la rencontre de Jérusalem. D'où un renforcement du grief fait assez couramment au trône oecuménique d'agir de son propre chef sans suffisamment tenir compte de l'opinion des Eglises-sœurs. Peut-être d'ailleurs un tel grief n'était-il pas totalement absent de certains membres de la hiérarchie du patriarcat constantinopolitain, et jusque parmi les membres du synode à l'égard du patriarche lui-même. Ceci expliquerait que manquent au bas du "*Tomos*" synodal certaines signatures.[7] On peut regretter cette attitude réticente mais on ne peut s'en étonner.

Il ne sera pas inutile de rappeler qu'à Rome même on est fort conscient de la difficulté qui résulte d'un certain manque de cohésion entre les différentes Eglises orthodoxes. Il y a là un fait qui paralyse singulièrement les efforts de rapprochement tentés tant du côté de Constantinople que du côté romain. Du moins ce fait fournit-il une occasion au siège de Rome de bien manifester que si naguère son attitude en face des Eglises orthodoxes a pu donner l'apparence qu'il tendait à appliquer la devise "*divide ut imperes*", il a désormais adopté l'attitude diamétralement contraire et que rien ne lui est plus à cœur que de favoriser — pour autant que cela puisse se faire de l'extérieur — la cohésion et l'unité des Eglises orthodoxes. Nous sommes assez bien placés pour dire que si les

---

[7]   En réalité, tous les métropolites présents à Istanbul furent invités à apposer leur signature au bas de ce document historique, et non pas seulement les membres du synode. Trois signatures manquent; ce sont celles des métropolites Maxime de Sardes, Maxime de Stravopolis et Jacques de Derkon. Il est important toutefois de préciser que leurs réserves ne portaient pas sur l'acte lui-même ainsi accompli mais sur la façon dont le patriarche avait procédé à l'égard des autres Eglises orthodoxes.

initiatives du siège de Constantinople en vue du rapprochement ont toujours été accueillies de la façon la plus bienveillante à Rome, jamais on n'y a manqué une occasion d'attirer l'attention du trône oecuménique sur les inconvénients que pourrait présenter une action unilatérale susceptible de créer des difficultés entre le patriarcat oecuménique et les autres Eglises orthodoxes.[8]

On ne pouvait s'attendre à ce que le geste accompli en commun par le pape et le patriarche soulevât le même enthousiasme — et même suscitât le même intérêt — dans les milieux protestants que dans les milieux catholiques-romains et orthodoxes. D'abord, parce que les événements visés de 1054 ne concernent pas, directement du moins, l'histoire de la Réforme et des Eglises qui en sont issues.[9] Ensuite aussi parce que, même les esprits qui sont grandement intéressés par le mouvement oecuménique, semblent toujours un peu chagrins lorsqu'ils enregistrent les étapes d'un rapprochement effectif entre l'Eglise orthodoxe et l'Eglise catholique-romaine, comme si un tel rapprochement devait nécessairement conduire à la constitution d'une sorte de front commun des Eglises de type dit "catholique" contre le bloc des communions dites "protestantes". Une telle crainte apparaît périodiquement dans l'attitude des cercles dirigeants du Conseil oecuménique des Eglises lui-même. Sans doute, en l'occurence, n'y eut-il pas de manifestation publique d'une telle crainte mais le moins qu'on puisse dire c'est que l'événement ne reçut pas, dans ces milieux, l'accueil qu'en lui-même il méritait comme un jalon posé sur la voie que l'on espère voir conduire à la réunion de tous les chrétiens.

---

[8] C'est une pente assez naturelle des esprits dans l'Eglise catholique-romaine de se représenter "l'*auctoritas*" du patriarche oecuménique dans l'Eglise orthodoxe entière à la manière de celle qu'exerce la papauté dans l'Eglise catholique universelle, ce qui n'est évidemment pas le cas. Céder à cette pente serait le plus sûr moyen de susciter l'animosité des Eglises orthodoxes, toujours portées, de leur côté, à suspecter une évolution dans ce sens du patriarcat oecuménique. La cohésion et l'unité qu'on peut attendre entre les Eglises orthodoxes ne peuvent être que conformes à la tradition propre de ces Eglises. On sait que la réunion de conférences pan-orthodoxes analogues à celles qui se sont tenues à Rhodes (1961 ; 1963 ; 1964) pourrait être une étape vers la constitution d'un organisme pan-orthodoxe assumant ce rôle de coordinateur dans l'unité collégiale des Eglises-soeurs.

[9] Nous disons "directement" car, si les événements de 1054 sont chronologiquement bien antérieurs à la Réforme protestante, nous pensons cependant être fondés à croire qu'entre autres graves conséquences de cette première rupture il faut compter précisément la crise religieuse du XVI siècle qui a divisé l'Eglise d'Occident. Il ne faut d'ailleurs jamais perdre de vue que ce que le protestantisme a rejeté de la tradition et de la structure hiérarchique sacramentelle de l'Eglise l'a tout autant, sinon même davantage, éloigné de l'Eglise orthodoxe. Il y a là, à notre sens, une donnée importante et même capitale du problème oecuménique à laquelle nous regrettons que, dans leur immense majorité, les milieux protestants se montrent jusqu'ici si peu sensibles.

6. PERSPECTIVES OUVERTES PAR LA "LEVÉE DES ANATHEMES"

Comme nous l'avons souligné, la déclaration commune a pris soin de présenter le geste de réconciliation accompli comme s'insérant dans une suite d'événements menant progressivement au rétablissement de la pleine communion entre l'Eglise orthodoxe et l'Eglise catholique romaine. L'événement initial avait été la rencontre de Jérusalem. D'autres devaient tout naturellement suivre et, effectivement, ont suivi. Ainsi se réalisait peu à peu la volonté ferme du patriarche Athénagoras d'en finir avec un oecuménisme fait trop exclusivement de bonnes paroles pour en venir à un oecuménisme d'actes positifs et concrets *réalisant* le rapprochement.

C'est à ce genre d'actes positifs et concrets qu'il faut rattacher l'échange, désormais devenu régulier, de lettres officielles entre le siège de Rome et divers premiers sièges des Eglises orthodoxes. C'est par un tel échange de lettres que se manifestait autrefois la communion de vie sacramentelle existant entre les différentes Eglises locales: lettres synodiques, par lesquelles le nouvel élu à la première charge d'une de ces Eglises faisait part de son élection aux titulaires des autres premiers sièges, et dans lesquelles il déclarait sa foi et, en conséquence, sollicitait la communion de ces autres Eglises; lettres aussi envoyées à l'occasion des deux grandes fêtes chrétiennes de Noël et de Pâques; lettres enfin suscitées par quelque événement exceptionnel survenu dans la vie de l'Eglise et mettant en danger soit la pureté de sa foi, soit la concorde fraternelle entre les Eglises locales. Il va de soi que l'échange actuel de telles lettres ne peut signifier une plénitude de communion qui n'existe pas. Mais du moins entendent-elles manifester la mesure de communion déjà existante ainsi que les bonnes dispositions réciproques entièrement et résolument tournées vers l'élimination progressive de tout ce qui fait encore obstacle à la communion plénière. Comme on doit bien le penser, le contenu de ces lettres est toujours très soigneusement étudié, la rédaction en est mûrement pesée dans le moindre de ses mots. Aussi se tromperait-on lourdement si l'on se contentait d'y voir de simples manifestations d'une politesse toute ecclésiastique mais sans aucune portée.

Actes très positifs aussi de bienveillance que la restitution à diverses Eglises orthodoxes d'insignes reliques d'apôtres ou de saints, naguère confiées aux bons soins de l'Eglise catholique-romaine pour les faire échapper à la profanation par les infidèles, telle la relique vénérée comme le chef de l'apôtre saint André à l'Eglise de Patras, le corps de saint Sabba au monastère du même nom en Palestine, le chef de saint Tite, disciple de saint Paul, à l'Eglise de Crète.

Mais, à coup sûr, ce sont les nouvelles rencontres du patriarche Athena-goras 1er et du pape Paul VI qui ont, jusqu'à présent, constitué les princi-paux maillons de cette chaîne d'événements jalonnant la voie de la pleine réconciliation.

Nous avons dit plus haut comment s'était tout d'abord révélée comme un obstacle à une première rencontre la difficulté qui s'opposait à ce que le pape Jean XXIII rendît la visite que le patriarche se déclarait disposé à lui faire. Il faut vraiment qu'un important chemin ait été parcouru — grâce au concile et aux démarches précédentes du trône oecuménique — pour qu'ait pu être envisagée, non plus seulement une visite rendue par le pape Paul VI au patriarche, mais bel et bien une visite faite — et très spontanément faite — par lui à Istanbul même. Ce n'est pas l'objet de cet article que d'en refaire le compte rendu; du moins nous sera-t-il permis de rappeler à quel point une telle démarche, de l'évêque de l'an-cienne Rome à celui de la nouvelle Rome, a favorablement surpris l'opi-nion unanime des Eglises orthodoxes. Pouvait-on imaginer un geste de rupture plus éclatante avec une tradition d'isolement dans laquelle cette même opinion était accoutumée de voir une manifestation de "l'orgueil romain", inspirateur de "sa constante politique de domination universel-le"? Mais, cette fois encore, les textes furent éloquents: aux discours, déjà pleins de substance, s'ajouta, d'une façon assez inattendue, un "message" du pape Paul VI où s'exprime très explicitement l'espoir de voir l'Eglise de Constantinople et celle de Rome se considérer de plus en plus comme des "Eglises-sœurs" ainsi qu'elles étaient accoutumées de le faire avant leur séparation.[10] Cet état de séparation ne doit pas les empêcher d'être sœurs et de se comporter comme telles dans toute la mesure permise par le trésor commun qu'elles ont hérité des apôtres. Quand on sait à quel point était sévèrement bannie du vocabulaire catho-lique-romain cette expression "Eglises-sœurs" même en parlant d'Eglises de la communion romaine, à plus forte raison à l'égard d'Eglises se trouvant hors de sa communion, on peut se rendre compte de quel souci de fidélité aux décisions les plus importantes du concile est animé le pape Paul VI, en particulier en ce qui concerne la revalorisation opérée par Vatican II de la notion d'Eglises locales et du principe collégial dans la structure hiérarchique de l'Eglise.

Peu de semaines devaient s'écouler avant que le patriarche Athéna-

---

[10]   On ne peut omettre de mentionner ici le geste du pape Paul VI s'agenouillant sur le sol lors de sa visite à Sainte-Sophie (devenue mosquée puis musée), et priant en réparation de l'acte accompli au même endroit en 1054 par les léats pontificaux durant la célébration de la sainte liturgie orthodoxe. En renouvelant ainsi le geste déjà accompli par le cardinal Bea lors d'une précédente visite au patriarche, le pape Paul VI en augmentait sensiblement la portée.

goras ne parte à son tour pour Rome afin de rendre au pape la visite reçue à Istanbul. Le fait que le pape Paul VI se soit déplacé le premier rendait singulièrement plus aisée la tâche du patriarche par rapport aux autres Eglises autocéphales: pouvaient-elles, en effet, faire désormais au patriarche oecuménique un grief de se rendre à Rome pour s'acquitter du devoir, que lui imposait la plus élémentaire bienséance, de rendre une visite qu'il avait reçue? Toutefois, tirant la leçon des événements antérieurs, Athénagoras 1er ne se rendit pas à Rome sans avoir pris d'abord un contract personnel avec quelques-uns des principaux patriarches orthodoxes. Seule l'Eglise de Moscou, avertie du désir manifesté par le patriarche oecuménique de se rendre auprès d'elle, lui fit savoir que le moment ne lui paraissait pas opportun et le pria de remettre au printemps suivant son voyage projeté en Union soviétique. En se rendant près des autres patriarches (Serbie, Bulgarie, Roumanie) le patriarche se mettait à même de s'informer sur leurs dispositions à l'égard du rapprochement souhaité par lui avec l'Eglise romaine. Il pouvait, en conséquence, mesurer les paroles qu'il se proposait de prononcer au cours de sa visite auprès du tombeau des apôtres et s'assurer ainsi, sinon le droit de parler en leur nom, du moins la certitude de n'en point recevoir de désapprobation. Ce que nous avons dit précédemment permet de comprendre le gain ainsi réalisé dans l'accord des Eglises orthodoxes par rapport aux démarches antérieures du représentant du trône oecuménique. Ne serait-ce qu'à cet égard, la visite romaine d'Athénagoras 1er a constitué une étape importante, dans le sens le plus heureux, sur la voie du développement du dialogue entre l'Eglise romaine et l'Orthodoxie. Mais du côté catholique-romain une nouvelle pierre était ajoutée à l'édifice par l'insistance mise à nouveau par le pape Paul VI, dans son adresse au patriarche, sur cette notion d'Eglises-sœurs dont nous avons toutes raisons de penser qu'elle constitue un axe majeur dans le dialogue entrepris en vue de la totale réconciliation.

On sait que le patriarche Athénagoras profita de son voyage en Europe occidentale pour se rendre auprès de Sa Grâce Michel Ramsey, archevêque de Cantorbéry, lui rendant ainsi la visite qu'il en avait reçue, et pour s'arrêter à Genève au siège du Conseil oecuménique des Eglises. Il n'entre pas dans l'objet de la présente étude d'exposer le détail de ces rencontres. Il nous suffira de les évoquer comme un témoignage de la volonté résolue du patriarcat oecuménique de ne point dissocier ses efforts de rapprochement avec l'Eglise catholique-romaine et les autres relations bilatérales récemment amorcées, de la conjoncture d'ensemble du grand et difficile problème de la restauration de la pleine unité entre tous les chrétiens.

11 janvier 1968

NOUVEAUX ASPECTS DE L'OECUMÉNISME

CHARLES MOELLER

Le titre de cette contribution en l'honneur de Georges Florovsky[1] "Nouveaux aspects de l'oecuménisme" peut sembler paradoxal. En effet dans la recherche de l'unité des chrétiens, nous nous proposons de redécouvrir une dimension trop négligée actuellement mais qui n'a rien de nouveau: celle que l'orthodoxie apporte plus particulièrement mais non exclusivement aux progrès de l'oecuménisme. Dans la première partie de cet essai sera exposée la fidélité de l'Eglise orthodoxe et, comme la littérature russe en fait foi, sa conscience aiguë du fait social. La position orthodoxe à la fois fondée sur la plus solide tradition et éveillée la première aux problèmes des hommes en société devrait servir de guide dans le dialogue

---

[1] Je me souviens de ma découverte de l'œuvre de Georges Florovsky. J'étais étudiant en théologie à l'université de Louvain. Le professeur Draguet consacra le cours de l'année 1937-1938, sur la théologie des églises orientales, au Congrès de la théologie orthodoxe tenu à Athènes en 1936, et dont les Actes venaient d'être publiés.

La lecture et le commentaire de cet article me fit prendre conscience que, non seulement en vertu du fait que le Nouveau Testament était écrit en grec, mais aussi par la place occupée dans la liturgie, la théologie, la spiritualité orthodoxe par les Pères *grecs*, il y avait une sorte de lien indissoluble entre certains aspects de la culture hellénique et l'annonce de la bonne nouvelle.

Le professeur Draguet attira notre attention, particulièrement, sur un thème qui, à cette époque, suscitait bien des recherches et discussions: celui de "l'essence de l'orthodoxie". Dans ce cadre, il signalait la contribution de Georges Florovsky: ce dernier marquait plutôt sa méfiance devant les tentatives de découvrir une "essence" de l'orthodoxie. En revanche, il soulignait un lien, selon lui fondamental, entre l'orthodoxie et la tradition patristique grecque. Il appelait ce fait "l'hellénisme chrétien".

Cette affirmation nous frappa d'autant plus que la plupart d'entre nous avaient pris connaissance de l'orthodoxie russe à travers le livre de Bulgakov, publié chez Alcan, dans une collection de forme austère, appelée "les religions". Nous connaissions aussi quelque peu le mouvement slavophile. Sans doute, les livres de A. Glorieux et de Samarine, parus en 1939, dans la naissante collection "Unam sanctam" allaient nous apprendre davantage. Mais, à travers la lecture d'œuvres de Nikolas Berdjaev, nous avions découvert ce monde extraordinaire, où la foi chrétienne voisinait avec certains thèmes de l'idéalisme allemand ou de la pensée slave. Nous n'avions qu'une assez vague connaissance de l'œuvre de Solov'ev, suffisante cependant pour entrevoir ce type de pensée prophétique, ouverte à la fois à la tradition liturgique la plus authentique, — celle de la "Div'ne liturgie" —, et à des vues un peu "apocalyptiques", — on parlait moins, alors, d'eschatologie —, sur l'avenir de l'Eglise en Occident. Enfin, évidemment, nous avions lu les principaux livres de Dostoevskij et y avions découvert le "messianisme orthodoxe" inscrit dans l'œuvre.

Le "nous" dont je parle ici représente la génération d'étudiants que nous étions vers les années 1935-1939, à la veille de la seconde guerre mondiale. C'était l'époque de la découverte de l'orthodoxie, à travers les écrits et les témoignages d'un certain nombre de philosophes et de théologiens russes de l'émigration.

Nous avions spontanément identifié l'orthodoxie avec la forme particulière qu'elle trouvait dans le mouvement slavophile. Comme Georges Florovsky était russe, nous identifions sa pensée avec celle des slavophiles.

L'étude de sa contribution au congrès de théologie orthodoxe d'Athènes fut pour nous une vraie découverte. Elle démontrait sans doute l'intérêt des approches de la foi orthodoxe en s'inspirant de certains aspects de la pensée russe et allemande. Mais elle mettait à jour aussi le caractère particulier et limité dans le temps et dans l'espace, de cette vision. Surtout elle indiquait l'aspect de "système de théologie" inhérent à cette conception.

Au contraire, en soulignant l'enracinement dans la patristique grecque, Georges Florovsky mettait à jour la continuité de la tradition profonde de l'orthodoxie. Ce dont cet "hellénisme" témoignait, ce n'était pas tant la spéculation d'un Origène, qu'il fallait ici mettre en avant, que sa "lecture" de la révélation biblique dans la tradition des églises grecques. C'était l'Origène commentateur de l'Ecriture par exemple, ou les homélies de Jean Chrysostome sur les épîtres de Saint Paul qu'il fallait considérer.

De voir ainsi l'orthodoxie russe, elle aussi, se rattacher à cette tradition de la patristique grecque, donnait à celle-ci une épaisseur dans le temps, une profondeur d'enracinement, qui plongeait jusque dans la Septante. La Systématisation, pour fascinante et importante qu'elle soit, reprenait sa place, au service de la Tradition vivante.

Je rencontrai le professeur Florovsky au centre *Istina*, à Boulogne-sur-Seine, après la seconde guerre mondiale, où il assistait à une rencontre oecuménique, à laquelle était présent Dom Lambert Beauduin. Une intervention du professeur Florovsky, toujours sur le sens de l'orthodoxie, témoignant d'une expérience vécue, profondément spirituelle, fit une fois de plus apparaître le même phénomène: lorsque des catholiques discutent avec des réformés, ils sont, sans doute, très loin les uns des autres sur un certain nombre de points, mais ils sont "proches", en ce qu'ils se servent des mêmes catégories de pensée. Durant ces discussions, les participants orthodoxes se sentent le plus souvent "étrangers"; tout se passe comme s'ils attendaient que, ces discussions terminées, l'unité, ou du moins le rapprochement étant fait, ils puissent alors participer au dialogue. Chaque fois qu'un théologien orthodoxe intervient, le problème antérieurement discuté entre catholiques et réformés change d'aspect, de problématique, "d'*impostazione*". Un exemple célèbre en fut donné au Concile Vatican II, lorsque l'évêque melchite Edelby aborda le problème de "Ecriture et Tradition", en faisant appel à "l'épiclèse" de l'Esprit-Saint, montrant que le rôle de la tradition vivante peut, en quelque manière, être éclairé de la sorte.

En cette lointaine soirée, à *Istina*, l'intervention de Georges Florovsky produisit le même renouvellement de perspectives. Dom Lambert remarqua avec la fine malice qui le caractérisait: "Nous sommes très loin les uns des autres, catholiques et protestants, sur une série de points; mais nous sommes proches, parce que nous usons des mêmes types de pensée; nous demeurons dans la dispute de famille. Au contraire, nous sommes infiniment proches des orthodoxes; que l'on songe par exemple à la doctrine de

oecuménique. A cette *rétrospective*, viendra se greffer dans la deuxième partie la *prospective*, c'est-à-dire la tâche qui confronte le monde occidental. L'urgence des problèmes qui accompagnent le bouleversement social appelle l'union des Eglises. Enfin la troisième partie, mesurant les progrès déjà accomplis, suggère que l'Eglise orthodoxe ayant la première réussi à se maintenir dans un milieu athée peut contribuer par son "génie propre" à résoudre les problèmes de Nouvel Humanisme.[2]

---

l'Eucharistie, de la succession apostolique; et, en même temps, nous nous sentons très loin les uns des autres, car la manière de penser, d'approcher les mêmes vérités, est tellement différente."

Georges Florovsky mettait en pleine lumière cet apport propre de l'orthodoxie. Il rappelait sans cesse la nécessité, dans le mouvement oecuménique, d'un dialogue "à trois", — disons même "à quatre" si l'on tient compte, comme on le doit, de l'Anglicanisme.

Tout cela met en évidence la nécessité de la participation de l'orthodoxie au dialogue oecuménique, non seulement parce qu'elle est une dénomination chrétienne importante par le nombre, — environ deux cent millions de fidèles —, mais aussi par son enracinement *privilégié* dans la tradition patristique grecque et syriaque.

On a souvent dit que, dans l'orthodoxie, il n'y avait qu'un intérêt réduit pour les problèmes posés par ce que l'on appelle "humanisme chrétien". C'est une affirmation qui ne répond pas à la réalité.

Vers les années 1944-1948, dans les discussions au sujet de l'approche humaniste de l'orthodoxie, on parlait de cette "humanité nouvelle" rayonnant sur le visage des saints transfigurés, comme par exemple Seraphim de Sarov. Les études du Père Cyprien Kern sur Palamas, celles de V. Losski, sur *La théologie mystique de l'Eglise d'Orient*, témoignaient de cette "lumière thaborique" rayonnant chez les saints, et se manifestant parfois, par un don extraordinaire, dans les gestes et les traits de l'homme. Des traductions françaises, enfin complètes, des *Frères Karamazov*, de Dostoevskij, révélaient, dans le Starec Zosima, inspiré d'un personnage historique, cette lumière mystérieuse qui rayonnait de ses paroles et de son comportement. La scène, narrée par le Starec, où il rappelle comment un soir, au bord d'un fleuve de Russie, un jeune homme très simple, mais très docile à la grâce de Dieu lui avait fait entrevoir comment toutes choses sont, ainsi, dans la paix du Logos créateur, manifestait cette vision propre de l'orthodoxie sur les "choses de ce monde". De même, le fameux chapître sur "l'odeur délétère", après la mort du Starec, révélait aux lecteurs quel critère original de la sainteté qu'était la conservation miraculeuse, dans une sorte d'intégrité, du corps du "saint". Alors que dans la vision latine, ce qui compte, c'est l'héroïcité des vertus.

[2] Dans une étude parue en 1946, j'ai proposé d'appeler cet aspect "humanisme eschatologique", en le distinguant de ce que je dénommais, d'une manière peut-être peu claire, "humanisme terrestre". Ces deux termes, quoi qu'il en soit, ont peut-être l'avantage de signaler clairement deux approches, distinctes, mais non contradictoires, de l'humanisme chrétien. Il va sans dire, du reste, que cet "humanisme eschatologique" est une donnée essentielle de la tradition occidentale dans le catholicisme. Il suffit de songer à la figure de François d'Assise qui "épousa Dame pauvreté": valeurs "profanes", — le rêve d'une beauté visible à laquelle dédier des gestes de "hautesse" —, et chrétiennes, — la pauvreté de Jésus-Christ —, se rejoignent ici si étroitement qu'on ne "peut les déchirer par pièces". Lorsque François Bernardone rencontra "Dame pauvreté", dans un seul regard, il découvrit le sommet de cet idéal de chevalerie qui était le sien, comme aussi celui de son temps, et la réalisation inattendue, venue *d'ailleurs* de Dieu, de ce même idéal en la figure de celle que tous les puissants de ce

1

Il est hors de doute que la vision de l'humanisme eschatologique fut redécouverte dans les milieux catholiques de l'Europe occidentale, en grande partie grâce au témoignage, aux contacts et relations, après la première guerre mondiale, avec les orthodoxes russes de l'émigration.

Autour de Berdjaev, et de Bulgakov, d'autres personnalités gravitant dans l'orbite de cette émigration ont contribué aussi à cette découverte. Comment ne pas évoquer ici l'archiprêtre Cassien, dont l'exégèse mystique de saint Jean fut, pour beaucoup, la vision d'un monde neuf?[3] Car c'est bien là que se dévoile un des apports essentiels de l'orthodoxie au

---

monde rejettent, la pauvreté.

Ce n'est point hasard si les orthodoxes reconnaissent en saint François d'Assise le saint qui, chez eux, éveille le plus d'échos en profondeur, car ils y voient ce "pauvre transfiguré" *qui erre toujours dans les sentiers de la Sainte Russie*, celui dont le Christ a dit: "Ce que vous avez fait au moindre des miens, c'est à moi que vous l'avez fait."

[3] Je me souviens comment, durant une visite à *Istina*, après la seconde guerre mondiale, nous eûmes l'occasion d'assister à une célébration de la divine liturgie, dans la cathédrale de la rue Daru: c'était la fête de l'Annonciation, dont on sait la place hors de pair dans le cycle liturgique byzantin, puisque, en cas de concurrence de la fête du 25 mars avec le vendredi saint, les deux offices sont combinés étroitement. L'incarnation et la rédemption apparaissent alors nouées si étroitement que les frontières entre la venue en ce monde, la mort à ce monde et la résurrection pour un monde nouveau, se mêlent et superposent leur signification.

Je me souviens encore de la communion, où je vis, pour la première fois, dans l'église orthodoxe, des parents communier avec leur petit enfant dans les bras; je voyais aussi ces mêmes parents, revenus de la communion, donner le baiser de paix à leurs enfants. Enfin, comment ne pas penser encore au sermon que l'évêque Cassien fit, qu'une interprète bénévole traduisait pour nous phrase par phrase.

Toujours dans la ligne de cet "humanisme transfiguré", le groupe auquel j'appartenais avait pu assister, la veille de l'Annonciation, à l'office de la vigile. Il ne se déroulait pas dans la cathédrale, mais dans une pièce rectangulaire, dont on nous dit qu'elle était un ancien garage. Ce qui frappait immédiatement, c'était comment cet espace sans aucune recherche de forme architecturale, prenait une sorte de grandeur sacrée, par les icones suspendues aux murs, les lampes allumées, l'iconostase, et les chants des officiants et du chœur.

Il y a là un aspect caractéristique des arts religieux byzantins. Les icones sont conçues selon d'autres canons que celui des perspectives tridimensionnelles de l'Occident récent. Le point de convergence des lignes ne se trouve pas dans le lointain de l'espace, mais dans l'oeil du sujet. Les lignes de la fameuse icone de la Troica de Rublev, que Georges Florovsky nous expliqua un jour, ne se rejoignent point dans l'espace optique du spectateur, mais bien dans son oeil. Malgré ce renversement de la perspective "classique", et sans doute à cause de celui-ci, les icones paraissent ouvrir une sorte d'espace intérieur, un espace cosmique, qui n'est pas le monde visible, mais un autre, entrevu à travers celui-ci.

On peut ainsi comprendre ce caractère à la fois *péregrinal et transfiguré* de la piété orthodoxe: ce garage transformé en église, comment ne pas voir une autre forme de cette "tente du témoignage" dont parle l'Ancien Testament?

mouvement oecuménique. Comme l'a dit Louis Bouyer, la liturgie byzantine fait pénétrer par des moyens invisibles dans le monde invisible. Elle réussit ce miracle. Ce n'est pas en effet l'image comme telle qui, en faisant penser au saint mystère représenté, aide l'esprit à s'élever vers ce dernier; c'est l'image elle-même, ce sont les chants, les gestes, les lumières qui progressivement introduisent le regard, le cœur, bientôt l'homme tout entier, dans l'entrevision d'un monde transfiguré. Le fidèle est debout; souvent il passe des heures, dans la foule, comme dans les églises de Russie, en 1967, dans des églises de village. Il regarde, il écoute. Il se laisse porter. D'aucuns, soucieux "d'engagement", diront qu'il rêve un peu, s'évade. Or, le fidèle, qu'il soit savant professeur à Saint-Serge, ou simple paysan de Tula, ne s'évade pas; il entre dans une vision décantée, dans une sorte de paix des yeux et des oreilles, un recueillement de tous les sens, qui sans aucunement l'arracher à ce monde, lui fait découvrir un monde autre, délivré peu à peu, ouvert à la lumière de la Jérusalem céleste.

C'est aussi en ces temps déjà lointains, aux alentours de la seconde guerre mondiale, que nous découvrîmes certains aspects peu connus de la littérature russe, ainsi la différence, allant parfois jusqu'à une véritable tension antinomique, entre Saint-Pétersburg, — comme elle se nommait dans ces écrits —, et Moscou. Dom Clément Lialine, moine du prieuré pour l'union à Amay-Chevetogne, expliquait cette opposition dans *Guerre et Paix*, de Tolstoj. La famille Rostov, généreuse, joviale, prodigue aussi, surtout en la figure du comte, incarnait les milieux moscovites. Nikolaj, Nataša: comment les oublier, au long de ces fêtes de famille, comme la Noël de l'an neuf? Puškin lui-même, disait Dom Lialine, quand il était à Moscou, se sentait meilleur, plus enraciné dans les souvenirs vivants de sa vieille "njanja" qui lui racontait des histoires un peu fantastiques, comme celle de la "Cabane sur pattes de poule". Au contraire Saint-Pétersburg paraissait plus brillant, plus froid, plus superficiel aussi dans *Guerre et Paix*. Ce fut à Saint-Pétersburg que Puškin se battit en duel et mourut de cette blessure froidement et très précisément infligée à lui par le baron d'Antès.

Gogol' surtout nous révélait des significations cachées. *Le Revizor* apparaît, à la fin, ce qu'il est, un menteur, prenant les apparences du véritable juge. Lorsque les fantoches du pitoyable village où il est venu sont devant lui, à la fin, saisis dans les plus grotesques positions de la servilité, on apprend soudain que le véritable revizor s'annonce, dont celui-ci n'était que la caricature mensongère. Tous alors s'immobilisent et le tableau final rend sensible la stupeur, le silence épouvanté qui, après tant de bruits et de fureur, tombe sur ce monde qui voit poindre son juge.

Le Revizor dans l'idée de Gogol', était une image de l'antéchrist; il devait rendre sensible la comédie humaine sous le signe du mensonge, de la servilité devant les puissances de ce monde.

Gogol' se désespérait de voir que personne, en son pays, ne semblait saisir cette signification proprement chrétienne, eschatologique oserait-on dire, de ses écrits. La seconde partie des *Ames mortes*, qu'il refit plusieurs fois, et, finalement, détruisit, devait dire cette vérité terrible, ce jugement, inscrit, lui aussi, dans son roman, mais dont la première partie, si bouffone, n'avait pas réussi à convaincre les lecteurs. Gogol' en fit un vrai drame spirituel; il craignait que son œuvre qu'il voulait témoignage de la foi orthodoxe, ne soit, au contraire, un témoignage à rebours, dont le démon se servait pour tromper plus encore les lecteurs.

Durant ses dernières années, Gogol' composa des méditations sur la divine liturgie, et sur les icônes. Lors d'un séjour offert par le Métropolite Nikodim, durant la conférence mondiale de Genève, *Eglise et société*, dès que la conversation se porta sur ces écrits de Gogol', une expérience commune, à la fois littéraire et chrétienne, se fit jour, autour des thèmes essentiels de la foi: péché, jugement, transfiguration.

L'exemple de Gogol' est d'une particulière signification. Il permet en effet de faire, dans l'ordre littéraire, et avec toutes les différences qui s'imposent entre une vision littéraire et l'action eucharistique, une découverte analogue de la sensibilité orthodoxe. C'est au cœur de la réalité humaine la plus quotidienne, la plus comique et la plus bouffone parfois, — car il ne faut pas oublier le génie satirique du "petit russien" qu'était Gogol' —, que se lit en filigrane cette absence de vérité et d'amour, ce creux, ce vide deviné derrière les masques qui font entrevoir par contraste le besoin du vrai juge, sauveur et pacificateur. Cette lecture "verticale" ou, si l'on préfère, polyphonique, à la manière d'une partition orchestrale, rend sensible l'humanisme eschatologique.

Dostoevskij conjoint à cette dimension, celle que, actuellement, on appellerait horizontale. *Les Frères Karamazov*, devait en effet se composer de trois parties, dont la première seulement fut achevée, les deux autres n'existant que sous forme d'ébauches, dans les *Carnets* laissés par le romancier. La première présentait Aleša "dans le monastère", auprès du Starec Zosima. Il y découvrait avec ferveur cette présence de la "Parole" dans le monde; il y entendait le Starec lui raconter comment un jour, voyant un soldat d'ordonnance frappé par son officier, il avait découvert le caractère sacré du visage humain, et l'intolérable affront fait à l'image de Dieu.

Seulement, Aleša ne sait pas encore combien son cœur est entraîné vers la violence, et l'obscurité de cette terre. Il porte en effet en lui l'hérédité des Karamazov. Celle-ci, dans l'idée de Dostoevskij, représente la pesanteur du monde, la violence partout présente, dont seul le long chemin vers la rédemption peut le délivrer. Aussi bien, Aleša devra "retourner dans ce monde". Après la mort du Starec, celle de son Père, le départ de Dimitrij en captivité, il quittera lui aussi l'enclos du monastère. Il prendra au sérieux la révolution. Il connaîtra la violence et la haine souffertes au nom de la société future.

Ceux qui ont lu *Les Démons*, savent le sens que Dostoevskij donne à l'entreprise révolutionnaire. Il ne peut la séparer de ce que son expérience lui avait appris, à propos du mystérieux Nečaev, qui hanta une partie de sa vie. Dostoevskij a donné de l'athéisme, dans cette lumière, quelques images d'une lucidité vertigineuse. Il avait en effet pressenti le sens de l'œuvre de Nietzsche. Ce qui nous intéresse ici, c'est la réponse orthodoxe aux problèmes "du monde de ce temps". Elle est orientée très différemment. Mais ce serait une perte sans rémission que d'oublier ce témoignage dont Dostoevskij a donné quelques images de feu.

Aleša doit donc passer par cette passion, faite d'espoirs humains et d'erreurs. La seconde partie du roman devait le montrer "se perdant" en quelque sorte dans un grand péché, devenant, si paradoxal que cela paraisse, une sorte de Stavrogin, singerie de l'agitation bavarde de Verxovenskij des *Démons*. Seulement, Aleša devait, dans la troisième partie du livre, retrouver la voie. Il ne retournait pas dans le monastère. Il demeurait "dans le monde". Seulement ce monde devenait "autre", par la vie sainte. On sait en effet maintenant comment, sous l'influence de Feodorov, un visionnaire du siècle passé, Dostoevskij, avait imaginé une transfiguration progressive de ce monde, sous la double pesée de la vie sainte des croyants, et des progrès d'ordre scientifique, vécus dans ce climat d'espérance eschatologique.

Il est difficile pour un esprit français de se confier au labyrinthe fascinant d'une espérance à la fois apocalyptique et terrestre. Notre intention ici n'est pas d'expliquer, moins encore de faire partager toutes ces idées, mais seulement de faire entrevoir, à travers l'œuvre projetée du grand romancier, cette vision d'humanisme eschatologique qui animait l'auteur de *Crime et Châtiment*. Il n'est pas de dialogue oecuménique avec l'orthodoxie qui puisse faire l'économie de cette dimension. Bien entendu, à travers les pages de Dostoevskij, nous en avons une image quelque peu particulière, fantastique parfois. Ce qui compte c'est de saisir le propos de l'écrivain, le témoignage qu'il donne indirectement d'une tradition plus large, plus simplement aussi, où se retrouvent les lignes "verticales" de la transcendance transfiguratrice de Dieu, et les lignes "horizontales" des efforts humains, au cœur du péché et de la grâce.

Cette dimension est "nouvelle", au sens de ces "*nova et vetera*" dont parle l'Evangile. Cette "nouveauté" doit être connue, vécue, spécialement durant ces temps humanistes et oecuméniques. Comme Paul VI l'a dit en son discours à la Curie, le 22 décembre 1967, l'Eglise se profile, en cette année 1967, selon deux lignes : celle du renouveau intérieur, des cœurs et des esprits, des institutions et des rites; celle de la présence, du dialogue avec le monde de ce temps. La visite de Paul VI au Patriarche Athénagoras, à Istanbul et la venue du même Patriarche à Rome, imposent cette redécouverte dans la tradition théologique occidentale, sous le signe de la Pentecôte. En ce sens, de Serafim de Sarov à François d'Assise, il n'y a pas tellement de chemin : c'est entre ces deux témoins et nous-mêmes, que la distance est immense.

Cette brève excursion dans la littérature russe ne nous a pas éloignés de Georges Florovski. Dans une brochure publiée par l'Institut Saint-Serge, intitulée *List of the Writings of Professors of the Russian Orthodox Institute in Paris, 1925-1954*, nous trouvons une série de noms que tous les oecuménistes de la première heure connaissent et vénèrent : S. Bulgakov, l'évêque Cassien, A. V. Kartašov, Rev. V. Zenkovskij, Rev. Cyprien Kern, Rev. N. Afanassiev, B. P. Vysheslavtzeff, G. P. Fedotoff, G. V. Mochulsky, W. W. Weijdle, V. N. Iljine, L. A. Zander, T. G. Spasky, S. S. Verkhovsky, P. E. Kovalesky, B. I. Sove, Rev. A. Schmemen, J. Meyendorff, Rev. A. Kniazeff. Parmi ces noms dont les premiers surtout représentent une génération dont il ne faut pas que le message se perde, figure celui de Georges Florovski, et dans la bibliographie qui le concerne, une section intitulée *Russian Thought*, sont cataloguées des études sur Tjutčev, Dostoevskij et Solov'ev. Il suffit de lire une de ses récentes études publiée en 1966, "Three Masters: The Quest for Religion in Nineteenth-Century Russian Literature", qui traite en particulier de Gogol', Tolstoj et Dostoevskij. Après une discussion minutieuse des vues religieuses de chacun de ces auteurs,[4] Georges Florovski résume la fin du

---

[4]   Georges Florovsky, "Three Masters: The Quest for Religion in Nineteenth-Century Russian Literature", dans *Comparative Literature Studies*, n. 2, pp. 119-137. A propos de Gogol', qu'il soit permis de citer quelques passages: "It has been suggested that Gogol apprehended Life *sub specie mortis* ... It means that life itself is deadly and deadening, a sort of impasse or illusion ... The earth is already inflamed with incomprehensible melancholy. Life is becoming more and more hardhearted. Everything is getting smaller and smaller. Only the gigantic image of boredom is growing in the sight of all, reaching day by day beyond each measure. Everything is hollow, and graves are everywhere" (p. 123).

On sait les images inoubliables que Gončarov a mises dans son roman, *Oblomov*, —

siècle dernier et le début de celui-ci en Russie, du point de vue des problèmes religieux, dans les lignes suivantes:

The 1890's were a critical period in the history of Russian thought and
literature. In this period of renascent romanticism and of symbolism, motifs
of hope and resignation, of expectation and despair, of faith and disillusionment
were strangely amalgamated in a new manner. By the end of the century
religious themes become conspicuous. The trend reached its peak in the first

---

au point que l'espèce d'ennui, et de nonchalence paresseuse du personnage a donné
naissance à un substantif, "l'oblomovščina", — et l'on n'a pas fini non plus de
découvrir dans l'ennui un des masques les plus subtils du désespoir *démoniaque*.

Aussi bien, Florovsky écrit: "The demonology of Gogol's early stories was probably
not quite serious, being derived from the Western romanticists, including Hoffmann,
and from folklore. The devils there are only grotesque and amusing. Still, in *The
Terrible Revenge* and even more so in *Vij*, the intrusion of evil spirits into human life
is presented with tragic sobriety. In the major works of Gogol evil spirits do not appear
in person, but their presence is assumed. They are operating everywhere, if usually in
disguise. By the end of his life he was overwhelmed with the feeling that evil, or the
Evil One, was omnipresent, as it were. Satan, he thought, had been unbound and
released so that he might appear in the world without even a mask. Although one may
be embarrassed by Gogol's phraseology, there can be no doubt that evil was for him a
superhuman reality charged with enormous power which could be conquered only by
'the mysterious power of the unfathomable Cross', the sole hope of Gogol in his later
years" (p. 124).

Citons encore quelques lignes sur Dostoevskij: "From his youth Dostoevski was
aware of human tragedy. He could discern the symptoms of spiritual anxiety, of
intensifying anguish and despair in human hearts, in human societies, on all level of
human existence. Modern man is an arrogant, rebellious creature; he may even make
blasphemous claims and assign God-like dignity to himself. And yet this rebellious
creature is a troubled and suffering being. In the turmoil of contemporary history, in
the face of growing revolt and apostasy, Dostoievski could discern the anguish of
unbelief. It was his deep conviction that it is unnatural for many to deny God's
existence: *quia fecisti nos ad te.* Man ceases to be truly human when he retreats from
God and claims to stand alone" (p. 131).

On éprouve, en lisant ces lignes, un sentiment de salubre rappel à la vision de
réalités essentielles. Il ne faudrait pas que le dialogue dont on parle tant actuellement
devienne un tiède compromis, dissimulant l'ampleur du drame spirituel que représente
l'athéisme contemporain, "le fait le plus grave de notre temps", disait Paul VI.

Dostoevskij n'ignorait du reste pas la difficulté de croire: "On the other hand,
Dostoievski knew only too well how difficult it is for man to believe. He used to claim
that his own faith was in no sense 'naive' or unaware of difficulties and objections, that
his hosanna had passed through the crucible of trials and temptations, had been tested
and proved. Indeed, he was himself affected by the doubts and hesitations of his own
turbulent and skeptical age. It was a long and arduous way from his early vague and
sentimental commitment to the Christ of history, to his definitive belief in Christ's
Divinity and in the decisive role of Incarnation in the redemtpion of man" (p. 131).

Florovsky mentionne la thèse de certains critiques selon lesquels Tolstoj serait
demeuré en dehors de sa génération: "Tolstoi does not belong psychologically to his
own generation; he was much behind it. He was in permanent opposition to the
course of history" (p. 135).

decade of the new century, on the eve of World War I. N. A. Berdiaev has rightly called the whole movement the Russian Religious Renaissance. On the whole, it held an odd mixture of insights and illusions, of honest search and irresponsible vagaries, in which were integrated various impulses from philosophy, art, and literature. As the heritage of older masters was rediscovered and reassessed in a changed situation and in a new perspective, the religious and prophetic message of Gogol', Dostoevskij, and Tolstoj came alive in the consciousness of the Russian intelligentsia. Later it assumed a new significance during the Revolution. One of the distinctions of the great Russian literature of the last century, the religious and prophetic note, was a mighty stimulus in the quest for ultimate reality and truth.[5]

2

La fin du siècle précédent fut, elle aussi, en France, dans le signe d'un renouveau spirituel et religieux, dans la littérature et les arts.

Seulement, le renouveau français se place sous le signe de la découverte du spirituel, dans la ligne de l'individu et de son histoire particulière. Le symbolisme, par exemple, demeura séparé de la situation sociale, et de la redécouverte des "mythes" au sens positif du terme.

Sans doute Claudel a-t-il célébré en ses héros chrétiens "les rassembleurs de la création"; il a parlé des risques de l'aventure baptismale. Seulement, rien de cela ne mène à des espérances où le social et le religieux essaient de se joindre. En d'autres termes, l'apport propre de la religiosité russe dans la culture au début de ce siècle, si bien marqué par Florovski, lui appartient en propre. La vision, souvent vague sans doute, mais étrangement convergente, où le péché et la grâce se heurtent, en cette passion qui conduit à une vision du monde où la société retrouve un sens authentique, — de n'être plus seulement unie par des idées abstraites, mais par une réalité commune, vécue dans la foi en l'Eglise —, manque totalement dans le renouveau spirituel européen du début du XXe siècle.

C'est précisément cet apport "russe et orthodoxe" que notre génération découvrait entre les années 30 et 40. Ceux qui n'ont pas participé à cette véritable initiation à un monde complètement inconnu jusqu'alors, ne peuvent mesurer la force d'impact qui l'accompagna. Faire de l'oecuménisme, en ce temps, c'était surtout découvrir cette spiritualité, cette liturgie, cette théologie orthodoxes qui nous apparaissent comme un bain de jouvence.

---

[5]   Florovsky, "Three Masters ...", p. 136.

Nous étions encore remplis d'illusions sur les possibilités, pour cette pensée et cette culture, de dialoguer avec les affirmations et réalisations de la révolution russe. Le titre donné, beaucoup plus tard par Jules Romains, dans *Les hommes de bonne volonté*, à cette génération, *Cette grande lueur à l'Est*, exprime assez bien l'espoir fort naïf de certains occidentaux, vers les années 1925-1930.

Gide, dans son œuvre la plus factice, sur Dostoevskij, n'avait pas réussi à faire oublier les analyses infiniment plus profondes et justes d'un Eugène Melchior de Voguë, en la *Revue des deux mondes*, de 1898, sur le roman russe. A travers les "belles infidèles" qu'étaient les traductions de Xal'perin-Kamenskij, nous entrevoyions quelque chose de cet apport prophétique, social, révolutionnaire et, malgré tout chrétien, de la génération de 1890 en Russie.

Tout cela aboutissait, comme on l'a dit au début de cet essai, à la découverte, à travers nos amis de l'Institut Saint-Serge à Paris, de l'orthodoxie tout court, dans le dialogue oecuménique et nous préparait à la lecture enthousiaste du petit livre de Bulgakov sur *L'Orthodoxie*, que le professeur Draguet, à la faculté de théologie de l'Université de Louvain, avait choisi comme texte de base pour son cours de théologie des églises d'Orient, en 1938.

Aujourd'hui, nous nous trouvons confrontés par un phénomène extraordinairement paradoxal: la deuxième guerre mondiale, le passage de la Chine au marxisme, les mouvements de libération nationaux et sociaux qui déchirent périodiquement les pays, et dominant tous ces problèmes, l'immense fait de l'incrédulité contemporaine.

Il semble que les mouvements de renouveau spirituels soient restés sans lendemain. En littérature, une série d'écrivains vivent et publient encore: Mauriac, Green, Graham Greene, Bruce Marshall, Heinrich Böll, etc. Mais *la relève n'est pas faite.* Sur le plan philosophique, la vague existentialiste, des années 1945 et suivantes, avait fait peur à de nombreux penseurs chrétiens. C'était en effet l'aile athée qui s'affirmait alors avec plus de force. Voici que, maintenant, la vague existentialiste semble passée, remplacée dans les pays de l'ouest européen par la vague "structuraliste". Certains, qui s'en réclament, prétendent tout expliquer, par exemple dans le domaine des mythes, sans que demeure le moindre résidu. Nous nous découvrons prisonniers de structures, de systèmes; la synchronie l'emporte sur la diachronie, le "toujours le même" remonte à l'horizon, aux dépens du "nouveau", de "l'événement libérateur".[6]

---

[6] Le "nouveau roman", qui dès les années 1958 avait enregistré, tel un sismographe, la venue de cette nouvelle onde, présente l'homme comme un être qui "est agi, est

En face de ce phénomène, — qui se rattache à un avatar du positivisme —, certains penseurs chrétiens éprouvent la nostalgie de "l'existentialisme, cette dernière "bonne hérésie chrétienne". En effet, on y recherchait de nouvelles définitions, de vieux concepts: liberté, responsabilité, Dieu, culpabilité, bien et mal. La négation même de ces valeurs leur prêtait encore une manière de réalité.

Petit à petit l'athéisme devient le fait majeur. On parle d'une "théologie de la mort de Dieu"; on publie des livres sous le titre "Dieu est mort?"; des numéros d'hebdomadaires, comme *Der Spiegel, Commonwealth, Time,* etc. sont consacrés à cette question.

Enfin, on parle de "christianisme sans religion", en s'inspirant, du reste non sans le simplifier, de Dietrich Bonhoeffer. On critique radicalement "l'institution" dans l'Eglise. On parle du "premier homme" qui veut maintenir au maximum tout l'ensemble des institutions; on parle du "deuxième homme", qui veut réformer, "*aggiornare*" l'institution, mais en demeurant fidèle à l'idée qu'il faut une institution en laquelle l'Eglise se manifeste et agisse. Le "troisième homme" est celui qui, devant ces discussions et disputes choisit d'être fidèle à un christianisme "évangelique": il quitte alors "l'Eglise institution" sur la pointe des pieds.

Nous sommes en présence d'une mise en question, infiniment plus radicale que celle qui se fit à l'époque de la Réforme. Du cœur de cette interrogation implacable, on a bientôt l'impression que les discussions au temps de Luther étaient "querelles de goupillons", réédition, sur grande échelle, du *Lutrin* de Boileau.

S'il est vrai que les controverses du XVIe siècle portaient sur quelques-uns des points les plus graves de la foi chrétienne, l'impression n'en demeure pas moins, invincible, qu'il y avait alors inconscience des questions qui venaient déjà "du dehors", galvaudage de richesses, de vérité et de charité, dilapidation d'un trésor. Cela n'en fait sentir que plus tragiquement la profondeur des questions présentes.

Ce que nous venons de dire au sujet de la littérature et de la pensée

---

parlé, est pensé". Dans *La modification*, de Michel Butor, nous sommes captifs de la rame de wagon, du compartiment dans lequel se fait le voyage de Paris à Rome. Au personnage qui accomplit le voyage "on" parle; on s'adresse toujours à lui, à la seconde personne; on l'interpelle: "Vous avez pensé ceci, vous avez dit cela." Mais qui parle? Qui est ce "on"? Jamais on n'use de la première personne, qui transporterait le lecteur dans l'intimité du personnage. Jamais non plus on n'use de la troisième personne, qui fait participer le lecteur, en une sorte de seconde vue démiurgique, du reste souvent illusoire, à la vie même du personnage, le dévoilant à nous-mêmes plus clairement qu'il ne l'est à lui-même. Non, implacablement au long des trois cent pages du "roman", nous entendons le "vous" anonyme, évasif, impersonnel.

philosophique ne doit pas faire négliger les apports de la sociologie, de l'économie et de la politique. Nous nous trouvons en face d'un ensemble de faits et d'aspirations que l'on nomme "le développement". "Le développement est le nouveau nom de la paix", a dit le Père Lebret; l'expression fut reprise par le pape Paul VI dans *Populorum Progressio*. Elle indique que le développement est une réalité extrêmement complexe. Elle implique l'ensemble des phénomènes déjà mentionnés, mais sous le signe d'une unité de progression humaine, individuelle et sociale, saisie dans un mouvement d'ascension culturelle dont l'ampleur se révèle de jour en jour.

La culture apparaît en effet tout autre chose qu'une activité de surcroît, quelque peu "inutile", liée à la formation d'individualités géniales; elle est processus d'acculturation, transformation du monde par l'homme, expérience de communauté, héritage du passé, tant technique qu'artistique; elle est prise de conscience de l'unité possible du genre humain, découverte de l'autonomie, c'est-à-dire du fait que chaque homme est responsable de la culture et, en un sens, "créateur" de celle-ci.

En face de cette immense espérance, le fait que les deux tiers du monde n'ont pas le minimum vital, le fait que l'écart entre les peuples "hyperdéveloppés" et les peuples en voie de développement va s'agrandissant sans cesse, apparaît comme la plus scandaleuse des injustices *au niveau cosmique*.

Naissent alors, dans la conscience de beaucoup de jeunes, par exemple les étudiants d'Université en Amérique latine, le sens aigu des "trois impératifs".[7] Il serait facile, trop facile, de voir là un nouvel avatar du "politique d'abord" de Charles Maurras: il s'agirait, cette fois, de "développement d'abord", "présence de l'Eglise au monde d'abord", "sociologique d'abord". On a parlé du reste d'une sorte de "sociologisme" qui

---

[7] Le premier, participer, comme étudiants d'université, au développement économique, social, du peuple; le second, la nécessité de prendre part au mouvement de *"politisiacão"*, c'est à dire au fait que tout, y compris l'université, se situe dans la société globale; le troisième, aider le peuple à prendre conscience qu'il est l'auteur de sa propre culture: au lieu de lui apporter une culture toute faite, il est nécessaire de l'éduquer à la prise de conscience de sa responsabilité dans la naissance, la conservation et le progrès de sa culture; c'est bien ce que, en Amérique latine, on nomme *"consciensisacião"*.

Il semble que, si l'on ne prend pas en considération ces "impératifs", toute action pastorale dans les milieux universitaires de l'Amérique latine sera vouée à l'inefficacité.

Ce sont souvent les mêmes qui, saisis par la mise en question radicale des vérités et institutions religieuses, se vouent tout entiers à cet impératif premier, selon eux, de participer au "développement".

envahirait bien des esprits, prenant le relai d'autres "ismes" comme "l'historicisme", le "psychologisme", qui passent peu à peu de mode.

Sans doute, le danger existe, de réduction de l'Eglise et de la foi chrétienne à n'être "que" le moyen, fut-il seul efficace, de réaliser ce "développement", ou du moins de l'aider puissamment. Mais il y a beaucoup plus, surtout si l'on considère que le concile Vatican II a voulu élaborer une Constitution pastorale sur l'Eglise dans le monde d'aujourd'hui, et que, par exemple le Conseil oecuménique des Eglises a consacré une conférence mondiale au thème "Eglise et société", à Genève, en juillet 1966.

En réalité ce sont toutes les églises chrétiennes qui se trouvent, ensemble, en face de cette double question: le sens du langage religieux, le sens du développement dans une perspective ecclésiastique de rédemption.

Dans cette situation nouvelle, les frontières de division ne se superposent plus à celles qui séparent les églises entre elles; elles délimitent au contraire des tendances divergentes, parfois opposées, à l'intérieur même de toutes et de chacune de ces dénominations.

Il y a ici un des aspects les plus importants de cette forme nouvelle de l'activité oecuménique. Celle que nous connaissions depuis les années que l'on a évoquées dans la première partie de cet essai, pourrait se nommer "rétrospective". Elle implique une confrontation de plus en plus précise des raisons qui, dans le passé, ont amené la division: motifs théologiques, liturgiques, facteurs non-théologiques. En d'autres termes, "l'anamnèse", ou souvenir de notre passé d'unité entre chrétiens doit nous faire découvrir aussi, de plus en plus clairement, le point exact à partir duquel nous avons commencé à nous différencier d'abord, ensuite à nous ignorer, puis à nous opposer, pour finir par la séparation.

Cette activité rétrospective demeurera toujours essentielle. Connaître par exemple en quoi nous sommes proches et lointains sur une question comme celle de la justification demeure capital; découvrir que sous des vocabulaires différents, — divinisation, justice extrinsèque, grâce créée —, l'orthodoxie, la Réforme et le catholicisme signifient une même réalité d'action de Dieu nous sauvant, est très pacifiant; les différences et oppositions viennent plus ici d'une méconnaissance progressive du sens initial de ces formulations que d'une véritable opposition entre les données de la foi. Les divergences, ou, mieux, "la" divergence majeure qui subsiste entre catholicisme et réforme, sur ce point, n'en apparaît que plus profonde, — elle est de l'ordre de ces "ensembles" qu'une vue synthétique saisit sans peine mais qui colorent de manière propre chacun des éléments

—; mais, en même temps, cette divergence, étant mieux située, le point exact de la recherche en vue de l'unité est en pleine clarté et le travail ne peut qu'y gagner.

Mais en face des problèmes que nous venons de définir et qui se posent à tous les chrétiens, l'Eglise se voit appelée sans doute à une forme nouvelle de la vocation oecuménique, en vue prospective. Ce terme, emprunté au Père Rahner, dit comment, étant tous ensemble en face des mêmes questions posées par "le monde", nous sommes comme forcés de sortir ensemble de nos camps retranchés et d'affronter ensemble la question commune.

Il ne s'agit pas de faire front commun *contre* quoi que ce soit; il ne s'agit pas de tactique, de quelque ordre qu'elle soit. Il s'agit seulement de la situation dans laquelle nous nous trouvons; il s'agit de la mission non seulement de mémoire, mais aussi de prophétie, qui est impartie à l'Eglise de répondre aux questions nouvelles, en puisant dans sa tradition les éléments permettant d'y répondre.

Voilà pourquoi les nombreux comités mixtes, qui se créent de plus en plus, ont sans doute pour but d'étudier des thèmes "rétrospectifs" comme "Catholicité et Apostolicité" par exemple; mais les problèmes actuels émergent aussi, comme par exemple ceux que la commission pontificale Justice et paix entreprend d'étudier conjointement avec le Conseil oecuménique des Eglises.

L'Eglise est "*ante et retro oculata*": cette image ancienne dit assez bien cette double orientation, vers le "passé", qu'elle assume et sauvegarde, et vers le "futur", qu'elle doit éclairer et assumer. L'Eglise est "*Gabe*", don reçu, et aussi "*Aufgabe*", tâche à accomplir.

On peut rassembler autour de deux axes ces problèmes communs, celui du langage religieux, et celui du développement.

Il n'est pas possible d'entrer dans le détail de la première question, celle du *langage religieux*. Démythisation, ou critique des images et des concepts religieux, soumis au feu des "maîtres du soupçon"; analyses psychologiques obligeant à une purification du comportement et du langage, de façon à éviter la mystification; analyses sociologiques des credos et rites religieux, tellement poussées, que l'impression naît d'une sorte de réduction à des systèmes sociaux préexistants; critique biblique par exemple des genres littéraires, paraissant mettre en doute l'unité fondamentale de la Bible etc.

Il suffirait de rappeler les parole du Dr. Visser 't Hooft, au comité central du Conseil oecuménique, à Genève, en février 1966, demandant ce que deviendrait le Conseil oecuménique si la théologie nouvelle introduisait dans la base même de ce Conseil, la Bible, un élément qui en ferait éclater l'unité.[8]

Il semble que la tension causée par la pluralité d'écclésiologies soit extraordinairement aiguë. D'un côté une critique raisonnable est inévitable: les questions se posent; l'homme moderne interroge l'Eglise. Et s'il demeure toujours primordial de s'occuper du *"Was"*, du contenu de la prédication et des vérités essentielles, comme le fit Barth, avec le génie que l'on sait, on ne peut négliger totalement le *"Wie"*, le comment de la prédication.

Entre ces deux axes, où est le point de rencontre? ou d'équilibre? Et qui le fixera? Le seul critère de la critique? de l'exégèse biblique? Qui fixera le terme? La voix d'une tradition ancienne, présente dans la "confession des Eglises"? Un "magistère"? Que seront alors les relations précises entre "magistère, foi et théologie"?

Ces situations, bien entendu, ne sont pas neuves, au temps de Pusey, Keble et Newman, à Oxford, il y avait risque d'éclatement entre un christianisme "libéral", soumis à une implacable critique, et un ritualisme

---

[8] On sait, par ailleurs, que certains, par exemple dans la section *Faith and Order*, estiment qu'il faut reconnaître une pluralité d'ecclésiologies dans le Nouveau Testament. Il faudrait en conclure, sur le plan du comportement en vue de l'unité, qu'il faut en prendre conscience, rester là où chacun se trouve, dialoguer et collaborer, car l'Esprit Saint, inspirant le Nouveau Testament, y inspire aussi cette pluralité dont il a été question.

La réunion du comité central du Conseil, à Héraklion, en 1967, a dû affronter le même problème. Le pasteur Carson Blake, nouveau secrétaire général, exposa la question. On se trouvait en face, d'une part, d'Eglises se demandant si la "théologie nouvelle" allait devenir celle du Conseil oecuménique: auquel cas, elles devraient s'en désolidariser; on se trouvait affronté, d'autre part, à une impatience de jeunes fractions d'une série d'Eglises, se demandant dans quelle mesure le Conseil allait prendre au sérieux cette même théologie nouvelle: au cas où le Conseil la rejetait, ce serait eux, alors, qui s'en iraient, impatientés devant cette lenteur et ce conservatisme.

Le pasteur Carson Blake, en son rapport, montra comment il fallait d'une part que le Conseil oecuménique réaffirme les vérités essentielles, — Dieu, la Trinité, Jésus Fils de Dieu incarné, la justification —; mais en même temps, il fallait prendre au sérieux, du point de vue pastoral, les questions posées par la théologie nouvelle.

Il faut aller plus loin, et constater que ces tensions au sein d'Eglises vont parfois jusqu'à une sorte de point de rupture. On sait par exemple que le mouvement "Kein anderes Evangelium", qui défend des positions "traditionnelles" dans l'Eglise évangélique allemande, a refusé de prendre part au "Kirchentag" de Hannover en juin 1967. Ce même mouvement vient de publier à Dusseldorf une sorte de charte-catalogue des points essentiels de la foi évangélique.

Ceux qui participèrent au "Kirchentag" de Hannover eurent le souci de sauvegarder la foi; maintes critiques faites devraient être au moins nuancées; par ailleurs, le mouvement conservateur, de tendance plutôt piétiste, est plus ouvert qu'on ne le croit à une saine analyse de raison. L'absence de la tendance "Kein anderes Evangelium" à Hannover, se traduisit du reste par un souci très marqué dans les discussions, par exemple sur la résurrection de Jésus, de tenir compte du point de vue des absents.

qui semblait vénérable, mais incapable d'affronter le courant de la pensée profane.[9]

Il n'est absolument pas dans nos intentions de triompher avec aisance, du point de vue catholique, des problèmes du langage religieux dont il est ici question. Il s'agit seulement de comprendre la situation. Il est possible que, devant le désarroi provoqué par cette question, surtout quand elle est traitée dans des journaux quotidiens par des "théologiens de la place publique", pour reprendre un mot du Père Congar, l'Orthodoxie ait éprouvé un besoin plus immédiat de communiquer plus étroitement avec l'Eglise romaine.

Mais, comme le répète souvent Mgr. Christophe Dumont, à qui cette section est très redevable, le dialogue exclusif fait courir le danger d'isolement; le dialogue à trois fait courir le danger de fronts doubles, contre le troisième, isolé: soit catholiques-orthodoxes en face de la réforme; soit orthodoxie-réforme, en face du catholicisme. Voilà pourquoi il faut sans cesse promouvoir le dialogue à quatre, — les Anglicans nous le rappelleraient si nous l'oublions! — et ne jamais diviser le problème œcuménique. Si les questions sont différentes, et doivent être distinguées, elles ne doivent pas être séparées.

Voilà pourquoi dans l'acte "d'affronter ensemble" que demande l'oecuménisme prospectif en face de la question du langage religieux, il faut à la fois sauvegarder la confiance mutuelle, la collaboration, et en même temps maintenir présente l'originalité de chacune des dénominations présentes. Les méthodes intellectuelles de recherche sont ici substantiellement communes: il s'agit en effet des critères scientifiques tels que celui de l'histoire. Le problème du "langage chalcédonien", par exemple, ne se peut éclairer à la seule clarté de la problématique actuelle. Il faut aussi, par exemple dans l'encyclopédie, *Chalkedon Geschichte und Gegenwart*

---

[9] Le mouvement d'Oxford est né de cette tension, de ce souci de sauvegarder une critique saine, sans doute, mais aussi de revitaliser la foi sacramentelle, la relation avec Dieu, le sens du salut que seul le Christ peut donner, car seul il *est* le Sauveur, enfin la redécouverte de la dimension religieuse de l'invisible.

Bien des Eglises sont ainsi écartelées, actuellement à l'intérieur d'elles-mêmes, autour de ces problèmes. Un malaise vague s'infiltre dans le peuple des croyants. On se surprend parfois à penser qu'un nouveau "mouvement d'Oxford" serait nécessaire. Ce qui bouleverse le plus ces "mouvements", — courants de grande profondeur —, c'est l'union étroite d'un courageux affrontement des questions critiques, d'un souci constant et vigilant d'affirmer sans cesse le "*Was*", ou contenu des vérités essentielles, et aussi, et peut-être surtout l'acte de prier ensemble.

Parmi les fidèles catholiques romains, il y a aussi, actuellement, des tensions: droite ou gauche, intégristes ou progressistes, etc.: termes qui, presque à coup sûr, provoqueront des mépréhensions sérieuses. Mais l'urgence du dialogue à l'intérieur de l'Eglise, entre les fidèles, — ce que Dubois Dumée nomme "dialogue de famille" —, est évidente.

(1951-1956), et dans l'ouvrage de Pannenberg, *Grundzüge der Christologie* (1964), étudier le "passé" de cette problématique. On voit ainsi que l'attitude "prospective" ne se conçoit pas sans "rétrospection". Le dialogue, en d'autres mots, est aussi ressourcement, la "prophétie" est aussi "mémoire".

La seconde question est celle du *développement*. Ici encore, les dénominations chrétiennes se trouvent en face d'une tension semblable, même si elle porte sur d'autres données.

Il semble que l'on découvre soudain la dimension cosmique de tous ces problèmes. Une sorte d'ivresse s'empare de beaucoup, à la pensée de la société post-industrielle que les prévisions des experts annoncent pour l'an 2000.[10]

Le développement porte avec lui ses propres problèmes, disons même ses risques de catastrophe. Mais en même temps, les possibilités positives sont inouïes. Il suffit de songer que "la société post-industrielle sera caractérisée par une liberté sans précédent de l'homme à l'égard des contraintes physiques, économiques, biologiques : quasi disparition du travail manuel, temps libre supérieur au temps de travail, abolition des distances, développement spectaculaire des moyens de culture et d'information, pouvoir décuplé sur la nature et sur la vie, etc."[11]

On comprend pourquoi certains estiment qu'il faut reconsidérer les catégories de pensée usuelles dans l'expérience chrétienne : une bonne quantité de celles-ci sont empruntées au monde agricole, alors que l'agriculture va reculer dans des proportions énormes, le monde de l'an 2000 étant de plus en plus caractérisé par une civilisation urbaine.

Ce point n'est mentionné qu'à titre d'indice de la secousse "géologique qui ébranle en leurs profondeurs les esprits de nombreux croyants. Certains disent que, jusqu'à présent, aucune église chrétienne n'a vraiment pris conscience de l'ampleur des mutations en cours. L'attrait profond qu'exercent l'œuvre et la personne de Teilhard de Chardin s'explique sans doute, en partie, parce qu'on y voit une intégration de cette mue radicale dans la vision chrétienne, d'où le Christ cosmique apparaît com-

---

[10] Les Etats-Unis, le Japon, le Canada, la Suède, s'il en faut croire Jean-Jacques Servan-Schreiber dans *Le défi américain* (Paris, 1967) seront alors à la pointe d'une avant garde d'une ère vraiment "neuve", par exemple par l'emploi devenu quotidien des ordinateurs, que l'on utilisera comme, aujourd'hui, l'eau et l'électricité dans les appartements privés.
  Les autres régions demeureront en arrière, — société de consommation pour l'Europe occidentale, civilisation ou société industrielle, société en processus d'industrialisation, société pré-industrielle —, et de terribles inégalités existeront, infiniment plus profondes qu'aujourd'hui.
[11] Jean-Jacques Servan-Schreiber, *Le défi américain*, 57.

me celui qui donne un sens ultime à cette genèse d'une "noosphère", où l'unité et la diversité se nouent étroitement.[12]

Le nom de Teilhard a le privilège d'éveiller dans les rangs de la pensée chrétienne l'enthousiasme ou la colere. Pour les uns, Teilhard est le penseur chrétien de ce temps, providentiellement apparu au moment où l'Eglise se trouve devant un développement sans précédent de l'homme et du monde; pour les autres, il est le plus grand danger que la société chrétienne orthodoxe ait couru depuis longtemps; il représenterait une nouvelle forme de gnose, dans laquelle s'effaceraient les contours précis, du naturel au surnaturel, de l'ordre de la création et de l'ordre de la rédemption, des imperfections inévitables du devenir et du péché.

Il n'est pas question ici de dirimer cette controverse extrêmement violente. On l'a mentionnée pour rendre sensible les tensions qui existent au sein de plusieurs dénominations chrétiennes en face du "défi" lancé par un monde dont, vraiment, nous avions mesuré très mal encore, jusqui' ici, à quel point il recèle de fantastiques possibilités pour l'humanité. Ici encore, les frontières ne se superposent pas aux divisions confessionnelles, mais les chevauchent sans cesse. On en avait pris conscience du reste déjà à la réunion mondiale du Conseil oecuménique, à Evanston, en 1954: le thème de l'espérance révéla alors cette urgence que Barth avait mise en lumière de manière prophétique.

Si Servan-Schreiber écrit: "147 journées de travail par an et 218 jours libres de travail dans une génération."[13] Il dit aussi: "Mais tout ne sera ni simple ni facile. L'un des grands problèmes qui nous est posé par cette

---

[12] Nous avons dit "expliquent en partie", car, si l'on en croit Henri de Lubac, dans *La pensée religieuse de Teilhard de Chardin*, l'auteur du *Phénomène humain* était hanté par le risque de la "captivité de l'humanité dans la bulle cosmique"; il parlait souvent à Madame de la Rochefoucault de son "angoisse" devant le monde présent. On aurait tort de réduire l'œuvre de Teilhard à une sorte de Physique de l'esprit, allant, comme nécessairement, vers la manifestation de l'union de l'humanité, sous l'attraction du "point Omega".

Certains théologiens orthodoxes de Russie y voient une approche chrétienne du grand élan de développement qui a marqué la Russie depuis le début de ce siècle. Une étude attentive, comparant la pensée de Teilhard et celle de certains penseurs russes comme Feodotov, déjà nommé à propos de Dostoevskij, serait sans doute éclairante.

De même, il est hors de doute que Teilhard est sans doute le seul penseur chrétien qui "intéresse" des penseurs marxistes. Il est pour eux la seule route qui leur rende possible un commencement d'intelligence de ce que serait la conception chrétienne. Bien sûr, on dira, et on a dit que c'est là, chez eux, risque de se méprendre sur l'essentiel, de réduire précisément le christianisme à une sorte de "philosophie de l'histoire". Si c'est à cette condition, dit-on, qu'ils s'y intéressent, mieux vaut qu'ils ne s'y intéressent pas du tout, car ils risquent ainsi non seulement de se tromper, mais d'entraîner les autres dans l'erreur.

[13] Jean-Jacques Servan-Schreiber, *Le défi américain*, 48.

nouvelle percée technologique est le fossé qui se creuse, de plus en plus, entre l'industrie américaine d'une part, le reste du monde de l'autre. Ceci ne posera pas seulement des problèmes, mais pourrait mener à des catastrophes ... C'est un monde nouveau qui s'ouvre, avec tous les aléas de l'aventure."[14] Ce qui frappe dans la réaction à ces prévisions, c'est l'unilatérisme des réponses: elles sont ou bien d'enthousiasme devant l'avenir, avec un appel aux chrétiens de s'y insérer au plus vite; ou bien elles sont négatives et pessimistes. Il est temps que ces oppositions stériles, que ces dialogues de sourds cessent. "Nous étions bien abusés. Je ne suis détrompé que d'hier", commence Pascal, dans *Les Provinciales*: les uns, enthousiastes de l'unique Teilhard, les autres, annonciateurs des dangers d'aveuglement, répètent à l'envi ces mots. Il faudrait s'élever au-dessus et chercher un point d'équilibre, mais aussi de tension prophétique, au sein de la rupture apportée par la Révélation. "Cette société sera-t-elle plus heureuse?, écrit encore Servan-Schreiber. C'est une autre question, qui ne comporte sans doute pas de réponse. Mais il est certain qu'elle représentera l'avant-garde de l'histoire humaine, et ceci nous regarde."[15]

Ici encore, toutes les églises, à des titres divers, se trouvent devant un problème commun. On se demande même si, en un sens, ce ne sont pas aussi les grandes religions du monde qui participeraient à cette mise en question. En l'an 2000, le Japon viendra immédiatement après les Etats-Unis dans l'avant garde de l'histoire dont il a été parlé; il faut avoir vu ces foules de jeunes étudiants et étudiantes, la chemise ou la blouse d'un blanc immaculé, dans les rues, les trains, les autobus de Tokyo; il faut avoir observé leur silence, leur sérieux, leurs yeux fixés sur un livre, leur marche rapide, leur discipline, pour se demander: que représente pour eux la religion bouddhiste et que sont encore les traditions Shintoïstes?

La réponse n'est pas dans un "acosmisme religieux" ou dans une immersion de la religion dans le temporel. Le bouddhisme Zen, par exemple, est très vivant au Japon, ainsi qu'un article de la revue *Concilium* vient de le montrer.[16] L'intériorité de l'expérience spirituelle se conjoint avec le sens de la responsabilité sociale, ainsi qu'il apparut dans le colloque de Oiso, du 27 mars au 1er avril 1967.

Cet exemple suffirait à montrer l'ampleur universelle de la question, mais aussi la nécessité d'y répondre en s'élevant au dessus de la conjoncture immédiate, pour joindre cette vision antinomique qui, seule, peut assumer l'ensemble du phénomène:

---

[14] Servan-Schreiber, *Le défi américain*, 101.
[15] Servan-Schreiber, *Le défi américain*, 51.
[16] *Concilium* (4e trimestre, 1967), n. 29, 131-147.

L'inquiétude de Dieu est commune à tous les hommes, écrit Georges Siegmund, dans le même numéro de *Concilium*. Elle est à l'œuvre aussi chez ceux qui se disent des incroyants. En dépit de tout le scepticisme qui barre la route à Dieu, en dépit de toutes les conceptions aberrantes sur Dieu, qui l'enveloppent d'obscurité, en dépit de la négation fréquente de Dieu, l'homme moderne, étranger à Dieu, porte lui aussi en soi une nostalgie de l'absolu. Elle lui est commune avec le bouddhiste. C'est pourquoi une analyse de cette inquiétude est la base à laquelle il nous faut revenir si nous voulons mener un dialogue authentique avec les non-chrétiens.[17]

L'oecuménisme "prospectif" se trouve ainsi en face d'une double question. Il semble que, pour l'affronter, toutes les dénominations chrétiennes sont invitées à se ressourcer, à retrouver, en une sorte de "renouement", leur expérience fondamentale d'Eglise. Doublement à l'écoute, et du monde, et de Dieu.

Oserait-on proposer ici trois thèmes qui forment la structure théologique de la Constitution pastorale *Gaudium et spes*? Ils offrent sans doute une invitation à une méditation concertée, théologique et spirituelle, de points essentiels du message. Une étude commune pourrait sans doute contribuer à cet affrontement commun des chrétiens, à leur témoignage apostolique, comme l'indique le décret conciliaire *Ad gentes*.[18]

Le premier thème est celui de l'homme créé à l'image de Dieu: il implique l'intériorité dont parle par exemple Saint Léon dans son sermon du quatrième dimanche de l'Avent, dans la liturgie latine; il signifie aussi que l'homme est appelé à dominer sur le monde, à le rendre plus humain; il signifie encore la nécessaire communauté des hommes, à laquelle tous sont appelés.

Le second thème est celui du Christ ressuscité. L'homme n'est pas seulement domination sur le monde; il est aussi passivité, erreur, mort et péché. Le serviteur souffrant d'Isaïe est aussi une "image de l'homme". Le Christ, "image de Dieu", fut aussi, en sa vie terrestre, un serviteur de Yahweh qui, s'étant "fait péché pour nous", a assumé les souffrances de l'homme. Aussi bien, par son obéissance jusqu'à la mort de la croix, il a été exalté au-dessus de tout nom. Dans l'humanité du Christ ressuscité, hypostatiquement unie à sa personne divine, rayonne la victoire totale du "Fils de l'homme" sur le péché, la mort et toutes formes de désordre. Là est l'archétype de l'humanité, créée à l'image et à la ressemblance de Dieu. En d'autres termes, l'image de Dieu qu'est l'homme n'est pas statique; elle est dynamique; elle se révèle pleinement dans le Christ, sauveur et ressuscité. On saisit dès lors l'importance du fait que chaque chapître

---

[17] *Concilium* (4e trimestre, 1967), n. 29, 130.
[18] *Ad gentes*, n. 15, §4.

de la première partie de *Gaudium et spes* se termine par un numéro sur le "mystère pascal". Nous sommes ici au-delà de toute réduction de l'espérance chrétienne à un espoir uniquement humain.

Enfin, le Verbe créateur et illuminateur. Ce thème johannique, — tout a été créé par le Verbe —, doit être rattaché à celui de la Sagesse, — qui est à la fois la loi de Dieu et un ordre mystérieux dans la création —. Or, comme l'a répété la tradition patristique, surtout grecque, le Verbe créateur est aussi le Verbe illuminateur. "Il était présent dans le monde avant son incarnation", dit Saint Irénée en un texte repris dans le chapître sur la culture, dans *Gaudium et spes*.[19] Dans cette perspective, on entrevoit comment une théologie de l'histoire est possible. La *"Weltgeschichte"* se révèle en relation avec la *"Heilsgeschichte"*. Le Verbe, mystérieusement présent dans le monde, et toujours présent de cette manière cachée, donne un sens religieux à ce qu'il y a de vrai et de bon dans la culture et dans les religions non-chrétiennes. Les anciens Pères n'hésitaient pas à dire que tout ce qu'il y avait de bon et de vrai, par exemple dans Platon, était un reflet de ce Verbe "caché" dans le monde.

Ces thèmes sont bibliques, patristiques; on les retrouve dans la liturgie de presque toutes les dénominations chrétiennes. N'y a-t-il pas là une manière de "mémoire" commune de toutes les églises, qui nourrit la "prophétie" que le monde attend?

3

"Le temps de l'oecuménisme facile, écrit Giorgio Girardet, dans *Nuovi tempi*, qui a caractérisé les six années depuis New-Delhi, est aujourd'hui fini."[20]

---

[19] *Gaudium et spes*, n. 57, §5.

[20] *Nuovi tempi* (24 decembre, 1967): "Informa diversa da quella prevista, il 1968 ripropone percio il problema dell'ecumenismo; non è piu il balletto ecumenico delle confessioni che si confrontanno, si inchinano e partono a bracetto, ma quello, ben piu vivo e impegnativo, dell'unita dell'popolo di Dio, lacerato verticalmente da convinzioni e impostazione profondamente diversi. Il problema dell'impegno politico e quello del cattolicesimo dovranno essere certamente affrontati, ma come aspetti particolari di quello della confessione della fede o della fede o della realizzazione della vita cristiana nel mondo" (*ibid.*, p. 8).

On ne verra, nous l'espérons, dans les lignes de Georges Girardet, à propos du ballet oecuménique, aucune critique désobligeante. Il ne faudrait pas que cet humour fasse perdre de vue le changement de climat que les rencontres récentes ont provoqué. Rien n'est plus important; sans une atmosphère de confiance et de respect, aucune confrontation ne se peut faire utilement.

Il faut même aller plus loin, et parler, à propos de la visite du Pape Paul VI ou de

L'unité se fera *"per viam acti"*, sans doute; elle se fera aussi *"per viam prophetiae"*; mais les problèmes centraux ne peuvent être évités. Et ils se posent, tous ensemble, et au plan de l'oecuménisme rétrospectif, — sens de la primauté du pape, signification du ministère dans l'Eglise, etc. —, et à celui de l'oecuménisme prospectif, — quel *sens* a l'enseignement des églises, quel est leur service dans ce monde des hommes? —.

J'ai sous les yeux, à nouveau, la brochure comportant la liste des travaux des professeurs de l'Institut orthodoxe de Saint Serge, entre 1925 et 1954. Je suis frappé par l'extraordinaire richesse de cette production, par sa variété, par son ampleur aussi, car elle entrevoyait déjà les problèmes actuels du sens du langage religieux et du développement.

A-t-on oublié que dès 1920 le patriarche oecuménique d'Istanbul proposait un plan de travail oecuménique? A-t-on perdu de vue que la génération qui a cinquante ans, actuellement, a presque tout reçu, en matière d'oecuménisme, de cette pléiade de théologiens orthodoxes russes, entre les années 1920-1948? Le Père C. Dumont rappelait encore récemment comment le professeur Kartashov, ayant été durant un an ministre des cultes dans le gouvernement provisoire, possède une expérience unique de la possibilité de maintenir l'Eglise chrétienne orthodoxe en un milieu politique athée.

Mais ce n'est pas seulement l'importance revêtue par le nombre même des penseurs orthodoxes, c'est aussi la *qualité* de leur apport, qui est remarquable. Il me semble qu'aujourd'hui, nous avons un besoin urgent de retrouver cette tradition orthodoxe dans son apport oecuménique. Elle doit nous aider à dépasser ce que le Père Congar appelait "le danger d'un certain horizontalisme", d'un oubli de la transcendance. Or il semble que le structuralisme nous invite à un sérieux examen de conscience, à une sorte de décapage radical.

Déterminer, montrer à quel point nous sommes insérés dans des structures linguistiques, sociologiques, ethnologiques, etc., c'est aussi nous inviter à mieux comprendre à quel point nous sommes "prisonniers des éléments de ce monde", et avons besoin d'une rédemption qui ne peut

celle du Patriarche Athénagoras, de gestes prophétiques, dont personne, voici cinq ans, n'imaginait la possibilité.

Ceci dit, le pasteur Girardet a parfaitement raison de rappeler que 1968 pourrait être une année cruciale pour l'oecuménisme. Par la réunion mondiale de Uppsala, en juillet 1968, sans doute; mais aussi parce que nous voici précisément arrivés à cet écartèlement entre l'oecuménisme de l'époque de l'entre deux guerres, dont on a vu comment, à propos de son aspect orthodoxe russe, il s'enracinait dans la "fin du siècle religieux" dont parlait Georges Florovsky, et l'oecuménisme actuel, affronté à la radicale mise en question que l'on a dite.

venir que de Dieu. Seule l'annonce de l'événement de la résurrection, —
en un sens le seul événement vrai de l'histoire —, peut nous délivrer de
la captivité de cet éternel retour qui hantait Nietzsche, et dont le nouveau
roman nous a laissé quelques pages obsédantes. De même, saisir le labyrinthe du langage dans lequel nous naissons, mesurer à quel point la
"synchronie" l'emporte sur la "diachronie", c'est aussi, par contraste,
retrouver mieux le sens de l'unique Parole de Dieu. Relire certaines
études orthodoxes de temps "lointains" à la lumière de ce dernier avatar
de la pensée européenne, serait sans aucun doute très révélateur. Cette
"mémoire" aussi pourrait être "prophétie".

Un des traits de l'orthodoxie a toujours été son insistance sur le
mystère pascal, et sur la participation du "cosmos" à la rédemption.
Frank-Duquesne, dans son livre *Cosmos et gloire* avait mis ce point en
lumière. Ce message est plus actuel que jamais. Lorsque fut demandé à
un symposium organisé le 8 novembre 1967, dans le cadre du General
Theological Seminary, quel point semblait le plus urgent actuellement
dans le travail œcuménique, Carson Blake souligna la nécessité de s'opposer efficacement aux barrières et inimités raciques, ethnologiques et de
couleur; mais il répéta avec une égale force la nécessité d'affronter ces
murs de haine avec la foi totale en la transcendance de Dieu agissant en
notre témoignage et en notre action. Le même jour le Dr. Schmeman,
après avoir esquissé la première voie de l'œcuménisme, rétrospective, puis
la seconde, prospective, où il semble ne plus être question de la présence
du monde, insista sur la nécessité d'une troisième forme de l'oecuménisme,
précisément celle qui assume les deux premières, dans l'affirmation du
mystère chrétien fondamental, la mort et la résurrection.

Nous avons esquissé les thèmes théologiques présents dans *Gaudium
et spes*. Ils sont communs à tous les chrétiens. Mais, en même temps, ils
éveillent un écho particulier dans la pensée orthodoxe.

Il est juste de faire remarquer ici que l'aspect de l'humanisme eschatologique, pour reprendre la terminologie proposée dans la première partie
de cet essai, aurait pu et dû être plus explicitement présent dans *Gaudium
et spes*. Un texte sur "l'humanisme des Béatitudes" a disparu après la
quatrième version; un paragraphe entier, consacré à l'action sacramentelle, par laquelle l'Eglise contribue, en transfigurant les réalités et les
signes, à "humaniser" le monde, n'est plus présent que par quelqués mots
"*Ecclesia, actione sua etiam liturgica, hominem ad interiorem libertatem
educat.*"[21]

---

[21]   *Gaudium et spes*, n. 58, §4.

Sans doute l'essentiel est dit quand il est précisé que, par sa mission divine, l'Eglise n'est pas, comme telle, appelée à civiliser, mais que, en accomplissant sa tâche propre d'évangéliser, elle civilise par surcroît.[22] Pie XI écrivait: "Il ne faut jamais perdre de vue que l'objectif de l'Eglise est d'évangéliser, et non de civiliser. Si elle civilise, c'est par l'évangélisation."

Il n'empêche, un dialogue et une collaboration avec l'orthodoxie, serait, sur ce point, vraiment importants. L'intervention de l'archiprêtre Vitalij Borovoj, à Genève, en 1966, aida à faire accepter par l'assemblée générale un chapître qui parlait en ce sens à propos de la théologie de la création.

Nous sommes ici à un carrefour oecuménique très ancien, s'il est vrai que la théologie anglicane, de son côté, par les liens qu'elle a toujours sauvegardés avec la tradition patristique grecque, spécialement Saint Irénée, apporte elle aussi son concours à cette vision de la résurrection-transfiguration.

La réunion mondiale de Uppsala, en juillet 1968, permet une autre approche de la même "actualité" de l'apport orthodoxe dans le nouvel oecuménisme. L'orthodoxie est entrée dans le Conseil oecuménique en 1961, à New-Delhi. Ce sera un des titres de gloire du secrétaire général, le Dr. Visser 't Hooft. Désormais l'orthodoxie a besoin d'avoir dans les structures du Conseil, une place qui corresponde mieux à son importance quantitative et qualitative. Elle l'a reçue à Uppsala.

C'est là un problème délicat, mais dont la solution doit promouvoir le bien de tous et de chacun. La question est connexe aux divers mouvements de "fédérations par Eglises" qui se sont développées ces dernières années. Ce qui, au premier abord, apparaîtra rupture d'un équilibre très difficilement obtenu jusqu'à présent, se révèlera plus tard, si ces restructurations sont faites, un équilibre plus stable, une forme plus efficace aussi de la collaboration.

Dans cette ligne, la prise de conscience, difficile, mais réelle, d'une plus grande unité au sein de l'orthodoxie, telle qu'elle se dessine au long des assemblées de Rhodes, contribue à donner à l'apport orthodoxe au Conseil œcuménique un plus grand poids, une plus grande force de témoignage. En particulier, — mais ceci est une opinion personnelle —, le "génie propre" de l'orthodoxie, précisément devant les problèmes du "nouvel humanisme", aidera toutes les églises membres du Conseil.

Une des originalités du projet de l'Institut Oecuménique d'Etudes Théologiques à Jérusalem, est de donner aux orthodoxes, dans le comité académique, une place qui corresponde à leur véritable importance: huit

---

[22] *Gaudium et spes*, n. 58, §4.

professeurs orthodoxes figurent aux côtés de huit catholiques, huit protestants, trois anglicans, deux pré-chacédoniens et un vieux catholique. Nous sommes d'autant plus heureux de signaler la chose que le professeur Florovski lui-même est un des membres de ce comité.

De même, dans le programme des recherches, et dans le choix des érudits appelés à diriger ou à visiter l'Institut, la présence d'orthodoxes est chaque fois prévue. C'est une des conditions essentielles pour que l'Institut, situé à Jérusalem, *Eglise, mère de toutes les Eglises,* puisse s'enraciner dans les traditions qui, depuis les origines, témoignent de l'espérance de la résurrection.

Par ailleurs, dans le cadre des diverses formes d'œcuménisme dont on a parlé, l'Institut ne sera pas œcuménique par les sujets de recherche, *mais par la méthode.* Les professeurs et étudiants y feront ensemble des recherches sur des questions communes à tous les chrétiens: la devise de l'Institut "*Mysterium salutis*" l'indique. Le thème du salut est biblique, patristique, liturgique, conciliaire et spirituel; à ce titre, l'approche "classique" s'impose ici, d'investigation positive et de réflexion. Mais, en même temps, par l'universalité de sa signification, qui éveille l'attention de tout homme, et aussi de l'homme de ce temps, — même si celui-ci déclare n'avoir précisément pas besoin du salut, être plus grand, plus authentiquement homme, de n'avoir pas besoin d'être sauvé —, une approche "moderne" est possible et nécessaire.

L'Institut doit promouvoir la recherche d'un projet de centre d'études pour étudiants déjà diplomés ("post-graduate students"); l'œcuménisme rétrospectif sera considéré, comment ne pas le faire s'il est vrai que nous divergeons aussi sur la vision du salut, mais ce sera l'approche prospective qui dominera.

De Jérusalem, ainsi, l'Institut pourra aider à cette nouvelle mission, vers une nouvelle Judée, une nouvelle Samarie et de nouvelles extrémités de la terre.

Il a bien souvent été question dans cet essai du thème "mémoire et prophétie." Les deux termes sont bibliques. Ils disent bien le lien profond existant entre les diverses formes d'œcuménisme, comme aussi entre la tâche de l'Eglise de répondre aux problèmes nouveaux, et de le faire en une fidélité profonde à tout ce qu'elle a reçu, à tout ce qu'elle est.

Il ne s'agit pas de cette forme nostalgique de la mémoire: celle-ci immobilise le passé; elle en néglige l'aspect réel, pour n'en conserver que l'image d'une félicité qui n'a jamais existé. L'attitude véritable n'est pas non plus celle de l'oubli, qui nous amputerait du passé: l'Eglise ne peut être cette mutilée qui a rompu avec ce qu'elle a été.

Cette mémoire est aussi prophétie, annonce des biens à venir, annonce de ce qui est "déjà" et de ce qui n'est "pas encore". Ainsi, l'Eucharistie, *mémorial*, est *communion*, dans la présence du Sauveur, et *espérance* de la consommation dans la plénitude eschatologique. Ces trois termes, déjà repris dans les documents de la commission Faith and Order, à Montréal, en 1963, se retrouvent aussi dans le décret conciliaire sur l'œcuménisme.

Enfin, si nous considérons la dimension horizontale, de la présence au monde, qui semble faire oublier tout le reste à bien des croyants, actuellement, et la dimension verticale, de la transcendance de Dieu et d'irruption prophétique de sa révélation et rédemption, nous n'oublierons pas, nous non plus, que Dieu n'est pas plus exclusivement présent dans la ligne verticale que dans la ligne horizontale. Il est partout, de sa présence d'immensité; il est présent dans l'appel qui demandait à son peuple, dans le Deutéronome, de pratiquer la justice envers le prochain, et de ne jamais oublier que la seule justice, finalement, est celle du Dieu juste.

Joindre la dimension horizontale et la dimension verticale, c'est dessiner une croix. La croix signifie, dans la symbolique du monde méditerranéen, l'universalité, les quatre points cardinaux. Reprise par les chrétiens, la croix signifie d'abord le gibet où Jésus fut crucifié et sa résurrection. Elle exprime l'espérance du salut, la certitude du salut, dans la foi.

La jointure de l'horizontale et de la verticale forment une croix. Signe de mort salvatrice. Signe aussi de résurrection.

PERSONALIA

ANDREW Q. BLANE
Associate Professor of History, City University of New York (Lehman)

THOMAS E. BIRD
Lecturer in Slavic Languages and Literature, City University of
New York (Queens)

GEORGE HUNTSTON WILLIAMS
Hollis Professor of Divinity, Harvard University

HARRY A. WOLFSON
Nathan Littauer Professor of Hebrew Literature and Philosophy (Emeritus), Harvard University

THOMAS F. TORRANCE
Professor of Christian Dogmatics, University of Edinburgh

JOHN MEYENDORFF
Professor of Patristics and Church History, St. Vladimir's Seminary,
Professor of Byzantine History, Fordham University

PETER CHARANIS
Vorhees Professor of History, Rutgers University

WILHELM KAHLE
Direktor der Kirchlichen Erziehungs Kammer für Berlin, Dr. theol. habil,
Privat dozent für Kirchengeschichte, Philipps-Universität, Marburg/Lahn

ERNST BENZ
o. Professor der Kirchen- und Dogmen-geschichte, Direktor des ökuminisches Institutes, Philipps-Universität, Marburg/Lahn

ROBERT STUPPERICH
Direktor der Ostkirche-Instituts, Universität Münster

SIR STEVEN RUNCIMAN
Honorable Fellow of Trinity College, Cambridge University

YVES M.-J. CONGAR, O.P.
Professeur aux Facultés théologiques, Le Saulchoir

NIKOS A. NISSIOTIS
Director of the Ecumenical Institute of Bossey, Professor of the Theological Faculty of the University of Athens

CHRISTOPHE J. DUMONT, O.P.
Fondateur du Centre "Istina", Professeur à l'Université Saint-Thomas, Rome

CHARLES MOELLER
Professeur à l'Université de Louvain, Sottosegretario della Sacra Congregazione per la Dottrina della Fede, Roma

INDEX